Moral Vision in International Politics

# Moral Vision
# in
# International Politics

## THE FOREIGN AID REGIME, 1949–1989

*David Halloran Lumsdaine*

PRINCETON UNIVERSITY PRESS

PRINCETON, NEW JERSEY

Copyright © 1993 by Princeton University Press
Published by Princeton University Press, 41 William Street,
Princeton, New Jersey 08540
In the United Kingdom: Princeton University Press,
Chichester, West Sussex

*Library of Congress Cataloging-in-Publication Data*

Lumsdaine, David Halloran.
Moral vision in international politics : the foreign aid regime,
1949–1989 / David Halloran Lumsdaine.
p.   cm.
Includes bibliographical references and index.
ISBN 0-691-07887-4 (CL) — ISBN 0-691-02767-6 (PB)
1. Economic assistance, American—Developing countries.
2. Economic assistance—Developing countries.   I. Title.
HC60.L86   1993   338.9'17301724—dc20   92-18508

This book has been composed in Linotron Sabon

Princeton University Press books are printed on acid-free paper,
and meet the guidelines for permanence and durability
of the Committee on Production Guidelines for Book Longevity of
the Council on Library Resources

Printed in the United States of America

10  9  8  7  6  5  4  3  2  1
10  9  8  7  6  5  4  3  2  1
(Pbk.)

*To my mother and father*

# Contents

*List of Tables and Figures*                                          ix

*Acknowledgments*                                                    xiii

*Abbreviations*                                                      xvii

PART I: *The Argument*

CHAPTER ONE
Do Morals Matter in International Politics?                            3

CHAPTER TWO
Why Was There Any Foreign Aid at All?                                30

PART II: *The Evidence*

CHAPTER THREE
Where the Money Went:
  Who Were the Main Recipients of Aid?                      73

CHAPTER FOUR
Who Paid the Bill:
  Similarities and Differences among the Donors            104

CHAPTER FIVE
Who Advocated Aid:
  Supporters and Opponents of Development Assistance       137

CHAPTER SIX
What Prepared the Way:
  Historical Antecedents of Aid                            182

CHAPTER SEVEN
How Aid Grew:
  Development of Regular Aid Programs                       221

CHAPTER EIGHT
How Aid Changed:
  Ongoing Reform in the Foreign Aid Regime                 253

PART III: *Conclusion*

CHAPTER NINE
How Shall We Then Live?                                              283

viii · Contents

*Notes*                                                    295

*Bibliography*                                             325

*Index*                                                    343

# Tables and Figures

TABLES

2.1 Volume of Aid Compared with Private Financial Flows to the Third World    35

2.2 Bilateral Aid Correlated with Trade    40

2.3 Aid and Commercial Flows, by LDC Income Class    40

2.4 DAC Aid Going to Multilateral Institutions, 1956–1989    41

2.5 Strong and Weak Aid Donors Classed by Domestic Social Spending and Private Charitable Contributions to Third World Development    41

2.6 Attitudes toward Increased Aid, by Church Attendance and Political Views    44

2.7 Best Predictors of Public Support for Foreign Aid    44

2.8 Perception of National Interest by Degree of Perceived Moral Duty to Give Aid    45

2.9 Degree of Tying of Aid    48

2.10 Percentage of Grant, Grant Element, and Interest Rate in Bilateral Aid, 1962–1988    48

2.11 DAC Countries Classified by Percentage of Aid Given to Multilateral Organizations    49

2.12 DAC Countries Classified by Grant Element in Aid over Time    49

2.13 Net Disbursed Aid by LDC Income Level over Time    50

3.1 Overlap between Top Aid and Trade Partners    76

3.2 Aid, Trade, and Investment in Major Aid Recipients    77

3.3 Share of Aid Going to Third World Countries Most Important in DAC Trade    77

3.4 Correlation Coefficients of DAC Bilateral Aid with Trade    78

3.5 Partial Correlation Coefficients of DAC Bilateral Aid with Trade, Controlling for Recipient Size    79

3.6 Correlations of Aid with Trade, for Individual Donors    80

3.7 Partial Correlations, Aid with Trade, for Individual Donors, Controlling for the Size of Recipient States    81

3.8 Aid to Former Colonies    83

3.9 Pacific Donors' Aid to Nearby Small States    87

3.10 Recipient Need and U.S. Bilateral Aid    92

3.11 Aid, Investment, and Trade by Recipient Income Class    95

3.12  Aid and Trade, Largest Third World Countries (1982)  95
3.13  Share of Aid, Exports, and Export Credits from OECD countries to Third World Countries by Recipient Income Class  96
3.14  Individual Donors' Bilateral Aid by Recipient Income Class  97
3.15  Percentage of Aid Going to All Poverty-Oriented Sectors  101
3.16  World Bank Resources Going to Poverty-Oriented Sectors  101
4.1  Comparison of Donors' Net Official Development Assistance and Net Private Financial Flows as Percentages of GNP, 1980–1989  106
4.2  Comparison of Donors' Net Official Development Assistance and Exports to, and Imports from, the Third World, 1980–1989  107
4.3  Foreign Aid, Domestic Government Social Expenditures, and Private Voluntary Contributions as Percentages of Gross National Product  122
4.4  Correlations of DAC Donors' Aid Spending with Domestic Social Spending and with Contributions to PVOs Assisting The Third World  124
4.5  Economic Aid to the Third World from Soviet Bloc Countries  129
4.6  Trends in DAC Donors' Net Disbursed Aid  133
5.1  Support for Aid Broken Down by Respondent Characteristics and Views  146
5.2  U.S. Support for Aid Classified by Respondent Foreign Policy Views  147
5.3  Percentages Favoring Increasing, Decreasing, Maintaining, or Cutting Aid, Broken Down by Regularity of Religious Attendance and by Political Self-Placement  149
5.4  Best Predictors of Support for Aid, Tested against Each Other  153
5.5  Perceptions of Moral Duty and of National Interest in Foreign Aid  157
5.6  Moral Duty, National Interest, and Support for Aiding Neediest Countries  157
5.7  Contracts for Japanese-Funded Aid Projects, by Nationality  160
5.8  Evolution of Japan's Aid Spending, 1974–1989  160
5.9  (English) Wording of Questions on *Euro-Barometers 13* and *20*  180
7.1  DAC Net Total Disbursements to UN Development Programs  246

8.1 Number of Donors at Various Levels of Aid Disbursements over Time 255

8.2 Percentages of Total OECD Aid Contributed Classified by Donor Grouping 257

8.3 Number of Donors Concentrating Aid on a Few Countries 258

8.4 Number of Recipients Receiving Various Percentages of Their Aid from a Single Donor, 1964 259

8.5 Number of Recipients Receiving Various Percentages of Their Aid from a Single Donor, 1978 259

8.6 Multilateral Percentages of DAC Aid, 1950–1989 261

8.7 Number of Donors with Various Levels of Support for Multilateral Aid 261

8.8 Degree of Tying in Aid: All DAC Countries and United States 263

8.9 Change In Tying Behavior between 1972 and 1982–1983 265

8.10 Grants, Grant Element, and Interest Rate in Bilateral ODA, 1950–1988 265

8.11 Number of DAC Donors with Various Levels of Grant Elements over Time 266

8.12 Net Disbursed Foreign Aid, Classified by Recipient Income Level: Importance in the Donor Aid Burden and in the Recipient Countries 267

8.13 Net Disbursed Foreign Aid, Classified by Recipient Income Level 268

FIGURES

4.1 Concern about Poverty Influences Both Social Spending and Foreign Aid 120

4.2 Concern about International Poverty Influences Charity and Foreign Aid 123

# Acknowledgments

HUMAN POVERTY and need of every kind has at least this possibility for good in it: by responding to others in need, and by receiving assistance, we may make manifest the love for one another that is a part of our main purpose and joy as human beings. Aid given and received can create bonds of fellowship and community which are among our most valuable possessions; happily, such debts of gratitude, though they may be reciprocal, are never canceled. It is a source of joy and of strength to me to be able to write this book with the kind and steady support of so many friends, and even help from strangers. This process itself, of which we are also in need, is an inexpressible gift for which I also give thanks.

I am particularly thankful for the support and criticisms of Steve Krasner, Bruce Russett, and Alex Wendt, who have aided me in this project with understanding and confidence, criticism and support, insight and sound judgment, and with great generosity in giving of their time. Their unfailing friendship has been one of the rewards of writing this book. I am grateful also for the help and the sound advice of other colleagues: David Abernethy, Malcolm DeBevoise, Arlee Ellis, William Foltz, Christopher Gacek, Alexander George, Donald Green, Bruce Johnston, Jack Levy, Walter Lippincott, Robert Packenham, Rogers Smith, Ian Shapiro, Edward Tufte, and Bradford Westerfield. Each of them made useful comments and helped generously in other ways. I have been greatly favored in my helpers and research assistants, too. I am grateful for the faithful, able assistance of Robert Griffin, Nicholas Kliment, and Adam Rothman, as well as for the support of Gabriel Casaburi, Cindy Crumrine, Ryan Dunch, Betsy Frey, Molan Chun Goldstein, Celeste Newbrough, and Eric Ressler. Jake Bowers, Leslie Eliason, Scott Johnson, David Kinsella, David Porteous, and Jeff Seward also assisted me briefly but very helpfully.

A much wider scholarly community has also provided invaluable assistance. The library, statistical, and computer, and Political Science Department staffs at Yale and Stanford were very helpful. Funding for my program was provided by Stanford University, by the MacArthur Foundation, through the Stanford Center for Arms Control and Disarmament, whose faculty and staff also assisted me in other ways, and through the Security and Arms Control Program at Yale, by the Yale Center for International and Area Studies, and by the Eisenhower-Roberts Foundation. The data used in this study were provided in part by the Development Assistance Committee of the OECD, through their *Public Data Base* and the figures in *Development Cooperation* and *Geographical Distribution of Financial Flows*. Without these data tapes and publications it would have been impossible to write this book. I am also grateful for data on *Direction of Trade* flows, provided by the International Monetary Fund and various data provided by the U.S. Arms Control and Disarmament Agency and the World Bank. Important parts of the public opinion data utilized in this book were made available by the Inter-university Consortium for Political and Social Research. The data for *Euro-Barometer 13* and *20* were originally collected by Jacques-René Rabier, Helene Riffault, and Ronald Inglehart. Neither the collectors of the original data nor the Consortium bear any responsibility for the analyses or interpretations presented here.

In addition to the professional support I have received, many friends not in my profession have assisted me in writing this book by their love, by their encouragement about this task, by their help with other tasks, by their putting up with my distraction, and often by their prayers. May this book serve in some way to advance our common concern that in this badly inflamed world, as Amos hoped, justice may roll down like waters and righteousness like an everflowing stream!

Each of these various communities has shown in different ways the goodness of human love, by which we are enabled to live together in peace and joy: it is to try to understand and extend this process that this book is written. In this world we desperately need reconciliation and healing, and that is perhaps most evident in our international relations, where we are apt to destroy ourselves as a species, and the world with us, and in the daily plight, amid great wealth, of this world's poor. At every level of being and of human social organization, generosity and cooperation are vital to life and to growth and restoration. Yet a special part is played in this by the need to help those who are poor. We determine our fate, individual and collective, in large measure by the ideas and values we place stock in, the ideas and values that we trust, prefer, value, and act on. That is why it is vital to place foreign aid on a firm moral foundation. But moreover—as the economic livelihood of the poor often is a matter of things beyond their control, as well as of their perseverance and values— so we have not the means to control the world's course, no matter what measures of cooperation and generosity we try: we are in need requiring all our moral capacities, but also requiring help we cannot command. May we be moved to help those who cannot repay us, just as we need help that we are unable to supply for ourselves. For this reason I see God's kindness in all who have helped me with this book, which I could not have written without their aid.

And in no community has that been more evident than in my own family, who have helped me in every way named above at one time or another, and in others as well. My brothers John and Peter have been a constant source of support to me, encouraging me and giving invaluable assistance. My parents, Arthur and Marion Lumsdaine, have helped me thoughout this enterprise even more; and first taught me how to think out problems in a scholarly and humanly responsible way. It is to them that this book is gratefully dedicated.

# Abbreviations

| | |
|---|---|
| ADB | Asian Development Bank |
| AfDB | African Development Bank |
| AFL | American Federation of Labor |
| ASEAN | Association of Southeast Asian Nations |
| CMEA | Council for Mutual Economic Assistance |
| DAC | Development Assistance Committee (of the OECD) |
| DOM | Départments d'Outre-Mer (Overseas Departments of France) |
| ECOSOC | Economic and Social Council (of the UN) |
| EPTA | Expanded Programme of Technical Assistance |
| ERP | European Recovery Program (Marshall Plan) |
| FAO | Food and Agriculture Organization |
| GATT | General Agreement on Tariffs and Trade |
| GDP | Gross Domestic Product |
| IBRD | The International Bank for Reconstruction and Development (the World Bank) |
| IDA | International Development Association (of the World Bank) |
| IDB | Inter-American Development Bank |
| IFC | International Finance Corporation |
| IIAA | Institute of Inter-American Affairs |
| ILO | International Labour Organization |
| IMC | International Missionary Council |
| IMF | International Monetary Fund |
| IRO | International Refugee Organization |
| LDC | Less Developed Country |
| LIC | Lower Income Country |
| LLDC | Least Developed Country |
| MITI | (Japanese) Ministry of International Trade and Investment |
| MOFA | (Japanese) Ministry of Foreign Affairs |
| NGO | Non-Governmental Organization |
| NIEO | New International Economic Order |
| ODA | Official Development Assistance |
| OECD | Organization for Economic Cooperation and Development |
| OEEC | Organization for European Economic Cooperation |
| OPEC | Organization of Petroleum Exporting Countries |

| PVO | Private Voluntary Organization |
| SCLC | Southern Christian Leadership Conference |
| SSA | Security-Supporting Assistance |
| SUNFED | Special United Nations Fund for Economic Development |
| TOM | Territoires d'Outre-Mer (Overseas Territories of France) |
| UAE | United Arab Emirates |
| UNDP | United Nations Development Program |
| UNHCR | United Nations High Commissioner for Refugees |
| UNICEF | United Nations International Children's Emergency Fund |
| UNIDO | United Nations Industrial Development Organization |
| UNRRA | United Nations Relief and Rehabilitation Administration |
| WHO | World Health Organization |

# PART I

# The Argument

## CHAPTER ONE

# Do Morals Matter in International Politics?

> I am sure that the power of vested interest is vastly exaggerated
> compared with the gradual encroachment of ideas. Not indeed,
> immediately, but after a certain interval; for in the field of eco-
> nomic and political philosophy there are not many who are influ-
> enced by new theories after they are twenty-five or thirty years of
> age, so that the ideas which civil servants and politicians and even
> agitators apply to current events are not likely to be the newest.
> But, soon or late, it is ideas, not vested interests, which are dan-
> gerous for good or evil.
>
> —John Maynard Keynes[1]

## IS CONSTRUCTIVE CHANGE IN THE INTERNATIONAL SYSTEM POSSIBLE?

How can the international system be changed to make the world a better
place? Can it be changed at all? Certainly changes occur; but if human
efforts cannot affect how things change, there is little hope of building a
better world. Some assume that everything in politics is a matter of calculated self-interest. Others hold that international anarchy and the distribution of power alone determine the basic character of international
politics. This book argues that efforts to build a better world can effect
significant change in international politics: vision, hope, commitment,
conviction sometimes make a big difference.

Many converging lines of evidence show that economic foreign aid
cannot be explained on the basis of donor states' political and economic
interests, and that humanitarian concern in the donor countries formed
the main basis of support for aid. The same conclusion emerges whether
one examines where donor countries spent their money, what countries
contributed a lot of aid, which groups and politicians supported aid, what
the public thought, how aid started, or how it changed over time. Support
for aid was a response to world poverty which arose mainly from ethical
and humane concern and, secondarily, from the belief that long-term
peace and prosperity was possible only in a generous and just international order where all could prosper.

Aid was pivotal in North-South relations. Foreign aid has been the largest financial flow to most less developed countries (LDCs) over the past forty years, far exceeding investment by multinational firms. Of course, aid was not completely pure: any program involving half a trillion dollars, a score of donor countries, many international agencies, and 120 recipient countries over half a century will involve mixed influences. As much as a third of aid mainly served donors' commercial, colonial, or strategic goals.[2] However, most foreign aid was based on donors' humanitarianism and their perception of the world as an interdependent community.

But the argument goes beyond the issue of foreign aid, important as that was. The underlying question is whether moral vision and commitment can help shape the global system. Most analytic theories of international politics deny this possibility or ignore the question. A growing scholarly literature engaging in moral reflection on world politics[3] often does not address empirical theories of international relations, and risks producing "purely theoretical discussions about ethics in world affairs."[4] This book seeks to bridge that gap. Most of the book is a detailed empirical analysis of how foreign aid came to be what it is, which is summarized in chapter 2. Readers more interested in foreign aid than in theories of international politics—and those so incredulous that they want some proof before they read further—should turn to that chapter at once. Yet in looking at foreign aid, I also aim to elaborate a more general understanding of how moral values can alter the tenor of international affairs.

This first chapter explores why the theoretically neglected factors of moral vision, values, and principles may play a large role in international affairs, by showing how states are able to go beyond their own self-interests. Many scholars assume nations act only to secure national self-interest, because of human selfishness and because only self-seeking states will thrive and continue to have influence. Selfishness and survival pressures are ubiquitous, but I argue that they are not absolute. Rigorous-sounding claims that self-interest is all-determining in world politics are often little more than plausibility arguments. States have significant choice and can modulate and counterbalance self-interest, destructive human impulses, and the pressures of the international system. The argument proceeds as follows. The next section of this chapter discusses the wide range of human nature expressed in international politics. The following section explores why genuine needs for prudence and wariness do not force states to be amoral calculators, despite Realist claims that systemic forces crowd out international public spirit and moral concern. A further section then presents an alternative understanding of the international system, building on arguments about human nature and about international anarchy to show how moral and political principles can structure international politics in important, lasting ways. Specifically, I argue that moral conceptions affect international politics in three ways: through the systematic transfer of domestic political conceptions of justice to international life; through social and moral dialogue that constitutes international society; and through normative meanings implicit in international regimes or practices such as foreign aid, meanings which shape the ongoing evolution of those practices.

All three effects show up repeatedly in the detailed quantitative and historical data on foreign aid. (1) This book shows that attitudes toward poverty in the development of the social welfare state paved the way for economic assistance to less developed countries. (2) Interactions with other states and of citizens with other people worldwide also influenced countries' aid policies. Growing popular awareness of poverty overseas, and the increasing numbers of professionals trained to work on problems of economic growth, affected aid. The fact that European countries had themselves received Marshall Plan aid helped overcome their initial reluctance to provide foreign aid to LDCs. The example of leading developed countries and the claims of LDCs in international forums also helped create a belief that developed countries had a moral obligation to provide aid. (3) The principle of help to those in great need implicit in the very idea of foreign aid led to steady modification of aid practices, which focused them more on the needs of the poor and moved them away from donor interest.

All three hypotheses also apply to issue areas other than foreign aid. Domestic attitudes toward conflict resolution should, if my broader argument is correct, influence attitudes toward international conflict. States that tyrannize over their own people may be ready to tyrannize over their neighbors. International society may encourage an atmosphere of cynicism and indifference to the rights of other peoples, or of hostility between groups, or of admiration of the ruthless use of force, or it may strengthen friendly relations and concern for international law. Many kinds of regimes and practices display a long-term evolution guided by their implicit social and moral meanings. The systematic effects of domestic values on foreign policy, of international society, and of moral meanings implicit in international practices constitute, I argue, a general program for research on ethical influence on the international system.

Thus moral reflection and leadership help shape what international life is like. The influence of domestic principles, of international public opinion, and of morally significant international regimes and practices is not automatic, and not always benign. But it is possible to labor to make international politics more responsive to considerations of justice and compassion. In the case of foreign aid, ethical influences have been crucial (despite many lamentable problems with aid), as the rest of the book shows in detail. The principle that the affluent should use their wealth to help those in dire poverty across international boundaries—a humanitarian principle clearly opposed to the rule of the strong for their own benefit—came to govern the largest financial transactions between rich nations and poor consistently and increasingly, over a period of more than forty years. Knowing that there are moral choices to make in international politics doesn't keep world politics from being vicious; but it does leave us responsible for the world we make.

## SELF-INTEREST AND HUMAN NATURE

Self-interest is not the inevitable determinant of international politics, about which we need, and can, do nothing. The contention that self-interest is inevitable takes two main forms. Some hold that human beings are inherently selfish, and intent on power. Others make a social-Darwinist argument that states must be self-interested, for only the strong survive in the international system. In this view, states' efforts to be just and generous build on sand: they can accomplish nothing in the anarchic international realm in which power is the prime mover and only ultimate reality. Both arguments are part of the Realist viewpoint that has dominated international relations scholarship in the past half century. Both imply that moral factors are negligible, that as E. H. Carr put it, "in the international order, the role of power is greater and that of morality less."[5]

Characteristic Realist emphases—a frank interest in the dynamics of power in anarchy, emphasis on the need for wariness in a dangerous world, caution about excesses, attention to ubiquitous drives for pre-eminence, a careful working out of the implications of self-interest—constitute an important theoretical and moral legacy for which we can be thankful; the argument here is not meant to downplay or contest the many fine insights of Realist thought. On the contrary, recognition of the power of the selfish and destructive elements in human nature and world politics is an essential part of my theoretical argument in this chapter, and is pivotal to the moral argument sketched in chapter 9. But many leading Realists go further, claiming explicitly or by implication that human venality and corruption, and the dynamics of power, preclude human compassion and idealism from being an important, modulating, force in international politics. Too easily, the single-minded pursuit of power and interest comes to be seen as inevitable, as natural, and as unproblematic. It is such deterministic and cynical views, which I think naive and unrealistic, that I aim to dissent from. This section of the chapter argues that human nature is more complex: self-interest, irrational destructiveness, and principle and compassion all play a role in international politics as well as in civil society and domestic politics. The following section addresses the claim that human nature is irrelevant because of the inexorable logic of the international system.

Though many contemporary Realists eschew all discussion of human nature, an accurate view of human potentialities is important to understanding the logic of international politics. Hans Morgenthau, "the founding father" of the discipline,[6] sees international politics as "governed by objective laws that have their roots in human nature." Claiming that "whatever man does . . . emanates from himself and refers again to himself," Morgenthau argues that "moral conflict between the self and others is . . . inevitable" because of the demands of scarcity. Unlike many later Realists, Morgenthau also sees politics corrupted by "the *animus dominandi*, the desire for power,"[7] a "psychological relation" based in a "tendency to dominate . . . [which] is an element of all human associations" and is present even in animals.[8] At the same time, Morgenthau says the national interest is objectively given by a state's international circumstances, for "objective laws" govern international politics, and "society in general."

The crucial concept of "interest defined in terms of power" is a "signpost" which enables "political realism to find its way through the landscape of international politics" and gives a country "foreign policy consistent within itself, regardless of the different motives, preferences, and intellectual and moral qualities of successive statesmen." Focusing on power enables the analyst to avoid "concern with motives and . . . ideological preferences," a "popular fallacy of equating the foreign policies of a statesman with his philosophic or political sympathies."[9] Pursuit of the national interest requires a chesslike, or even Machiavellian, rationality—cleverness in attaining power with limited means. As Spykman put it, "the struggle for survival, and the improvement of the relative power position becomes the primary objective of the internal and external policy of states," for "power means survival, the ability to impose one's will on others . . . [and] to dictate to those who are without power." Accordingly, the

> statesman . . . can concern himself with values of justice, fairness, and tolerance *only to the extent* that they contribute to or do not interfere with the power objective. They can be used instrumentally as moral justification for the power quest, but they must be discarded the moment their application brings weakness. *The search for power is not made for the achievement of moral values; moral values are used to facilitate the attainment of power.* In this kind of a world states can survive only by constant devotion to power politics.[10] (emphasis added)

Power as a means to survive in a hostile world dictates the state's ends as well as its means, and this externally given end displaces other ends and controls state values.

Realism entails an "exclusion of morality from politics"[11] because international affairs are a realm apart, determined by exigencies of power politics alone and thus exempt from moral judgments. International politics is discontinuous from everyday life and domestic politics, particularly in a liberal democratic society, and requires different thinking.[12] Morgenthau deplores any "depreciation of power politics" as unclear thinking based on the "domestic experience" of the middle class in the nineteenth century. Attention to power is inevitable, but paradoxically it is also a virtue, for the concept of an objective national "interest defined in terms of power" provides the statesman with "rational discipline in action."[13] Lippman, Kennan, Spykman, Herz, Carr, and other classical Realists warn against the pernicious influence of "utopianism," "idealism," and "moralism," which derail the sensible pursuit of national interest and lead to dangerous excess. National security and acquisition of power are the only appropriate norms for a country's international conduct. A Realist understanding that moral and political principles cannot shape international politics protects foreign policy from the perilous, destabilizing, and immoral effects that non-Realist principles may induce.

In sum, the inevitability of self-interest in international relations is portrayed by classical Realists as a necessary consequence both of a uniformly selfish human nature and of the exigencies of power in anarchy. International politics is and should remain an autonomous sphere, immune from ordinary moral considerations and governed by objective laws. The inflexible dictates of international power politics determine national interests, which are ascertained by a technical, politically and philosophically neutral, rationality. Wise statesmanship is a matter of strategic skill, of mastering a calculus of advantage, a technical game for experts.

I demur. Self-interest undoubtedly plays a commanding role in the world's affairs. It is only natural that human beings individually and jointly seek to advance their interests. Unsure of just what threats we will face and of what our needs and desires will be, we want not only specific goods but power and control in general. Further, human beings are profoundly self-centered, and our egotism affects almost all we do, often corrupting even our genuine love for family and friends. The allure of wealth and pleasure, security and prestige, are obvious and powerful. We find it hard to see others' points of view or acknowledge our own faults. We attend to our own welfare when we should consider others' needs. But a view of human action that sees only self-interest is far too simple. It errs in leaving out the dark side of human character, often astonishingly powerful, as well as in ignoring the strength of compassionate feelings, or hatred of injustice. Principled refusals to do wrong, and acts of love and compassion, are common, as are folly, unnecessary hatred and domineering, and self-defeating behavior. Human beings are a mixture of self-interest, idealism, and pointless destructiveness. All three elements operate, in varying proportions, in civil society and politics and in international affairs as well as in the life of the individual.

Much of what people do is simply destructive. Selfish actions intended to make us better off are often counterproductive. We easily become prisoners of grasping, power-conscious, domineering, or overcautious attitudes that serve our interests poorly. Openly self-defeating acts and attitudes are not unusual: resentments, desires for domination or revenge, paranoia, outbursts of annoyance and unkindness, and settled animosities often undermine the goals we seek. Human self-centeredness goes far beyond the rational pursuit of goals that enhance the individual's well-being or pleasure; it includes addictions, pointless antagonisms, distorted priorities, and desires for dominance. The point is not that self-destructive acts satisfy no impulse whatever; acts of that kind are rare. But acts which predictably result in frustrating and debilitating consequences are all too common.

Destructive and unnecessarily hostile actions are common in group relations and international politics as well as in personal life. Much violence—in international, as in civic and familial life—serves no one's interests. Futile obsessions, feuds, and unjustified distrusts abound. Selfishness often lies behind foolish egocentrisms, but it is hard to call such behavior self-interested. While there are genuine security interests which develop in ethnic groups' strife, internationally and nationally, antagonisms between Israelis and Arabs, Greeks and Turks, Armenians and Azerbaijanis, and even Argentines and Brazilians are not simply rational responses to threat; they involve personal antipathies that help neither side. Conciliation may be difficult even if everyone would benefit. These irrational dislikes may be inflamed by minor incidents more than by genuine increases in threat.

Yet life is also full of principle and heroism, patriotism, costly honesty, compassion for people in need, and devotion to worldwide peace and justice. Mencius observed that "it is a feeling common to all mankind that they cannot bear to see others suffer. . . . This feeling of distress [at the suffering of others] is the first sign of humanity." Parents try to overcome children's self-centeredness and to extend their sympathies for others. Religious and ethical teaching enjoins us to "consider not only your own interests, but also the interests of others," to be honest, and to respect moral limits. Principled, altruistic behavior exists at every level from personal life to the international system. A few individuals open their hearts to engage in daring acts in defense of others, as Raoul Wallenberg did, or are gripped like Mother Theresa's Sisters of Charity by a lifelong dedication to the poor, the homeless, and the dying; but smaller acts of honesty, kindness, or courage are more common. Many people make sacrifices for the common good, or for strangers, in daily life. Kohn draws on a growing literature to document widespread altruistic and prosocial behavior: on people giving time, money, and blood, on empathetic distress, on concern about justice, on bystander intervention in emergencies, and so forth.[14] Hornstein, Fisch, and Holmes note that 50% of people will mail back an apparently lost wallet.[15] The Carnegie Foundation Hero Fund Commission commends dozens of "outstanding acts of selfless heroism" in the United States and Canada each year.[16] Fellner and Marshall observe that many people donate a kidney to a stranger without consideration of anything about the recipient except that without it he will die.[17] Staub cites examples ranging from minor assistance to cases where people risk their lives to save strangers.[18] Krebs likewise concludes that "a substantial amount of research indicates that people may behave prosocially to maintain equity and justice in interpersonal relations."[19]

Group relations, also, can be informed by principled concern for fairness and for disadvantaged groups. No society is without vast amounts of selfish behavior, and power and unbridled self-interest may be even harder to curb in society than in the life of the individual. But the degree to which unnecessary social viciousness, kindness, reform, and principle are present varies widely. There are notable examples of groups and communities acting in organized ways for the sake of others, as the villagers of Le Chambon in France did, in shielding thousands of Jews from the Nazis at risk of their own lives as a part of their vision of the social meaning of their Huguenot faith.[20] Generosity can operate socially on a regular basis as well as in crisis. Richard Titmuss's book *The Gift Relationship* showed that systems of voluntary blood donation worked extremely well, providing sufficient amounts for hospital needs at higher quality than did systems relying on monetary or other incentives to donors. Attempts to supplement donations with purchased blood tended to undermine the voluntary provision.[21] Concern for justice can shift power in society toward the powerless, sometimes with the consent of the powerful who have come to acknowledge the demands of justice. Significant devolution of power from privileged groups and classes has altered older, exclusionary forms of rule. Tocqueville's claim that the world had become more democratic with every succeeding half century since 1500 still holds true. Representative government, restraints on state power, extension of suffrage, the rule of law, awareness of civil and human rights, and the provision of social welfare benefits seem to be increasingly widespread. Martin Luther King showed the power of moral force, combined with effective pressure, in successful nonviolent demonstrations that galvanized American conscience. Unaffected people of goodwill from across the country marched for racial justice in the South, and white legislatures and courts overturned legal segregation and mandated remedies for past wrongs. Many university and other communities embraced affirmative action out of conviction. Christopher Mooney observes that by "a 71% to 21% margin . . . white Americans agreed that 'after years of discrimination it is only fair to set up special programs to make sure that women and minorities are given every chance to have equal opportunities in employment and education.'" Courts and lawmakers sensed a rare "unified national interest in regard to a specific moral principle" and effected an unprecedented "transformation both in the distribution of opportunity and the obligations of government."[22]

International politics particularly involve violence, the struggle for power, group self-centeredness, and indifference to the rights and fates of others. Power without law, morality, or social restraints especially characterizes relations between nations for many reasons: lack of a sovereign, an absence of acknowledged rules, ethnic prejudices, national pride that legitimates violence, fears of unlimited consequences that could lead even to death and enslavement. Interstate relations are often ruled by force, violence, and brutality, and understandable self-reinforcing expectations of anarchy. International politics is the one arena in which group differences are routinely settled by organized mass killing, by war.

Yet appeals to conscience have effected some significant changes even in international politics. Wilberforce and the English evangelicals worked tirelessly and effectively for the abolition of slave trading and slavery in the British Empire. Henry Dunant, horrified at wounded soldiers dying unattended at the Battle of Solferino, stirred the conscience of the world with his writing, in a way that succeeded in establishing the Geneva conventions on warfare as well as the Red Cross. Fridtjof Nansen gained lasting international commitments to assist refugees by his persistent appeals to the conscience of world leaders, and his successors established international status for stateless persons, a permanent office for refugees, and a presumption of international support for them which is now taken for granted.[23] Mohandas K. Gandhi, Martin Luther King's model, expelled the British from India, while preserving democracy and fostering norms of equality within, by determined and self-sacrificial moral suasion. Amnesty International and other groups have strengthened international support for human rights and given regimes notorious for their abuses a pariah status.

The notion that national self-interest must be a country's exclusive motivation is curious, in a way, because the effective pursuit of national interests presupposes idealism on the part of individuals. Existence of a sovereign possessing a monopoly of force does not guarantee effective government. A country can be run despite cynicism and hostility toward the government and its laws, but it cannot be run well. Laws serving the interest of the holders of power alone seldom command wide assent; illegitimate governments may find it hard to get effective compliance even with legitimate, constructive, demands. Morale, loyalty, conviction that the national interest is worth serving are vital to the state. Unless residents of a country sense common interests and destiny, it is hard to resolve intergroup tensions which are bound to arise: some of the differences between national and international politics have disappeared. Effective administration also demands foresight and creative problem solving, which are needed to keep many complex factors in balance. Intelligent and loyal public service that keeps the country on track requires people with strong principles and ideas, who are willing to exercise independent judgment and risk disapproval in order make things work well. The effective functioning of the state relies in many ways on sustaining idealism and national loyalty. National self-interest, like commitment to international goals of peace and justice, requires principled idealists committed to the common good.

And idealistic people needed to serve the government are apt to have strong commitments not only to the nation but to mankind. Good citizens and officials have many sets of concerns: they may be strong adherents of a party, have strong aims for society, strong views about international questions, and so on. They seek to balance and reconcile official duties, personal goals, and broader principles so that all may be served. Finding ways to advance broader human interests consistent with national interests requires the same ingenuity and inspiration in balancing various loyalties that the running of the country does. The national state itself would be weak indeed, then, without the ideals and capacities that also make commitment to international peace and justice possible. And thoughtful, devoted support, including willingness to make sacrifices if need be, is elicited by worthy and inspiring goals, so that the idealism and public assent needed for effective national government may itself be strengthened by a broad, idealistic international vision.

## System-Level Determination of Self-Interest

But does the diversity of human motives and social structures affect international politics? Most contemporary Realists eschew discussing human nature, and base their arguments upon the logic of the international system instead. To the extent that survival pressures tightly constrain states' behavior, internal characteristics cannot seriously affect state conduct, and discussion of the self-interested, destructive, and principled elements in human nature and society is irrelevant. So it is argued that the international system inexorably shapes what states do, by presenting states with overwhelming incentives, or by eliminating states that fail to pursue self-interest relentlessly. This systemic conditioning and natural selection may also be supplemented by a competition for influence: states that follow realpolitik maxims grow and those that irrationally ignore the mandate to egoism decline and lose all influence (except as examples of folly, warnings not to be beguiled by a seductive idealism). States may enter into regimes, agreements, and cooperative behavior at times, but only as doing so furthers their self-interests. Is there such an inescapable, anarchic, self-help international system, which forces states to engage in self-interested foreign policy and makes international politics a realm apart, unaffected by the range of human motives and social structures?

Kenneth Waltz, perhaps the "father" of neo-Realist thinking, has elaborated this line of thought. His 1959 book, *Man, the State and War*, helpfully classifies analyses of international politics as first, second, or third image: those locating explanation in human character, in the internal structure of states, and in international anarchy, respectively. He begins by asking, "Can we have peace more often in the future than in the past?" and concludes that since human nature and the morality of individual states will always be imperfect, nations will inevitably settle disputes by warfare and act out of self-interest alone.

> The third image . . . avoids the tendency of some realists to attribute the necessary amorality, or even immorality, of world politics to the inherently bad character of man. . . . No matter how good their intentions, policy makers must bear in mind the implications of the third image . . . : Each state pursues its own interests, however defined, in ways it judges best. Force is a means of achieving the external ends of states because there exists no consistent, reliable process of reconciling the conflicts of interest that inevitably arise among similar units in a condition of anarchy. A foreign policy based on this image of international relations is neither moral nor immoral, but embodies merely a reasoned response to the world about us.[24]

Waltz's 1979 *Theory of International Politics* amplifies the same line of thought. There he claims it is a kind of theorem that in an anarchic system composed of functionally similar units the distribution of power alone determines that system's fundamental parameters: thus international politics is inevitably a self-help system. Main conclusions of classical Realism, including its deprecation of morality as impossible and unrealistic in international affairs, are reformulated as part of an inexorable systems logic. Even more than in Morgenthau, international politics is a realm apart, utterly distinct from human character and domestic society.[25]

These extreme claims of structural determinism are incorrect for at least five reasons: survival pressures do not tightly constrain state behavior; the system itself can be altered by changes in the views and practices and relationships of its constituent units; realpolitik policies are not always those which reward states best; the moral tone of a state's international policies is a factor in its strength; and the ideas and domestic social values states hold are essential to reckoning their interests.

1. *States can choose to be public-spirited*, despite system constraints. States have to be wary, of course, but that leaves them a lot of slack. All organizations, all people, must exercise a reasonable prudence and care for themselves in order to survive. But they can pursue goals other than survival. The argument that structural pressures make system transformation impossible presumes that exigencies of survival in the system tightly constrain states, which must pursue self-interest single-mindedly or decline. "The international imperative is 'take care of yourself!'" Waltz tells us. "With each country constrained to take care of itself, no one can take care of the system." But the international system often does not tightly constrain states: it leaves them discretion, which can be used to aid those in need or to work on building a better international order.[26]

The fact that the world is a dangerous place and that states must exercise prudence and be wary is not, in itself, an argument for Realism. The knowledge that the world is full of dangers can be used as the starting point for many different kinds of arguments. Idealists like Woodrow Wilson inferred the need for collective security arrangements, the importance of world public opinion, and the need to establish stable democracies on the basis of self-determination. One can argue that adherence to fundamental moral principle is the best guide to prudent policy: that genuine commitment to making a just and generous world society is the best foundation for long-term peace and prosperity. The idea that a dangerous, sovereignless world makes a self-help system inevitable is not self-evident.

Situations of anarchy, in which actors face potentially serious security threats which no sovereign polices, are not always "self-help" systems in which no one cares for the public interest, or the interests of others. Michael Taylor reviews substantial evidence on primitive and other communities that provide collective goods and maintain social order without sovereign enforcement, and gives a theoretical account of how this can happen. What happens in anarchy depends on the character of the units and on their process of interaction.[27] Josiah Royce's research on California mining camps bereft of state authority illustrates these points. Law-abiding Americans in an initial anarchy were able to combine to protect against wrongdoers. Harsh extralegal justice against malefactors and a prolonged absence of a settled social life, not the inability to organize under anarchy, undermined social order over time. The sources of order and disorder had less to do with the anarchic structure and absence of sovereign enforcement than with individual character, the sense of community and common identity, the role of law, and the tendency for quasi-legal violence, once initiated, to become habitual.[28]

Biological and economic selection pressures do not always force units into a single mode of survival. Firms and households behave quite variously despite the constant competitive pressure of market forces. Households must provide for themselves in an economic "self-help" system, but exigencies of survival do not keep people from taking risks and spending time and money to promote causes they believe in, or to spite people they hate. Firms do not just adjust to market forces; entrepreneurs, moved by ideas, create innovations like personal computers, as Schumpeter argued. Brian Arthur, Paul David, Douglas Puffert, and others explain how, where there are increasing returns to scale, the market leaves many technological and economic outcomes indeterminate; the final balance is an accumulation of small choices.[29] Similarly, Gould and Eldredge show there is no single fixed path in biological evolution; no unique equilibrium predetermines what is "fittest." Contingent events can send species and ecosystems down this path or that. "Organisms are not putty before a molding environment or billiard balls before the pool cue of natural selection. Their inherited forms and behaviors constrain and push back; they cannot be quickly transformed to new optimality every time the environment alters."[30] Organisms develop and retain characteristics not immediately useful for survival. The biological environment places some powerful constraints on organisms but does not tightly determine them.

Krasner argues that the states' system, like the marketplace and biological world, is contingent and may show great institutional persistence. The nation-state persists as a form, even where it is not efficient. This may consign us to a world that destroys itself for lack of cooperation, he argues.[31] Indeed it may. But if so, the problem is not an inevitable result of international anarchy, but results from human blindness and institutional inflexibility. Nothing about an anarchic system as such makes pure self-help logically inevitable. The international system does not tightly constrain what states do; they have some slack, discretion, to build the world they choose.

2. *The system itself can change.* The international system is constructed from the interacting behavior of parts. The "system" is not a mystic entity exerting forces on the parts; only the behavior of the parts, past, current, and anticipated, provides the individual units with "sys-

temic" incentives. Thus, any factor that changes the way many units act changes the system, also. Where units and the system arise from the interaction of the units, forces at the systemic level and internal forces that affect the units' behavior are codetermining.

Most accounts in which the character of international politics is determined by anarchy presume that changes in units cannot alter the fundamental nature of the system or alter the basic quality of international life. Waltz specifically argues that self-help, realpolitik behavior is structurally required where functionally identical units compete in anarchy. "Some have hoped that changes in the awareness and purpose, in the organization and ideology, of states would change the quality of international life. [But in vain] . . . The only remedy for a strong structural effect is a structural change."[32] But this is simply erroneous, unless it is defined so as to make it tautologous. Axelrod, in his well-known *Evolution of Cooperation*, displays a system of competitive, functionally identical units of equal capacity within which the kind of behavior that pays off depends not upon the distribution of power but upon the distribution of policies.[33] In Axelrod's model, cooperative behavior becomes more profitable for all actors when a number of units adopt more cooperative policies. Increasing returns to cooperation mean that moves toward more cooperative policies can snowball. Moreover, he shows that under some circumstances, actors with policies which would not do well in the existing equilibrium of a system can "invade" it; by sticking together, states with cooperative policies can support one another in order to thrive in a less benign world and, ultimately, to alter it.[34]

The idea of increasing returns to cooperative conduct in international affairs is implicit in a number of classical arguments for cooperation. Both Saint-Pierre and Kant argued that if some states adhered to a defensive league, other states would face increased incentives to join.[35] One can imagine other, similar propositions. If democracies don't fight one another, the spread of democracy alters states' incentives. If social-democratic states are moved by human compassion to help states suffering internal calamities instead of exploiting their weakness, that affects the amount prudent states will spend on armies. If a sense of common identity allows states in an area to develop a common currency, or free trade, we live in a potentially different kind of system from one in which such a thing is an unthinkable loss of control. On the other hand, if states have enduring animosities based less on strategic vulnerability than on memories of historic wrongs, that also affects the system. If states that domineer over their own people present a greater threat to the people of nearby states, changes in domestic government can induce a more hostile, fearful system. Changes in interstate process and in the domestic character of states, if widespread, may alter the tenor of the international system for good or ill.

Changes in foreign policy can set in motion dynamics that change the functioning of the international system. If domestic political systems affect foreign policies systematically, worldwide changes in domestic political systems may change the tenor of international politics. If political systems model their behavior on one another, changes of habits may snowball to make the system different. If citizens see themselves as part of a worldwide human family, or feel bound in their international dealings by moral and political principles that govern domestic politics, changes in "international society" can alter the basic quality of international politics.

*3. Cooperative behavior often pays off.* The existence of payoffs to cooperation does not disprove the idea that state behavior is egoistic. Much of the theoretical literature on international cooperation in the last ten years shows why cooperation can occur even among hard-shelled rational egoists. In itself, the existence of important returns to cooperation need not weaken the conclusion that unit behavior is determined by the exigencies of survival in a competitive system. Demonstrations that cooperation can pay are not claims that cooperation is inevitable.

But the claim that egoism is determined by the system does presume that the behavior the system rewards is realpolitik: ruthless, unprincipled, unfaithful, competitive, concerned with triumphing over others, unrestrained except by countervailing power or incentives. Waltz holds that insecure states "are compelled" by the nature of the international system to concentrate on relative, rather than on absolute, gains. "Structural constraints explain why the [same] methods are repeatedly used despite differences in the persons and states who use them." These are realpolitik methods whose elements, "exhaustively listed, are these: The ruler's . . . interest provides the springs of action; the necessities of policy arise from the unregulated competition of states; calculation based on these necessities can discover the policies that will best serve a state's interests; success is the ultimate test of policy, and success is defined as preserving and strengthening the state."[36] But if there are strong returns to prosocial as well as to self-centered behavior, states can seek to develop their interests in a way consistent with principled support of a better world. If the benefits of behaving like isolated units indifferent or hostile to others are often outweighed by the benefits of being cooperative, realpolitik behavior is not systemically compelled. No one doubts that there are pressures on actors to behave selfishly. Where there are returns to cooperative behavior as well, though, the system is ambiguous, providing mixed incentives, and may permit reasonably successful states to pursue different kinds of strategies, according to the choices they prefer.

Some benefits accrue to cooperative behavior in one-on-one interactions even without specific agreements. Axelrod has shown how in long-term interactions actors who act cooperatively (but with reciprocity) can do better than actors who pursue their gains at the expense of others in a greedy or aggressive way.[37] There may be benefits from reputation: if actors can gain from having a reputation for "toughness"[38] they may also gain from reputations for trustworthiness, reasonableness, cooperativeness, or even generous good faith toward partners. Such reputations are the more valuable where there is much to gain from mutual bargains, and considerable fear of being let down. The benefits from being a partner others can trust are also amplified if specific cooperative arrangements end up creating international networks of policymakers.[39] Even with a single partner, cooperation on some issues may well also lead to the development of institutional links, which make further cooperation easier and cheaper.[40]

However, finding a sustainable mutually beneficial arrangement among a group of actors often requires establishing international regimes—understood as principles, rules, norms, and decision-making procedures around which the behavior of states converges—and other kinds of cooperation under anarchy.[41] The existence of such expectations changes state behavior because they alter states' incentives from what they would be in the absence of the regimes. Opportunities to find mutually beneficial deals are often missed in the absence of institutionalization of some kind. Clear delineation of expectations (including a framework of legal liability), the reduction of transaction costs, and the provision of information (particularly high-quality symmetrical information) to allow monitoring and coordination are all factors that can facilitate the creation and maintenance of cooperation.[42] The greater the issue density and the greater the number of potential areas of cooperation among actors, too, the more opportunities there are for cooperation.[43] The availability of adequate information is important so that actors can assure themselves that cooperation continues to be in their own best interests and that others are doing their part. Mutuality of interests, the shadow of the future, and the number of players will all affect how easy it is to find and agree upon cooperative solutions.[44]

Payoffs to cooperation can occur whether or not the actors are aware of them, and cooperation can sometimes evolve whether the actors are aware of its benefits or not. The payoffs to cooperation do not presuppose rational egoism. But cooperation will be slower to occur where actors doubt its viability or focus unnecessarily on relative gains. Axelrod's work shows that even quite sophisticated actors are in fact often mesmerized by short-term relative gains, even when this focus serves them poorly in the struggle for survival. A grasping attitude is often an impediment to self-interest as well as to cooperation.[45] Thus, since several kinds of strategies are consistent with the state's survival, the individual and domestic political ethos can be important in choosing less or more cooperative strategies.[46]

*4. A country's strength may be increased by deeply held ideals*, for a variety of reasons. The presence of strongly held ideals may work to unify a nation, just as it may serve as a "glue" holding together coalitions.[47] Countries are strengthened by "republican virtue," by citizen willingness to obey laws, pay taxes, and make sacrifices in time of need. A country whose internal legitimacy is damaged faces serious problems, no matter its coercive resources. Promoting the idea of the country as a good citizen in a larger world is consonant with promoting good citizenship at home. High purpose and ideals in a state's external dealings tends to attract dedicated, idealistic, bright public servants, which the state needs for all its goals. Articulation of a clear, compelling vision for the nation helps different elements of the country to work together more effectively. Idealism may foster insight into building constructive relations abroad.

Ideals and strong principles of domestic government may also restrain states from folly. Robert Osgood argues that states which ignore moral strictures are apt to become involved in self-destructive excesses. Jack Donnelly, in a powerful paper, "Thucydides and Realism," argues that just such unrestrained egotism, or *pleonexia*, led to the downfall of Athens.

> Pursuit of power, interest and gain causes them, in the end, to lose all, largely because of the growing Realism of their policy. To renounce ethical restraint in foreign affairs, whatever the intention, is in practice likely to give free reign to passionate, grasping desire. In principle, rational long-term self-interest may check desire. In practice, this is unlikely, "unrealistic" in the ordinary sense of that term. As Robert Osgood notes, "it is certainly utopian to expect any great number of people to have the wit to perceive or the will to follow the dictates of enlightened self-interest on the basis of reason alone. Rational self-interest divorced from ideal principles is as weak and erratic a guide for foreign policy as idealism undisciplined by reason." . . . Without ethical restraints, the pursuit of interest is not clarified and purified, as Realists would have it. Rather, it degenerates into an uncontrollable grasping desire that in the end destroys even the desirer.[48]

Rousseau's critique of Saint-Pierre's proposed peace plan, similarly, locates the problems not in international anarchy, nor in the true interests of states, but in the irresponsible passions and folly of kings. Monarchs love "war and conquest without and the encroachment of despotism within" to the detriment of their countries' strength as well as of their citizens' well-being.[49] Kant, accordingly, held that members of a defensive league for "Perpetual Peace" should be republics, since states that conduct their internal affairs rationally rather than by sovereign fiat would tend to be more peaceful and just in international conduct.[50] Wilson's view that the spread of democracy would promote peace continued the same line of reasoning.

Both the rationality of the state and its strength are often functions of its moral fiber. Pursuit of just and idealistic policies may provide the state reserves of commitment and of thinking unavailable to a cynical, exploitative, or realpolitik state. Genuine idealism and moral resolve are not simply unprofitable luxury items, although they cannot be manufactured to order when it is realized that they are useful. They provide a source of strength in domestic and international affairs, while also imposing some costs.

*5. State rationality is not independent of philosophical outlook.* The idea that structural constraints govern state behavior presupposes that statesmen know and respond to the requirements the system imposes. It therefore presumes that states' rationality is a matter of calculating their interests, defined in terms of power. Social philosophy is irrelevant, for "changes in the awareness and purpose, in the organization and ideology, of states" cannot change the "quality of international life," according to Waltz.[51] Everything depends upon system structure; rationality consists in seeing the plain facts of power clearly.

But the facts of power are not plain and clear and do not lend themselves to objective perceptions of self-interest. Deciding how to serve even selfish interests depends upon one's general outlook on international politics and requires judgments about what to think, trust in, and value. The great difficulties of rationality are not those of calculating what to do in a known world, or even of assessing probabilities among known alternatives. The real difficulties are those of understanding what the main features of the world are like.[52]

Consider the problems scholars have in constructing accounts of international politics. Different scholars employ diverse basic models, based on Realist, Marxist, Liberal, and other paradigms. These disagree about whether the state, the international system, classes, or individuals are principal actors, about how actors are constituted, and about how they act.[53] Different paradigms often explain different things, with different evidence. Evaluating their relative accuracy is no easy matter and depends on judgments about what phenomena are most important. But judgments of what is important depend upon theorists' value emphases, so that mutually supporting descriptive and normative theories are often worked out together. Similarly, politicians, or voters, differ not only in their goals but in the way they see the world. The emphasis on distinct paradigms can be overdone, as can partisan differences in national policy debates. But the cardinal role that varying interpretive frameworks play in scholarship and in political life arises not from scholarly obscurantism or unnecessary partisanship; it inheres in the fact that the social world is difficult to interpret, and understandings of it are bound up with one's moral and political outlook.

Any rationality with which states conduct themselves is not (as Waltz seems to imply) some inexorable realpolitik wisdom dictated by the international system (mysterious, invisible, yet more real than the things that are seen). Leaders are not demigods unswayed by human passions, philosophies, political interests, or moral concerns (as Morgenthau suggests). The rationality relevant to international politics is no mere matter of calculating payoffs from alternative futures with ascertainable probabilities and valuations. It is just this imaginative, imperfect, ideologically charged, outlook-dependent understanding that actual scholars, politicians, and publics have to use. So national self-interests emerge from a social process of choice and self-definition whose character and objectives are influenced by people's basic values and views of life. Therefore, political assumptions and practices of domestic political life may systematically affect international politics. Parties and countries that differ in domestic politics will differ predictably in international politics. Their choices will be influenced by their moral and political outlooks, or by their inattention to ethical questions, and not simply by the technical implementation of some inevitable, structurally determined national interest. They are choices for which people are morally responsible.

## An Alternative View of the International System

The same factors that indicate why action is not systemically determined also give clues in seeing how the richness of human motivation and thought, and of human society and relationships, have structural effects on the international system. Because there is slack in the system, actors' views and preferences as well as their survival needs affect their choices, and long-term, nonobvious strengths and weaknesses of different outlooks have time to make themselves felt. Because the international system is built up of the behavior of its units, value-based foreign policy choices can reinforce prosocial behavior and resist sliding toward a system whose norms are determined by its worst members. Because there are benefits to acting cooperatively, fairly, and with restraint, developing long-term positive relationships with other countries and prosocial international conduct is more possible than at first appears. Because shorter-term advantages can glitter more than solid long-term gains, even cooperative policies that serve states' self-interests may occur only when supported by public-spirited ideals, and leaders with strong convictions may be needed to provide reasoned arguments, vision, and reminders of principles easily laid aside. Because analyses of the political and moral realm are based not just on complex calculations but on one's general outlook on human society as well, the vision and insight with which nations and statesmen approach international relations will reflect their overall moral and political outlooks, including their domestic political views.

Thus international politics reflect actors' principles and moral vision, or lack of them, as well as incentives and structures that the international system presents. This central point suggests three more specific hypotheses:

1. The beliefs, values, and practices of daily moral discourse and domestic political life tend to be transferred to one's understanding and conduct of foreign affairs.
2. A country tends to be influenced, both in its international dealings and in its domestic political institutions, by its experience and role in international society.
3. International regimes and practices often have an inherent social meaning, so that the change in those international practices which are constituted around well-grounded moral norms tends to be ongoing, norm-governed change.

The three subsections that follow discuss these three hypotheses in turn. The first hypothesis, about the influence of domestic norms on international politics, is an "inside-out" explanation; the second, dealing with the influence of international society, is an "outside-in" explanation.[54] The third, emphasizing how the social meanings of practices influence their evolution, is an explanation at the level of the international system; however because such "reflectivist"[55] or "constructivist" explanation involves social and moral meanings, it involves issues of human character.

## 1. Systematic Domestic Influences on Foreign Policy

The values and practices of domestic political life are apt to be preferred in international politics. Citizens and leaders who favor certain principles in domestic politics are more apt to approve their worth and see their usefulness in international affairs, or to use their assumptions and models without reflection. Familiar and valued methods of organization seem plausible, while no one feels comfortable with untried, "foreign" methods. For instance, leaders of a democracy might well value democratically structured inter-nation dealings, such as an assembly of nations modeled on a democratic legislature. In addition to this, they would be more likely to think of such a model, and see its incidental practical advantages, than would officials of authoritarian countries.[56] The transfer of domestic democratic values to international relations may be one way of explaining the now well-established proposition that democracies seldom fight one another.[57] Similarly, a country familiar with particular economic arrangements domestically may be readier to cope with similar arrangements internationally, even where there is no strictly logical connection between the two. A country is prone to model international institutions and mechanisms and objectives on its domestic ones both because they accord with what it values and believes in and because they seem familiar and workable.

The influence of domestic political values, beliefs, and practices on a country's international policies should be clearly distinguished from the important idea that the desires and needs of domestic factions, and the outcomes of internal political bargaining, impinge on international policies. A country's needs to protect farmers, or placate its officer corps, or lower taxes may affect its international positions. The army or navy may insist on standard operating procedures even in moments of crisis. Capitalists may use the state to promote business interests abroad, and insecure holders of state power may reinforce their grip on power by seeking international support and prestige even if this is not in the national interest. Bureaucratic bargaining and domestic political demands certainly affect international affairs.[58] But the influence of such subnational interests is quite different from the structuring of international policies to reflect the values and beliefs and practices of national life. Jangling subnational interests are unlikely to move the conduct of international affairs in a systematic direction and cannot be expected to produce congruences between the forms of domestic and international life. They do not derive from general principles and are unlikely to lead a country to act public-spiritedly abroad. The impact of domestic factions and the clash of particularistic local interests impedes any broad international, or even national, vision. But the translation of principles of domestic cooperation into the international sphere can lead toward a higher-level rationality in which pursuit of the national interest is modified to take account of global human interests.

The creation and maintenance of foreign aid programs illustrates this transfer of domestic principles and practices to international politics in several ways. The countries with strong domestic social-welfare programs were the steadiest and most generous foreign aid donors. Politicians, parties, interest groups, and academic authors who disliked the welfare state disliked foreign aid; those who supported domestic redistributive and antipoverty measures supported foreign aid. Opinion polls show that citizens who felt strongly about alleviating poverty at home were more likely to favor foreign aid. Those who made private donations to charities dealing with overseas poverty also tended to favor foreign aid. Aid was referred to as a kind of international welfare state measure by supporters and by critics, and arguments used to justify the welfare state were used, by popular speakers and by professional philosophers, to justify international aid. The idea of international assistance was originated by strong advocates of domestic welfare measures, and was possible only after there was widespread consensus that the government ought to assist poor people in domestic society.

The same idea can readily be extended to many other possible transfers of domestic norms and practices to a country's international dealings. One might hypothesize that countries and individuals that favored laissez-faire economic policies domestically were more inclined to favor free-trade policies abroad. Liss argues that nineteenth-century Latin American trade links with Britain and the United States reflected influence of the doctrines of liberalism on the thinking of Latin American elites.[59] Attitudes toward colonialism may tend to reflect domestic racial attitudes and colonialism probably reinforced domestic racism. The colonialisms of the sixteenth century and of the nineteenth century seem to have involved establishing stereotypes of the conquered nations as racially inferior. Determined opposition to colonialism in this century has often been linked to struggles against racism,[60] while the stiff criticism of colonialism by the sixteenth-century Spanish church involved opposing claims that American Indians were less than fully human. The Just War theory that the theologians at Salamanca used to impugn the Spanish conquest of the New World was based in part on an analogy between justice among persons and justice among states or human communities.[61] Third World support for dependency theory and for delinking from the world capitalist economy in the 1960s and 1970s were based on socialist critiques of domestic economic political economy. There is a wide field for research in testing and refining the general proposition that domestic political practices and beliefs "systematically" affect foreign policy and interpretation of the international system.

## 2. International Society as an Influence on State Behavior

Practices and norms of international life also influence states' international conduct. Governments perceive their own state as a member of a society of states, and often seek to act in customary ways, or gauge their own nation's policies by those of other respected states, or conform to regional and worldwide norms. Citizens may see the state as operating in a worldwide human community, and judge state conduct based on human reactions to problems foreigners face. Cross-national friendships and common enterprises among professionals, businessmen, scientists, and students lead to personal bonds as well as to shared understandings of correct international practice.

The influence of international society must be clearly distinguished from that of incentives of the international system understood merely as interaction among states calculating tangible costs and benefits of various courses of action. All theorists agree that states belong to an "international system" in which they make choices based at least in part on anticipations of how other states will react. Realism, however, depicts this system as utterly different from domestic society because, lacking a sovereign to keep order and restrain violence, it must be a self-help, "anarchic" order. In this view, states deal with other states not on the basis of likes or dislikes, trust or distrust, friendship or emnity, but on the basis of calculations of interest and concerns about the international distribution of power. Each state has this a-social character, so states cannot develop noninstrumental relationships with other states. Deals are struck but states, unlike natural persons in civil society, do not respond to each other in more than a calculating way, and do not expect others to do so. Each state's behavior is geared to calculation of its advantage; hence attempts to develop lasting friendships with other states are futile, even if some oddball state should want to try.

A view of the international environment as international society, on the other hand, presupposes that states may care how they are regarded by others, even when this makes little difference to their own prospects. They conform to customary practice not just to avoid injuring their interests but because they do not like to be thought odd. If states were calculating and incapable of more than instrumental relationships, they would not care if states they dealt with were odd, and thought them odd.[62] Thus one must distinguish emulation and prestige which can be explained on Realist, or on rational egoist, grounds from emulation and prestige which presuppose a complex social awareness as an influence on states. Having a reputation as powerful, tough, reliable, honest, or even reasonable in its deals might serve a state's international interests. But having a reputation as sympathetic to the poor or as committed to upholding the international order cannot, unless the idea of state interest is defined in terms of broadly moral values as well as of power and wealth. When a state seeks to behave as neighbors or other admired states do, not to enhance its wealth and might but because such behavior is considered virtuous or indicative of an advanced social order, such emulation cannot be accounted for as an attempt to achieve success and security by emulating successful states.[63]

Yet Ireland and Finland started giving foreign aid partly to feel that they were members of the peer group of nations they used in defining their own identity. There is no evidence that other states disapproved of Finland's or Ireland's neglect of foreign aid, nor reason to think Finland and Ireland would have been hurt by such disapproval had it existed. And such disapproval would have made little sense from other egoistic states, for they would not have gained from Irish or Finnish aid. Countries like Norway and the Netherlands that donated high levels of aid also sought to define themselves as model donors. If the Norse and the Dutch sought to be seen as laudable, it is either because moral applause with no tangible benefits was important to them or because other states were willing to reward behavior they thought moral on behalf of third parties.[64] Again, country after country adopted strict worldwide standards for aid, despite the absence of any binding international agreement.[65]

The hypothesis that states tend to conform to expected or approved behavior also suggests investigations in other issue areas and fits in with some existing findings. Thomson finds that the way in which states conduct war is stylized and involves important social norms.[66] Two centuries ago it was acceptable to wage war with hired foreign mercenaries; now it is not. Killing and enslaving inhabitants of conquered countries, a common if brutal practice in Thucydides's day, would make a state an utter outlaw today. Wars to acquire territory, normal enough in the seventeenth century, are increasingly regarded as unacceptable. Colonial policies that seemed natural in the nineteenth century would incur powerful international condemnation in the twentieth. In the sixteenth century, countries could employ a citizen of a foreign country as an ambassador; today such behavior would be impossible. Domestic practices, too, may be objects of international scrutiny, even when they do not affect international security. Countries that repress domestic minorities, torture prisoners, utilize disapproved political and economic systems, or practice open racism may be subjected to international pressure or even sanctions. On the other hand, countries seek the accoutrements of modernity—airports, modern hotels, a steel industry—whether or not these costly items advance their power. Also, advanced democracies, communist states, Third World states, socialist states, Islamic states, and Latin American, African, Arab, European, and Scandinavian states each cultivate special links with each other and try to conform to group-approved practice as well as to standards enjoined by world society at large.

## 3. Development of Meaningful International Practices

Changes in international practices such as foreign aid are influenced not only by domestic interests and international pressures but also by the essential concepts implicit in the practices themselves. Games like baseball and chess, John Rawls argues,[67] are constituted by their rules, which are unlike rules of thumb or ad hoc agreements; these practices make sense only when understood "from within" in terms of those rules. Not only specific games but broad human institutions such as promise keeping and punishment for wrongdoing are constituted by their rules; how they can be set up or changed is restricted by human and ethical meanings that these rules embody. Engaging in such meaningful practices strengthens the underlying norms they embody, and the practices themselves tend to evolve in accord with these norms. Ferejohn argues that voting, when instituted in one context, may change the way politics is conceived, leading to the extension of the practice.[68] Social welfare institutions have strengthened the principle that they embody, that of caring for citizens' economic needs, and thus create pressures to alter and extend the welfare state. International practices too are subject to a "law of the instrument," by which norms and standards implicit in them affect their subsequent evolution. Walzer argues, for instance, that states feel a need to justify their wars, and find themselves constrained by those justifications, which have their own stubborn logic.[69] In general, as various "reflectivist" theorists have argued, understanding the social meaning of international practices is important to grasping why those practices persist or change.[70]

Many factors operated to make foreign aid practices evolve in accord with their "inner logic" or implicit meaning.[71] Announcing programs directed to particular purposes created rhetorical momentum.[72] Foreign aid programs were presented as development assistance to poor countries, from Truman's first articulation of the Point Four program onward. Putting aid on such a rhetorical footing made it easy to criticize aid for failure to help the poor, and harder to criticize aid for failure to serve other goals.[73] Public scrutiny and criticism of aid strengthened this momentum. The OECD's Development Assistance Committee (DAC), set up with independent professional staff and candid mutual criticism, helped recruit donor countries, but it also created ongoing pressures on donors to conform by making aid beneficial to recipients. Both in the UN bodies and in Western-dominated agencies like the DAC and World Bank, finding common ground in debate required appealing to general principles rather than to particularistic interests. Thus, setting targets for aid volume, concessionality, and attention to the neediest states played an important part in moving aid donors toward policies focused on recipients' developmental needs, too, despite an absence of formal agreements and highly variable levels of compliance with guidelines.

Support for aid depended in considerable measure upon its connection with wider spheres of moral and political reasoning. In the absence of definite agreements and sanctions, shared ideology or normative understanding can be particularly important.[74] The implicit norm of alleviation and long-term amelioration of poverty played an important role in foreign aid. The growth within the donor countries of aid professionals and others committed to Third World development was one aspect of this. To have aid programs at all required staff with expertise, commitment to developmental goals, and professional standards.[75] Obtaining high-caliber leadership entailed finding people with independent judgment and broad influence who were committed to the eradication of global poverty, and not merely to national interests. The shared understandings of experts were part of a broader shared understanding in society. NGOs, groups of intellectuals, of churches, and of labor or labor-oriented parties with commitments to issues of equality and/or helping the poor all played a role in promoting foreign aid. Groups of citizens concerned with poverty, development, and international cooperation were formed because these issues found roots in the broader moral and political traditions of their societies. The plausibility and indeed conceivability of international cooperation and economic assistance rested upon the broad legitimacy that attached in domestic political affairs, and in everyday ethical life, to cooperative solutions, to compassion for the disadvantaged, and to inclusionary, democratic relations.

This tendency for important international practices and institutions having inherent social meanings to grow and develop along the lines of principles already implicit in them, as part of a wider society, may be observed in other international practices as well. The growth of the European Community was not just a series of specific deals; it depended upon the gradual creation of a strengthened sense of European identity. The development of the idea of world government from a few pre–World War I institutions, through the League of Nations, to the UN and its agencies, reflected a long-term development of norms of international cooperation and equality. This involved not only formal sovereign equality but a growing belief that an ethnocentric or Eurocentric worldview was biased and wrong.

## Conclusion

Realism has long contended that international politics is profoundly and inherently conflictual. The bases for this claim vary from aggressive human nature to the character of the state or of the international system. I have argued (1) that human nature is highly varied, and can produce destructive, merely self-interested, or principled and altruistic deeds, and (2) that the international system does not require prudent states to concentrate so exclusively on their own needs that no one can take care of the system, or of weaker neighbors. Systemic forces do not entail any one way of coping, but permit a range of state behavior and various types of international systems. The ambiguities which give states significant choices suggest that philosophical and ideological differences can shape how states behave. Principles and values systematically affect the world system, and waxing or waning ethical concerns and changes in domestic political systems can significantly alter the overall character of international politics.

This opens up several distinct lines of investigation and hypothesis testing, about domestic influence, international norms, and the inherent meanings of various international practices. Each of these hypotheses involves denying that the processes of international politics are discontinuous from the social and moral character of personal life and civil society. Moral factors can alter the tenor of international life, not only in peripheral ways, but by changing the character of the system.

Cooperation stems not just from incentives but from underlying attitudes and values. Insofar as cooperation is simply making mutually advantageous (pareto-improving) deals, there is nothing particularly fine about it: it may tend toward or away from peace or the restraint of oppression or concern for the needy. Cooperation is valuable where it involves an ethic of working together to promote essential and humanly beneficial change. Understanding cooperation narrowly conceived of as cooperation among rational egoists is not alternative but complementary to moral factors, because practices of cooperation once begun have an inherent logic that may lead states in self-interested cooperative arrangements toward broader cooperative values. But for just these reasons it is important to start developing analytic conceptions of cooperation that show their relationship to the moral bases of society.

The forty-year history of foreign aid shows how many concepts discussed in this chapter worked out in practice. Differences in domestic political principles, among leaders and publics, best explain systematic differences between the aid programs of different states and the reasons that aid got started. The role of international society was at work, both in the dialogue between less developed countries and aid donors and in the sense of appropriate behavior that constrained the donors as members of the OECD. That practices once undertaken had their own momentum, and grew and changed influenced by the meanings that constituted them as practices, may be seen both in the developments that prepared the way for aid and in the evolution of foreign aid practices.

Strong humanitarian convictions shaped this large, novel, and important aspect of international economic relations. Foreign aid is a paradigm case of the influence of crucial moral principles because of its universal scope, as assistance from well-off nations to any in need, its focus on poverty, and its empowerment of the weakest groups and states in the international system. For the book as a whole argues what chapter 2 presents in summary: foreign aid cannot be explained on the basis of the economic and political interests of the donor countries alone, and any satisfactory explanation must give a central place to the influence of humanitarian and egalitarian convictions upon aid donors.

## CHAPTER TWO

# Why Was There Any Foreign Aid at All?

> The very idea that the developed countries, in all their dealings
> with underdeveloped countries, should show special consider-
> ation for their welfare and economic development, and should
> even be prepared to feel a collective responsibility for aiding
> them, is *an entirely new concept dating from after the Second
> World War.*
>
> —Gunnar Myrdal[1]

## THE THEORETICAL PUZZLE OF FOREIGN AID

Why did the developed democracies provide economic aid to less developed countries from the 1950s onward? The net economic foreign aid
from the developed countries has exceeded $500 billion over the last forty
years. Net aid has been greater than net investment by multinational corporations in the Third World every year since the fifties, and has often
exceeded all net foreign commercial investment and lending combined to
less developed countries. Donor participation has been widespread. Denmark and Austria, New Zealand and Germany, Britain and Finland, and
ten other countries have foreign aid programs larger, as a percentage of
GNP, than that of the United States. Nearly all poor countries have been
regular recipients of aid. Donors have maintained aid programs steadily
since the fifties, and most programs have gotten stronger over time. But
regular programs of foreign aid were completely unheard of before the
end of the forties. What led to this sudden and historically unprecedented
departure from past practice?

This book argues that foreign aid cannot be accounted for on the basis
of the economic and political interests of the donor countries alone; the
essential causes lay in the humanitarian and egalitarian principles of the
donor countries, and in their implicit belief that only on the basis of a just
international order in which all states had a chance to do well was peace
and prosperity possible.

Such a thesis will provoke incredulity on the part of many readers, yet
the evidence is rich and varied both for the negative proposition that the
economic and political interests of the donor states do not explain foreign
aid and for the affirmation that humanitarian concern and public-spirited

commitment to building a better world were the mainsprings that made foreign aid go forward. Official statements advocating aid, from Truman's Point Four in his inaugural speech to the Brandt Commission Report and beyond, which speak of aid both as a moral duty and as an essential component of a newly interdependent world's economic and political health, could be merely a mask for national self-interests. But evidence about what donor countries did and about which countries and persons supported aid shows again and again the role played by humane concern, domestic welfare values, and a commitment to being a constructive part of a sound international society. Donors spent aid moneys mainly on poor countries of little strategic or economic value (chapter 3). The countries with strong aid programs were not those with strong interests in the Third World but those with strong domestic social programs (chapter 4). Public opinion favored giving aid to needy, not economically or strategically useful, countries, and public support was based on moral concern and commitment to domestic welfare concerns. The parties, politicians, and writers who supported aid were those who supported measures to help the domestic poor, while those who opposed aid tended to be cold warriors and staunch advocates of laissez-faire capitalism (chapter 5). The circumstances that led to the creation of aid programs suggest that their roots lay in the development of the welfare state and of a broad internationalism (chapter 6). The ways in which aid changed over time suggest that aid was regularly reformed to make it more useful to the poor and the developing countries, and less useful for the promotion of direct donor interests (chapters 7 and 8). These chapters, and the argument of the book, are summarized in more detail later in this chapter, in the section entitled "The Evidence about Why There Was Foreign Aid."

That does not mean that donor self-interest never played an important role: of course it did. It would be astonishing if only one set of factors played any role in programs sponsored by some 18 donor states and a score of international agencies, and directed to some 120 recipients over a period of more than forty years. Critics on the left have assailed foreign aid as simply a tool of cold-war interests and as a way of promoting the destructive inroads of capitalism in the Third World. Critics on the right have assailed foreign aid as a boondoggle, an inappropriate use of tax dollars, an instrument that props up inefficient socialist regimes and encourages state planning, and the tool of self-serving bureaucrats. Realist commentators have fit aid comfortably into the box of promotion of national self-interest.[2] Each group makes points important both to understanding aid and to reforming it. It cannot be stated too strongly that self-interested motives did play a part in foreign aid from time to time. It was hard to keep constituent and state economic interests out of aid, although the effort was increasingly successful. Even private charities concerned with Third World development have a self-serving side, as Brian Smith points out.[3] Human action at every level of human society is a mixture of principled and humane, of self-interested, and of pointlessly destructive actions. In this mix it is all too common for selfish and destructive elements to dominate, particularly in international affairs. But for just this reason, it is essential to understand the range of variation and the way in which the more positive side of human nature can come into play, in international affairs as elsewhere.

One must not lose sight of the overall picture by applying an unrealistic standard. If we apply too exacting a standard of "true democracy," we will find there are no true democracies in the world; that does not mean there is no difference worth considering between England and Iran, between India and China, or between Frei's and Pinochet's Chile. Indeed, it would not be conceptually useful to hold up a standard of perfection in examining whether a commercial firm is intent on profit or a major army concerned with winning wars. In any large enterprise, some people will be concerned with goals other than the enterprise's essential purpose. If foreign aid is measured against the purity of heart of Saint Francis or Mother Theresa, it will be found terribly imperfect; if it is measured against the normal practice of international affairs, it will be seen as a very hopeful phenomenon, in which humane concern figured most importantly, though by no means exclusively. Foreign aid was imperfect and too often reflected donor interests, true. Reforming and improving development assistance is a pressing need. But one seeks to reform and strengthen only enterprises whose fundamental purpose is sound.

Judged by any reasonable standard, the evidence shows that, despite all the admixtures, the fundamental purpose behind aid was a strongly humane one.[4] Perhaps as much as a third of the money classed as economic aid primarily served commercial concerns, cold-war rivalry and fear of communism, support for allies, maintenance of colonial and regional ties, or attempts to promote market economies, which all played an important part from time to time.[5] But aid programs were tailored primarily for the promotion of economic development, alleviation of poverty, and creation of a just and workable international order. Without principled support, aid would never have been started and would have ended quickly; and where there was strong, principled support for aid the influence commercial and strategic concerns had on aid decreased and the volume of aid increased. For the effective support for aid came almost exclusively from an inclusive, humane internationalism, which perceived a responsibility on the part of the developed countries to help fight poverty in the less developed, and which conceived of the world as an interdependent whole whose problems were the concern of all peoples.

*Basic Facts about Aid*

Before turning in more detail to evidence about the causes of foreign aid, it is necessary to define the phenomenon and to present a few basic facts about it. "Aid" or "foreign aid" or "development assistance" or "ODA" (overseas development assistance) are used here interchangeably to denote *gifts and concessional loans of economic resources, such as finance and technology, employed for economic purposes provided to less developed countries by governments of the developed democracies*, directly or through intermediaries such as UN programs and multilateral development banks. "Developed democracies" here refers to the countries that were members of the Development Assistance Committee (DAC) of the Organization for Economic Cooperation and Development (OECD), namely, Canada and the United States, Austria, Belgium, Denmark, England, Finland, France, Germany, Ireland, Italy, the Netherlands, Norway, Switzerland, Sweden, Australia, Japan, and New Zealand, which will also be referred to as "OECD" or "DAC" donors. Commercial loans, or loan-like transactions by multilateral organizations such as the market-rate lending of the World Bank, are not included; this means that almost none of the activity of the International Monetary Fund (IMF) counts as aid by the standards of this book.[6] In practice, the figures used are those provided by the DAC, and the figures used in the book are net disbursements, unless otherwise stated, so that the figures in discussion are approximately net transfers, as explained in more detail in the notes.[7] The main points are that military aid and loans at near-commercial terms, and all official export credits, are excluded; that aid from communist countries and OPEC countries is not what is being explained (though it will be discussed); and that the explanation is of aid to less developed countries (LDCs), not, for instance, of Marshall Plan aid to Europe. In sum, *the foreign aid referred to here is concessional economic assistance, direct and indirect, from the developed democracies to the Third World*.

Foreign aid of this kind was virtually nonexistent before 1949. Strong states have seldom promoted outward flows of financial and technological resources; they have sought tribute or "protection money" from weaker states instead. States often seek to prevent outflows of investment and technology even on commercial terms, since possession of capital and technology have been seen as advantages for the state that possessed them. The liberalism of the nineteenth century was unusual in eschewing mercantilist policies by advocating and allowing more-or-less unhindered commercial flows of resources. The free or near-free provision of technology and finance to weaker states is an extremely anomalous and recent departure from all past practices.

During and after World War II American policymakers started assuming concern for economic conditions worldwide. The twentieth century had seen a growth of internationalist sentiment and of national welfare states pledged to the eradication of poverty. These trends came together in the thirties and forties in an idealistic commitment to establishing a world with "freedom from want" as well as "freedom from fear"[8] and in a belief that "poverty anywhere constitutes a danger to prosperity everywhere."[9] The way for aid to the less developed countries was paved by wartime and immediate postwar programs for relief and reconstruction, like the UNRRA, and by the establishment of the IMF, the IBRD, and the UN and its economic and social council (ECOSOC). Concessional aid to Europe in the Marshall Plan, or European Recovery Program (ERP), also set an important precedent after the war. The Marshall Plan was important in that it was in principle open to all in the region, and important also for the later development of foreign aid because of its impetus in establishing the OEEC. Still, nothing like a general program of assistance to less developed countries was undertaken, or conceived of.

In January 1949, the fourth point of President Truman's inaugural address contained a surprising call for a "bold new program" of economic and technical aid to poorer countries. Within three years of Truman's Point Four proposal not only had a U.S. program of ongoing aid been adopted, but the Colombo Plan for South Asia had been sponsored by Britain, Canada, and other countries; and in the UN calls for further development programs had found their first fruits in establishment of an Expanded Programme of Technical Assistance (EPTA). In addition, the World Bank (or IBRD) had shifted its lending from European reconstruction to Third World development, starting primarily with loans approved in January 1949, only days before Truman's speech.

Since that time, foreign aid has been an important phenomenon, a highly significant and long-lasting part of the financial relations between LDCs and advanced capitalist democracies, as table 2.1 shows. Indeed, it is surprising that theories of international political economy have not paid more attention to it. Total foreign aid from 1950 to the present by developed democracies has been over $500 billion; reckoned in constant 1988 dollars, the total is around $1.1 trillion. Net foreign aid has been larger than OECD direct foreign investment in the Third World in every year since the midfifties; indeed in most years, and in the aggregate, it has been more than twice as great. Total net private investment in the Third World began to match aid only with the ballooning of commercial lending that followed the oil shock of 1973, and has fallen below aid levels in recent years. It is not yet clear which will be the larger flow in the next decade. Even these figures understate the relative impact of foreign aid in most LDCs, however, because private investment, both transnational eq-

TABLE 2.1
Volume of Aid Compared with Private Financial Flows to the Third World

| Net Financial Flows, Current Billions | 1950–55 | 1956–60 | 1961–65 | 1966–70 | 1971–75 | 1976–80 | 1981–85 | 1986–89 | Total 1961–89 |
|---|---|---|---|---|---|---|---|---|---|
| Net foreign aid (ODA) | 11.7 | 20.3 | 30.1 | 32.7 | 50.7 | 98.4 | 139.2 | 173.1 | 524.2 |
| Net private investment of which: | — | 13.5 | 12.1 | 26.3 | 51.4 | 158.6 | 164.8 | 108.0 | 521.2 |
| FDI (multinationals) | — | — | 9.8 | 13.3 | 32.4 | 50.0 | 51.7 | 69.0 | 226.2 |
| Aid (constant billions) | 79 | 115 | 146 | 144 | 145 | 170 | 208 | 184 | 1,146 |

*Sources:* Computed from OECD, *Development Cooperation* and *Development Assistance,* various years: 1961, p. 19; 1964, pp. 106–9; 1967, pp. 184–85; 1970, pp. 172–73; 1974, p. 232; 1977, p. 188; 1978, p. 216; 1981, p. 196; 1982, p. 218; 1985, pp. 334, 336; 1986, p. 284; 1990, pp. 264, 267–68; 1991, pp. 197–98.

*Notes:* Table entries are in billions of dollars, all current save the last line, which is in 1988 (billions of) dollars. ODA figures before 1960 include other official flows, but these are relatively small. The constant figures are in 1988 dollars, computed using a GNP deflator.

uity and lending, is highly concentrated in a few newly industrializing countries, while aid is much more widely spread. In the dealings of most LDCs with the West, and of most Western countries with most LDCs, then, aid is by far the preponderant financial flow.

Despite the initial U.S. lead, aid was not primarily an American project but a broadly based international effort by the developed countries. The United States, the Colombo Plan donor countries (England, Canada, Australia, and New Zealand), and France were joined in aid giving in the late fifties and early sixties by virtually all the remaining industrial democracies. The OEEC, or Organization for European Economic Cooperation, that had been originally the instrument of Marshall Plan aid to Europe, was reorganized in 1961 as the OECD, the Organization for Economic Cooperation and Development, with Third World development an explicit priority and with a special Development Assistance Committee (DAC) to guide and order and monitor aid practices. U.S. aid was about a quarter of the DAC total for many years; more recently it has declined to a fifth or sixth of all DAC aid. And since the midsixties the United States has been a relatively uncommitted aid donor; other developed countries have devoted a substantially larger proportion of GNP to foreign assistance. By 1978–83 the United States share of foreign aid was about one quarter of the aid total; by the end of the eighties, a fifth or a sixth. By the midseventies, the Netherlands and Scandinavian donors combined contributed more aid than any single donor but the United States. By the early eighties, small donors provided three fourths the aid the United States did.[10] Throughout the late sixties and seventies, also, the emphasis shifted toward aid more focused on the poorest countries and poorer sectors within countries, and to aid channeled through multilateral institutions. The IBRD added a concessional finance facility, the IDA (or International Development Association), in 1960 and was joined by regional development banks, also with soft-loan windows, over the following decade. After long pressure, the rich countries agreed to fund a UN Development Program at a substantial level, starting in the midsixties, as well.

Indeed, however one explains the puzzling occurrence of foreign aid, any satisfactory explanation must look at the aid policies of all the developed countries together, since most industrial democracies had a working aid plan by 1957, a mere four or five years after the Point Four program actually began operation. The sudden appearance of aid in the postwar period cannot be understood on a case-by-case basis. Looking only at French aid, one could hypothesize that it sprang from France's unique pride in disseminating its cultural traditions; looking just at Swiss aid, one could argue it showed the special place of Switzerland's international banking industry; U.S. aid alone could be attributed to U.S. hegemony or to American exceptionalism in foreign policy; and Japan's aid might have been a tool of its export promotion strategy. But explanations of this kind do not explain why aid policies arose in all these industrial democracies at once, in a single decade, and have remained for nearly half a century. Clearly an element of imitation or diffusion was at work here; however, that is not an explanation but a restatement of the problem. Nations copy ideas they reckon appealing; the question posed by the approximately simultaneous appearance of multiple aid policies is why so many nations found the idea attractive. While there was some variety in aid policies and motives among the industrial democracies, the key to the development of aid is to be found in common causes and in factors that influenced the whole tenor of the times.

### Distinctive Characteristics of Aid

The aid policies of the OECD countries also have a complex common structure which attests to a systemic influence at work that requires common explanation. The OECD aid policies that emerged suddenly in the fifties shared a host of distinctive features, all related to the alleviation of poverty and fostering of economic development. And these features have been strengthened regularly through the forty years that aid policies have been in place.[11] This continuity of policy and these common distinctive properties that reliably characterized OECD aid further underline the novelty of aid and add to the need to find a common explanation for the emergence of the foreign aid of the developed democracies.

Aid funded by DAC countries was large-scale, regular, and ongoing; publicly given, internationally monitored, often multilaterally channeled, and generally available to any poor nation; concessionally financed, and usually untied to explicit military, economic, or diplomatic bargains;[12] and provided for projects of economic betterment (usually development rather than relief), designed by technical experts and economists, and subject to formal conditions to assure attainment of humane or developmental purposes or (allegedly) sound economic policies in recipient countries, not to their foreign policies or other external behavior.[13] These many common features or characteristics may be grouped roughly in four main sets, which can be elaborated a bit more fully: aid was substantial or solid, public, concessional, and developmentally oriented.

*Aid has been solid, or substantial,* in three respects that distinguish it from the few previous instances of official international transfers. It has been large in scale—generally exceeding donor direct foreign commercial investment in the Third World, for instance, and ranging up to 1% of donor GNP or more. It has been provided on a regular basis, continuing with slight fluctuation from year to year. And it has been ongoing in the sense that, once started, aid has continued until now. Both the size of aid and its reliability have been important aspects of its usefulness as a tool of development.

*Aid has been a public or open process*, rather than a set of private transactions between individual donor and recipient states. Amounts and forms of aid are published by OECD countries and multilateral agencies and are collated, analyzed, and defined by technical experts in the DAC. Much aid (up to 30% in recent years) has been channeled through multilateral agencies, such as the IBRD and UNDP, which are run by international civil servants. Some of these organizations are responsible to the donor nations as a whole; others are responsible to the developed countries or to the full UN. Moreover, it has been presumed that less developed countries of every sort were candidates for aid: aid is conceptualized as being for poor countries at large, not only for special friends or allies.

*Aid has been concessional*, in two main respects. It has been offered as grants or as loans bearing such low interest as to have a very high grant element.[14] And these grants or soft loans are generally not linked to reciprocal international behavior by recipients: there is no explicit quid pro quo. In the nineteenth century, a richer state occasionally supplied a poorer one money (or even the right to sell bonds) in exchange for a diplomatic concession on terms such that if the state receiving the money changed its policy, the money might be demanded back. Such a thing would be unthinkably opprobrious in the context of the aid regime. Clearly, pressuring goes on at times, especially by the larger bilateral donors, involving an explicit or implicit threat of suspending future largesse. And a portion of aid is openly tied to purchases from the donor nation. But these are exceptions to the general principle, not the standard they were for the few transfers of earlier centuries.

Finally, *aid is oriented toward economic development and alleviation of poverty*. It is provided for particular recipient domestic tasks, directed toward the growth of the recipient's economy or the alleviation of poverty as a rule. It is often provided in the form of "project aid" geared to a particular economic development undertaking, and also provided as "program aid" supporting a wider range of the programs in some sector of the recipient's budget.[15] Whereas international reciprocation is not ordinarily a condition for foreign aid, its proper domestic use, for purposes of economic development and the like, is. And the personnel and the structures of aid agencies, bilateral and multilateral, are organized and chosen with this in view. Also, over time, development lending has moved more toward projects, such as agricultural and rural development, that will have more impact on the poor within a recipient country.

## THE EVIDENCE ABOUT WHY THERE WAS FOREIGN AID

One way of assessing what lay behind aid programs is to look at how donors allocated their aid resources—at where the money went. Evidence on this point is examined in detail in chapter 3. Aid money went not primarily to countries of economic and political importance to donors but to recipient countries with great needs; and aid programs were set up and administered not to maximize donor influence but to promote economic development. Aid was not directed primarily to countries that traded heavily with the developed countries, as table 2.2 makes clear. While there was some correlation between aid and trade, it was small and fell quickly; furthermore, when one controls for the fact that a large country like Bangladesh has more substantial trade and aid because of its size than does the Maldive Islands, the correlations are near zero or even negative. It is true that statistically several major bilateral aid donors show a significant relation between trade and aid, and not between aid and poverty of recipient, but the correlations are low. But the total figures on aid, bilateral and multilateral, show significant poverty orientation. Even in the early years, most concessional economic assistance was directed toward poor countries with relatively low trade and private investment and relatively low growth prospects. India has been a big recipient of aid; Mexico and Brazil have not. Table 2.3, showing the aid, trade, and private investment of OECD states to recipients classified by level of income, makes the point concisely; a more detailed treatment is given in chapter 3. This directing of aid to states with low income and private transactions contrasts markedly, too, with the distribution of official export credits. Such credits, which were clearly given as an export promotion tool, went to states with high GNP, trade, and private investment.

Most aid programs required that funding go only to specific, developmentally relevant projects; over time, there were attempts to emphasize projects and sectors that would benefit the poorest people in recipient countries. Aid administration was not undertaken by diplomats but by economic and technical specialists, usually in an administratively separate aid agency; those who made line-level aid decisions were not those with an interest in politics but those trained in economic development. True, initially some states tied much of their aid to purchases in their own country, but even these tied purchases did not cover the cost of providing the goods; and aid tying declined markedly over time, and has applied to

TABLE 2.2
Bilateral Aid Correlated with Trade:
Plain and Partial Correlation Coefficients between Bilateral Aid and Trade
between the Third World and the OECD as a Whole

| Aid Correlated with | 1968–73 | 1984–88 | Type of Correlation |
|---|---|---|---|
| Donor exports | .345† | .249† | Simple correlations |
| Donor imports | .286† | .156 | Simple correlations |
| Donor exports | .105 | .011 | Controlled for recipient size |
| Donor imports | .012 | −.110 | Controlled for recipient size |

Sources: Data from tables 3.4 and 3.5.
Notes: Number of Third World countries: N = 105.
† significant at a .01 level (unmarked correlations are nonsignificant at a .05 level).

TABLE 2.3
Aid and Commercial Flows, by LDC Income Class (Percentages)

| Type of Flow | Period | Middle and High Income LDCs | Low Income LDCs | Least Developed Countries |
|---|---|---|---|---|
| Bilateral Aid | 1968–82 | 40 | 60 | 19 |
| Multilateral Aid | 1968–82 | 30 | 70 | 28 |
| Export Credits | 1968–82 | 84 | 17 | 3 |
| Exports of OECD | 1968–77 | 86 | 15 | 3 |
| Exports of OECD | 1978–81 | 82 | 18 | 3 |
| Private Capital | 1971–76 | 86 | 14 | 2 |
| Private Capital | 1978–81 | 87 | 13 | 2 |

Sources: Data from tables 3.11 and 3.13, and from OECD, Geographical Distribution of Financial Flows, various years.
Notes: Figures for low income countries and for middle- and high-income LDCs may total to slightly more than 100% due to rounding error. "Least developed countries" is a subcategory of "low income countries."

a minority of aid in recent years, even counting all gifts of food aid and donor provision of technical assistance in the "tied aid" category.

Also, a growing proportion of aid was given by the donor states to multilateral institutions such as the United Nations Development Program, the Social Trust Fund of the Inter-American Development Bank, and the International Development Association (IDA), the development fund of the World Bank, as table 2.4 shows. Aid channeled through these sources—almost a third of the total—could not even be identified as coming from any particular donor. Many donors consciously undertook to direct a large proportion of their aid to the neediest recipients, and multilateral institutions tended to favor large, poor recipient states even more

TABLE 2.4
DAC Aid Going to Multilateral Institutions, 1956–1989 (Percentages)

|  | 1956 | 1960 | 1970 | 1980–84 | 1985–89 |
|---|---|---|---|---|---|
| Aid from all DAC countries | 7 | 13 | 14 | 31 | 28 |
| United States aid | 4 | 8 | 12 | 31 | 20 |

Source: Data from table 8.6.

Note: Figures through 1970 are based on percentages of net total official flows, since separate ODA data are not available before that date.

TABLE 2.5
Strong and Weak Aid Donors Classed by Domestic Social Spending and Private Charitable Contributions to Third World Development

| ODA/GNP | Domestic Social Expenditure | | ODA/GNP | Private Charitable Donations to Third World Development | |
|---|---|---|---|---|---|
|  | High | Low |  | High | Low |
| High | 7 | 2 | High | 6 | 3 |
| Low | 2 | 6 | Low | 2 | 6 |

Source: Data from table 4.3.
Note: Table entries show numbers of DAC donors. Ireland is not included.

than bilateral aid programs. Probably about one third of aid can be attributed to direct donor self-interest.[16] If aid had been intended to serve the economic or foreign policy of donor states, it should have been more fully tied, all bilateral, and directed primarily to economically and strategically important states. What we see in fact is what should have happened if aid was intended for purposes of economic development: aid administered by professionals, often multilaterally channeled, directed primarily to poor states with low commercial potential.

Another way of assessing what lay behind aid programs is to look at which countries were strong aid donors—at who paid the aid bill. Evidence on this point is examined in detail in chapter 4. Among the developed democracies, the country with the strongest overseas political interests, the United States, was not a vigorous aid donor, measured in terms of aid per capita or aid as a percentage of gross national product (ODA/GNP). Countries with strong colonial or financial connections to Third World countries were middling in their aid spending. The stronger donors tended to be those with strong domestic social welfare programs and those with strong private contributions to private voluntary organizations, as table 2.5 illustrates. Donors like Norway and Sweden, with strong domestic social programs and aid programs of high quality, focused on the poorest countries and groups, and tended also to commit much higher percentages of GNP to aid. The United States, with its mixed humanitarian and strategic rationale for aid, declined in its commitment over time; while countries that increased their volume of aid also tended to improve aid quality.

The entire set of developed democracies, furthermore, showed as a group a kind of commitment to aid that no other group of countries did. While the Soviet Union and Eastern European countries (through their organization CMEA, or Council for Mutual Economic Assistance) initiated "aid programs" after the West did, the programs were much smaller in scale, usually involved only loans, were fully tied to equipment from the CMEA countries, had virtually no multilateral component, and, especially after the first few years, focused almost exclusively on a few, close strategic allies—Vietnam and Cuba primarily. There was nothing similar to the widely dispersed, concessional aid that all democratic donors supplied. Yet some of the potential Eastern European donors, such as East Germany, were at least as developed as the poorer Western donors, some of which, like Ireland, Finland, and New Zealand, joined in regular aid giving only in recent years. Engaging in publicly monitored, widely dispersed, concessional, multilaterally channeled aid programs was characteristic not of states that were economically strong nor of those involved in world politics but of states with strong commitments to responding to poverty at home.

These interstate comparisons receive additional confirmation from an examination of what led people to favor aid and of what kinds of people and groups supported aid programs—of who advocated aid, and why. Evidence about public opinion and about what kinds of parties, factions, interest groups, politicians, and scholars supported (and opposed) aid is detailed in chapter 5. Just as *countries* with strong domestic social spending and high private voluntary contributions to Third World concerns tended to favor aid, so *individuals* who thought domestic poverty and inequality serious problems tended to favor aid. Organized aid constituencies, such as church, university, and labor, and charitable groups asked both for purer aid and more aid; groups that wanted to subordinate aid to commercial or strategic purposes were either indifferent to aid funding or actively hostile to it. Notable international advocates of aid—Harry Truman, Harold Wilson, Lester Pearson, Willi Brandt—were not cold warriors or apologists of international capitalism but strong partisans of the domestic welfare state and, usually, of a pro-peace, cooperative internationalism. In almost every developed democracy, political parties and politicians committed to strong domestic social programs tended to favor stronger aid spending and reducing the commercial element in aid. In the early sixties, Goldwater argued that aid should be cut and restricted to military aid to U.S. allies; Hubert Humphrey advocated that aid be increased, for reasons of compassion and the promotion of a more stable world, and made this a centerpiece of his foreign policy program. Usually, when in power, pro-aid politicians actually improved aid in quality and quantity. Few politicians were as openly anti-aid as Goldwater, but those who cut aid, such as Reagan and Eisenhower, tended to be strongly anti-communist and hostile as well to the programs of the welfare state; they sought both to reduce aid and to subordinate it to narrow national interests. In the eighties, Mitterand, a socialist, within the first few days of taking office committed France to providing more aid, better focused on economic development, and he followed through. Margaret Thatcher disparaged aid as "handouts" in a way that drew sharp criticism from even her own party; she both cut aid and sought to make it serve British commercial interests more. Strongly conservative scholars, and particularly those committed to the sufficiency of market capitalism—Milton Friedman, Edward Banfield, P. T. Bauer—openly argued against aid, and in doing so explicitly compared it to the domestic welfare state; while renowned supporters—Gunnar Myrdal, Barbara Ward, Paul Hoffman—also compared foreign aid to helping the domestic poor, but by way of commending the practice. And advocates of aid invariably based their support of aid on strong humane and idealistic principles of some sort: socialist, religious, or simply humanitarian.

The same patterns of support for aid show up in systematic public opinion data, as chapter 5 also details. Publics, when asked, consistently said aid should go to needy countries that would use it well rather than being used to promote narrow national interests. In one poll of ten European countries, 75% favored giving aid to the neediest LDCs rather than those of strategic, political, or economic importance to their own country. People who favored aid tended to be people with exposure to the needs of the Third World and those who favored domestic programs of redistribution. Students, the young, the well-educated, people on the Left, and those with strong religious convictions tended to favor aid more than others did, while those with strong convictions of any sort tended to favor aid more than those who expressed no opinion on political or religious matters, as table 2.6, based on another multi-nation European poll, shows. Table 2.7 shows that those who had personally contributed to Third World causes, those who expressed negative sentiments about colonialism, those who wanted to reduce domestic inequality all tended to be strongly pro-aid. Those with strong national security concerns did not particularly favor aid. Most notably, however, in the ten-country study mentioned, the strongest predictor by far of support for aid was agreement with the statement "we have a moral duty to help" Third World countries; this item alone accounted for an astonishing 37% of the variance in support for aid.

TABLE 2.6
Percentages Favoring Increased Aid, by Church Attendance and
Political Views

|  | Church Attendance | | |
| --- | --- | --- | --- |
| Self-Placement on a Left-Right Scale | Regular | Rare | No Answer |
| Left | 34 | 29 | 25 |
| Right | 25 | 17 | 13 |
| No answer | 22 | 18 | 9 |

Source: Data from table 5.3.

Note: These are 1983 survey data from ten European countries. A more complete explanation of the data is also found in table 5.3.

TABLE 2.7
Best Predictors of Public Support for Foreign Aid

|  |  |  | Measures of Association with Support for Aid | |
| --- | --- | --- | --- | --- |
|  |  |  | Bivariate | Multiple |
| Variable Number | Statement That Respondents Agreed or Disagreed With | Percentage Agreeing | Correlation $R^2$ | Regression Beta |
| (121) | We have a moral duty to help poor nations | 74 | .61 | .36 |
| (123) | It's in our own interest to help poor nations | 70 | .50 | .21 |
| (155) | Aid needy states, not those useful to us | 70 | .38 | .18 |
| (115) | These countries don't really want to work | 26 | .35 | .15 |
| (157) | I've contributed myself to help the Third World | 60 | .28 | .12 |
| (043) | Helping poor areas in our country is important | 74 | .28 | .09 |

*Estimated Equation*

Support for Aid = $Var_{121} + Var_{123} + Var_{155} + Var_{112} + Var_{157} + Var_{43}$ + Error Term
(Four-item index)

Source: Data from tables 5.1 and 5.4, which also give details of the construction of the four-item support-for-aid index.

Notes: Table 5.9 gives the exact wording of the questions.

Beta = standardized multiple regression coefficient. The overall explained variance of model as a whole: $R^2 = .51$. Model and each regressor is significant at a .01 level.

Also, those who were strong supporters of aid were far more likely to support aid which went to needy recipients. Most of those who favored using aid to promote national self-interest were at best indifferent about whether aid should be given at all. It is true that agreement that "aid is in our own interest" was also a strong predictor of support for aid, however, those who agreed with this statement tended to be largely those who agreed with the idea that aid was a moral duty, as is shown in table 2.8.

TABLE 2.8

Perception of National Interest by Degree of Perceived Moral Duty to Give Aid (Percentages)

| Is Aid in Our Own Interest? | Is It Our Moral Duty to Give Foreign Aid? | | | |
|---|---|---|---|---|
| | Fully Agree | Agree to Some Extent | Disagree to Some Extent | Fully Disagree |
| Agree | 87 | 78 | 42 | 29 |
| Disagree | 9 | 16 | 53 | 66 |

Source: Data from table 5.5.

Notes: Columns total less than 100% because some people offered no opinion. Total number of respondents: $N = 9718$. Table 5.9 gives the exact wording of the questions.

Moreover, those who saw aid as "in our own interest" were *less* likely than others to think aid should be used to promote trade or strategic interests; this is true even when one controls for the association with a sense of "moral duty to aid." The idea of "national interest" that aid supporters had in mind was one which reckoned national interest as including things that would promote the welfare of the people in the Third World, whether or not there were any direct national benefits to the donor country. That is, support for aid was based on a sense of global citizenship, a sense that defense of the human interest was inherently in the national interest.

The prehistory of foreign aid also suggests that the source of the thinking that led to aid came from the growth of labor and social democratic ideas, and from the development of a climate of humane internationalism, as chapter 6 documents. The rise of the welfare state throughout the century reflected the rise of organized labor and social-democratic parties, which were consciously internationalist from the start and which placed advocacy of the needs of poorer citizens on a basis of universal human rights. The development of the domestic welfare state drew also on the influence of private humanitarian movements to help the poor, and the increasing awareness of the problems and the need for structural solutions, which was fostered by social critics, reports on the conditions of the poor, and the churches particularly. The first systematic assessments of levels of nutrition worldwide began in the thirties, and people began to call for attention to economic needs worldwide. In the twenties and thirties the International Missionary Council began to call for more attention to the poverty of the less developed regions and advocated an international order that would hold to a high moral standard and better "reflect the mind of Christ." The International Labour Organization (ILO) gave economic needs of less developed countries special importance in its Philadelphia Declaration of 1944, which was incorporated in the ILO charter. Programs of international relief following the First World War and continuing efforts by the League of Nations to deal with the needs of refugees and other international social problems were followed early in the Second World War by plans for reconstruction of Europe, through the UNRRA and a planned World Bank. The World Bank, however, was meant for purposes of both reconstruction and development, with the Latin American delegates to the 1944 Bretton Woods conference, which wrote its charter, insisting upon a greater focus upon the ongoing, development needs of poor countries. The idea of worldwide concern for economic needs was mooted repeatedly in liberal and humanitarian circles during the late thirties and forties, with the Carnegie Foundation, Eugene Staley, people from the Brookings Institution, Secretary of State Cordell Hull, Wendell Willkie, Harvard economist Alvin Hansen (writing for the National Council on Social Studies), and Vice President Henry Wallace increasingly thinking in terms of what one writer called a "World New Deal." Churches, labor groups, international organizations, charitable foundations, and academics concerned with questions of world poverty and peace first broached the ideas of assistance to less developed countries. These ideas found vague but influential expression in Roosevelt's articulation of the Four Freedoms, including freedom from want, as goals of the wartime effort, and in the subsequent endorsement of the goals of freedom from want as well as freedom from fear in the Atlantic Charter of war aims signed by Churchill and Roosevelt in August 1941 and endorsed by twenty-six countries in a "Declaration of the United Nations" the following New Year's Day.

The historical developments leading up to aid also included a growing internationalism, and one that included a commitment to ideas of self-determination and a repudiation of racial and colonial ideologies, and thus included a far less Eurocentric focus. The growth of international institutions, culminating in the foundation of the League of Nations in 1919, was accompanied by a rise in internationalist sentiments. The League devoted over half its budget to economic and social programs and laid the foundation for the later UN Economic and Social Council. At the same time, dissatisfaction with what the League did in these areas caused the major international agencies dealing with economic and social problems to form the Bruce Commission, whose influential 1939 report seems to have had its effects in the formation of the UN and its Economic and Social Council (ECOSOC), in particular. The decision to establish a United Nations organization whose scope included economic as well as security matters set in motion a process in which it was natural that the Latin American nations would press in the ECOSOC for consideration of their problems, even as attention was being given to European reconstruction. The Marshall Plan, which provided assistance to European countries without expectation that the money would be paid back, clearly reflected both the perception that without the creation of an economically prosperous Europe chaos would ensue, and the compassion that Americans felt for the people living in a destroyed continent. By its wise focus not just on immediate needs but on long-term reconstruction as well, it became a model poorer countries could use in pressing for later concessional assistance.

Thus President Truman's initial call for aid to less developed countries in his January 1949 inaugural address reflected internationalism and humanitarianism extending across national boundaries, awareness of world poverty, and support for social welfare, which had been developing over the previous half century or more. As chapter 7 details, his suggestion for a "bold new program" of technical assistance to poorer countries, coming as it did into a situation in which the support for ideas of economic assistance was already latent, led to a groundswell of support for such programs among church groups, economists, advocates of internationalism, and labor groups. Programs of foreign aid expanded rapidly, with the British Labour government creating a Colombo Plan, the UN creating the Expanded Programme of Technical Assistance, and the World Bank moving almost exclusively to development lending in the year after Truman's speech. The adoption of aid programs by many of the European countries was consolidated by the reformulation of the Organization for European Economic Cooperation (OEEC) as the Organization for Economic Cooperation and Development, with a Development Assistance Committee (DAC) in which most of the developed countries reviewed their development programs regularly, and by the proclamation by the United Nations, at President Kennedy's suggestion, of the sixties as the Development Decade. The process of moving aid programs toward greater commitment of funds, less dependency of recipients on donors, more multilateral channeling of funds, and more concessional assistance, was pushed along both by the internal criticism of the DAC countries themselves—including the setting of (nonbinding) standards for foreign aid by the DAC, which appears to have had a great effect on most member countries—and by the pressure in international forums by the less developed countries that led to the creation of a UNDP and to the World Bank's soft-loan window.

The changes in the way in which aid was given during the sixties, seventies, and eighties, after aid was well established, also provide clear evidence that aid drew most of its support from humanitarian and egalitarian ideas, as chapter 8 demonstrates. Most countries consistently revised their aid in a variety of ways that made aid less useful to donors for any particularistic purposes of their own but more useful for purposes of economic development in donor states. Aid became far more multilateral,

TABLE 2.9

Degree of Tying of Aid: All DAC Countries (Percentages)

|  | Untied | Fully Tied |
|---|---|---|
| 1950s and early 1960s (rough estimates only) | 25 | 67 |
| 1972 | 35 | 35 |
| 1980 | 56 | 32 |
| 1988 | 57 | 31 |

Source: Data from table 8.8.

Notes: Figures for early years are very approximate, due to sketchy data. Figures for intervening years are roughly between those for years shown. Rows do not total 100% because some aid was partially tied; that is, while it did not have to be spent in the donor country, there were some restrictions on where it could be spent.

TABLE 2.10

Percentage of Grant, Grant Element, and Interest Rate in Bilateral Aid, 1962–1988

| Measure of Concessionality | 1962 | 1968 | 1979 | 1988 |
|---|---|---|---|---|
| Percentage of grants | 60 | 51 | 71 | 73 |
| Grant element | — | 58 | 76 | 89 |
| Loan interest rate | 3.6 | 2.9 | 2.6 | 2.7 |

Source: Data from table 8.10.

Notes: All figures in the table are percentages, but of different kinds. The percentage of bilateral aid is simply a percentage of aid given; the grant element is an imputed percentage. The interest rate is a rate of growth. The "grant element" is the percentage of aid given as grants plus the proportion of the low-interest loans which would be grants if each loan were decomposed as a pure grant plus a loan at commercial rates. Interest rates shown are the nominal interest rates. Because of high inflation and a steady nominal rate, real interest rates on ODA loans were falling, and frequently negative, from the late sixties through the middle eighties.

with the multilateral share of aid moving from 6% or less initially to 30% or more by the mid seventies, thus insulating the recipient countries from their influence, as table 2.4 shows. Aid became less tied to purchases in the donor country, as table 2.9 shows. While originally almost two thirds of aid was restricted to purchases in the donor country, by the eighties almost 60% was without purchasing conditions, and another 10% had only some conditions on it. Again, aid moved from being a mixture of loans and grants to being almost wholly concessional, as table 2.10 shows. Aid consistently became less concentrated, with donors giving aid to a wider variety of states and recipients becoming far less dependent on any one aid source. More aid was directed toward the poorest countries, and toward the poorer sectors within recipient countries. Aid to the poor-

TABLE 2.11
DAC Countries Classified by Percentage of Aid Given to Multilateral Organizations

| Donor's Contribution to Multilateral Organizations as Percentage of Its ODA | 1960–61 | 1970–71 | 1980–81 | 1988–89 |
| --- | --- | --- | --- | --- |
| over 30 | 4 | 5 | 10 | 12 |
| 20–29.9 | 4 | 7 | 7 | 4 |
| 10–19.9 | 3 | 5 | 1 | 2 |
| under 10 | 2 | 0 | 0 | 0 |
| DAC countries not included | 5 | 1 | 1 | 0 |

*Source*: See sources for table 8.7.

*Notes*: Table entries are numbers of countries in each percentage range. In early years countries that later joined the DAC are not included; usually those countries had no aid programs in the earliest years.

TABLE 2.12
DAC Countries Classified by Grant Element in Aid over Time

| Grant Element (Percentage) | 1965–66 | 1970–71 | 1980–81 | 1988–89 |
| --- | --- | --- | --- | --- |
| 95–100 | 4 | 5 | 10 | 11 |
| 85–94.9 | 4 | 5 | 5 | 4 |
| 60–84.9 | 4 | 6 | 2 | 2 |
| Below 50 | 3 | 1 | 0 | 0 |
| DAC countries not included | 3 | 1 | 1 | 1 |

| Central Tendency: Grant Element for all DAC Foreign Aid (Percentage) | | | | |
| --- | --- | --- | --- | --- |
| DAC total | 84.0 | 83.1 | 89.7 | 91.6 |
| Median | 83.6 | 86.0 | 96.6 | 98.7 |

*Source*: Derived from data in table 8.11.

*Notes*: Main table entries are numbers of countries in each percentage range. In early years countries that later joined the DAC are not included; usually those countries had no aid programs in the earliest years.

est countries was almost entirely pure grants not tied to purchases in the donor country.

The changes in the way aid was provided were not the result of changes in a few countries only. Despite the fact that at any one time there was a wide range of degrees of tying and of financial concessionality, there was steady movement by the entire DAC donor community in the direction of less tied, more concessional aid, as tables 2.11 and 2.12 show. The same is true of the rise in multilateral shares of aid, and of its poverty orienta-

TABLE 2.13
Net Disbursed Aid By LDC Income Level over Time (Percentages)

| Recipient Income Class | 1960–61 | 1970–71 | 1982–83 | 1986–87 |
|---|---|---|---|---|
| Upper middle income countries | 41.5 | 26.2 | 23.5 | 21.1 |
| Lower middle income countries | 11.8 | 17.4 | 17.3 | 16.3 |
| Low income countries | 46.5 | 56.2 | 59.3 | 62.5 |
| Memo item: Least developed countries | 6.5 | 10.2 | 24.6 | 28.2 |

*Sources*: Data from table 8.12.

*Note*: Column totals may differ from 100% due to rounding. "Least developed countries" is a sub-category of "low income countries."

tion, as chapter 8 documents in detail. Table 2.13 shows the strong aggregate movement toward directing aid to the poorest countries.

If aid had been given to secure economic advantages or political leverage, it would have been sensible for the donor countries to move aid in exactly the opposite directions. The way in which aid was revised by nearly all donor countries suggests that the humane values which motivated most domestic advocates of aid and which were accepted in principle in international forums of donor countries, such as the DAC, affected the actual spending of most donors, even though they were not a part of any binding agreements and the degree of adherence to them was not at a uniform level, but varied from donor to donor.

## OTHER MOTIVES AND EXPLANATIONS FOR FOREIGN AID

There is no doubt that motives other than concern for the poverty of the recipient states entered into foreign aid. While most national aid agencies were staffed by professional economists and technical experts, and insulated from direct pressure from their countries' foreign offices, the decision of where aid went was influenced by political considerations. While an increasing portion of aid was untied to purchases in the donor country, a substantial portion of aid was tied, particularly in the early years of aid. Legislatures and business constituencies wanted some assurance that the money spent for aid was not spent solely to enrich foreign competitors. Up to half of U.S. bilateral aid (a third of all U.S. aid) was explicitly set aside as security supporting assistance, going to special allies of the United States—Vietnam, Israel, Egypt, El Salvador—and serving security purposes; U.S. aid also was denied to countries that allied themselves closely with the Soviets or seemed to constitute a threat in U.S. eyes. A substantial (though declining) portion of French official spending overseas was in the form of support to overseas territories and departments, and other French aid was closely directed to former colonies. Japanese aid before the late seventies was probably directed mainly at targets of commercial interest. The question is how important these motives are in accounting for the existence of foreign aid.

The fact that other motives played a part in aid allocation is not in itself evidence that they were very important in causing aid to come into being. Once a major government program is decided upon, there are many compromises that are made with potentially opposed factions to secure passage, and many groups that attempt to cash in on the money to be spent. Adoption of a program is the creation of a "field of play," on which those who wanted the program must contend with others over the details of spending and administration. For instance, it is clear that U.S. military spending is influenced by the attempts of members of Congress to get or maintain contracts and bases in their districts, by the concerns of the branches of military service to expand their purviews and maintain weapons systems to which they are committed, and to some extent by the possibilities of military sales abroad or the demands of allies, apart from the fundamental constitutive reason that justifies military spending, the provision of defense and maintenance of order. The degree to which congressional influence determines where the aid budget will be spent is not necessarily a good indicator of the degree to which the military spending exists for pork-barrel as distinct from legitimate defense purposes.

There are clear examples in which political conditions as well as attempts to serve domestic constituencies piggybacked on aid. West Germany adopted a rider on foreign aid appropriations making countries which recognized East Germany ineligible for its aid. This Hallstein Doctrine remained in force until the two Germanies reached an accommodation during Brandt's chancellorship. But the rider seems to have been parasitic upon aid expenditures and not an important underlying motive, for German foreign aid did not decrease when the doctrine ceased to function. Chancellor Brandt's foreign policy placed an emphasis upon interdependence and the needs of the Third World as well as upon East-West accommodation; aid increased in the period after the Hallstein Doctrine lapsed. Similarly, Senator Hickenlooper passed an amendment that U.S. aid could not go to countries which expropriated U.S. firms. But Hickenlooper, a noted conservative, was no friend of aid; the amendment, though very hard to vote against, does not seem to explain U.S. aid, even apart from the fact that U.S. net aid represented an investment two to four times greater than all net investment in the Third World by U.S. multinationals.

Foreign aid was affected by motives other than a humane internationalism, but these other motives were insufficient to justify donors' becoming involved in the aid effort, and quite inadequate to explain their sustaining and augmenting their programs. The other motives also do little to account for the variation among states or to explain the domestic politics of aid. While other motives inevitably entered in, only the humane internationalism that was, as a matter of fact, usually given as the motive also accounts adequately for the actual behavior of the donor states. This becomes clear if we examine other possible arguments one by one.

## Interests of Individual Donor States

It is difficult to account for aid as attempts by individual donor states to secure advantages for themselves, for four reasons which emerge from patterns of aid spending, although undoubtedly donor commercial interests played a part. First, many of the donor states had few commercial interests in the Third World and were unable to secure any kind of international influence. These include the states that had the strongest aid programs as a percentage of national income. Second, a substantial portion of all OECD aid was channeled through multilateral organizations. It is hard to see how states could have hoped to gain advantages for themselves from the money that went there. Third, the associations of bilateral aid with trade are weak, and many of the states could not have hoped to obtain useful political influence from their aid. Fourth, aid was given in a way that makes perfect sense if the aim of the aid was to promote development, but no sense if the aim was to gain advantages for particular donor states. That is, aid was channeled increasingly to poor sectors, went increasingly to the poorest countries, was more and more in the form of pure grants, was less and less tied, and so on.

While the aid almost certainly provided some benefits within the donor countries, these benefits were insufficient to justify the aid expenses, and indeed, the countries whose aid may have provided them with the most internal rewards were those which were least committed to aid. But countries which increased the quantity of their aid also tended to increase aid quality, as France and Japan did in the eighties, while those countries which decreased their aid in the eighties, such as Britain and the United States, at the same time focused aid more narrowly on achieving trade and strategic objectives. These patterns are the more significant because they tally exactly with evidence about public opinion and about the parties and groups and politicians and scholars who supported and opposed aid. Just as countries which gave purer aid made more of an aid commitment, and countries which increased or decreased quality increased or decreased the quantity of aid provided, so those opposed to aid tended to favor tying what aid was given to donor interests, while strong supporters of aid favored aid less tied to donor self-interest as well as more abundant aid.

## Collective Interests of Donor States

If the contribution aid made to individual donors' self-interests was insufficient to justify its costs, perhaps there were benefits to the Western countries as a group that were worth the costs the donors paid. Collective gains to OECD donors from their joint aid programs might have included resisting communist influence and extending capitalism to the Third World, or exerting discipline over LDCs, for instance with respect to their payment of debts. Multilateral aid, so hard to justify on the basis of each country's gains from its own contribution, could be understood in this way as a public good for which donors agreed among themselves to share the costs. But such explanations must grapple with well-known problems about collective action or the voluntary provision of public goods: if the benefits were joint while the decision making was by individual donors, each of which bore its own costs, each donor would have been tempted to free-ride, enjoying the benefits but not contributing, since the absence of its own contributions would not significantly alter the degree to which it benefited from the effects of aid. For on this view, the gains foreign aid secured were public ones, from which donors that did not contribute could not be excluded.

But there are ways in which international public goods might have been secured. Collective goods might have been provided by the United States as the largest state, because its immense size meant that the effect of its own aid on its gains from aid might have justified its investment. Or the United States as hegemon, and as leader of the free world and of the Western alliance, might have pressured other states to do their part. Or the donor states might, even without U.S. leadership, have struck some sort of bargain, or formed a regime, in which each participated because of a joint understanding to which each donor country adhered because of concern for its reputation and because its behavior in upholding the bargain could be monitored.

## The Influence of the United States as Hegemon

It could be argued that aid served the strategic purposes of the United States, which used aid to support its overall aims in building an order favorable to it in two ways: by integrating Third World countries into the international capitalist system and by providing inducements for them not to develop close relationships with the Soviet Union. The United States during the fifties and sixties introduced the concept of "burden sharing," the idea that other allies needed to pick up more of the costs of the Western alliance and, in particular, of foreign aid. One could argue, then, that the foreign aid participation of non-U.S. donors was a response to U.S. pressures that its dependent allies pick up the responsibilities for aid which secured the good of the alliance or other goals the United States saw as valuable: to secure world political stability, resistance to communist infiltration, or continuing trade and prosperity. This explanation faces several problems which make it an implausible explanation of the aid behavior of other OECD countries.

One problem is that aid from most donors steadily increased, as U.S. aid contributions steadily declined, and as the hegemonic leverage of the United States declined also. The United States did play a part in promoting aid policies in the other OECD states initially. The United States effected the reorganization of the OEEC as the OECD and the establishment of the DAC, and pressed the recuperated democratic market states to provide more foreign aid. But this does not explain why other countries continued "bearing the burden" as the United States continued to decrease its load, and as they became more independent in other ways. Still less does it explain the marked increases in aid as a percentage of GNP on the part of most of the other OECD nations in the seventies and eighties. If countries were influenced by U.S. pressure to give aid, their aid should have varied with the strength of U.S. influence and with the degree of U.S. commitment to the goal of providing foreign aid. But in fact, they varied inversely to U.S. strength and U.S. commitment to aid.

A further problem with this explanation is that the burden other countries shouldered was not exactly the one the United States wanted them to assume. European aid tended to favor countries perceived as egalitarian, such as Tanzania, which were also persistent critics of the international system. Some aid went to countries the United States reckoned as enemies, such as Vietnam or Cuba. Other aid, such as Australia's to Papua New Guinea, went to countries which, while not obnoxious to U.S. sensibilities, were not a U.S. priority. Another difficulty is that while donors sometimes spoke in terms of doing their part in promoting development, they rarely spoke in terms of satisfying U.S. demands or aiding in objectives of promoting world trade or resistance to communism, as is detailed in chapter 5. The actual policy discussion about support for aid in other DAC countries emphasized developmental objectives, and never U.S. leadership in strategic objectives. Also, if the collective goods were economic, it is hard to see why donors sought to extend capitalism in the system as a whole rather than simply concentrate on their own trade. Finally, explanation that donors sought the extension of capitalism faces the problem that aid went increasingly to countries which had little potential as trading partners, to the poorest states, rather than to countries which were economically important to the donors.

## The Bipolar World and Competition with Communism

A concern for stemming the spread of communism was a central part of United States policy to the Third World. The postwar world was one dominated by bipolarity, and the cold war conflict between the United States and the Soviet Union. Do these factors explain foreign aid? Certainly, concern about communism played a role in U.S. aid policies. A process of strengthening countries against disorder, of improving their standard of living, and of demonstrating the advantages of a noncommunist, democratic, market-oriented way of life was a motivation that played an important part in U.S. foreign aid. It is entirely possible that neither the Marshall Plan nor the Point Four program could have been sold to the Congress without the imminent threat of communist takeovers. A strategy of strengthening noncommunist countries formed part of the idea of containment that Kennan outlined in his early policy statements; and the idea of resisting subversion and reversing anti-Americanism in Latin America probably played a role both in the reinforcing of aid in the last years of the Eisenhower administration and in Kennedy's emphasis upon the importance of foreign aid. The anticommunist motive also entered into the thinking of British and Australian and some other leaders in the early years, and seems to have had a mild influence on the selection of aid recipients by a number of donors. Yet while competition with communism played a role in getting aid off the ground, it does not explain OECD foreign aid, for many reasons.

First, within the OECD itself, the goal of using aid to contain communism was extremely controversial. Some DAC members, like Sweden and Switzerland, had long traditions of neutrality; others, like Austria and Finland, were so situated as to make neutrality essential; yet others, like Germany and England, while involved in formal alliances to block Soviet expansion, renounced the idea of using aid in that way. Concern about the spread of communism was mainly an American fear; there is little evidence that this motivated European or Japanese programs of foreign aid. Indeed, several strong OECD donors (notably Sweden), feeling aid should go to egalitarian regimes, have favored not only socialist regimes, such as Tanzania, or Marxist regimes, such as Allende's Chile, but actual communist allies, such as Cuba and North Vietnam, as well, in their aid policies.

Arguments from bipolarity also fail to explain the differences between the West and the communist countries in providing aid. If aid was an effective means of international political influence in a crucial global struggle, why did the Soviet bloc not employ it in a similar way to the OECD? Soviet aid was very limited, despite initial more lavish offers.

Russian and Iron Curtain aid was much smaller in size than OECD aid, and for the most part went only to closely allied states: Afghanistan, Cuba, Vietnam. Virtually none was multilaterally channeled, through UN organizations and the like. Only a quite small fraction went to India and a few other nonallied states. If aid chiefly constituted a newly effective means of political influence for superpowers, blocs, or individual nations, it would be surprising to find groups of competing nations behaving so differently. This is shown when Soviet aid is examined in detail in chapter 4.

Bipolarity and cold war arguments also do very badly at predicting which OECD donors supported aid strongly and who advocated aid within the states' domestic polities. The most staunchly anticommunist country, the United States, has been relatively slack in its support for aid. Many donors which supported aid most strongly tended to be favorable to leftist regimes in the Third World. Those countries which have maintained a strong aid commitment have not eliminated or reduced aid now that there are no fears of communist expansion, and are not expected to. While American commitment to aid declined, support in Europe rose, especially in countries least sympathetic to the cold war. A look at support for aid within countries shows why. Those individuals and groups most concerned about the spread of communism were, in general, those least favorable toward aid both in the United States and elsewhere. Individuals, groups, parties, and statesmen more on the left tended to be particularly strong supporters of foreign aid; and in Europe, communists and those on the far left were particularly strong supporters. Even in the United States, the original impetus came from New Dealers and people committed to broad internationalism; aid was consistently advocated by liberal Democrats and opposed particularly by the right wing of the Republican party. Public opinion data from country after country also show that strong aid supporters did not want aid used to further strategic interests.

Introduction of an anticommunist motive may ultimately have weakened support for aid by undermining the real, humanitarian bases of support, as Gunnar Myrdal had argued all along; it was impossible to secure active support for aid from anticommunists and conservatives, and compromising the character of aid eroded the support of humanitarian advocates who were its only consistent champions. Initial attempts to gain support for aid as prophylactic against communist influence also undercut later U.S. support for aid because this rationale appeared more and more implausible. During the seventies and eighties it became clear that nominally Marxist Third World states, such as Angola, were not necessarily menacing to Western interests and also that providing aid did not necessarily reduce the chances of radical revolutions. While U.S. aid continues to weaken due to lack of domestic support, most OECD countries have increased their aid. Support for aid seems to have fared better when not linked to anticommunism, perhaps because it was not eroded when accumulated experience undermined antiradical rationales for aid. And there is little reason to suppose that European or Japanese aid, which held constant or increased over the last decade, will fade away in the nineties now that any threat of communism as a worldwide force is effectively removed. If foreign aid was driven by concern about communism, it should have declined as the threat of communism in the Third World declined and the prospects it would be useful in counteracting communism dimmed. It did just the opposite.

In sum, the cold war and bipolar rivalry of the United States and the Soviet Union do not explain aid. Competition with communism played a role in sustaining U.S. interest in aid and in U.S. attempts to interest other developed democracies in "sharing" the aid "burden," although even there it can be argued that concern with communism was simply used by people with genuine concerns about Third World poverty to generate support for aid policies and placate critics. But it cannot account for the aid of any of the other donors, nor for the bases of support for aid, even in the United States. It mispredicts where aid was allocated, and cannot explain which donors were strong in their support, either. In fact, on each count the evidence suggests that opposition to communism hindered aid as much as it helped, apart from the important transitional role it played in the United States.

## Collective Economic Interests of the Donors

OECD countries might have agreed to further their collective interests even without U.S. leadership in the aid area, or after that leadership waned. Krasner and others[17] discuss how regimes can lead even self-interested states to cooperate, particularly where a dominant power helps set up regimes. Keohane[18] elaborates conditions under which public goods can be provided and other forms of cooperation can occur, internationally, through mutually beneficial bargains among parties with common interests, even in the absence of hegemonic power, or especially after its decline. Axelrod and Keohane,[19] and other contributors to Oye's[20] edited volume *Cooperation under Anarchy* provide further elaboration of this line of discussion. The possibility of constructing regimes and other pareto-improving bargains as a way of overcoming free-rider problems in the provision of public goods helps in understanding a variety of important international economic arrangements—the GATT, the IMF, and cartels like OPEC—as well as some collective security arrangements. Cooperation among the donors, in the limited sense of such pareto-improving deals, might support collective interests of the cooperating, or colluding, parties, without having in view any broader values or humane aims, as Keohane[21] rightly emphasizes. Thus it would have been possible to set foreign aid up as a joint arrangement in which all developed countries chipped in to support collective interests in promoting trade with LDCs, without regard to the effects on the LDCs.

But the conditions for this kind of bargain were in fact missing in the case of aid. Where what is involved in maintenance of a public good is a well-defined action—refraining from certain behavior or contributing at a known and fixed level—states can create a regime or collective agreement for mutual benefit. In such circumstances, a regime reduces costs of bargaining over individual levels of participation, and monitoring prevents cheating. But no aid bargains were struck and there was no accepted standard as to what countries' overall aid contributions should be, although contributions to replenish IDA capital were worked out in periodic negotiations. The DAC proposed various targets and goals, but these operated as guidelines, not as definite commitments on the part of the donor countries, and compliance varied by such large amounts that countries were really free from constraints. Different donors' levels of aid varied widely, ranging in a given year from .2% to 1.1% of GNP. The percentage of multilateral aid and tied aid varied widely. There was also broad variation in the extent to which aid was directed to poorer nations. Such disparate levels of participation made it possible for a country to ride free on the rest of the OECD. Aid was monitored and targets were set, but no country could be said to be in violation of a specific agreement. This makes it hard to see why a country would feel strongly compelled to raise its aid contribution, since no matter the contribution, it would not suffer from a reputation of failing to honor its commitments.

The rates at which particular countries participated in aid also make the free-rider objections to this hypothesis the more formidable. For the country, generally, that has the largest stake in the maintenance of such a regime is the large power; it is unique in being able to break the regime single-handedly, or feel the effects of its own contributions redound to itself. But the United States, while it initially pushed foreign aid and participated vigorously, has, as we noted, been the laggard since. It is even harder to see why countries like Norway and the Netherlands, whose aid was well above the DAC targets, continued to raise levels of aid funding. Again, since aid totals were essentially unaffected by the presence of the smallest participants, and aid was a well-established practice that showed no signs of going away by the midsixties, it is hard to see how securing collective goods could have motivated new countries to join the DAC and start aid programs, as New Zealand, Finland, and Ireland did.

Further difficulties appear in considering what specific collective gains a consortium of OECD nations might have sought, other than seeking the humane goals of promoting economic development and alleviating poverty. Had the aim been to extend OECD prosperity through promoting capitalist economies, trade, and foreign investment, why would states not bound by a mutual agreement have done this to advance common interests rather than simply furthering their own trade and investments by means of foreign aid? Yet states provided growing shares of their aid to multilateral institutions. Also, if the collective interest was in extending trade and capitalism, it made poor sense to invest in poor countries without major economic value. India, which receives far the greatest flow of aid, and from many sources, increased exports to the OECD slightly more than fourfold from 1965 to 1980 and imports from the OECD slightly less than fourfold to half a billion dollars per month. Third World countries as a whole have increased both nearly tenfold, to $20 billion a month. Brazil's growth of trade has kept par with the Third World average; Mexico's and Hong Kong's have exceeded it considerably; Korea's and Singapore's trade show nearly a hundredfold increase. Yet Brazil and Mexico combined get only half of the aid that India does, even though Brazil does over twice, Mexico three times, the trade with the West that India does. Hong Kong and Singapore receive a percent or two of India's total in aid, though they each import from and export to the OECD substantially more than does India, a populous and needy country.

The problems in the collective economic interest hypothesis become worse when we look specifically at the distribution of multilaterally channeled aid. Multilateral aid has been focused more narrowly than bilateral on least developed countries, which engage in far less OECD trade and have less potential for it than middle-income or industrializing LDCs. This has been the result of a deliberate policy, which has tightened that focus over the years. Furthermore, the focus has been sharper in the largely OECD-controlled World Bank group than in the largely LDC-controlled UN development programs. Donor funding has, it is true, yielded to Third World insistence in giving increased funding over to the recipient-dominated UNDP and remains relatively steady in funding the donor-dominated World Bank Group. But as UNDP funding increased, Bank Group funding held fairly steady, and in any case, the increased DAC funding for recipient-controlled multilateral institutions is even harder to reconcile with an argument from DAC collective self-interest.

The argument that aid furthered collective interests is hard to reconcile with the distribution of aid to recipients, the policies of multilateral institutions not designed to further OECD goals, or the variations of support among donors. And it is particularly hard to see how the incentives that sustain regimes based on mutually advantageous bargains among the contributors could have sustained aid. The variable levels of funding, the existence of customary behavior that did not depend on each donor's fulfilling a customary level of compliance, and the absence of reputational considerations that would affect a donor's power or trustworthiness, all make the ordinary sort of collective-interests argument hard to sustain.

### Unspecified Influence, Prestige, and Other Arguments

Occasionally other miscellaneous arguments are suggested as a basis for aid programs. The sudden widespread appearance of aid may be attributed to bureaucratic interests, to the diffusion of the idea of aid, or to a "competition for influence" factor that would leave nonparticipants disgraced. The participation of small donors especially may be said to be due to the fact that they have no other role to play internationally or that they seek "prestige."

These arguments share two main defects, which are related. While they offer mechanisms—diffusion or bureaucratic interest, for instance—by which aid policies may have been advanced, they do not provide autonomous driving forces that would set these in motion. Bureaucracies may seek to enhance their power, but they need reasons for doing so that will appeal to an audience larger than themselves. Ideas do diffuse, but only when their implementation is perceived, for other reasons, as being desirable. This applies, too, to retention of colonial or mandate relationships: there must be a reason why should they be retained. Similarly, to the extent these categories offer even vague impulses that might affect various sizes of nations—prestige, keeping international or regional presence, "keeping up with the Joneses" or "playing a role"—they do not indicate why nations suddenly choose to do this by giving away money rather than by more traditional, and plausible, means such as developing small high-tech or other industrial sectors, a more powerful army or shipping industry, or even some cultural or scientific distinction. Still less do they give a clue as to why all the rich industrial democracies chose to enhance prestige, to copy and then surpass the hegemon's behavior, to seek "a role" or "presence" internationally, or to indulge their bureaucracies in just the same way. It includes any conceivable behavior, and therefore does not distinguish certain kinds of causes from others.

It might be said that if politicians sought to promote Third World development as an end in itself, they did so because they sought re-election. Or, that if publics sought this goal, they did so because they wanted to have national prestige. Or that they wanted to feel that they were doing the right thing. And these are counted as national interests. To treat these things as self-interested makes a hash of any analytic attempt to discuss international relations, because it confounds tangible benefits a nation may hope to reap with the process by which decisions are made. I will treat these three cases in reverse order, and then enunciate the general principle.

When a country undertakes a course of action because it thinks that is the moral thing to do—because others will benefit, or because duty requires it for other reasons—rather than because it thinks the country itself will benefit, this should not be referred to as acting in the national interest. For to do so makes "national interest" an analytically useless concept, since any purposive behavior that is approved falls under it. Such a usage fails to distinguish pursuit of military strength, diplomatic position, economic gain, and the like from pursuit of the welfare of other states, or principles of justice. In claiming that a nation undertakes *certain* actions from the pursuit of national strength and wealth, or even undertakes *all* actions from those motives, it is necessary to admit a conceptual category of actions that are *not* undertaken for these goals if the claim is to be more than a tautology.

A similar problem attends the use of a concept of "prestige." If by the pursuit of "prestige" we mean that a country is seeking a reputation for a particular thing—military might, or unwillingness to give in on certain matters, or the like—and that this reputation may later be convertible to concrete material advantages of the same kind that wealth or military might confer, then it is clearly a (sophisticated) form of pursuit of national interest. However, the "prestige" sought ordinarily proclaims, in this case, the factor of power or interest that it is associated with. Thus a reputation for effective military operations—one kind of "prestige"—draws its desirability from the desirable aspects of possessing military capabilities. A reputation for making fine electronic products or machine tools draws its desirability from the desirability of being an economic leader. If a nation seeks to undertake an activity for a means of international prestige, that says something about what that nation wants to be seen as: what sort of an actor it is in the international system, and what sort of actor it wants to be seen as, is proclaimed *not* by the fact that it seeks prestige or reputation but by *what* it seeks reputation *as*. Thus to say that Sweden, for instance, "sought prestige" as a generous donor of foreign aid is to raise the question of *why* it wanted to be seen as that sort of an actor. *If* what the international system favors is power, and if nations seeking to advance their interests seek those capacities that give them wealth and power, then to seek "prestige" as a donor is not to seek to advance national interest.

Finally, to say that politicians sought to promote aid because publics wanted it is to distract attention from the question of what sorts of policies promoted strictly national interest and to turn instead to the question of how exactly policies (leaning one way *or* the other) were selected. In fact, it is probable from the evidence that in most cases publics were less interested in policies of foreign aid than politicians and other elites were. But whether or not this was true, and if so whether or not the politicians were more internationally minded, or more gullible than publics, is not required in our inquiry here. The question of how nations came to adopt and to reform foreign aid policies depends on the goal of the policies, not on whether the policymakers were the originators of the goals or simply the transmission belt of the public's desires.

## FOREIGN AID AND MORAL INFLUENCE IN INTERNATIONAL POLITICS

The first chapter argued that the character of international politics is not wholly determined in advance by an unvarying human nature or international system but reflects moral choices which become embodied in the regular patterns of international affairs. Human beings are capable of selfish and self-interested behavior, of generous and just deeds, and of pointless follies, animosities, and self-destructiveness, in personal life and in domestic and international politics. Calculations of national advantage based on pressures of survival or satisfaction of interests do not determine how states act, in part because states are not tightly constrained but can choose many different objectives, and in part because rational consideration of how to attain objectives is not a technical process of calculation or optimization, especially in new, large-scale, unreplicable, long-term situations. How one conceives of the future and what will work out well is closely bound up with one's interpretation of the world and one's value perspective. Thus, the contestation between different approaches to international politics is a contestation between different understandings, different moral perspectives, about international politics. Actors' rationality in international politics is not some process of calculation from facts of known weights, at which mathematicians are best, or in which statesmen's political and philosophic views are irrelevant, as Morgenthau claimed: rationality is not simply a chesslike power calculus. Being rational requires political and moral insight, vision and practice. The direction that careful, thoughtful, wise, rational policies take reflects both their goals and their assumptions about what the world is like, and about the values to trust in.

Individual national policies and the international system reflect moral choices, good and bad, which are bound up with differing outlooks and interpretations of what international politics is about. For international politics is not some realm apart, wholly governed by its own laws and, in particular, by considerations of power and of objective national interests.

States have latitude in what to trust in, what to value, whether to seek to act with justice and mercy: no one strategy is the one that obviously works best in a complex long run; there is no theorem that pragmatic cynics do better than pragmatic idealists. Such differing wisdoms and values are not the product of lone individuals or lone states' calculations: they are social products that draw upon and interpret existing practice. Thus I argued that (1) a country's international politics will systematically be linked to the values and assumptions and practices of its domestic politics, (2) a country's international politics will reflect the world society in which it finds itself, and (3) the practices of international politics are not simply devices to be taken up or abandoned as technical instruments to national ends but are meaningful actions whose logic, once the practices are adopted, influences and modifies states' goals and vision.

The idea that rationality in international politics must be understood in terms of moral choice[22] and not simply in terms of some hypothesized pure calculation of advantage thus leads to specific lines of investigation which can be researched empirically in a wide variety of areas: types of economic structure, policies on race and colonialism, attitudes toward domination and freedom, and so on. These ideas are followed out specifically in this book in the issue area of foreign aid, where one can trace these three general hypotheses at work: domestic values influence the values states adopt in international politics; states base their international policies on their perception of international society and how it defines respectable and appropriate conduct; and international practices once adopted influence ideas of acceptably just conduct and thus lead to progressive refinement of practices in accord with their moral meaning. The next three subsections of this chapter specifically trace how we see these processes at work.

### Domestic Political and Individual Moral Influences

The evidence that countries provided aid out of humanitarian concern and not out of a desire to obtain specific advantages is quite strong, and it reveals the links between views about international relations and moral reasoning in everyday life and in domestic political matters.

Countries with high levels of public support for foreign aid tended to give more aid and to raise the level and quality of aid spending and keep it high. When one looks at public support, it appears that the general public was influenced primarily by moral considerations. Lindholm notes that only 18% of Swedes who strongly agreed that "securing a good living" was life's most important goal favored raising aid spending, while 53% of those who strongly disagreed favored raising aid.[23] In ten European countries, those who had themselves contributed to assistance to the

Third World were more likely to favor aid. Seventy-five percent of the general public in these ten countries felt aid should be given to the countries that needed it most rather than to suppliers of raw materials, potential importers of their own country's goods, or countries of strategic importance. The 25% who did not favor directing aid to the poorest countries were much less favorable toward giving aid. Other polls from the United States and Britain suggest the same, though the questions were less focused. Those with strong convictions tended to favor aid more, and those who attended church regularly or were on the left, particularly, as well as current students, the well educated, and those who favored domestic redistribution and help for the poor, tended to favor aid. The single best predictor of support for aid, which accounts for almost 40% of the variance by itself, was inquiring whether "we have a moral duty to help" Third World countries. Reasons for opposition to aid were interesting, too: all centered on waste, the idea that recipients were lazy, or concerns about the effectiveness of aid; no one seemed to be concerned that aid, though effective in reducing poverty of those in need, would not gain any concrete advantages.

If these were the feelings of the general public, it is not clear why public officeholders should be motivated to support strategic aid instead. Those who hold the reins of government are, of course, in a sense less insulated from the pressure of daily events than is the general public, and more apt to want to tailor policies to the exigencies of the present moment; lawmakers are more apt to be pressured by particularistic national interests. Probably aid was often bent a bit to serve pressing needs of the economy or of foreign affairs (especially in larger states with a worldwide foreign policy). In the United States, where congressional support for aid was difficult to obtain, there is no doubt that anticommunist and other foreign policy rationales were mixed in to gain support for aid. However, in terms of the overall purposes of aid, politicians and other officials were drawn from the general population and favored similar goals, and also had to satisfy the public with their policies. In fact, evidence from almost every aid-giving democracy indicates that those politicians who favored higher aid levels were also supporters of aid more geared to the needs of recipient countries and tended to be those on the left, those associated with strong moral causes, and those concerned about domestic poverty. All the internal evidence suggests support for aid stemmed from the same sources as attempts to provide for the poor at home.

Direct evidence about aid spending indicates that what countries did with their aid was done primarily to promote recipient economic development, and that the interest in recipient development was based on domestic political values, too. Those countries with strong aid spending were those with strong domestic social programs, and those whose citizens had in fact individually contributed to private charities concerned with the Third World. Countries with high volumes of aid as a percentage of GNP tended to have programs that were high quality in the sense of being highly multilateral, directed more toward the poorest countries and the poorest sectors in countries, being free from tying, and being at highly concessional terms. Generally speaking, when a given country increased its aid, it improved quality also, as Japan did in the seventies; when countries decreased their aid, they tended to cut quality also.

The way in which aid first came about also suggests the same humane motivations. The earliest precursor programs were found in private voluntary efforts at overseas relief: church efforts, the Red Cross, refugee aid, and Belgian Relief efforts. The programs which led up to aid—colonial development programs, technical assistance to Latin America, the World Bank, the Marshall Plan, the UN—were the work of liberals like Bevin, Keynes, Marshall, Rockefeller, and White and were opposed by those who, like Robert A. Taft, later opposed aid. Early advocates of programs for world economic planning tended to be those concerned with domestic poverty and humanitarian causes as well.

## The Influence of International Society

The process leading up to aid also reflected a growth of internationalism. Advocates of programs of international assistance thought of rational social organization and of building a better world in terms of constructing a positive international order as well as in terms of the welfare and needs of people overseas. Throughout the twentieth century advocates of assistance to those in need have made the arguments that (in the words of the Philadelphia Declaration of the ILO in 1944) "poverty anywhere constitutes a danger to prosperity everywhere" and that freedom from want and freedom from fear are linked goals as Churchill and Roosevelt presented them in the Atlantic Charter.

This sense of the interconnectedness of peace and justice and prosperity appears to have been not a calculation of benefits so much as the expansion of national and personal identity. Those who favored foreign aid were likely to feel that giving aid "is in our interests," but those who felt aid was "in our interests" were more likely than others to repudiate giving aid to countries of strategic or economic importance and to favor giving aid to needy countries instead, as public opinion data show. Like soldiers who say, "We all gain through each of us having the courage to fight for what is right," what is involved here is not individual "interests" in the delimited social science sense that analyzes how a "public good" can suffer in a free-rider problem but a sense of the common good with which people identify. Citizens of small countries who favored foreign aid as "in our interests" but eschewed seeking any specific interest were saying that as they were willing to pay taxes for national goals, as part of the nation, so they were willing to have their country contribute to the building of a better world, of which they felt they were a part. Commitment to the construction of a better international order rested upon building a sense of communality, of common fate and interest, with others around the world.

The establishment of an international forum in the United Nations, what Senator Arthur Vandenberg called the "town meeting of tomorrow's world," necessarily led to the concerns of the less developed nations being brought forth to public attention and concern in a new way. The years prior to the announcement of Truman's Point Four plan, the first foreign aid in the modern sense, are full of the Latin American and other less developed countries pressing in the UN's Economic and Social Council for substantial programs of development assistance. The new awareness of the existence and needs of the underdeveloped countries awakened in many people in developed countries a desire to do something; in the context of a world in which the developed countries had already decided that peace and prosperity were linked to the recognition of the needs and rights of all countries, the demands presented were ones to which the developed countries' leaders, even when they did not like the demands, felt a need to respond.

Also, as aid became established as a practice, it became a mark of proper participation in the responsibilities of the developed countries. Ireland sought both to define itself in its own estimation and to establish itself as a developed country by committing itself to have an exemplary aid program and, finally, by joining the DAC. New Zealand and Finland similarly, in joining the DAC at a time when no one was pressing for it, moved toward establishing themselves as full members of the society of developed nations. Japan responded to criticism of its international role, in part, by changing its aid policies, which had been exceptionally laggardly throughout the seventies, not only markedly increasing the volume of aid but also increasing the multilaterally channeled share of aid, reducing aid tying, and moving away, to some extent at least, from an earlier commercial orientation to aid. More generally, the aid-giving countries submitted themselves to mutual criticism in their aid policies by joining the DAC, which set standards from time to time which seem to have influenced most of its members to move toward targets for improving and increasing aid. This also led some countries, such as the Dutch and the Swedes, to consciously see their role in the aid process as one of seeking to set higher standards, to reform and correct the aid process by example.

It may be objected that Japan sought to improve its foreign aid to look good to other countries, that Sweden was concerned with being perceived as a leader in virtue, that Ireland wanted to be like other developed countries, and Finland like other Scandinavian states. Perhaps so, yet even if this was the case, it suggests both the power of international society and the power of moral concerns to influence it.

Realists argue that the character of international politics makes it different from daily life or domestic politics: in the former, perhaps, generous motives may come into play, but in the latter the pressure of political forces requires each state to act in a realpolitik manner. There are really two arguments here: that the philosophy, or sympathies, of the statesman (and by extension, the nation) cannot enter in to international politics; and that the pressures of international life force countries to behave selfishly. Both arguments are wrong, although no one would deny the pervasive power of international pressure or a state's need to look after its own interests. Not only do domestic concerns about international poverty and desires to make a stabler world affect foreign policy; international concern about these matters does also. States are concerned about whether they are doing well or poorly by international standards, and there is an attempt to act virtuously in a general way, and not only to fulfill definite, agreed-on obligations clearly monitored. Where that results in states acting more public-spiritedly or compassionately than they would if left to their own devices, international society is shown to have power to improve state conduct. International pressures operate not just to make states more self-centered and realpolitik but also to exert a beneficial power of public opinion. If public opinion has power in this way, international society is more like domestic society than most theorists acknowledge.

It should be pointed out that if countries are swayed to do what is right by the pressure of international opinion, this shows the power of moral concerns in international politics. That power, like the impetus to seek military prestige, or revenge, or economic dominance, is not something that operates simply at the level of individual motivations: it has a systemic element, which is made manifest in states' copying or conforming to behavior deemed virtuous. Such conformity often reflects strong domestic pressures for more public-spirited international policy, too: domestic advocates seize on international opinion and standing to press their case. But even apart from domestic advocacy, even if the conformity was only for the sake of looking good in the eyes of other countries, it would show the power of moral ideals. La Rochefoucauld states that "hypocrisy is the tribute that vice pays to virtue." But where hypocrisy consists not of pretending to do one thing and doing another, but of actually doing something costly and right but doing it out of a desire for approbation, the acknowledged standards show their power nevertheless. Where the tribute paid is not dissimulation but externally virtuous action perhaps without conviction, virtue has nevertheless showed its power to levy tribute. This is precisely power such as Realism, and all rational action theories that limit effective state motives to improving the situation of the state itself, must deny that moral principle has. Moral principle, like self-aggrandizement, has effects in international politics both because people are naturally drawn to it and because of environmental pressures on the state.

### Ongoing Change as the Development of Meaningful International Practices

The history of foreign aid also clearly supports the hypothesis that international practices once put in place develop according to their own inner logic. The features of foreign aid that set it apart from anything before it—its ongoing and reliable scale; its open, public, and multilateral character; its concessionality; and its focus upon economic development in poor countries—all bore witness from the beginning of the aid process to an underlying concept of international solidarity between people and between countries, which centered on alleviating poverty and raising standards of living. The aim was to create a world in which all could pursue basic goals cooperatively with reasonable prospects of success. The same elements characterize the welfare-state internationalist thinking in the early twentieth century, in which one can see an elaboration of ideas and programs that finally led to aid in 1949. And the defining characteristics of aid were ones which, after its inception, showed steady, ongoing, norm-governed change.

As chapter 6 shows, there was a steady growth of welfare state measures, labor movements, and social-democratic parties through the century. The role of the ILO and the positions of labor parties and socialist writers before the start of aid all show a strong internationalism which, by the forties, increasingly included a concern for the poverty in underdeveloped countries. A series of international relief efforts of successively broader scope—the Red Cross, Belgian Relief, the UNRRA, the World Bank, the Marshall Plan—and the institutionalization of international concern with economic matters in universal membership organizations, culminating with the UN Economic and Social Council, also show steady growth in international concern for economic problems of foreign countries. There was growth of domestic humanitarian movements and, later, of associated international charitable undertakings, including increasing involvement in economic as well as health problems overseas by missionary organizations. Such humanitarian concern often combined addressing concrete and immediate problems with advocacy of more permanent structural solutions.

Upon the introduction of aid, there was an immediate upsurge in interest in the problems of the developed countries. Popular books full of enthusiasm about the new challenge of aid to poor countries appeared.

Economists took up development as a major interest in the discipline. Organizations were formed to deal with world hunger. More importantly, governments adopted aid programs which, over time, were steadily modified to make them more focused on recipient poverty, as chapters 7 and 8 will show. Aid as a percentage of GNP rose toward proposed targets of .7% or 1% of GNP. The share of multilateral aid rose, and more multilateral aid, as time went on, went through organizations like UNDP, which were primarily subject to Third World, not to developed country, control. Aid tying decreased, especially among those countries which acknowledged a need to cut tying. The concessional element of aid grew, finally approaching 100%. A conscious and successful effort was made to direct larger percentages of aid to poorer states and, above all, to the least developed countries; efforts were also made to see that aid reached the poorest people in countries that were assisted.

## CONCLUSION

Foreign aid was the largest financial flow to the Third World consistently through the postwar period, and was greater than all other flows combined, except in the period roughly from 1973 to 1985. The sudden appearance of aid from nearly a score of developed democracies in the fifties, and their steady commitment to aid since, cannot be explained by the individual or collective economic and political interests of the donor states, though those interests did sometimes influence aid. Evidence about aid spending, about which countries had the strongest aid programs, about public support for aid, about the origins of aid, and about ongoing changes in aid suggests instead that the real bases of support lay in humanitarian and egalitarian concern in the donor countries. Such concern was usually combined with an internationalism which held that the only secure basis for world peace and prosperity in the long run lay in providing all states with a chance to make progress toward a better life; but this kind of internationalism tended to be held only by those who were committed to the welfare of poor countries for other reasons, and was generally opposed to the use of aid to support narrow national interests.

As just discussed, the practice of foreign aid from 1949 to the present also accords with the more general arguments developed in chapter 1 about the ways in which moral factors can influence international politics. There was regular influence of domestic concerns with poverty upon international aid efforts. A sense of world citizenship led individuals to support assistance to the Third World, and perceptions of international society led developed country governments to pay attention to international norms and standards, to the kind of identity they wanted to develop, to the opinion of other developed states, and to the complaints of Third World countries.

# PART II

# The Evidence

## CHAPTER THREE

# Where the Money Went:
## Who Were the Main Recipients of Aid?

> Among our century's most urgent problems is the wholly unacceptable poverty that blights the lives of some 2,000 million people in the more than 100 countries of the developing world. Of these 2,000 million, nearly 800 million are caught up in what can only be termed absolute poverty . . . a condition of life so degrading as to be an insult to human dignity.
>
> —Robert S. McNamara[1]

THE REASONS for which aid programs were instituted should show up in the objects on which donor countries expended their resources. Various theories about the purposes of foreign aid are tested, in part, by where the money went. I will argue that the choice of aid recipient supports the overall contention of this book: that aid cannot be anything like fully accounted for on the basis of donor economic and political interests, and that a commitment to promoting economic development, worldwide, was an important factor in aid policies, as well. The focus on poverty that McNamara advocated should, if I am right, show up in where aid was spent.

To be sure, not all aid went for purposes of economic development: colonial, trade, and strategic motivations also played a part. The question is how these diverse motives affected aid spending. In some cases the various factors competed and should be viewed as rival, incompatible, explanations; in other cases different motives—developmental motives and colonial ties, for instance—worked together and should be seen as supplementary rather than alternative explanations. Thus, a country might have been moved to undertake aid programs by humane motives, but have decided to concentrate aid in countries to which it had historic ties; or a country might have sought to strengthen a potential ally, but have been moved by humane considerations to do so by offering development assistance rather than military assistance. Although the implication of the different hypotheses may overlap in a particular case, and different causal factors sometimes may have worked together in practice, the different possible explanatory factors listed have different implications in principle.

To the extent that aid was provided by donors in the hope of furthering their trade and investment (and in particular their exports) in the Third World, it should have been directed to Third World states where there were reasonable expectations of securing important commercial and financial advantages: those with relatively large or fast-growing trade and investment. This chapter considers this explanation particularly, because the evidence of where aid was spent makes it quite improbable that most aid could have been a sensible policy instrument to advance donor trade and investment. Clearly, donors made some effort to have their aid assist their own economies. But equally clearly, this was a distinct minority of aid, even reckoning aid that served both donor economic interests and developmental goals as primarily given for the former reason. And it is quite possible that very little "dual-purpose" aid was provided primarily to support donor economic interests; usually such interests merely piggybacked on existing aid appropriations.[2]

Again, to the extent that aid was intended to provide strategic influence for donors, it should have been focused fairly sharply on those states that a particular donor sought to influence or strengthen. And to the extent that it was designed to strengthen or retain colonial ties, of course it should have been focused on former colonies. Again, clearly such political concerns of donor states strongly influenced where *some* aid money was spent, or withheld. Money *was* directed toward, or away from, particular countries in attempts to influence, support, or oppose recipients or to maintain special relationships especially with former colonies. United States aid to Vietnam, to Israel, to Egypt, and to El Salvador, and recent U.S. attempts to influence recipients or boycott undesirable countries, are notable examples. Other interesting cases of attempted influence are available, such as Germany's Hallstein Doctrine. These cases, while important and distinctly political in motivation, constitute a fairly small portion of all OECD aid funding, however. The desire of the colonial powers to maintain influence in former colonies and the desire for regional influence are motives of a somewhat different kind, which will also be explored.

While it is very important to recognize the economic and political objectives that aid was used to secure, these account for a minority of foreign aid funding. Moreover, there is positive evidence that the patterns of aid spending are those which would be expected if aid funding sought to promote Third World economic development. The patterns of aid spending are consistent with the hypothesis that a substantial majority of aid was largely motivated by concerns with recipient poverty; the patterns are hard to account for apart from genuine donor concern for poverty and development.

## ECONOMIC INTERESTS OF THE DONOR STATES

One major interest of donor states in the Third World could have been promotion of their own trade. Where this motivated their foreign aid, that aid should have gone toward Third World states that had large potential as trade partners, or to those whose trade with the industrial countries, or particular donors, was largest or showed most significant growth.

Even at a glance, this explanation faces some tough obstacles. In recent years, Bolivia has received more economic assistance than has Mexico, and Botswana far more than Nigeria.[3] Such aid was not proportioned to economic advantages potential recipients offered donors—nor indeed to the political importance of the recipients. This suggests that it is worth taking a more systematic look at the distribution of OECD aid compared to Third World trade.

One way to assess how donors spent aid money is to look at the largest aid recipients and examine how important their trade was to donors; or, to look at major Third World trade partners of donor states and ask how important their aid loomed. Table 3.1 shows what the overlap was between DAC countries' top ten trade (import or export) partners in the Third World and the ten that they provided the most aid to. There is little overlap between the lists: about two to three recipients per donor, on average, were both top aid receivers and either top export or import partners of the same donor. Also, many of the overlapping instances were large, poor, states such as India that would often appear on both lists, even if aid were given solely on the basis of recipient need. Donors' most important aid recipients were not usually important trade partners (importers or exporters); top trade partners were rarely among a donor's aid priorities.

Another revealing measure is the proportion of OECD Third World trade conducted with top aid recipients, shown in table 3.2. The ten most major recipients of DAC bilateral aid accounted for about 40% to 50% of the aid (58% in the earliest period), but these Third World states engaged in only a fairly small part of the trade with DAC countries. The top ten recipients of multilateral aid largely funded by DAC countries similarly received about 40% to 50% of the multilateral aid and small shares of total DAC trade. Important aid recipients were not terribly important to developed country imports or exports.

Important aid recipients also received few developed country official export credits. That was not, however, because no countries had that kind of special importance in OECD trade with the Third World. A look at the percentage of trade going to the top importers and exporters, in

TABLE 3.1
Overlap between Top Aid and Trade Partners: Number of Times a Top Aid Recipient of a Given Donor Was a Top Import or Export Partner (out of 10 Possible)

| Donor | 1969–73 | 1974–78 | 1979–83 | 1984–88 |
|---|---|---|---|---|
| Australia | 4 | 4 | 3 | 5 |
| Austria | 4 | 4 | 4 | 6 |
| Belgium | 2 | 3 | 2 | 2 |
| Canada | 3 | 2 | 1 | 2 |
| Denmark | 0 | 1 | 2 | 2 |
| Finland | 1 | 1 | 1 | 1 |
| France | 6 | 5 | 5 | 2 |
| Germany | 5 | 2 | 2 | 5 |
| Italy | 2 | 1 | 2 | 2 |
| Japan | 6 | 6 | 6 | 5 |
| Netherlands | 4 | 3 | 4 | 5 |
| New Zealand | 3 | 1 | 2 | 2 |
| Norway | 1 | 0 | 0 | 0 |
| Sweden | 1 | 1 | 0 | 1 |
| Switzerland | 1 | 1 | 0 | 1 |
| United Kingdom | 5 | 1 | 1 | 1 |
| United States | 5 | 5 | 4 | 2 |

*Number of Times an LDC is Both a Top Trade Partner and Top Aid Recipient (Totaling over All of the 17 DAC Donor Countries [out of 170 Possible])*

| | | | | |
|---|---|---|---|---|
| All LDCs | 53 | 41 | 39 | 44 |
| Very needy, large LDCs[a] | 11 | 14 | 10 | 12 |
| Other LDCs | 42 | 33 | 29 | 32 |

*Sources*: Computed from OECD, *Geographical Distribution of Financial Flows*; from OECD, *Public Data Base*; and from International Monetary Fund, *Direction of Trade*.

[a] India, Indonesia, Pakistan, and Bangladesh, which have fairly high trade despite extreme poverty because of their vast size.

table 3.3, shows that it was quite high, usually 40% to 50% of DAC imports and exports to the Third World, and sometimes more. Significantly, official export credits, a financial instrument used by OECD countries to promote sales of their own exports, were highly concentrated in the Third World countries that were important trade partners and, predictably enough, especially in those countries that were important markets for exports. Official export credits went, in conformity with their stated purposes, mainly to sites likely to be important in expansion of trade. But foreign aid did not. A low proportion of bilateral aid, and even less multilateral aid, especially after the early seventies, went to those

TABLE 3.2
Aid, Trade, and Investment in Major Aid Recipients

| | Percentages of Various Flows Going to Top 10 Multilateral Aid Recipients | | | Percentages of Various Flows Going to Top 10 Bilateral Aid Recipients | | | |
|---|---|---|---|---|---|---|---|
| | DAC Exports | DAC Imports | Multilateral DAC Aid | DAC Exports | DAC Imports | Official Export Credits[a] | Bilateral DAC Aid |
| 1969–73 | 27.5 | 28.2 | 44.1 | 25.2 | 23.1 | 11.4 | 58.0 |
| 1974–78 | 11.2 | 12.1 | 44.7 | 18.2 | 16.9 | 14.5 | 50.5 |
| 1979–83 | 17.0 | 17.0 | 47.5 | 17.7 | 17.1 | 18.2 | 45.7 |
| 1984–88 | 15.2 | 11.4 | 48.7 | 24.1 | 20.9 | — | 43.1 |

Sources: See sources listed in table 3.1.

[a] The periods for export credits are 1968–72, 1973–77, and 1978–82. These refer to official government funded credits only, not private credits.


TABLE 3.3
Share of Aid Going to Third World Countries Most Important in DAC Trade

| | Percentage of Aid and Trade Going to Top Third World Importers | | | | | |
|---|---|---|---|---|---|---|
| | DAC Exports | DAC Imports | Official Export Credits[a] | DAC Bilateral Aid | Multilateral Aid | Total Aid |
| 1969–73 | 43.1 | 38.4 | 45.6 | 25.2 | 27.1 | 25.5 |
| 1974–78 | 45.8 | 48.5 | 42.0 | 6.1 | 4.7 | 5.7 |
| 1979–83 | 45.4 | 44.5 | — | 12.6 | 7.3 | 11.0 |
| 1984–88 | 52.6 | 50.5 | — | 25.4 | — | 24.5 |

| | Percentage of Aid and Trade Going to Top Third World Exporters | | | | | |
|---|---|---|---|---|---|---|
| | DAC Exports | DAC Imports | Official Export Credits[a] | DAC Bilateral Aid | Multilateral Aid | Total Aid |
| 1969–73 | 34.5 | 44.4 | 26.9 | 30.2 | 33.6 | 30.8 |
| 1974–78 | 42.1 | 56.3 | 32.7 | 13.4 | 8.5 | 12.1 |
| 1979–83 | 56.4 | 42.1 | — | 11.0 | 5.7 | 9.5 |
| 1984–88 | 58.6 | 48.2 | — | 11.7 | 8.7 | 10.9 |

Sources: See sources listed in table 3.1.

[a] Official government funded export credits, not private credits. The time periods for official export credits are 1968–72 and 1973–77.

important LDC trading partners of OECD countries. Overall, export credits were sensibly proportioned to the end of promoting trade. If aid had been intended to promote the economic interests of the donor states, it would have been directed to economically important Third World States, as export credits were. It was not, because that was not its goal.

This is borne out by the low correlations between aid and trade. For the DAC as a whole, and for most individual donors, any positive correlations are fully explained by the very proper need to direct aid to large countries. The correlations between total Third World trade with OECD countries and aggregate DAC bilateral development assistance to more than 105 aid recipients in four five-year periods from 1968 to 1988 are given in table 3.4. The correlation coefficients ($R$) are low, especially from the midseventies on. There is an association between aid and trade, but it is quite weak. The explained variance ($R^2$) in those periods is in no case as high as 12%; by the mideighties trade explains less than 1% of variation. Even these figures are somewhat inflated, however, because part of the association between aid and trade stems simply from the varying sizes of recipient states. That is, if aid were given in equal amounts to each individual in the Third World, there would be a correlation between aid and trade to states because of the uneven size of countries: countries such as India, simply because of their larger size, would have more trade and more aid than would countries like the Maldive Islands. The partial correlation figures between aid and trade controlled for recipient country size, given in table 3.5, yield much lower coefficients. However, even without this additional consideration, it is clear that the association between aid and trade is at best weak.

Of course, aggregate figures for the OECD could hide the association of aid and trade by intermixing the aid and trade figures for different donors. It might be that Denmark does most of its trade with Brazil, and

TABLE 3.4
Correlation Coefficients of DAC Bilateral Aid with Trade

| Correlation of Aid With | 1968–73 | 1974–78 | 1979–83 | 1984–88 |
|---|---|---|---|---|
| OECD exports | .345† | .221* | .223* | .249† |
| OECD imports | .286† | .153 | .174 | .156 |
| Observations: $N =$ | 105 | 107 | 108 | 108 |

Sources: See sources listed in table 3.1.
Notes: Correlations are between all OECD bilateral aid to a given potential recipient in a given period and the total exports or imports of all OECD (DAC) countries to or from that recipient.
† Significant at a .01 level.
* Significant at a .05 level (unmarked correlations are nonsignificant at a .05 level).

TABLE 3.5

Partial Correlation Coefficients of DAC Bilateral Aid with Trade, Controlling for Recipient Size

| Correlation of Aid With | 1968–73 | 1974–78 | 1979–83 | 1984–88 |
|---|---|---|---|---|
| OECD exports | .114 | .054 | .124 | .072 |
| OECD imports | .001 | −.014 | .089 | .003 |
| Observations: $N =$ | 105 | 107 | 108 | 108 |

Sources: See sources listed in table 3.1.

Note: No correlations were significant at a .05 level. "Size" refers to population size.

directs its aid there, while Italy concentrates aid and trade on Mexico, giving a summed OECD total in which the differences cancel out. What, then, are the associations between aid and trade for individual OECD donors? Correlations of aid and trade for individual donor countries are given in tables 3.6 and 3.7. A few donors, notably Belgium, France, and Japan, had noticeably higher correlations between their aid and trade, particularly their exports, than the OECD average; a few other donors, Australia, Austria, Germany, New Zealand, were also somewhat high. On the whole, however, there is no hidden association. In fact, many donors had lower correlations of trade and aid than the DAC average; a quarter of the signs are negative, and only about 40% are significant (even without controlling for recipient size). Most donors' correlations declined over time; and with the exceptions of Japan and Belgium, and of France in earlier periods, even the highest correlations explained no more than a fifth of the variance. And again, the partial correlations, controlled for the size of the recipient country, are substantially lower, and often negative, especially in later periods, as shown in table 3.7.

In summary, trade considerations, though they seem to have played some part in the foreign aid of about half of the DAC states, can explain at most a small fraction of DAC bilateral aid overall and can provide virtually no explanation of the aid of many of the smaller DAC donors. While even for those donors, aid was not completely insulated from the effects of pressures to expand trade, the economic self-promotion effect was so small that it could not provide a sensible justification of aid, even on the most optimistic assumptions. For those donors where economic interests played a less negligible role, the role was still fairly small, except in the case of Japan, and was in almost every such case declining. (And as chapter 4 will show, the donors that had larger economic interests were generally not the more vigorous donors but the laggards in per capita spending.)

TABLE 3.6
Correlations of Aid with Trade, for Individual Donors

| | 1968–73 | | 1974–78 | | 1979–83 | | 1984–88 | |
| | Donor's | | Donor's | | Donor's | | Donor's | |
| | Imports | Exports | Imports | Exports | Imports | Exports | Imports | Exports |
|---|---|---|---|---|---|---|---|---|
| Australia | .23˙ | .58† | .13 | .35† | .12 | .34† | .18 | .32† |
| Austria | .09 | .03 | −.00 | .08 | .36† | .25† | .33† | .32† |
| Belgium | .88† | .50† | .66† | .25† | .66† | .18 | .49† | .12 |
| Canada | .21˙ | .40† | −.06 | .19 | −.12 | .01 | −.05 | .13 |
| Denmark | .02 | .03 | −.05 | .05 | .03 | .03 | .03 | .14 |
| Finland | −.02 | .10 | −.04 | −.02 | −.06 | −.00 | −.08 | .02 |
| France | .66† | .78† | .26† | .59† | .28† | .50† | .26† | .38† |
| Germany | .38† | .45† | .19˙ | .34† | .12 | .23˙ | .25† | .39† |
| Italy | .05 | .25˙ | −.11 | −.29† | −.07 | −.04 | .00 | .06 |
| Japan | .58† | .61† | .71† | .54† | .68† | .50† | .66† | .42† |
| New Zealand | .14 | .39† | .06 | .43† | .31† | .35† | .17 | .20˙ |
| Netherlands | .16 | .32† | .00 | .16 | −.03 | .11 | .02 | .16 |
| Norway | −.00 | .01 | −.06 | −.02 | −.07 | −.02 | −.10 | −.03 |
| Sweden | −.04 | −.02 | −.07 | .02 | −.10 | −.04 | −.11 | .08 |
| Switzerland | .12 | .04 | .09 | −.02 | −.04 | −.03 | −.11 | −.06 |
| United Kingdom | .40† | .45† | .23˙ | .17 | .17 | .30† | .11 | .34† |
| United States | .19 | .34† | .02 | .19˙ | −.01 | .14 | .00 | .14 |

Sources: See sources listed in table 3.1.

Notes: The N, the number of trade and aid partners, varies from 80 to 105, except for New Zealand, where it is as low as 64 before 1979. The N tends to be higher for larger donors and later years.

† Significant at a .01 level.

˙ Significant at a .05 level (other correlations are nonsignificant at a .05 level).

## SPECIAL RELATIONSHIPS BETWEEN DONOR AND RECIPIENT

In examining the economic link, one fact that emerges is that quite a lot of aid went to relatively few recipients. This by itself is what would be expected on almost any hypothesis because of the uneven distribution of population among Third World countries. Two countries contain about half the population in the Third World, and five more contain a third of the remainder, leaving a hundred or so more with, together, only a third of the population. And of these, half the population is contained by a dozen or so countries more. This uneven distribution of sizes—on a hypothesis of aid directed to promote donor trade, or to promote donor political power, or to promote recipient economic growth—naturally would lead to a highly skewed distribution of aid. Some of the cases in

TABLE 3.7

Partial Correlations, Aid with Trade, for Individual Donors, Controlling for the Size of Recipient States

| | 1968–73 | | 1974–78 | | 1979–83 | | 1984–88 | |
|---|---|---|---|---|---|---|---|---|
| | Donor's | | Donor's | | Donor's | | Donor's | |
| | *Imports* | *Exports* | *Imports* | *Exports* | *Imports* | *Exports* | *Imports* | *Exports* |
| Australia | .27† | .62† | .14 | .41† | .13 | .39† | .18 | .34† |
| Austria | .05 | .01 | −.01 | .08 | .35† | .24* | .32† | .31† |
| Belgium | .88† | .50† | .66† | .25† | .66† | .16 | .49† | .10 |
| Canada | .05 | −.11 | −.12 | −.13 | −.17 | −.22* | −.16 | −.19* |
| Denmark | −.04 | .00 | −.08 | .02 | −.10 | −.04 | −.21* | −.01 |
| Finland | −.03 | .09 | −.03 | −.01 | −.06 | .00 | −.08 | .03 |
| France | .66† | .78† | .26† | .59† | .28† | .50† | .23* | .35 |
| Germany | .34† | .39† | .15 | .30† | .06 | .15 | .12 | .22* |
| Italy | .04 | .24 | −.12 | −.30† | −.06 | −.04 | −.05 | −.00 |
| Japan | .55† | .59† | .69† | .51† | .61† | .39† | .50† | .15† |
| New Zealand | .09 | .35† | .04 | .44† | .31† | .37† | .18 | .23* |
| Netherlands | .08 | .24* | −.10 | −.02 | −.09 | −.04 | −.10 | .05 |
| Norway | −.05 | −.02 | −.07 | −.07 | −.10 | −.06 | −.14 | −.07 |
| Sweden | −.06 | −.07 | −.11 | −.02 | −.13 | −.05 | −.16 | −.02 |
| Switzerland | −.02 | −.05 | −.02 | −.08 | −.12 | −.12 | −.21 | −.20* |
| United Kingdom | .30† | .33† | .14 | .08 | .06 | .19 | −.01 | .17 |
| United States | .15 | .30† | .00 | .18 | −.01 | .13 | .01 | .15 |

*Sources*: See sources listed in table 3.1.

*Notes*: The N, the number of trade and aid partners, varies from 80 to 105, except for New Zealand, where it is as low as 64 before 1979. The N tends to be higher for larger donors and later years.

† Significant at a .01 level.

* Significant at a .01 level (other correlations are nonsignificant at a .05 level).

which aid was high for individual countries are of this sort: India, Indonesia, Pakistan, Bangladesh, and occasionally Brazil and Nigeria. There are other instances in which special relationships between particular donors and recipients did not necessarily reflect self-serving donor interests. Switzerland devoted special attention to Nepal, for instance; the Swiss, residents of a small landlocked mountain state, chose a special aid relationship with a country whose situation they would be particularly able to understand. Many smaller donors decided that they would be more effective establishing ongoing aid and consultative relations with a small number of recipients, often very poor ones. But in other cases, aid was concentrated on a country out of proportion to its size or economic development needs. This section considers such cases—Israel, Vietnam, Zaire, Reunion, Papua New Guinea and so on. I will first examine aid that arose out of relations between colonial powers and their former colonies, and then regionally focused and strategically linked aid relationships.

## Colonial and Former Colonial Aid Relationships

Most DAC donors—Ireland, Switzerland, Austria, Finland, Sweden, Norway, Denmark, New Zealand, and Canada—had no colonial ties or none that substantially affected later aid giving, as was the case with Germany, which lost its colonies after World War I. But Britain, France, Belgium, the Netherlands, and Italy were DAC donors with ongoing colonial connections[4] that affected their aid giving. Table 3.8 gives the extent of their aid involvement with their former colonies, at four time periods from 1960 to the present.

To show that a donor's aid served its self-interests, one must identify concrete benefits it received from the aid, whether the aid went to former colonies or elsewhere. Simply the fact that a special tie—here a colonial tie—was involved in aid does not show how that tie served donor self-interest. In the case of some special ties, it is evident that the aid given in support of them was *not* based to any significant degree on an interest in furthering Third World economic development as an end in itself, and was based on other national interests. U.S. aid to Vietnam or to Israel and Egypt was clearly given basically in support of political, security, alliance, or perhaps peacekeeping objectives, and will be taken here as simply self-interested.[5] It is somewhat less obvious what colonial powers got out of the retention of friendly ties with their former colonies. For if the "friendship" established provided current tangible benefits to the former colonial power, such as military bases or trade or votes in international forums or formal alliance, then these should be evident. But there were not important bases or alliances involved in most of strongest colonial links shown in table 3.8: France with Algeria, England with India and Kenya, Belgium with Zaire, the Netherlands with Indonesia, Italy with Somalia. In most of these cases, the prospects of trade advantages could not possibly have loomed very large either.

Of course there is another class of motivations: a desire to have a world role, a cultural mission, prestige, and so on. If these terms refer to something that conferred exercisable power, then that something should be specified. But if they mean simply that aid policy was motivated by a desire to take a positive part in world affairs, or to be praised for doing so, then this is precisely the kind of thing—though not the only thing—that I claim was happening in foreign aid. Similarly, it may be claimed that the maintenance of colonial ties secured the friendship and goodwill of the former colonies. If such "friendship" took the form of definite benefits the

TABLE 3.8
Aid to Former Colonies (Percentages of Donor's Total Aid)

| Donors and Former Colonies | 1960–61 | 1970–71 | 1980–81 | 1988–89 |
|---|---|---|---|---|
| Belgium | | | | |
|     Zaire | 61.3 | 39.9 | 25.0 | 17.4 |
|     Burundi | 7.2 | 7.4 | 4.3 | 2.6 |
|     Rwanda | — | 9.0 | 5.5 | 4.2 |
| France | | | | |
|     Algeria | 45.6 | 8.7 | 1.8 | .9 |
|     DOM/TOM | — | 28.3 | 36.2 | 27.1 |
|     Other former colonies | — | 20.3 | — | — |
| Italy | | | | |
|     Somalia | 13.4 | 4.0 | 3.9 | 5.4 |
|     Ethiopia | 6.4 | 2.8 | 1.7 | 5.5 |
| Netherlands | | | | |
|     Indonesia | 47.7 | 22.1 | 5.1 | 8.2 |
|     Surinam | — | 11.9 | 6.6 | 1.2 |
|     Netherlands Antilles | — | 11.0 | 5.0 | 2.9 |
| United Kingdom | | | | |
|     India | 12.5 | 20.5 | 12.1 | 5.3 |
|     Kenya | 11.9 | 4.0 | 2.7 | 3.0 |
|     Other former colonies | 41.9 | 34.8 | — | — |

Sources: OECD, *Development Cooperation, 1985*, pp. 306–14; and OECD, *Development Cooperation, 1990*, p. 234.

Notes: Tables fail to include some small items. Dashes indicate missing data. Figures are percentages of a donor's total aid, bilateral and multilateral.

colonial power could reap, these should be demonstrated. But if the benefits of "friendship" meant only that ex-colonies applauded the colonial power's largesse, this would not confer any concrete advantages on the ex-power unless those ex-colonies were strongly influenced by sentiment or a sense of obligation. But if the former colonies could be influenced by sentimental motives, so could the donors. And if motivations of this kind can have more than tiny and occasional effects on international relations, this seriously modifies the world depicted by Realist theory as one based on the pursuit of power and advantage.

In the case of Belgium, Italy, and the Netherlands, the colonial possessions were relatively few, and it is easy to examine the effects of the colonial relationship on aid giving. The case of Britain and France is different, for the British and French empires had included large portions of the globe, and many of their former colonies merited very substantial aid on humanitarian grounds alone. It is unclear why Britain or France, had they been motivated solely by humanitarian concerns, should have extended aid beyond their former colonial domains, which in both cases included an important portion of the world's neediest countries, and which they knew well. It is best to stipulate that aid given to ex-colonies was motivated by the donor's desire to retain its power and influence wherever the aid exceeded what would have been reasonable in the absence of a prior colonial relationship. But where the aid went to countries that would have been fitting recipients of the amount of aid they received simply on humane and developmental grounds, it is hard to see the fact of a prior colonial relationship as an explanation for aid if the relationship did not bring the colonial power some other concrete benefits. However, even with this stipulation, aid to former colonies need not loom terribly large in the analysis.

The aid of the smaller colonial powers does not seem to have had its long-term motivation in any relations with former colonies, despite an initial concentration on these countries. Italian aid to its former colonies fell very quickly, and had never formed a major part of its aid. Its aid to Yugoslavia, about a third of Italian aid in the early sixties, would be a more likely candidate for attempted influence, but that also fell rapidly and was under 10% by the start of the seventies, and was negligible a decade later, when Italian aid began to climb rapidly as a percentage of GNP. Italian aid, which historically had hovered around .10–.15% of GNP, rose to more than twice that by the mideighties. The percentage of Dutch aid to its former colonies also fell rapidly, from 60% in 1960–61 to 45% in 1970–71 to around 12% by the end of the eighties. Much of that was aid to Indonesia, and was amply justified, as Indonesia is a lower income country and the fourth largest of the LDCs in population. This was the time of the most rapid increase of Dutch foreign aid commitments, which moved from .5% to over 1% of GNP in a little over a decade, under the leadership of Jan Pronk as aid minister, who was strongly committed to Third World causes and opposed in principle to any sort of neocolonialism. The share of Belgian aid going to its former colonies also fell rapidly, decade by decade, from 78% to 56% to 35% to 24%. Belgian aid as a percentage of GNP did rise rapidly about the start of the sixties, but then fell off and climbed gradually, from .42% in 1966 to about .58% by the early eighties. Belgian aid to Zaire remained around 20% of the aid budget, but again a good case can be made that this reflected responsible use of aid money to assist a country with serious needs and one for which Belgium properly felt historic responsibility.

Thus by the end of the seventies, aid to former colonies had fallen to a very low level for two of the three lesser colonial powers, and for the third was a modest share of aid expenditures. Further, a rapid increase in Italian and Dutch aid spending came just as concentration of aid on former colonies ceased; in Belgium, aid spending rose gradually as concentration on its old colonies fell. The *allocation* of aid money by the smaller colonial states was influenced by colonial ties in the early years, but their long-term *motives* for providing aid must have been different, for aid to former colonies has been only a small share of their aid in the last two decades, and their aid commitments increased as their colonial focus declined.

British bilateral aid did tend to be concentrated on former colonies; but it is not clear what different distribution of aid would have been more responsive to the needs of the recipients. India has consistently been the recipient of more British bilateral aid than has any other country; but it is hard to see why this shouldn't be the case. India is one of the poorest LDCs, with roughly a quarter of the population of the Third World; one could argue, as the World Bank in effect has, that India should receive 20% of all aid; by these standards, the problem is that Britain has only rarely devoted as much of its aid as it should to India's needs. Nigeria, Pakistan, and Bangladesh are the fifth, sixth, and seventh most populous countries in the Third World, with Pakistan and especially Bangladesh among the world's very poor countries. Other British colonies in Africa are also among the world's neediest states. Thus, it is sensible for Britain to concentrate its bilateral aid on poor states among its former colonies, whose administrative and legal systems the British know, and with which it will be possible to work efficiently. In addition, there is some feeling that Britain bears a particular historical responsibility for former colonies. Under these circumstances it is hard to see how the British bilateral aid distribution shows any great bias toward British interests in the extent to which it focuses on former British colonies. In addition, the multilateral percentage of British aid rose in the seventies and eighties, and was often 40–50% of the British aid total.

French aid is a somewhat different matter. French aid was quite high from the beginning, and initially reflected the French determination, which continued at least through the first Indochina conflict in the early fifties and the Algerian war in the late fifties, to retain French colonies, and even to make them part of a greater France. In pursuit of this aim, France spent heavily on its colonies originally, and devoted substantial aid to Algeria in the early sixties; even today it retains a substantial number of small islands and territories as Overseas Departments and Overseas Territories of France (called DOM and TOM) that receive substantial subsidies from France, often amounting to a thousand dollars or more per capita, which France has sought to classify as foreign aid but which other donors have considered as part of France's internal affairs, not as aid. This quasi-aid constituted up to about 40% of the French aid total in years as late as the early eighties. It is reasonable to consider the part of

French aid devoted to DOM and TOM as not primarily aimed at economic development; in any case, it is, in a sense, not *foreign* aid at all.[6] The remainder of French bilateral aid has tended to be concentrated on French former colonies as well, with the multilateral component of French aid remaining very small relative to that of most other DAC donors. The French connection with the French colonies is stronger, furthermore, than that of almost any other colonial power, in terms of the influence of language and culture, orientation of the colony toward the metropolis, ongoing military influence, and currency management, with most countries in Francophone Africa having currencies pegged to the franc. It is reasonable to see French concerns for maintaining influence in former colonies as a very prominent motive in French aid, even apart from the quasi-aid given to DOM and TOM.[7]

Even here, however, other factors seem to be at work. With the accession of the Mitterand government, there was a commitment to increase the level of aid funding, remove DOM and TOM from the aid calculations, and pay particular attention to the needs of the Third World. This set of humanitarian and poverty-oriented concerns, to which the French Socialist party was committed and which Mitterand emphasized as a particular priority, went together with a reversal of the steady decline of French aid that had been going on from the late fifties through the end of the seventies. The explicit program of the Mitterand government led to a 30% increase in (non-DOM/TOM) aid, a falling share of aid going to French possessions, a marked rise in the share of aid going to multilateral organizations, and aid to LLDCs rising to meet the DAC target of .15% of GNP, with the share of aid to other low-income LDCs also rising. This conjunction of explicit commitment to policies favoring the Third World, to newly rising aid totals, and to increasing volumes of aid suggests that while former colonial and commercial interests had an important place in French aid, Third World development was an important motive as well, and indeed the one which has proved capable of generating fresh support for aid as colonial ties dwindled.[8]

## Special Relationships and Regional Emphases of Japan, Australia, and New Zealand

Australia was never a colonial power, but Papua New Guinea was made a Trust Territory under the aegis of Australia in the League Mandates system. This has led to a special relationship between Australia and New Guinea that has had some of the features of a colonial relationship. Australia's bilateral foreign aid concentrated upon Papua New Guinea rather exclusively for a good many years, and aid to New Guinea still looms large in Australia's aid program. Almost two thirds of all foreign aid from

Australia went there in 1970–71, with this figure dropping to about 40% by the beginning of the eighties and to under 25% by the end of the decade, while the share of aid channeled through multilateral institutions had tripled to 30% of the total. This aid amounted to some $90 per New Guinea inhabitant, an amount all out of proportion to the normal scale of aid. The rest of Australia's aid appeared more or less normal, although there was some emphasis in bilateral aid toward countries in the South Pacific region.

New Zealand's aid, despite the absence of a colonial past, shows some similar features: it is concentrated on neighboring island countries, although much less so and with a modest decline in concentration over time. About half of its bilateral aid has gone, over the last fifteen years, to these tiny island states.

TABLE 3.9
Pacific Donors' Aid to Nearby Small States (Percentages of Donor's Aid Total)

| Donor<br>Recipient | 1970–71 | 1980–81 | 1988–89 |
|---|---|---|---|
| Australia | | | |
| Papua New Guinea | 66.9 | 42.9 | 23.3 |
| Other Oceania[a] | 0.5 | 3.8 | 4.3 |
| Indonesia | 8.2 | 7.0 | 7.3 |
| Other Far East and Southeast Asia | 6.7 | 10.6 | 10.7 |
| New Zealand | | | |
| Cook Islands | 12.6 | 12.6 | 8.5 |
| Other Oceania[b] | 25.5 | 25.6 | 21.8 |
| Indonesia | 5.4 | 5.4 | 2.2 |
| Other Far East and Southeast Asia | 2.5 | 5.3 | 1.4 |
| Japan | | | |
| Indonesia | 22.9 | 11.2 | 13.1 |
| Philippines | 4.4 | 4.7 | 5.4 |
| Korea | 19.8 | 6.9 | 1.1 |
| China | 0 | .4 | 7.4 |
| India | 10.2 | 2.2 | 3.1 |
| Thailand | 2.9 | 4.1 | 1.8 |
| Burma | 3.5 | 3.6 | 2.8 |
| Pakistan | 7.9 | 5.0 | 3.9 |

Sources: OECD, Development Cooperation, 1985, pp. 306–14; and OECD, Development Cooperation, 1990, pp. 235 ff.

Notes: Tables fail to include some small items. Figures are percentages of a donor's total aid, bilateral and multilateral.

[a] Includes Fiji, Western Samoa, and the Solomon Islands.

[b] Includes Fiji, Western Samoa, Niue, Tonga, Tokelau, and Papua New Guinea.

These aid priorities are clearly not means to promote trade, for the recipient countries' trade is not a large proportion of that of the donor countries, but they may be seen as a means to exert regional influence or to fortify nearby island states against disorder. Although it seems at first that these priorities are not a sensible approach to economic development, it can be argued that they are. Small donors may see venturing all over the world to try to assist Third World development as self-defeating. To work out successful development plans with a limited number of major recipients may be thought of as a more sensible way of using aid, and of creating a learning experience about how to use aid effectively. This has, indeed, been the conclusion of most small donors: sizable portions of Scandinavian and Swiss aid, for instance, have been consciously directed to a few priority countries. Given that, the concentration on neighboring states may be justified as more efficient than attempts to conduct programs halfway around the globe. In fact, New Zealand has held up its program of aid to Fiji, at times, as a model of success in development aid. This rationale is more dubious in the case of Australian aid to New Guinea, whose high per capita concentration on a few recipients seems a doubtful means to development, as does the French concentration on Reunion or Martinique (though not to the same degree).

Japanese aid poses explanatory problems of a different sort. Japanese aid did not go to small recipients whose need for extensive aid can be questioned. The main recipients of Japanese aid were all countries with largish populations (30 million or more), and in each period noted in table 3.9 the largest recipient was Indonesia, the third most populous Third World country, with India the fourth largest recipient in earlier years, and China the second largest in the latter period. Indonesia and India together account for about a third of Japanese aid in earlier years and, together with China, for only slightly less than a third of Japanese *bilateral* aid in the latter period. Aiding these countries is eminently sensible on humanitarian and developmental grounds. However, almost another third, in the first two periods, went to regional countries whose GNPs were considerably higher, such as the Philippines and Korea, resulting in the high correlation between aid and trade that was observed earlier. This gives some grounds to wonder about the overall priorities expressed in Japan's aid program. Even the expenditures in India, China, and Indonesia may be seen as the development of good regional relations for Japan. Other aid expenditures, in wartime South Vietnam and more recently in Egypt, may be seen as a way of building good relations with the United States, and of mitigating various U.S. annoyances by furthering U.S. goals and policies.

It is widely acknowledged that for its first twenty to thirty years, Japanese aid was largely designed to secure trade advantages and, secondarily, to show its proper participation as a member of the Western alliance, although some observers feel that humanitarian concerns were mixed in from an early stage.[9] However, the focus of Japanese aid has changed some over time. Some scholars state that the emphasis in Japanese aid moved from trade to efforts to cultivate good relations with others, and then to attention to basic human needs.[10] It is notable that Japan's aid spending in the last decade, following an initial plea by Prime Minister Fukuda, has both risen rapidly in volume and increased markedly in quality, supported by public opinion which, according to Orr, responded strongly to the spectacle of African drought in 1984–85.[11]

The changed consensus has been reflected in changed aid spending. Japan's aid spending has markedly increased in the last decade, from .23% of GNP in 1974–79 to .34% in 1986–89, and has done so just as it markedly improved in quality. While total Japanese aid has risen by about 50% as a share of GNP over the last decade, bilateral aid rose only by about 25%, while multilateral aid more than doubled, from .06% to .14% of GNP over this same period. Bilateral aid to LLDCs as a percentage of all Japanese ODA rose from 5% in the early seventies to about 15% at the turn of the decade to around 20% by the late eighties.[12] And Japan now concentrates only 40% of its bilateral aid in its local region, compared with an earlier 50–70% (depending on whether South Asia is counted as local). Furthermore, Japan has opened up its aid procurement practices in the last few years, resulting, as Orr shows, in the actual percentage of Japanese contractors in aid contracts falling from 57% in 1982 to 27% in 1988, with the percentage of LDC and local cost contractors rising from 27% to 50% and that of other OECD members rising from 15% to 22%.[13] This strongly suggests a change in Japanese priorities in aid which downplays Japanese commercial interests at precisely the moment that aid is being expanded and directed more to poor recipients.

No one would claim Japanese aid is a model of purity yet. The percentage of tied aid, and the commercial element in Japanese aid, could well stand to be further reduced. The share of aid to least developed countries is well below the .15% DAC target. The grant element in Japanese bilateral aid is low. And aid remains strongly correlated with trade. It would not be hard to argue that Japan's aid has been, throughout most of the last forty years, the program most oriented to donor advantage, as well as one of the least vigorous programs measured as a percentage of GNP. And much Japanese aid probably still serves commercial purposes. However, the changes just noted constitute a significant, though far from complete, decommercialization of aid. Public statements that Japan must pay more attention to the poor nations, and public opinion which supports more aid and focusing aid on poor countries, indicate that in Japan as elsewhere public support for aid reflects humanitarian concerns. The conjunction of an improvement in aid quality with a sharp increase in Japanese aid levels suggests that such humanitarian bases of support have increasing influence on the actual administration of Japanese aid.

## U.S. Security-Supporting Assistance

Starting with the Foreign Assistance Act of 1961, there was a fairly clear distinction made between aid provided by the United States for security reasons, designated Security-Supporting Assistance, and other foreign aid. The proportion of Security-Supporting Assistance (SSA) in the U.S. aid budget varied, but was generally one third to one half of U.S. bilateral aid. McKinlay and Mughan have shown that while the correlation between SSA and military aid or arms sales was high and highly significant throughout the years from 1950 to the present, the correlation between arms transfers and sales or military aid, and economic aid not so designated was weak and often statistically nonsignificant.[14] In early years (1960–61) about 25% of U.S. aid went to Korea, Turkey, Vietnam, Taiwan, and Iran, for instance. In 1970–71, over 10% went to Vietnam and another 10% to Korea, Turkey, and Israel. In 1982–83, a quarter of U.S. aid went to Israel and Egypt, with another 6% to El Salvador and other Central American and Caribbean countries, and 4% to Turkey.

Aid of this kind is best conceived as motivated not by goals of economic development but by American security concerns. Aid to Israel, even if spent on development projects, can be reasonably construed as essentially budget support to a small, middle-income ally[15] that the United States aims to assist not on account of its poverty but because of its militarily threatened position; and aid to Egypt, even if it ends up furthering economic development, should be understood as compensation offered to protect Egypt from the ill effects of loss of Arab aid due to its adherence to a political compromise with Israel, which the United States promoted. Aid to El Salvador also clearly resulted from strategic and military-political commitments. Aid to other Central American countries was perhaps a bit different: while it reflected a current preoccupation with one area of the world, it may have been part of ongoing development efforts. Nevertheless, these moneys probably result less from a commitment to development in any form than from attempts to forestall immediate or looming political crisis.

A number of studies have shown an association between U.S. aid and economic or strategic interests. This includes the work of McKinlay and Mughan, the cross-country study of Maizels and Nissanke, and other articles reviewed by Poe, as well as the superb, careful cross-country study of Bencivenga discussed below.[16] The strongest finding of Poe from his review of much of this literature is that aid increases with recipient population. Studies also usually find greater aid going to countries sharing a border with the Soviet Union, though it is hard to interpret just what the result signifies, since the set seems limited to Turkey, Iran, and Afghanistan. A series of strategic-related variables, and a series of variables on trade with the communist bloc do not yield results significant at the .05 level, except for the 1961–64 period, although about half of these series are "significant at the .10 level"; and many do not find the correlation in the predicted direction. McKinlay and Mughan, whose book is not among the works reviewed by Poe, do get high significant correlations with four clusters of variables they take to indicate self-interest; but their results are hard to interpret both because they include as "self-interest" (specifically "power capability") variables per capita GNP and population, which are generally, and more reasonably, taken as measures of recipient need, and because they include dozens of explanatory variables, which weave in and out of their results with the signs varying a good deal.[17] In the articles Poe reviews, aid from other donors and growth of exports in recipients also seem not to be reliably related to U.S. aid. Aid and trade are reliably and positively related in these studies; however, these relationships may be mostly a result of recipient size, as there is no reliable relation between trade and per capita aid. Poe, in addition, does not find much evidence of a relationship between aid and recipient poverty.

However, if one disaggregates U.S. economic aid into Security-Supporting Assistance and other aid, one finds that non-SSA bilateral aid was quite responsive to recipient poverty. U.S. non-SSA economic aid was highly correlated with recipient country population throughout the history of U.S. aid. Correlations with measures of recipient country poverty are positive throughout, although low and insignificant before the seventies; however they rise sharply in the early seventies and become significant in 1974, usually remaining significant thereafter. The change in 1974 is particularly interesting because in 1973 Congress passed the New Directions legislation, mandating an emphasis on recipient need, after growing dissatisfaction with U.S. foreign policy at the end of the Vietnam War and during the Watergate period, which made a permanent impact in orienting U.S. aid more toward poor nations. Table 3.10 shows correlations of non-SSA aid with recipient population, recipient poverty, and their product, taken as a measure of recipient need for aid. The results here are presented using the reciprocal of GNP per capita as the poverty variable, but other measures of poverty give similar results.[18] Early high correlations with the "need" variable arise from aid being directed toward populous countries. Following the New Directions legislation, correlations with poverty and size are both important, jointly explaining over half the variance in non-SSA aid allocation through the seventies.

TABLE 3.10
Recipient Need and U.S. Bilateral Aid (Not Security Supporting Assistance):
Association of Non-SSA U.S. Bilateral Foreign Aid with Recipient Population,
with Two Measures of Recipient Poverty, and with Overall Need

| | Simple Correlations with Single Variables | | | | | Multiple Correlation‡ |
| | Recipient Size | Recipient Poverty | | Overall Need (Size*Poverty) | | Size and Recipient Poverty, regressed together |
| | | 1/GNPC | −logGNPC | Pop/GNPC | | |
| | R | R | R | R | R² | R² |
|------|------|------|------|------|------|------|
| 1970 | .86† | .08 | .11 | .81 | .66† | .73† |
| 1971 | .89† | .10 | .12 | .86 | .74† | .79† |
| 1972 | .38† | .18 | .18 | .41 | .17† | .16† |
| 1973 | .39† | .14 | .15 | .38 | .14† | .16† |
| 1974 | .71† | .25* | .27† | .73 | .54† | .53† |
| 1975 | .75† | .18 | .22* | .76 | .58† | .58† |
| 1976 | .53† | .20 | .22* | .52 | .27† | .30† |
| 1977 | .48† | .23* | .26* | .45 | .21† | .26† |
| 1978 | .61† | .29† | .28* | .60 | .36† | .40† |
| 1979 | .61† | .29† | .29† | .60 | .37† | .41† |
| 1980 | .57† | .23* | .29† | .56 | .30† | .37† |
| 1981 | .64† | .22* | .29† | .64 | .41† | .44ˡ |
| 1982 | .28† | .21* | .28† | .34 | .11† | .14† |
| 1983 | .28† | .18 | .27† | .32 | .11† | .13† |
| 1984 | .27† | .19 | .28† | .32 | .11† | .13† |
| 1985 | .22† | .28† | .35† | .28 | .08† | .15† |

*Sources*: Computations from *U.S. Overseas Loans and Grants, and Assistance from International Organizations*, various years. (These are reports to Congress, which serve as Statistical Annex I to the Annual Development Coordination Committee Report to Congress: CONG–R–0105.

*Notes*: The N, the number of trade and aid partners, varies from 81 to 91. The N tends to be higher for later years, and is always 86 or above after 1972.

† Significant at a .01 level.

* Significant at a .05 level.

‡The model as a whole (NonSSAaid = $a + b_1$*SIZE + $b_2$*POV + Error term), and the size term were significant at a .01 level in all years. The poverty term was significant at a .01 level in 1985, and at a .05 level in 1974 and 1978–84; it was near-significant in 1975–77.

Both continued to be important, but were attenuated, during the extremely conservative, anti-aid, cold-war-oriented, pro-business Reagan administration, which also sharply cut back the quantity of aid and reduced aid quality in other ways, too. Comparing the distribution of SSA and non-SSA aid by recipient income level shows the same thing. Sanford observes that the percentages of all U.S. "economic" aid, including SSA, going to the world's poorest countries was only in the 11–20% range, averaging about 16%, while the percentage of U.S. "development assistance," not including SSA, ranged from 20% to 50%, and averaged about 41%.[19]

U.S. Security-Supporting Assistance certainly was used primarily, and avowedly, to support allies and to further U.S. foreign policy goals. However, SSA constitutes only about half of U.S. *bilateral* aid during the fifties and eighties, and a third of U.S. bilateral aid in the sixties and seventies.[20] Since the sixties, it has been only a quarter to a third of all U.S. aid, bilateral plus multilateral. The apparent lack of correlation of U.S. bilateral aid with measures of recipient poverty results from lumping SSA together with aid designated primarily for economic purposes. SSA was directed primarily at countries that the United States avowedly sought to support for security reasons, and although it, too, took the form of economic development assistance, it naturally was allocated not based mainly on recipient economic needs. However, allocation of U.S. bilateral non-SSA, generally greater than SSA, was strongly influenced by recipient need.

## WHERE AID WENT: AID AND POVERTY

Donor economic interests do not go very far toward explaining where foreign aid went, except in the case of Japan. Colonial, regional, and strategic interests account for a distinct minority of bilateral aid money, and are relevant for less than half the aid donors. These political interests on a generous accounting explain perhaps half of the bilateral aid of the United States and France, a smaller fraction of Australian and Belgian aid, and a still smaller part of the aid of other former colonial powers.

What, then, are alternative explanations of where aid went? One place to start, in examining this question, is with a puzzling fact that came up in comparing trade and aid. For many donors, the correlation of aid with trade was actually slightly negative, particularly after taking account of recipient size. This in itself is at first glance odd. Yet generally the association of donor exports and aid was stronger than that of aid and donor imports. It is as if even when there were factors leading toward some association of aid with trade, and particularly with donor exports, there were other, stronger factors leading to a negative correlation.

On the hypothesis of donor economic interests being important in the decision to give aid, one would suppose a strong positive association between aid and donor economic interests. On the hypothesis of donor political interests being important in the decision to give aid, one would look for a strong concentration of aid on politically or strategically important and problematic countries. On the hypothesis of aid given out of a general resolve to promote Third World development, what would one expect?

An association between where aid went and those countries with the greatest needs for development assistance. And just that was in fact the case. Aid went preponderantly, and increasingly, to those countries where the poorest people lived, and where a lot of them lived. Aid tended to go to poor, and especially to large, poor, countries. This renders the tendency toward a negative association between aid and trade or investment intelligible. The poorer countries on the whole tended to be those with less capacity for trade and investment.

Table 3.11 shows where OECD aid, investment, and trade went among Third World countries classified by their income level. The poorer countries received the substantial bulk of aid—almost 60% of bilateral aid and almost 80% of multilateral aid, just as the commitment-to-development hypothesis would predict; while the main part of trade and investment went to the more advanced, or affluent, Third World countries. The same picture emerges if the data are disaggregated further by recipient income, separating least developed countries from low income countries in general, or separating NICs (or newly industrializing countries) from middle- and upper-income LDCs. It is the most economically advanced countries that get the trade and especially the investment; it is the least advanced countries that get the most aid, especially multilateral aid.

Aid levels varied with level of economic need in a striking way among the largest states, also, as shown in table 3.12. There are eight countries in the Third World with over 70 million inhabitants, according to 1981 OECD figures; after that there is a break, then many countries from 55 million on down. The eight largest are China, India, Indonesia, Brazil, Pakistan, Bangladesh, Nigeria, and Mexico. Brazil, Mexico, and Nigeria, markedly more prosperous than the other large states, received, despite their economic and strategic importance to the West, relatively low levels of aid—less than was spent in smaller and poorer countries of minor global importance, less than in Tunisia or Upper Volta, less than in Bolivia or Peru, far less than in Burma or Thailand (though these in turn received far less than the large *poor* states we are considering: Indonesia, Bangladesh, Pakistan, as well as India and China). Nigeria's extremely low aid funding is relatively recent, and probably temporary: it received $80–100 million annually through most of the seventies, and $30–60 million in the late seventies and early eighties. The decline in aid to Nigeria in the eighties accompanied Nigeria's relative lack of need for outside capital because of its petroleum industry. The proportioning of aid to poverty or financial need is present in both the bilateral and the multilateral figures, but is more pronounced in multilateral assistance. Among the largest and most important recipients, as among recipients as a whole, the emphasis in aid has been upon need, where need has been measured primarily by degree of poverty and, to a degree, by population.

TABLE 3.11

Aid, Investment, and Trade by Recipient Income Class (Percentages)

| Type of Transaction | Low Income Countries | | | Middle or Higher Income Third World Countries | | |
|---|---|---|---|---|---|---|
| | 1981 | 1982–84 | 1985–88 | 1981 | 1982–84 | 1985–88 |
| Net Foreign Aid | | | | | | |
| Bilateral | 57 | 56 | 63 | 42 | 43 | 37 |
| Multilateral | 79 | 81 | 85 | 21 | 19 | 15 |
| Net Commercial Investment | 24 | 11 | 24 | 75 | 89 | 76 |
| FDI (multinational firms) | — | 14 | 5 | — | 86 | 95 |
| Portfolio | — | 5 | — | — | 95 | — |
| Trade | | | | | | |
| OECD exports | 18 | 23 | 24 | 82 | 77 | 76 |
| OECD imports | 20 | 20 | 20 | 80 | 80 | 80 |

Source: Computed from OECD, Geographical Distribution of Financial Flows, various years, summary tables at end.

Note: The percentage distribution of gross foreign aid and commercial investment is approximately the same as the distribution of the net flows.

TABLE 3.12

Aid and Trade, Largest Third World Countries (1982): Largest Countries' Population, GNP, Aid, and OECD Commerce and Finance

| Country | Population (millions) | GNP per Capita (dollars) | Foreign Aid ($ millions) | OECD Trade ($ millions) | Private Investment ($ millions) |
|---|---|---|---|---|---|
| Bangladesh | 93 | 140 | 970 | 980 | − 24 |
| India | 719 | 250 | 1,852 | 7,482 | 229 |
| China | 1,008 | 310 | 627 | 12,897 | 1,414 |
| Pakistan | 87 | 380 | 667 | 2,579 | 60 |
| Indonesia | 153 | 580 | 742 | 8,471 | 3,286 |
| Nigeria | 90 | 870 | 49 | 13,717 | 1,370 |
| Mexico | 73 | 1,360 | 133 | 24,438 | 5,589 |
| Brazil | 130 | 2,240 | 103 | 9,403 | 6,515 |

Source: OECD, Geographical Distribution of Financial Flows, 1980–1983, country pages and summary tables at the end.

Note: Aid figures refer to net disbursed aid.

While the emphasis upon foreign aid directed to the neediest recipients has been increased in recent years, and varies from donor to donor, the basic pattern, implicit in the concept of foreign aid from the start, has been fairly consistent throughout the postwar period, as shown in a more comprehensive summary of aid, over a fifteen-year period, in table 3.13.

TABLE 3.13
Share of Aid, Exports, and Export Credits from OECD countries to Third World
Countries by Recipient Income Class: 1968–1982 Summed (Percentages)

| | Bilateral Aid | Multilateral Aid | Export Credits | OECD Exports[a] |
|---|---|---|---|---|
| Least developed countries | 19 | 28 | 3 | 3 |
| Other low income countries | 41 | 42 | 14 | 12 |
| Lower middle income LDCs | 25 | 21 | 27 | 33 |
| Upper middle income LDCs | 8 | 8 | 45 | 22 |
| Higher income LDCs | 6 | 0 | 2 | 6 |
| Oil rich countries | 1 | 1 | 10 | 25 |

Sources: See sources listed in table 3.1.
Notes: Columns may not add to 100% due to rounding error.
[a] Exports taken for period 1968–77.

And what holds true in the aggregate, and in the cases examined above, also holds true if the data are disaggregated by time period, by donor, and by (population) size of recipient state. This provides some assurance that the results are not artifacts of recent trends, of one or two large donors, or of a correlation of population and income level. Actually, the aggregate figures understate the degree to which most donors directed aid to poorer recipients. Table 3.14 breaks down the overall data about income class of recipients of aid by donor, to see whether the patterns just seen in OECD aid as a whole hold for particular DAC donors. The median DAC figures, giving a measure of what most donors did, are more skewed toward aid to the poorer or poorest recipients than are the total (or mean) figures given above. However, despite some important variation among donors, the emphasis upon directing foreign aid toward the poorer countries was nearly universal among DAC countries. Only three donors directed less than 50% of their aid to the poorer LDCs. A solid majority (ten) of the DAC countries directed two thirds or more of their aid to those poorer countries. Most DAC countries directed at least a quarter of their aid to the neediest countries, the least developed countries (LLDCs). Yet these countries were of little economic importance to the donor states: the share of donor exports to the Third World received by LLDCs was less than 5% for every DAC donor; the share of Third World exports to all lower-income LDCs combined was less than 20% for every DAC donor but Australia. On the other hand, Third World recipients with large trade and investment potential—upper middle income LDCs, which accounted for over half the exports of most (eleven) donors—received only small amounts of aid. Only six donors spent as much as 10% of their aid on upper middle income LDCs, and only Austria over 25% of its aid

TABLE 3.14
Individual Donors' Bilateral Aid by Recipient Income Class: Percentages of Total, 1968–1982

| | Detailed Breakdown in Four Categories | | | | Summary |
|---|---|---|---|---|---|
| | Least Developed (LLDC) | Other Low Income (OLIC) | Lower Middle Income (MIC) | Upper Middle Income (UMIC) | All Low Income Countries (LICs) (LLDCs + OLICs) |
| Denmark | 41 | 45 | 12 | 1 | 86 |
| Norway | 40 | 43 | 11 | 6 | 83 |
| Sweden | 35 | 48 | 15 | 2 | 83 |
| Belgium | 23 | 58 | 15 | 4 | 81 |
| Switzerland | 37 | 40 | 16 | 7 | 77 |
| Canada | 28 | 49 | 18 | 5 | 77 |
| United Kingdom | 26 | 48 | 18 | 7 | 74 |
| Finland | 42 | 31 | 25 | 2 | 73 |
| Netherlands | 25 | 43 | 14 | 18 | 68 |
| Italy | 33 | 34 | 15 | 18 | 67 |
| Japan | 13 | 45 | 38 | 4 | 58 |
| France | 22 | 34 | 27 | 17 | 56 |
| United States | 12 | 43 | 21 | 23 | 55 |
| Germany | 22 | 30 | 23 | 25 | 52 |
| New Zealand | 9 | 29 | 59 | 2 | 38 |
| Austria | 4 | 25 | 28 | 43 | 29 |
| Australia | 7 | 18 | 75 | 0 | 25 |
| TOTALS | | | | | |
| DAC bilateral | 19 | 41 | 25 | 16 | 59 |
| DAC median | 25 | 43 | 18 | 6 | 68 |
| Multilateral | 30 | 32 | 21 | 17 | 62 |

*Sources*: See sources listed in table 3.1.

*Notes*: The total labeled DAC bilateral is the figure for all DAC aid funds taken together, not the mean of the individual figures in the column above.

The median figures are medians of the columns: they do not add up horizontally, as do the DAC bilateral and the multilateral figures.

Half the DAC countries had totals above, half below, the median figures.

The multilateral total is the mean for all aid funds given by the major international aid agencies.

Rows may not add to 100% due to rounding error.

total. The concentration of aid on LLDCs, and on poorer recipients generally, reflected a choice to send aid to poor states rather than to economically important ones, and it was apparent in the aid programs of virtually all donors.[21]

Although aid has gone more to large, poor countries, it is important to be aware that there is often a "small-country bias" to aid per capita: larger countries tend to receive more aid, but not in proportion to their size, so that aid per capita tends to fall with rising size. There are various ways of explaining this pattern: one can argue that countries get some aid simply by virtue of existing, and having embassies able to solicit aid; that larger countries have larger internal markets and smaller countries therefore have more acute need for aid; that many small countries are the poor countries of Africa; that it simply seems unbalanced, despite the great needs, to give the majority of all aid to India and China, which together have half the population of the LDCs and two-thirds that of the lower income LLDCs. Also, the countries considered neediest, the LLDCs, have a combined population of only 300 million, less than a tenth of the Third World total, but receive a quarter of all aid.

The poverty orientation of aid is also borne out in a qualified way by regressions analyzing how donors allocated their aid. First, it should be recalled that a third of donor aid over the last twenty years has been allocated through multilateral organizations. There is uniform consensus that such aid was directed to large, poor states. Auerbach confirms this even in the sixties for four multilateral aid organizations, although the emphasis on poverty is weaker for the IDA in those years.[22] However, the IDA has subsequently focused particularly on the poorest countries, and has a policy of seeking to direct 40% of its lending to the largest very poor countries, India and China; the share of IDA funds going to the poorest countries has risen from 79% in 1969–70, to 85% in 1975–80, to 90% in 1981–87.[23] Maizels and Nissanke also find that their "recipient interest" model of multilateral per capita aid is successful for the two periods they study, 1969–70 and 1978–80, while their "donor interest" model is not. Thus, a third of donor aid was allocated to organizations focusing on poor countries and effectively buffering most donor influence.

Dowling and Heimenz, using a sample of ninety countries where "aid allocations have been relatively free of gross political overtones" during the seventies, find for bilateral and for multilateral aid that there is a small-country bias, and a bias toward low-income countries, although there was a subset of very poor countries that received relatively little aid.[24] However, Maizels and Nissanke find that their "donor interest" model for per capita aid for four of the major bilateral donors, the United States, the United Kingdom, France, and Japan, is confirmed, while their "recipient interest" model is not. However, their "interest" variables include regional concentrations, which are not necessarily easy to interpret, and also include an "availability of strategic materials" variable, sometimes with positive and sometimes with negative coefficients. Their discussion does not help greatly in sorting out the relative importance of the various components, and the per capita aid variable, unweighted, is not a measure of where donors chose to spend most of their money, but certainly these results show that donor interest factors limited the impact of recipient need in aid allocations.[25]

By far the most detailed and extensive regression-type studies of bilateral aid allocations are those of Bencivenga, who models aid from each of the seventeen DAC donors in the years from 1969 to 1977. She models choice of recipients and allocation of aid among recipients separately, and does so separately for grants and loans, using probits and tobits. Her overall results for the way donors allocated aid are explained extensively, concisely, and clearly in a summary publication, "Motives for Bilateral OECD Aid to Developing Countries."[26] In summarizing her results, I will place more emphasis than she does, however, on allocation of grants, since grants constituted the vast majority of net DAC bilateral aid, rising from 59% of all aid in 1969 to 71% by 1977 (and 78% by 1987).[27] Bencivenga finds population size positive and significant in all loan and grant probit and tobit estimations, although there is a small-country bias for about half the donors. She finds the coefficients of GNP grants tobits negative for all the Nordic donors, Switzerland, Belgium, the Netherlands, Australia, and Japan throughout, and becoming consistently negative for Canada, France, Britain, and Germany in the later years she studies. The United States also showed a movement from positive to negative effect of GNP, consistent with my findings on U.S. non-SSA aid above, although these were not statistically significant in most cases. Austria and Italy alone had positive coefficients for GNP in the grants probits. In sum, she finds development the dominant motive for Denmark, Norway, Sweden, the Netherlands, and the most prominent one for Canada, Australia, and New Zealand although the latter two also responded to economic ties with recipients. Belgium responded to poverty "only in its allocation of grants," and also favored countries with economic ties at first but not later; grants, however, were 85% to 90% of Belgian aid.

Bencivenga says that "economic goals appear to have been most important to Japan" in these years; this finding is consistent with other studies, and there is little reason to doubt it. Although she finds some responsiveness to poverty in allocation of grants, the reverse is true of loans, and at this period grants were only a third to a quarter of Japanese aid. The same pattern was true of Germany, although German aid was about 50% grants. In the German case, there was also some responsiveness to foreign exchange shortage, another indicator of recipient need. France and England also found economic goals important, but she notes that "both were guided by poverty in their selection of recipients and in their allocations of grants in the later years of the sample," and grants were 80–90% of net ODA for France throughout, while English grants evolved from 59% of net ODA in 1969 to over 95% in 1976–77. Bencivenga also finds other factors playing an important role: colonial ties in the case of France and England; small-country bias in the case of large donors other than Japan; the legitimacy of the recipient government in the policies of Australia and New Zealand; and cold war considerations in the case of Australia, Britain, France, the United States, Belgium, and some others, for instance.[28] In the case of the United States she finds no predominant factor: economic ties were unimportant; ties to the communist bloc were a negative factor for recipients; recipient growth rate carried a positive weight, which she notes is "consistent with, if not strong evidence of, the United States' long-standing principle that self-help should be a factor in aid allocation"; and recipient poverty was a negative factor in loans, but evolved from negative to positive in allocation of grants, which made up 60% of U.S. aid by the end of the period.

The poverty orientation of aid is also borne out by the attempts made to reorient development assistance to those sectors most likely to reach poor people. Ian Little observes that "the World Bank has come to include concepts of 'basic needs' in its policy utterances, and Robert Mc-Namara has been emphatic in his appeals to increase aid and direct it, and development in general, toward the mass of the poor. . . . Similarly the Development Assistance Committee of the Organization for Economic Cooperation and Development has endorsed the idea that basic human needs should be a central purpose of development cooperation." Little notes that these emphases are, in his view, "attempts to create a moral community that transcends national sovereignty," although he notes that even liberal elites from Third World countries tend to resist this emphasis.[29] This poverty orientation is clearly reflected in the steady shift of development assistance toward those sectors which would be most likely to reach poorer people within recipient countries—agriculture, and "social sectors" or "poverty-oriented sectors" other than agriculture, such as rural development, small-scale industry, water supply and sewerage, urbanization assistance, education, and population planning, health and nutrition, as shown in tables 3.15 and 3.16. While just what expenditures count as falling within those sectors is a tricky matter, and the ways of aggregating these figures are not consistent from source to source, it is clear that assistance to these sectors has increased markedly both from bilateral and multilateral sources.

## WHERE AID WENT: SUMMARY AND CONCLUSIONS

The way donors spent their money cannot be explained on the basis of donor economic and political interests alone, though these certainly played a part; concern for economic development and for helping people escape poverty clearly had a large influence as well. The vast majority of

TABLE 3.15
Percentage of Aid Going to All Poverty-Oriented Sectors

|  | 1971–72 | 1975–76 | 1988 |
|---|---|---|---|
| U.S. bilateral |  |  |  |
| Social sectors | 2.4 | 1.9 | 23.4 |
| Agriculture | 2.1 | 8.6 | 8.9 |
| DAC bilateral |  |  |  |
| Social sectors | 5.5 | 10.1 | 24.9 |
| Agriculture | 2.9 | 8.1 | 10.8 |
| Multilateral |  |  |  |
| Social sectors | — | — | 19.9 |
| Agriculture | — | — | 23.2 |

Source: OECD, Development Cooperation, various years.
Note: The sectoral data offer problems of comparison from one year to another; the figures may not be fully comparable to one another.

TABLE 3.16
World Bank Resources Going to Poverty-Oriented Sectors (Percentages)

| | Early Period | | | |
|---|---|---|---|---|
| Combined World Bank Lending (IBRD plus IDA) | 1948–60 | 1961–65 | 1966–72 | 1973–74 |
| Lending to agriculture | 6 | 12 | 17 | 24 |

| Agricultural Credit as a Percentage of All World Bank Lending to Agriculture | 1948–63 | 1964–68 | 1969–73 |
|---|---|---|---|
| | 19.1 | 44.8 | 54.9 |

| | | | Later Period | | | | |
|---|---|---|---|---|---|---|---|
| IBRD Lending | 1968–70 | 1971–73 | 1976–78 | 1979–81 | 1982–83 | 1984–85 | 1986 |
| Agriculture | 16.1 | 13.3 | 15.8 | 13.4 | 11.5 | 14.7 | 15.6 |
| Rural development | 3.2 | 7.6 | 16.5 | 15.3 | 13.1 | 9.4 | 13.7 |
| Other poverty sectors | 1.8 | 7.7 | 10.9 | 14.2 | 12.8 | 7.3 | 15.5 |

| IDA Lending | 1976–80 | 1981–87 |
|---|---|---|
| Agriculture and rural development | 42.4 | 37.1 |
| Other poverty sectors | 12.8 | 21.2 |

Sources: The separate IBRD and IDA lending figures are from Jonathan Sanford, 1989, "The World Bank and Poverty: A Review of the Evidence on Whether the Agency Has Diminished Emphasis on Aid to the Poor," American Journal of Economics and Sociology, reprinted by permission. The combined IDA and IBRD figures for earlier periods are from World Bank publications.

foreign aid money went to needy countries of relatively low economic importance to the donors. Thirty percent of all aid was given to multilateral institutions from the midseventies on, which buffered any leverage aid could give the donors. Almost all aid was administered as development assistance by development professionals and was carefully monitored, not simply given to recipient governments. Aid was not pure: not given with an eye only to fostering economic development and eliminating poverty. Certainly, there was some connection between aid and trade for a number of important donors. France and Britain concentrated aid on former colonies to a considerable extent; a half to a third of U.S. bilateral aid was given as Security Supporting Assistance, allocated on the basis not of recipient needs but of U.S. strategic objectives. Some other donors also tended to disfavor radical and communist regimes and others considered illegitimate or authoritarian. At the same time, it is hard to explain most aid on the basis of these weak connections to economic and strategic interests; and there is abundant evidence that in multilateral, and in most bilateral aid, recipient need was an important factor which led donors to favor aid to larger, poorer, LDCs.

Some countries had more altruistic aid programs than others, but in no case is it easy to account for aid wholly on the basis of donor self-interests. The orientation toward recipient poverty was particularly strong in the case of some of the smaller bilateral donors, especially the Netherlands, Switzerland, Sweden, Norway, and Denmark; and to some substantial degree in the aid of Canada, Germany, Belgium, and Australia. But even the bilateral aid of the most self-interested donors appears to have been influenced to some extent by considerations of recipient poverty. The United States, some of whose aid was certainly, and indeed avowedly, used for economic support for countries on the basis of U.S. concerns for security, directed the non-SSA portion of bilateral aid—generally half to two thirds—toward needy, large, and poor recipients. Japanese aid has been generally understood as simply an instrument of Japanese commercial policy, and this was probably more or less true through the late seventies. However, in the last decade, Japanese statements about the need to assume moral responsibility for poverty have accompanied improvement in quality—a higher multilateral share, greater poverty orientation, and a smaller share of actual Japanese procurement—just as the volume of Japanese aid rose dramatically. In the case of France, too, strong advocacy of the needs of the Third World in the Mitterand years was accompanied by a dramatic improvement in the quality of French aid, as well as by a marked increase in quantity. And even if one wholly discounts bilateral aid from these donors as self-interested, it is hard to account for their multilateral aid on the same basis.

At the same time, donors differed substantially in the vigor of their aid programs, and in the extent to which these reflected their own or recipient interests; donors changed in these respects over time, as well. Generally, those donors with average or above-average shares going to poorer LDCs tended to be those donors that gave more aid than average as a percentage of GNP; and a given donor's aid quality and quantity tended to wax and wane together. These differences and changes provide another kind of hard evidence that concern for alleviating poverty and fostering development formed the basis of support for foreign aid, and will be explored in chapters 4 and 8.

## CHAPTER FOUR

# Who Paid the Bill:
## Similarities and Differences among the Donors

> Once our moral vision has expanded sufficiently to recognize our
> duties to *all* our compatriots—once we have come to appreciate
> the moral case for the welfare state—it is logically very difficult
> indeed not to be drawn "beyond the welfare state" . . . and ex-
> tend similar protections to the needy worldwide.
> —Robert E. Goodin[1]

LOOKING AT WHO paid the aid bill ought to give important clues to why
aid was given. The donors that spent more on aid should have been the
most motivated. If aid was given to promote donor economic interests in
the Third World, those countries having greater investments and heavier
trade with the Third World should have tended to spend a higher percentage of GNP on aid. If the aid was given to secure political influence, those
with global political interests, or special interests in the Third World,
should have tended to have stronger aid programs. If aid was primarily
given to promote colonial ties, aid should have come mainly from the
former colonial powers and should have tended to fall off as those ties
weakened. But if aid arose mainly from a humane commitment to Third
World economic development, donors that showed the most commitment
to Third World development and to elimination of poverty and inequality
should have supported aid most strongly.

The differences among the DAC donors should not obscure their similarities. DAC donors had broadly similar aid policies, which were quite
different from the aid policies of other states, or from any previous interstate transfers. The striking similarity among seventeen or eighteen DAC
donors in consistently pursuing a novel set of policies is a starting point of
this book's whole inquiry; the distinctiveness and coherence of DAC donors as a group will be discussed at the end of the chapter. But policy
differences within the DAC provide important evidence about what motivated aid, and that is this chapter's main focus. The very factors that set
the DAC donors apart from other countries, and accounted for their distinctiveness as a group, also varied within the group and account for the
within-group variation.

## Possible Donor Self-Interests

### Economic Interests of Individual Donor States

If each state undertook aid programs to support its foreign trade and investment, aid programs ought to have had more appeal to states with more to gain. States with much to gain economically would tend to be those with considerable trade and investment interests in the Third World.[2] If aid was designed to promote states' overseas commerce, it would be odd if states with much to gain made little of the opportunity, while states with less to gain spent a lot on aid.

Two OECD countries had by far the highest investments in the Third World as a percentage of GNP: Switzerland and Britain. Switzerland, known for its international banking, invested amounts ranging up to 5% of its GNP in the Third World in the late seventies and early eighties, but provided less than .3% of its GNP in foreign aid in the eighties, well below the DAC average. Throughout most of the postwar period, Swiss aid was far lower, despite the large Swiss investment in the Third World.[3] The United Kingdom, with private investments in the Third World in the late seventies sometimes ranging up to 3% of GNP, had only a moderate aid program. The really vigorous donors—in terms of aid as a percentage of GNP—(Norway, the Netherlands, Sweden, and Denmark) had middling private investment at best. There is no simple relationship between commercial financial flows and a country's support of foreign aid programs, as is set out in table 4.1. And in fact, donors' aid as a percentage of GNP during the decade of the eighties was negatively correlated both with net total private financial flows ($R = -.04$) and with net foreign direct investment (FDI), that is, with investment by transnational firms ($R = -.39$) taken as percentages of GNP, although the correlations are not significant.

To see aid as a means to promote investment in the Third World is also problematic because for most donors, net aid was greater than all net private investment in the Third World in most years. Net aid was almost always greater than net investment by a country's multinational firms. Table 4.1 shows that for most countries, total net private flows were less than aid flows: only Belgium, the United Kingdom, France, Switzerland, and the United States had private flows greater than or equal to net concessional aid. And as noted in chapter 3, most aid went to countries receiving little of a donor's private investment, and could not reasonably have been spent as a way of promoting national gains from finance there. Aid would have been a fantastically inefficient way to subsidize private investment.

TABLE 4.1

Comparison of Donors' Net Official Development Assistance (ODA) and Net Private Financial Flows (PFF) as Percentages of GNP, 1980–1989

| | Foreign Aid and Private Financial Flows to Third World as Percentage of GNP | | | Net Private Flows as Percentages of Net ODA | |
| --- | --- | --- | --- | --- | --- |
| | Net Foreign Aid | Net Private Finance | | | |
| | ODA/GNP | PFF/GNP | FDI[a]/GNP | PFF/ODA | FDI[a]/ODA |
| Norway | 1.03 | .35 | .04 | .34 | .04 |
| Netherlands | .99 | .44 | .19 | .44 | .19 |
| Denmark | .89 | .15 | .08 | .18 | .10 |
| Sweden | .87 | .31 | .11 | .36 | .13 |
| France | .73 | .52 | .11 | .71 | .15 |
| Belgium | .51 | .58 | .19 | 1.14 | .37 |
| Canada | .46 | .20 | .04 | .43 | .69 |
| Finland | .45 | .11 | .06 | .24 | .13 |
| Australia | .44 | .27 | .20 | .61 | .45 |
| Germany | .43 | .41 | .12 | .95 | .28 |
| United Kingdom | .34 | .66 | .41 | 1.94 | 1.20 |
| Italy | .32 | .21 | .09 | .66 | .28 |
| Japan | .30 | .46 | .21 | 1.53 | .70 |
| Switzerland | .29 | 1.33 | .48 | 4.59 | 1.66 |
| New Zealand | .27 | .10 | .09 | .37 | .33 |
| Austria | .25 | − .06 | .03 | − .23 | .12 |
| United States | .22 | .23 | .12 | 1.05 | .55 |
| DAC total | .36 | .35 | .15 | .98 | .44 |

Source: OECD, Geographical Distribution of Financial Flows, various years.

[a] Net foreign direct investment (net investment by multinational corporations).

The relationship between aid and trade with Third World countries, given in table 4.2, also shows that those countries with the most to gain in promoting Third World trade were not those with the highest aid spending. Few top aid donors had high exports to the Third World. Belgium, Switzerland, Australia, and New Zealand had particularly high exports to the Third World, yet all but Belgium had smallish aid programs, and Belgium's was a third of the way down the list. Countries with very weak Third World exports, like Canada and Finland, were fairly strong aid donors, and of the top four aid donors only one, the Netherlands, had above-average exports to the Third World. The correlations between aid per GNP and Third World exports and imports are not close to statistical significance, with the coefficient for exports negative and that for imports positive. Exports and imports to the Third World as percentages of total exports and imports both correlate negatively with aid per GNP. (The former is statistically significant at a .05 level; the latter, though close, is

TABLE 4.2

Comparison of Donors' Net Official Development Assistance (ODA) and Exports to, and Imports from, the Third World, 1980–1989

| | | DAC Country's Third World Exports and Imports | | | |
|---|---|---|---|---|---|
| | Foreign Aid (ODA) as Percentages of GNP | Percentages of GNP | | Percentages of DAC Country's World Exports and Imports | |
| | | Exports | Imports | Exports | Imports |
| Norway | 1.03 | 2.7 | 2.7 | .09 | .10 |
| Netherlands | .99 | 3.9 | 4.9 | .08 | .11 |
| Denmark | .89 | 3.1 | 2.9 | .11 | .10 |
| Sweden | .87 | 3.0 | 2.2 | .11 | .08 |
| France | .73 | 3.1 | 2.4 | .17 | .12 |
| Belgium | .51 | 5.9 | 5.5 | .10 | .09 |
| Canada | .46 | 1.8 | 1.9 | .07 | .08 |
| Finland | .45 | 1.9 | 1.8 | .08 | .07 |
| Australia | .44 | 4.0 | 2.5 | .29 | .17 |
| Germany | .43 | 3.6 | 3.3 | .13 | .15 |
| United Kingdom | .34 | 3.0 | 3.0 | .15 | .13 |
| Italy | .32 | 2.7 | 3.1 | .15 | .16 |
| Japan | .30 | 3.5 | 2.4 | .32 | .28 |
| Switzerland | .29 | 4.5 | 2.4 | .17 | .08 |
| New Zealand | .27 | 4.9 | 3.2 | .21 | .14 |
| Austria | .25 | 3.2 | 3.1 | .13 | .10 |
| United States | .22 | 2.0 | 2.8 | .31 | .30 |
| Ireland | .20 | 3.2 | 3.4 | .05 | .06 |
| DAC total | .36 | 2.8 | 2.8 | .19 | .18 |

Sources: computed from OECD, Development Cooperation, various years; and from IMF, Direction of Trade Annual, various years.

Note: The last two columns give a country's exports (imports) to the Third World as a percentage of its total exports (imports). Total DAC GNP is approximately $9,543 billion.

not.) The overall story is the same as that for investment: there is no apparent relationship between those countries which had the greatest stake in increased Third World trade and those which had vigorous aid programs. In fact, just as with private investment, if anything, the donors with lower exports to the Third World gave more aid.

## Colonial Interests of the Donors

The colonial powers might have had an interest in retaining special ties with their former colonies. How far can this explain foreign aid? To start with, there is some problem about ascertaining what "interest" colonial powers had in retaining such "special ties," apart from concrete economic advantages that they thought would accrue. The figures just looked at, and those of chapter 3, suggest that these economic interests do not explain aid well. It is also hard to pinpoint just what concrete political interests the colonizers had in their ex-colonies, especially after the first few years. But if instead the "interest" of former colonial powers simply refers to bonds of culture, language, or friendship of some sort, then it is not clear why bonds of "wanting to help out," which were more or less the stated purpose of aid, should not have played a similar role; for the vague hypothesis of sentimental ties is equally a departure from Realist or other self-interest paradigms. There is reason to suppose that such vague bonds did play some role in the first years following decolonization; for instance, Britons, in public opinion polls, expressed the view that they bore particular responsibility to alleviate poverty in their former colonies. But without going into these things further, I will simplify the argument here by stipulating any special interest by colonial powers in their former colonies as self-interested. Even making that strong assumption, the amount of such colonial influence that can be detected as a basis for foreign aid is small.

Very few donors' aid programs can be explained on the basis of colonial ties, no matter what the nature of those ties was. England and France had extensive colonial holdings; the Netherlands, Belgium, and Italy rather limited ones.[4] And as mentioned in the last chapter, the percentage of aid from Belgium, Italy, and the Netherlands, to former colonies soon declined to a fairly low figure, while their aid programs held constant or increased over the long term. Some other special relationships between donor and recipient could have included attempts to develop regional influence. Australia concentrated a great deal of aid on Papua New Guinea, for which it had been a trustee under the League Mandates system. New Zealand gave a good deal of aid to small neighboring island states that it might have sought to influence. Of course, a special relationship is not, in itself, evidence of an interest in influence. Several of the smaller donors that had no possibility of acquiring regional influence sought long-term cooperative relationships with Tanzania, Nepal, India and other poor states. Certainly the French, British, Belgian, and Dutch programs initially drew mainly on the strength of old colonial ties; it is less clear that this created a sensible way for these or other former colonial powers to pursue definite or even plausible interests in their old colonies. But even if regional relationships that the Western Pacific donors—Japan, Australia, and New Zealand—developed with Third World countries in their regions are included together with colonial ties, and all are stipulated as self-interested, little of the variation in foreign aid is explained.

For one thing, this could explain at most the aid programs of a minority of donor states, for only a minority had colonial or reasonable regional interests to pursue. But furthermore, the countries with strong aid ties to former colonies or smaller regional states were not strong aid donors and, indeed, were rather weak ones, with the possible exception of France.[5] The Netherlands had a strong aid program, but as explained in chapter 3, only a small part of Dutch, Italian, or Belgian aid in recent years has gone to former colonies. Even if we make the extreme assumption that aid to former colonies was solely for the sake of preserving the colonial ties, it predicts very poorly which countries had large aid programs and, in any case, cannot account for the aid of any substantial number of the seventeen DAC donors.

## Global Security Interests and Anticommunism

What of the cold war and the bipolar nature of the system as an explanation of foreign aid? Was aid provided mainly as an instrument in the competition between the West and the communist countries for influence in the Third World? If so, it is hard to understand why the Soviet Union and East European countries did not make more use of it, a point that will be explored at the end of the chapter. But this explanation also cannot account for the differences in support for aid among DAC donors.

If aid was meant to resist communism, the United States should have been particularly the leader in foreign aid policies, both because it was the leader of the Western alliance, and had most to gain, and because it was the most anticommunist. Other threatened states and those most adamant in their opposition to communism might perhaps have been other important supporters of aid. Or perhaps middle powers, not having incentives such as free trade to support an alternate order, might see it as in their interest to join together with the large power whose pole they gravitated to, to oppose gains of influence by the rival bloc. But that is simply not what happened.

Cold war and anticommunist considerations played an important role in U.S. foreign aid, although I argue in chapters 5 and 6 that neither the initial impetus nor the domestic bases of support for most aid lay there. But the United States, after an initial, and important, period of enthusiasm, was among the weakest of the aid donors. A number of formally neutral states—Sweden, Austria, Switzerland, Finland, and Ireland—chose to be part of the aid regime. While most of these were only moderate donors, Sweden was among the strongest in its giving. Also, many of the strongest donors, rather than giving aid to resist the proliferation of leftist or communist governments in the Third World, pursued aid policies directly at odds with the U.S. antileft penchants. Left-leaning Third

World countries such as Tanzania, which were viewed as socially responsible and egalitarian, and which were vocal critics of the West, were particularly favored by many of the European donors. Sweden began to provide aid to Cuba in 1970, and was joined by Finland, Belgium, and later
Norway, the Netherlands, and Canada. Many of these same states provided aid to socialist Vietnam and to Sandinista Nicaragua. However
much the sympathies of these DAC donors lay with the United States and
the Western alliance in Europe, however opposed they may have been to
Soviet repression, these sentiments did not carry over to fear of socialism
or radicalism in the Third World, and cannot explain their foreign aid.

If the interest in aid was a response to a bipolar world, the support for
aid ought to have varied as the cold war thawed and refroze. But instead,
the period of détente was the period in which aid rose the most, as a
percentage of GNP, in most of the donor countries. That increase slackened in the tenser climate of the late seventies and early eighties. Had aid
been an artifact of the cold war, one would also expect a rapid falling off
of aid after the end of the cold war; but that has not happened, although
U.S. aid continues its long downward drift. In addition, the people who
originally advocated aid, and those who later supported aid, were not
strong anticommunists and, indeed, tended to be people on the left, opposed to the cold war, as chapters 5 and 6 document. Moreover, even if
aid had been motivated by cold war considerations, it is hard to see how
this would have sustained the aid effort, since there were no agreements
about which countries should give aid, and any of the small or middle
donors might have slackened its aid support considerably without too
much fear that this would undermine the aid regime and its beneficial
consequences for that donor of strengthening the world system, politically or economically. Britain in fact did so, as did the United States, while
the regime stood firm. Some other factors must have motivated the
donors.

To recognize the limits of East-West conflict and anticommunism as an
overall explanation of foreign aid or of the behavior of most of the participants is not to minimize the role these factors had in some particular
cases. As mentioned in the previous chapter, a substantial amount of
*United States* bilateral foreign aid was set aside as Security-Supporting
Assistance. It is possible to construe some of the remainder as having
served this purpose also. It is possible to interpret Australia's strong aid
relationship with neighboring countries, especially Papua New Guinea,
and some of the aid of Japan and New Zealand as also having served
security objectives connected to stopping the spread of communist influence. It is not necessary to interpret even Australia's aid to Papua New
Guinea in that way, but there is certainly evidence that, at the start of
Australia's aid program, that sort of consideration was taken very seri-

ously. Nevertheless, this argument seems to be of rather limited value in accounting for the aid of many OECD donors, and it certainly does not help in predicting which OECD countries funded aid at higher levels.

### The Structure of the International System: Interests of the Hegemon and Others in Free Trade

One prevalent argument about the politics of international economics emphasizes the way in which interests in retaining a system of free international trade, or the ability to do so, may differ from nation to nation and change depending upon the distribution of capabilities in the system. Briefly, the ability to keep an open system of free trade, or the interest in doing so, rests with a major power—the hegemon—that takes, or can take, on itself the responsibility for keeping the system of free trade going. In one variant, one might expect the hegemon itself to bear the costs of preserving a system of open trade. In other variants, small states, which share the hegemon's interests or are subject to its suasion might also take a part in upholding the free trade order. In any of the variants, chief responsibility and capacity to sustain the order would rest upon the hegemonic state.

Now foreign aid serves various purposes in the economies of recipient states, but one of the important ones is that by alleviating shortages of foreign exchange, it facilitates purchases of the exports of other states, particularly from those Western states whose firms have important technology, capital goods, and other items, and require hard currency in payment. By alleviating a Third World country's "balance of payments constraint," foreign aid can increase the recipient's trade, particularly its imports, and, in the long run, its general participation in the international capitalist economy. Because of this, one might argue that foreign aid benefited the trading order and, hence, that the hegemon and others with an interest in preserving an open trading order had interests of that sort which their provision of foreign aid was designed to serve. In this section I examine that line of reasoning.

To the extent that foreign aid was a device to preserve or extend open trade relations in the international system, aid should have been given primarily by those states most able and motivated to preserve that order, or most apt to the influence of the hegemon that is so motivated. Then aid should be most strongly supported by the United States and, next, by states over which it had strong influence. In general, aid with such a basis would be expected to wane over time, if the hegemon loses interest in the regime, given its costs, or loses power to enforce it. Declines in U.S. power and in U.S. interest in foreign aid would both erode support for foreign aid as a means to an open trading order. But this is inconsistent with the patterns of support for aid actually observed. The United States did, in large measure, initiate the aid regime, as this theory might predict. But this did not last long. From the late sixties onward, U.S. commitment to providing aid declined steadily, and U.S. power also declined. Insofar as the aid regime relied on hegemonic support and power, foreign aid from other donors should also have declined for both reasons. But, apart from Britain, in economic decline of its own, this was not the case; in fact, most donors actually increased their aid as a percentage of GNP. The United States was not the leader but the laggard in providing foreign aid, and the most committed aid donors, the standard setters for the regime, were small states often critical of U.S. policy, such as Norway, the Netherlands, and Sweden.[6] Thus the predictions of a structural economic theory of aid as a means of promoting an open order are inconsistent with the patterns of support for aid among donors.

## A Cooperative Regime Based on Common Economic Interests (without Hegemonic Influence)

International regimes and other arrangements of mutual benefit to participating nations can emerge, or at least can survive, even in the absence of hegemonic leadership and enforcement, despite the costs participation in cooperative arrangements imposes on individual participant states. The very concept here presupposes a particular dilemma: a structure of incentives in which the best solution for all is one that requires participants to give up maximizing their individual opportunities for the sake of some kind of common benefit. In the absence of strong enforcement, each participant would be likely to do so only if convinced that the overall results were better, given its own goals, than the results of it and all others going their own ways and responding separately to the incentives faced. In this way, it is possible to account for cooperation in the presence of incentives not to cooperate without departing from the national self-interest premises concerning the behavior of states in the international system.

Typically, the enforcement of such a pact lies in each knowing that his failure to live up to the agreement results in a loss of confidence or in other sanctions from other members of the pact, or that this sort of withdrawal will soon be copied and cause the pact to unravel, to his own net disbenefit. In either case, the enforcement depends not only on the visibility of "cheating" but on clear-cut and stable definitions of compliance or noncompliance. For where this is not the case, a lack of effort on the part of one would not lead to the undermining of the pact or to censure of the one giving less effort. On the other hand, if this is in fact the mechanism underlying support of the pact, declining compliance could be expected to erode, increasingly, the compliance of others. Indeed, were this not the case, no incentive to comply would be left!

OECD states might have sought to further common economic interests by the maintenance of a foreign aid regime as described in the preceding two sections. There may have been a common economic interest in the preservation and extension of the capitalist system, and in keeping the Third World countries from withdrawing from that system. So I will consider what the implications of this sort of "regime" structure might have been for patterns of regime support, and whether this gets over any of the difficulties of supposing common interests hinged upon the continuing support of a hegemon.

This argument does get around some of the previous objections to the failure of the contributions to correspond to the size of the participants in the way that is expected in some structural theory. Middle powers, as well as the hegemon, might have an interest in the preservation of a capitalist order around the world, and might have sought to preserve it by a regime that gave incentives to Third World countries to participate in the world economy. Some smaller states, too, might have had incentives to preserve the capitalist order in this way. Taken in this way, however, it is hard to see that there is any prediction about what states would have been contributors.

One possible prediction would have been that larger states would have incentive to participate because they would capture more of the externalities accruing from their behavior. But as shown above, such was not the case. Or one could argue that those more involved in trade would be the strongest aid participants. But again, as came out in the examination of individual incentives, such was not the case. Overall, however, it is not clear that this theory yields *any* prediction about which states should have participated more. In this sense, it gets over some of the problems raised by the failure of middle powers to be the regime "breakers" and of the hegemon to be the regime "maker" that came up in our previous discussion of economic interests at the system level.

This sort of theory in which an aid regime is based on fear of regime decay *does* suggest, however, that the incentive to *continue* in the regime depended upon the setting of clear, collective standards of acceptable participation. And this was clearly not the case. It might be argued that the declining participation of the United States could have been accepted by or justified to other DAC countries on the basis of other U.S. global responsibilities, including the defense support upon which all of the democratic states, whether formally allied or not, might be claimed to have been, to some extent at least, leaning. But even leaving out the United States as an exception, the *unevenness* of aid support, both between countries and across time, makes it hard to reconcile the facts with an explanation which holds that DAC donors felt a need to conform to DAC norms lest they be injured if the aid regime collapsed. Different OECD countries differed considerably in their levels of foreign aid (as a percentage of GNP)—often by a factor of two or three. True, this was generally a small variation if one compares it with the difference between any of the DAC donors and any prewar aid efforts, or between the DAC donors and other consistent groups of donors. But I will examine the implications of the similarities as well as of the differences later in this chapter.

Not only was there variation between donors but variation over time. For one thing, when donors reduced their aid support, though they may have been chided by other DAC countries at the annual aid reviews, there is little evidence of fear that the whole regime would collapse. But moreover, a good number of donors with already exemplary records chose to increase their participation. This is something hard to account for, if the motive for participation was that failure to adhere to minimum standards would precipitate withdrawal from the regime by others.

## Two Senses of Support for Common Interests

Distinguish, in passing, however, between the idea that the aid regime was motivated by common security or economic interests in the sense that self-interested participants kept participating because of fear of regime collapse, and the idea that OECD nations participated because of a willingness to do their part in assuring a peaceful and prosperous future for the world or the West, and one in which they themselves would have a share. These two rationales for aid, so similar seeming at first, imply or presuppose radically different theoretical frameworks. To say that nations agreed, explicitly or implicitly, and kept their agreements for fear of having their pact collapse does not take us beyond the scope of Realist arguments, though it perhaps softens their hard edge, and does not cover the facts here. To say that nations adhered, sometimes in a supererogatory way, to understandings they had reached out of loyalty to a common good whose appeal to them depended in part on the fact that it was relevant to their condition and their future—whether or not it covers the facts here; and it at least does not conflict with them—is to leave the Realist type of explanation altogether and acknowledge that loyalties secured not by the prospects of cost to one's own nation but by concern for a larger order of which the nation was a part could influence national decisions.

Both of these paths of influence could reasonably be described as a national concern for "milieu goals" or as "the national interest in the peace and prosperity of the international system" or as "participation in a regime, based on common interests." But they refer to essentially different logics of action. My aim is not to try to reserve these terms for one type of consideration or the other, or even to advocate that they should be used in a single way. However desirable consistent usage might be, it is apt to prove impossible, for these phrases are too close to common speech to be reliably reserved as technical terms. Ordinary usage will tend to creep in, creating ambiguity. It is important to be aware of the ambiguity and its likely occurrence, so as to be able to distinguish the two phenomena for purposes of analysis.

There is little doubt that nations were influenced by the argument that foreign aid was an element in doing their part to sustain an international order that would be beneficial to all. But there is little chance that they did so under the illusion that they would suffer if they decided to ride free.

## THE SOCIAL PHILOSOPHY OF THE DONOR COUNTRIES: AN ALTERNATIVE EXPLANATION OF DIFFERENTIAL DONOR SUPPORT OF AID

This book argues that foreign aid was largely a product of humanitarian ideas and values in the developed democracies which found support in the domestic political arrangements and religious and moral traditions of the West, and which issued in an emphasis on international cooperation and a commitment to remedying poverty for humanitarian and egalitarian reasons. If so, what should follow? On this hypothesis, support for aid should have varied as the concern for poverty and inequality *within* donor states varied. States with democratic and social-democratic traditions and strong support for government assistance to poor people at home should have been more apt to provide foreign aid. And public humanitarian sentiment and concern about poverty in the Third World should have been reflected in higher levels of aid funding, also. Each of these propositions finds strong confirmation in the variation in aid funding among donor states, which shows an association between domestic and international spending concerned with poverty. States acted just as if their commitment to aid flowed from public concern about domestic and international poverty.

The predicted association of foreign aid with donor social spending and with other measures of concern about poverty is confirmed by the evidence of this chapter; the operation of concern about poverty in undergirding aid can be traced in domestic political processes that led to aid spending as well. Chapter 5 shows that the publics in donor countries were concerned about Third World poverty, and that this concern was critical to their support for aid. That chapter also shows that the politicians, political parties, and academic writers who supported aid also supported measures to alleviate domestic poverty and inequality, while those who opposed aid were also cool toward doing anything about domestic poverty; and that the organized groups which supported aid were all humanitarian. Chapter 6 shows that the way for aid was prepared by the growth of a climate of opinion which favored welfare spending and international measures for alleviating suffering abroad, both as an end in itself and as a necessity for creating international order. The evidence of this chapter is complementary to that in the rest of the book in other ways, as well. Chapter 2 showed that there was considerable unity among the democratic advanced states; and further supporting evidence, contrasting these states of the OECD with other donors or potential donors, is given at the end of this chapter. This section will look at how strength of donor support in the OECD countries covaried with humanitarian and egalitarian concerns for poverty, as expressed in domestic social spending and politics, in private commitment to aid, and in public opinion about aid.

## Public Opinion as an Index of Social Philosophy

The link between social spending, private voluntary contributions, and foreign aid, and the hypothesized cause of all three, was the concern of people in the donor countries that their governments do something about poverty. Concerns of this kind were not limited to mass publics; special interest groups, more active and informed citizens, and policy elites shared them, as chapter 5 shows. Comparison of aid funding levels and opinion data here suggest that the public's concerns about poverty played a part in the link. The data are not systematic, but they are very suggestive. Of eleven DAC donors in which people were asked in the period around 1983 whether they favored their country giving foreign aid, the highest levels of public support were in the Netherlands and Denmark (89% and 86%), the countries out of the eleven with the highest levels of aid (1.02% and .85% of GNP, 1984 figures). Italy, the United Kingdom, France, Belgium, and Germany have levels of public support ranging from 83% to 79% with aid at .33%, .33%, .77%, .56%, and .45% of GNP respectively. The level of public support is markedly lower in New Zealand (70%), Australia (65%), the United States (50%), and Austria, whose aid was .25%, .46%, .24%, and .28% of GNP respectively.[7] Thus, of these eleven countries, three of the four with low public opinion support have the lowest levels of aid funding as well. Yet surveys consistently show that publics support aid because of their concern for poor people. If the level of aid funding tends to vary with the level of public support, this suggests that aid was given in response to concerns about recipient poverty. Where good data are available, the strength of public support for aid roughly lines up with the vigor of actual aid programs.

The dynamics of aid over time also suggest that sustaining a commitment to foreign aid depends upon generating public support for this kind of humanitarian program. For instance, although Italy had only moderate levels of aid funding despite high public support in 1983, when the poll in question was taken, aid rose to .40% of GNP by the end of the eighties, starting from some .16% in 1980–81. Similarly, of the two non-DAC countries with very high levels of support for aid that were included in the 1983 Euro-Barometer survey, Ireland (86% support) joined the DAC in 1985, and Luxembourg (87% support) more than doubled its aid from .12% to .29% of GNP during the eighties, though it did not join the DAC. In addition, in those countries where polls are reported which show strong public support for increasing aid, there have been marked increases. In Italy and Luxembourg in 1983, 40% more favored increasing aid than decreasing it; the rapid increases there have been noted. From 55% to 80% of Finns favored increases in aid in the early eighties; aid rose from .22% to .61% of GNP in the course of the decade. In Switzerland, 36% favored increasing aid in a 1984 poll; aid increased from .22% to .31% in the eighties. Japanese polls consistently showed public support for increasing aid in the late seventies and early eighties; and Japanese aid increased from .22% in 1975–76 to .35% in 1985. In the Netherlands in 1970, 47% favored an increase in aid; and aid increased from .50% in 1969 to .74% in 1975 to .97% in 1980. Support for increases in aid was more moderate in other cases in which aid stayed relatively constant. And unfortunately, in three of the countries with low public opinion support, Australia, New Zealand, and the United States, aid has been in decline since the midseventies. In the United States, where support for aid has been weakest, and where opinion data have consistently shown stronger support for decreasing aid than increasing it, aid has in fact declined in recent years from .60% of GNP in 1963 to .15% to .23% of GNP, the lowest level in the DAC, except for Ireland. In the fourth country with low support, Austria, aid has stayed at a low level and has been of low quality—mostly bilateral, weak in its concessionality, less directed than that of other donors to the poorest countries. Public support for aid seems to lead to stronger aid programs.

This accords quite well with Mosley's findings that when aid is more directed to the need of recipients, donors often, though not invariably, support aid at higher levels. Mosley looks both at "supply-side" factors, affecting constraints to providing aid, and "demand-side" factors. He hypothesizes that the quality of aid, understood as orientation to recipient needs, ought to affect donor country public demand for aid, since publics consistently wanted aid to help the poor. He shows, among other things, that high aid quality was a factor leading to increased aid spending in some OECD countries, where aid quality is defined as the sum of four measures: the proportion of aid given to least developed countries, the proportion of aid given to agriculture and to social infrastructure, the proportion of untied aid, and the grant element in the total aid flow. Using data on nine DAC countries from roughly 1961 to 1979, he finds that a country's aid expenditures are influenced significantly upward both by its own past disbursements and by the expenditures of other OECD donors.[8] He argues as well that expenditures are elastic with respect to a country's relative income, that is, its income as a share of the income of other donors. Understandably, the health of the domestic economy also appears to be a factor, as Robertson also argues.[9] But most interestingly, he finds that the quality of a donor's aid program often makes a difference to its commitment to providing foreign aid. For one group, including the Netherlands, Norway, and the United States, higher quality appears to contribute to higher aid spending. Sweden, Canada, and West Germany show a correlation between aid quality and that part of aid spending not explained by various supply-side factors he identifies; this, he argues, suggests that public concern for quality of aid leads governments to increase aid quality in these countries. Mosley thus concludes that public concern for humanitarian purposes in aid was an important factor in total aid volume.

The history of French and Japanese aid in the eighties strongly supports this argument, although Mosley's figures show no association for these countries in the period he studies. High Japanese officials, starting in 1979, argued the importance of responding to global human needs, and public opinion was mobilized by concern over African famine. In the period since, Japanese aid expenditures have risen markedly, as discussed in chapter 5, at the very time that aid quality has risen sharply, with Japanese aid to multilateral institutions and lower income countries increasing as a percentage of the Japanese aid total, and both formal tying and the actual share of Japanese aid going to Japanese contractors decreasing rapidly. The French story is similar; Mitterand made a commitment to policies sensitive to the needs of the Third World prior to his election, which he reaffirmed in the first few days after his election. Since then, French aid has increased rapidly in volume and quality, as is discussed in detail in chapter 5. The multilateral share of French aid and the share going to least developed countries increased, as the total rose and the amount of aid not directed to DOM and TOM rose by nearly 50%. For both France and Japan, the largest increases in aid quality in their histories occurred after the period of Mosley's study, at the time of major increases in aid funding, after explicit statements by government leaders of intentions to be more responsive to Third World needs.

## Social-Democratic Political Strength

The strength of social-democratic or left parties also seems to be associated with foreign aid spending. Such parties, traditionally in favor of measures to improve the situation of the working classes and to diminish inequality in society, were a natural organized political group in which to find concern for worldwide poverty, as is discussed in chapters 5 and 6. Countries that never had labor or social-democratic governments—the North American countries, New Zealand, and Japan—had low aid spending compared to the rest of the DAC: three of the four were in the bottom third of aid giving both at the start and end of the eighties. On the other hand, states with the strongest record of aid giving, such as Norway and Sweden, were states dominated by social-democratic rule. The strength of social-democratic parties is often closely aligned with social spending; however, each variable adds some information where the two differ. In some cases where the strength of social-democratic parties differs from social spending (higher in Norway, lower in Belgium) it seems closer to actual aid levels; in four other cases, social spending predicts better. Also note that in both Britain and the United States, the strongly conservative, procapitalist, and anticommunist governments of Thatcher and Reagan cut foreign aid expenditures and sought to use foreign aid more and more openly as an instrument of economic and/or political influence. By contrast, the Mitterand administration in France reversed a long-term decline in levels of foreign aid funding and also moved to channel aid much more through multilateral institutions, altering long-established French practice. These examples suggest, though they do not prove, that more right-wing parties are less disposed to aid, and that the party in power, which can change more rapidly than levels of social spending, is a useful supplementary indication of how a willingness to employ government to alleviate problems of the domestic poor can help dispose people favorably toward foreign aid.[10]

## Domestic Social Spending

Domestic social spending provides a particularly good indicator because it permits comparisons between countries and across time. It allows assessment of the idea that foreign aid came out of humanitarian and egalitarian concerns, by comparing aid spending with spending on domestic policies relevant to poverty. If those countries that were most interested in aid were those more interested in the domestic alleviation of poverty, this lends some support to the idea that it was alleviation of poverty that motivated foreign aid. Why should we expect foreign aid spending to covary with domestic social spending and other indicators of attempts to reduce poverty? Both arise from concern for alleviating and reducing poverty. It is true that these concerns are on "different levels of analysis." Domestic social policy emerges not just from the compassion of individuals but from the social and political dynamics of the society. International policies such as foreign aid likewise reflect the dynamics of international power and organization and not just root desires on the part of policy elites in the donor countries, much less mass opinion or feeling. Nevertheless, the hypothesis of this study is that ideas and values did affect international process. While the mechanism by which they had their influence—on domestic and on international policy—involved organizational decisions and events that had little to do with those ideas, it also drew upon those ideas and values. Since concern about poverty and inequality, and belief in the wisdom of dealing with problems by including the less fortunate rather than suppressing them, influenced thinking about both domestic and international policy, there should be a relationship between the two (see fig. 4.1). States with strong concern for poverty as expressed by domestic social spending and other indicators should also have been strong supporters of aid.

FIGURE 4.1
Concern about Poverty Influences Both Social Spending and Foreign Aid

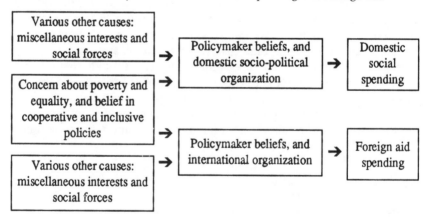

Social expenditures are strongly associated with foreign aid spending. The social expenditure variable indicates social spending as a percentage of GNP, and rose rapidly during and just prior to the main increases of foreign aid spending in the seventies. Social expenditures in part reflect concern about poverty and a willingness to have the government spend to address social needs; thus they tap attitudes toward poverty and government economic programs which, according to the rationale developed in chapter 1, should carry over from domestic affairs to international relations. This hypothesis receives some confirmation on the micro level from public opinion data, reviewed in chapter 5, which suggest that people concerned about domestic poverty and inequality tended to favor foreign aid.

At the macro level, the strongest supporters of aid, consistently, were states with particularly strong domestic social welfare spending. The five donors at the top of the 1982–1983 ODA/GNP list show strong domestic commitment to social welfare as measured by social spending as a percentage of GNP, including the top four domestic social spenders[11] (see table 4.3). Similarly, of the bottom seven aid spenders, two had lowest social spending, and two more were in the bottom five social spenders. Norway, the Netherlands, Sweden, and then Denmark have been the strongest donors over the last fifteen to twenty years, consistently and by a substantial margin; all have strongly social-democratic polities, and all (except, by some measures, Norway) have very high domestic social spending. France and Belgium have been next[12] and also have high domestic spending. The United States and Italy, Austria, Finland, Japan, New Zealand, and Switzerland have been the weak donors; of these, the United States, Japan, and New Zealand have weak domestic social spending, while Italy's is not high. Finland's aid has risen spectacularly since the early eighties and now stands as fifth strongest in the DAC in percentage of GNP, more closely in accord with its social spending. High domestic social spenders were big aid givers, with the very highest usually being the very biggest, and low domestic social spenders gave less aid.

The percentage social expenditures of the donor states have been strongly and significantly correlated with their aid spending from the midseventies onward. Other, less accurate and less complete social expenditure data available yearly from 1960 to 1981 yield slightly lower but consistently positive correlations, ranging from $R = .23$ upward in the early seventies, and are significant or nearly significant from 1973 onward. The correlations using what are probably the best social expenditure data for 1975, 1980, 1982–1983, and 1985 show correlations that are highly significant and explain over 25% of the variance in aid spending (see table 4.4). Countries with strong welfare programs also had strong aid programs.

## Private Voluntary Contributions
### to International Economic Assistance

A different sort of independent variable is provided by levels of private contributions to nongovernmental organizations involved with helping Third World countries. Such voluntary contributions reflect citizen con-

TABLE 4.3

Foreign Aid, Domestic Government Social Expenditures, and Private Voluntary Contributions as Percentages of Gross National Product (1982–1983 Averages)

| | | Foreign Aid | Domestic Social Spending | Private Voluntary Contributions to the Third World |
|---|---|---|---|---|
| NO | Norway | 1.03 | 28 | .0069 |
| NE | Netherlands | 1.00 | 35 | .0071 |
| SW | Sweden | .94 | 36 | .0055 |
| DE | Denmark | .75 | 33 | .0018 |
| BE | Belgium | .59 | 35 | .0032 |
| AL | Australia | .53 | 18 | .0017 |
| GE | Germany | .48 | 29 | .0052 |
| FR | France[a] | .48 | 29 | .0005 |
| CA | Canada | .43 | 22 | .0042 |
| UK | United Kingdom | .36 | 23 | .0016 |
| FI | Finland | .31 | 28 | .0028 |
| JA | Japan | .31 | 14 | .0002 |
| AU | Austria | .29 | 25 | .0019 |
| SZ | Switzerland | .28 | 14 | .0045 |
| NZ | New Zealand | .28 | 20 | .0026 |
| US | United States | .25 | 20 | .0039 |
| IT | Italy | .24 | 26 | .0001 |

| | | Domestic Social Expenditures | | Private Voluntary Contributions | |
|---|---|---|---|---|---|
| | | High | Low | High | Low |
| | | BE DE FR GE NE NO SW | AL CA | BE CA GE NO NE SW | AL DE FR |
| Government Foreign Aid Expenditures (ODA/GNP) | High | 7 | 2 | 6 | 3 |
| | Low | 2 | 6 | 2 | 6 |
| | | FI IT | AU JA NZ SZ UK US | SZ US | AU FI IT JA NZ UK |

Sources: OECD, Development Cooperation, 1985, p. 130; and OECD, Development Cooperation, various years.

[a] France's ODA/GNP is given excluding aid to DOM and TOM; including that aid, the percentage would be 74%; this would not change France's position in the fourfold tables.

FIGURE 4.2
Concern about International Poverty Influences Charity and Foreign Aid

cern for Third World development. If concern for economic justice and about poverty in the Third World is an important factor causing foreign aid, and if private voluntary contributions give a good indication of public support for efforts to alleviate world poverty, then such contributions should be associated with levels of government aid, since both have a common cause whose strength may vary from donor country to donor country (see figure 4.2). How well do PVO contributions predict levels of foreign aid spending?

Data on private voluntary expenditures for assistance to the Third World, also as a percentage of GNP, represent amounts raised by private organizations such as church charities, Oxfam, CARE, and so on for assistance overseas; they do not include money received by these organizations from governments. Thus, they are an index of strong citizen concern about Third World economic conditions, and one on which we have more systematic comparative data than we do for public opinion polls. The relationship between PVO contributions and support for foreign aid also receives micro-level support from public opinion data, which indicate that people who say they have contributed to voluntary organizations concerned with Third World poverty are substantially more apt to support foreign aid than those who have not.

Of course, the intercausation between PVO levels and government aid spending can be complex. Government attempts to build up awareness of the problems of developing countries may have had a positive effect on PVO contributions, just as the public concern expressed in those contributions may have affected government policy.[13] In either case there is evidence that foreign aid spending was perceived as benefiting from public concern about overseas poverty—either because the government responded to popular concerns or because it thought the creation of popu-

TABLE 4.4
Correlations of DAC Donors' Aid Spending with Domestic Social
Spending and with Contributions to PVOs Assisting The Third World

| | Simple Correlations with ODA/GNP | | | | | | Regression Equation for Both Variables | | | | |
| | Domestic Social Spending | | | Private Voluntary Contributions | | | | | Significance Level | | |
| | R | $R^2$ | signif. | R | $R^2$ | signif. | $R^2$ | Adj. $R^2$ | Model | Social | PVOs |
|---|---|---|---|---|---|---|---|---|---|---|---|
| 1975 | .50 | .25 | (.041) | .35 | .12 | (.160) | .34 | .25 | (.050) | (.049) | (.170) |
| 1980 | .57 | .32 | (.016) | .40 | .16 | (.109) | .47 | .39 | (.012) | (.014) | (.075) |
| 1982[a] | .69 | .48 | (.002) | .60 | .36 | (.010) | .65 | .59 | (.001) | (.005) | (.022) |
| 1983[a] | .63 | .40 | (.006) | .64 | .41 | (.006) | .63 | .58 | (.001) | (.010) | (.009) |
| 1985 | .54 | .29 | (.024) | .63 | .40 | (.006) | .70 | .66 | (.000) | (.002) | (.001) |

Sources: OECD, 1985, Social Expenditure, 1960–1990, pp. 79–97; OECD, 1988, The Future of Social Protection, p. 10; OECD, Development Cooperation, 1985, p. 131; and ibid., various years.

Notes: Significance levels are given in parentheses. $N = 17$ throughout; all DAC countries but Ireland are included. Data use French expenditures excluding DOM & TOM.

[a] Social expenditures for 1982 and 1983 are the 1982–83 average; separate figures were available for ODA and PVO only in those years.

lar concern in favor of development a way to undergird its aid policy politically. The association between official development assistance and private voluntary spending on Third World economic development thus adds some further weight to the evidence that aid responded to concern in the DAC countries about Third World poverty.

Countries where individual citizen concern about Third World poverty was strong also tended to have strong aid programs, especially after the midseventies. Those countries with the most vigorous aid programs, Norway, Sweden, and the Netherlands, were just those with very substantial levels of PVO contributions, as appears in table 4.3, while those with very low PVO contributions had low levels of ODA/GNP, except for France. Those with "intermediate" levels of PVO support ranged from very weak ODA support to quite substantial. The PVO indicator fails notably in five main cases. Denmark, France, and Australia had low levels of PVO contributions (.0018%, .0005%, and .0017% of GNP) but had high levels of ODA. They were ranked fourth, sixth, and eighth in 1982–83 ODA/ GNP, if France's aid to DOM and TOM is excluded; including that aid, France would be roughly tied for fourth. The United States and Switzerland, on the other hand, had fairly high levels of PVO contributions (.0039% and .0045%) but quite low levels of ODA/GNP. However, France's level of PVO contributions, though still low, tripled as a percentage of GNP over the decade from 1975 to 1985, while its aid rose substantially, and U.S. and Australian levels of PVO contributions, like U.S. and Australian aid, have been declining. Also it is worth noting that in all these cases except Australia, social spending was high where PVO contributions were low, and vice versa.

The combination of social expenditures and private voluntary contributions to Third World development is particularly powerful in explaining aid spending, as table 4.4 indicates. Correlations between aid and private charitable expenditures are positive from the start of the data we have on them, around 1970, and become significant in 1977 and from 1981 onward, hovering close to significance (.10 or less) from 1976 on, while the correlations of social expenditures and aid are also strong, as noted above. Taken together, PVO contributions and social spending as percentages of GNP give remarkably good estimates of aid spending, particularly in recent years. The PVO percentages are positively correlated with social expenditures also, but not strongly, so that regressing aid spending on social expenditures and private voluntary contributions explains 40–70% of the variance in aid spending in the early to middle eighties in years that there is good data for both predictor variables.[14] Public concerns about poverty, expressed in domestic social spending and donations to international charitable causes, give strong, and increasingly strong, explanations of differences in aid spending between donors.

## Explanation of Deviant Cases

What kind of an explanation is there for the deviant cases: for Switzerland and, to an extent, the United States, on the one hand, which have low foreign aid spending despite high public commitment as measured in PVO contributions; and on the other, for France, which has relatively high levels of aid despite low PVO contributions, or for Austria and especially Finland, with low levels of aid despite high or relatively high social spending and social-democratic influence in government? Such explanations are necessarily conjectural, and run the risk of becoming ad hoc; nevertheless, an "analysis of the residuals," a look at cases that are farthest from prediction, can be helpful, and can even increase our understanding of some systematic influences at work.

One way to start is to reconsider our measure of aid commitment: net foreign aid (or ODA) as a fraction of GNP. Foreign aid, although for the most part carefully culled by OECD sources to eliminate military or non-concessional aid, does include some kinds of aid to particular recipients that are at best doubtfully related to economic development, as noted in chapter 3. Prime among these are U.S. aid to Israel and, earlier, to Southeast Asia, and French aid to its overseas territories and departments. Possible doubtful cases would include any expenditure suspiciously high in aid per capita by a patron country to a fairly exclusive recipient, espe-cially one not needing specially high levels of transfer. This would also make the extent of Australian funding to Papua New Guinea questiona-ble, for instance.

In the case of France, there has been dispute for some time in the DAC about whether it is legitimate to count as foreign aid French expenditures in its overseas departments and territories (DOM and TOM). The depart-ments legally are part of France just as Normandy is, though they are not geographically contiguous. Can the U.S. government count as foreign aid its expenditures in Alaska, the argument goes or, more reasonably, Italy its expenditures to improve the economic conditions of Sicily? In many recent DAC reports, the opening table in the statistical annex, "ODA Performance of DAC Countries in Recent Years,"[15] has given ODA and ODA/GNP figures for France both including and excluding "aid" to DOM and TOM. The latter figures, ranging from .42% to .52% of GNP, are much lower than the former, which are in the .58% to .77% range, and are mostly at the upper end. Taking this into account, France, rather than being one of the top donors, is a middle range donor, as would be expected from its social spending, and is closer to what would be ex-pected from its low PVO contributions and few years of social-demo-cratic rule, on the hypotheses set forth earlier. That France's commitment to DAC goals may be less than it at first appears is also indicated by the low extent of its multilateral aid spending, which for years has been markedly below the level customary in DAC countries.

It is interesting to note that there has been change in French aid policy under Mitterand. The socialist French government has rapidly increased the percentage of multilateral aid spending. It has also reversed the de-cline in French aid spending, which had been quite steady since the late fifties, reaching a low of .57% of GNP in 1978 (including DOM and TOM), and which rose to .77% of GNP by 1984 and has stayed roughly constant since, with aid excluding DOM and TOM rising from .38% of GNP in 1979 to .52% in 1984.

Australia's aid, in the middle range despite an absence of socialist rule (except for three years) and low PVO contributions, may also be dis-counted on the grounds of its extraordinary concentration on near neigh-bors—especially Papua New Guinea—and its lack (until recently) of a large share of multilateral aid.

On the other hand, what is the explanation for low Swiss aid contribu-tions despite high Swiss private voluntary contributions and the fact that social democrats were often part of the government and occasionally held the position of prime minister? It is to be noted that the quality of Swiss aid seems to be exemplary, directing aid especially to the poorest recipi-ents and, notably, to those among them with large populations. This seems consonant with the high level of concern expressed in private voluntary development efforts.

Two factors may come into play here, both related to traditional Swiss attitudes. Switzerland has for many years had a particularly vigorous tradition of voluntary aid to those in need: the first Red Cross was created by a Swiss, Dunant; World Red Cross headquarters are still in Switzerland, as are the headquarters for the coordination of worldwide relief for disasters.[16] At the same time, the Swiss have a resistance to central government and international entanglements, an independence that is legendary and keeps the Swiss even yet from joining the United Nations. Thus, high *private* efforts to aid poor lands might be expected to coexist in Switzerland with lesser *governmental* efforts at development. After all, despite the relatively large inclusion of social democrats in the government, social spending and government expenditure in general are about tied with Japan's for lowest in the DAC (as a percentage of GNP) and are far lower than those of the next lowest nation.

Somewhat similar things may be said about the United States as regards resistance to governmental spending and emphasis on nongovernmental organizations. The United States's foreign aid is very low, in comparison to that of other DAC donors. It remains so even if the percentage of ODA is reckoned relative to central government expenditure (CGE) rather than to GNP, to take account of the United States's relatively small governmental sector. In this respect, considering the anti–central government traditions in the United States provides less of an explanation for its low aid spending than it does for Swiss spending. But of course less explanation is needed: the United States has no social-democratic participation in government at all. What the United States's history does help explain is the relatively high level of private voluntary support for development. The United States, at least since the time of Tocqueville, has been noted for the strength of its private associations, and is somewhat noted as well for its compassionate responses to earthquakes, floods, and other disasters. This at least in part accounts for the discrepancy between PVO and government support of Third World economic development.

## SIMILARITY AMONG DAC DONORS: THE DAC'S UNIQUENESS

Just as one can ask why one DAC donor and not another was a strong aid donor, one can ask how the set of DAC donors compares to other donors or possible donors, and what the implications of this comparison are. While this book is concerned with explaining the foreign aid of DAC donors, it is important to look at how DAC donors compare with other donors or possible donors. For one thing, restricting our attention to DAC countries, and treating them as a group and their behavior as part

TABLE 4.5
Economic Aid to the Third World from Soviet Bloc (CMEA) Countries (Millions of U.S. Dollars)

| From the Soviet Union | 1970 | 1971 | 1972 | 1973 | 1974 | 1975 | 1976 | 1977 | 1978 | 1979 | 1980 | 1981 | 1982 | 1983 |
|---|---|---|---|---|---|---|---|---|---|---|---|---|---|---|
| To CMEA countries[a] | 565 | 574 | 541 | 613 | 628 | 1,185 | 1,200 | 1,200 | 1,225 | 1,490 | 1,640 | 2,015 | 2,060 | 2,110 |
| To other allies[b] | 173 | 173 | 175 | 174 | 172 | 104 | 64 | 62 | 76 | 144 | 438 | 363 | 259 | 315 |
| Repayments | -100 | -100 | -100 | -100 | -100 | -110 | -135 | -135 | -135 | -135 | -135 | -140 | -140 | -140 |
| Net to allies[c] | 638 | 647 | 616 | 687 | 700 | 1,179 | 1,129 | 1,127 | 1,166 | 1,499 | 1,943 | 2,238 | 2,179 | 2,285 |
| To non-allies[d] | 351 | 374 | 453 | 517 | 374 | 389 | 410 | 440 | 449 | 437 | 384 | 376 | 301 | 290 |
| Repayments | -215 | -241 | -246 | -281 | -316 | -344 | -460 | -368 | -375 | -381 | -393 | -409 | -411 | -415 |
| Net to non-allies[d] | 136 | 133 | 207 | 236 | 58 | 45 | -50 | 88 | -74 | 56 | -9 | -33 | -110 | -125 |
| Memo items | | | | | | | | | | | | | | |
| Scholarships | 25 | 26 | 29 | 32 | 30 | 45 | 60 | 70 | 105 | 155 | 180 | 220 | 252 | 250 |
| Multilateral aid | 4 | 4 | 5 | 5 | 5 | 5 | 6 | 5 | 6 | 7 | 7 | 6 | 4 | 4 |

| From Eastern Europe | 1970 | 1971 | 1972 | 1973 | 1974 | 1975 | 1976 | 1977 | 1978 | 1979 | 1980 | 1981 | 1982 | 1983 |
|---|---|---|---|---|---|---|---|---|---|---|---|---|---|---|
| To CMEA countries[a] | 150 | 150 | 125 | 150 | 125 | 125 | 192 | 152 | 152 | 152 | 310 | 330 | 370 | 370 |
| To other allies[b] | 1 | 0 | 2 | 0 | 2 | 1 | 8 | 11 | 22 | 52 | 58 | 66 | 56 | 55 |
| Repayments | -20 | -20 | -20 | -20 | -20 | -20 | -30 | -30 | -33 | -33 | -33 | -33 | -33 | -33 |
| Net to allies[c] | 131 | 130 | 107 | 130 | 107 | 106 | 170 | 133 | 141 | 171 | 335 | 363 | 393 | 392 |
| To non-allies[d] | 125 | 174 | 163 | 159 | 184 | 219 | 200 | 209 | 234 | 307 | 230 | 205 | 144 | 105 |
| Repayments | -77 | -86 | -95 | -104 | -115 | -119 | -126 | -136 | -148 | -155 | -164 | -170 | -175 | -177 |
| Net to non-allies[d] | 48 | 88 | 68 | 55 | 69 | 100 | 74 | 73 | 86 | 152 | 66 | 35 | -31 | -72 |
| Memo items | | | | | | | | | | | | | | |
| Scholarships | 17 | 19 | 19 | 21 | 20 | 26 | 46 | 50 | 74 | 120 | 130 | 140 | 165 | 165 |
| Multilateral aid | 2 | 2 | 3 | 3 | 4 | 5 | 5 | 5 | 5 | 6 | 7 | 7 | 6 | 5 |

Source: OECD, Development Cooperation, 1984, pp. 242–43.
Notes: Figures are in millions of U.S. dollars. All categories but repayments and subtotals are gross figures.
[a] Soviet bloc countries (Council for Mutual Economic Assistance, or CMEA).
[b] Other close Soviet allies: Cuba, Afghanistan, and Mongolia.
[c] Cuba, Afghanistan, Mongolia, and CMEA, net of repayments.
[d] Non-allied refers to all LDCs other than Cuba, Afghanistan, Mongolia, and CMEA.

of a regime to be explained requires explicit justification. Also, although there were substantial differences among DAC donors, these should not be allowed to obscure the even more striking uniformities among these countries. The contrast with other donors and possible donors illustrates graphically the distinctiveness and uniformity of the DAC countries as a group. At the same time, the norms developed by the DAC countries have influenced others, and that influence is a part of the development of norms that a practice like foreign aid generates.

The DAC countries were the center of the foreign aid regime in two senses: they provided the bulk of the foreign aid, considered by any standards, and they were characterized by the properties that, as set out in chapter 2, set foreign aid apart from past economic foreign policy: aid was substantial, international, public, and concessional and had an economic-developmental focus. DAC donors chiefly differed from OPEC and communist donors in many of these same respects: the aid was a larger and/or more reliable source; it was much more international, given to more recipients, and more publicly; and it was provided from a much more diverse base.

OECD aid began in the fifties, and most DAC donors gradually increased their aid over time.[17] Aid was made available to almost all developing countries—the few exceptions have largely ceased—and increasingly from diverse sources and through a multilateral process. Soviet bloc aid (referred to as aid from the CMEA, or Council for Mutual Economic Assistance), on the other hand, started up in the late fifties at a much lower level, was often promised but not delivered, was offered in many cases on terms that were nearer commercial than concessional rates, came mostly from the Soviet Union and hardly at all through multilateral channels, and increasingly was cut back to a few countries of obvious strategic value to the USSR. OPEC aid is an in-between case. It started in a big way in 1973 (although there had been a bit of aid from Kuwait before) and attained extraordinary volume as a percentage of GNP at first, but it later declined sharply; and the distribution was primarily bilateral, largely directed to Arab states, and increasingly funded by Kuwait and Saudi Arabia.

A brief look at the breakdown of foreign aid from Eastern Europe and the Soviet Union over the period from 1970 to 1983, given in table 4.5, shows that its character was utterly different from that of OECD aid. The total amount of net Soviet and East European aid was tiny: about the same as the contributions of private voluntary organizations in the West, about a third of Western contributions to multilateral organizations, about a tenth of the Western aid total, and a third to a half of OPEC contributions. The amount of Soviet and Eastern European multilateral contributions was negligible, averaging less than $10 million per year, compared to a Western $9 billion in 1983, for instance. Of the bilateral total, 80% to 90% came from the Soviet Union, as opposed to some 25% of OECD aid from the United States (or 55% at the height of U.S. aid hegemony in the late fifties and early sixties), or as opposed to some two thirds of OPEC aid from Saudi Arabia. Most strikingly, this aid was distributed preponderantly to close allies, and only these allies seem to have received aid on highly concessional terms. In early years, over 80% of net bilateral aid (excluding scholarships, whose distribution is not available) went to five close allies: Cuba, Vietnam, Mongolia, Afghanistan, and North Korea. As time went on, the amount of net bilateral aid to other countries declined further, becoming negative in six out of the last eight years given for the Soviet Union and negative for aid from Eastern Europe in the last two.[18] Gross bilateral aid to countries other than the few close Soviet allies also declined, ending up around 10% to 15% of the Soviet "foreign aid" total. Net bilateral aid to countries other than the five countries just mentioned was less than the net bilateral aid of Finland for the same period. Two thirds went to Vietnam and Cuba alone. In sum, Soviet bloc aid was small in volume, not multilaterally channeled, and heavily concentrated on a half-dozen strategic allies; and "aid" to other countries does not appear to have been on concessional terms.

OPEC aid has been much closer to having the characteristics that made OECD aid distinctive. OPEC aid is not as easy to explain in self-interested terms as Soviet aid is. OPEC aid has been sizable, particularly since 1973; it has fluctuated substantially, however. Rising from a total of $385 million in 1970 to $5.4 billion in 1975 and $9.5 billion in 1980, OPEC aid has fallen sharply since 1981, to some $1.5 billion in 1989. Throughout the seventies and early eighties, aid as a percentage of GNP was 3% to 6% in Saudi Arabia, Kuwait, and the United Arab Emirates (UAE); but by the end of the eighties, Saudi aid was 1–2% of GNP, Kuwait and Libya about .5%, and the UAE down to .1% and, in 1988, to even negative net disbursements. Libya also had an aid program early, and has continued it at a very respectable .3% to .5% of GNP level. Other OPEC donors, however, had negligible programs, if any, before the rise of oil prices in the seventies, and had declined to percentages under .2% of GNP by 1984. It remains to be seen whether OPEC aid will be lasting. This of course is not altogether to OPEC's discredit: the forces that permitted very high levels of aid earlier—the huge oil bonanzas of the seventies—have been replaced by weaker and fluctuating oil prices. And the aid programs of Saudi Arabia, Kuwait, and the UAE were for a time far more ample (as a percentage of GNP) than anything in the West since the Marshall Plan; Saudi Arabia has continued a very high, even though reduced, level of funding.

OPEC aid has been considerably more parochial than OECD aid in a variety of ways. Saudi aid, 40–60% of the OPEC total in the seventies,[19] rose to 75% by the mideighties and ranged as high as 90% in the late eighties. The multilateral part of aid was at most $1.5 billion; but multilateral aid provided through institutions of broad membership (the UN, World Bank, or regional development banks—as opposed to exclusively Arab, Islamic, or OPEC institutions) was never above about $0.5 billion. On the other hand, multilateral aid does continue to be about 14% of Arab aid, with Kuwait, Libya, Algeria, and Qatar providing half or more of their aid multilaterally in 1988–89. Arab bilateral aid, and the aid from specifically Arab multilateral agencies, was concentrated rather narrowly, insofar as figures were made public. In 1983–84 about one third of OPEC bilateral aid consisted of Saudi treasury grants for which no breakdown is available; one third went to Jordan, Syria, and Bahrain (all with GNP per capita over $1,500); one third to all other countries. This last third was itself fairly concentrated. Similarly, in 1984–87, 36% of Arab bilateral aid was reported without a specified destination, and another 37% went to upper middle income countries. In 1981–82, aid for which there are available figures show the Arab bilateral and Arab agency aid together as distributing over 85% of their aid to twenty countries of small size; some 6% went to Bangladesh, Pakistan, and India combined (population 900 million, GNP per capita about $300); 42% went to Syria and Jordan (population 12 million, GNP per capita about $1,650). Six and a half percent went to Oman and Bahrain (population 2 million, GNP per capita above $5,000); 22% went to Morocco, Yemen, Sudan, and Lebanon. The concentration on Arab countries raises questions about whether the purpose of the aid was an attempt to buy friendship and influence, and to diffuse criticism of the concentration of wealth in a few Arab states, concerns that showed their importance visibly in the 1991 Gulf War. At the same time, OPEC aid to broadly based multilaterals, at 10–15% of the total, is more clearly directed to development; and Arab countries have allocated a nonnegligible share of aid to least developed countries (about 16% of their total aid, 26% of the amount whose allocation is known, in 1984–87).[20]

Thus, there are several reasons to focus upon OECD aid. It constitutes some four fifths of aid over the last decade. Further, here is aid that has been consistent over a period of thirty to thirty-five years. It is the main source of aid that is available to most potential recipients. It constitutes a large set of somewhat independent cases—as opposed to the CMEA countries, whose aid consisted largely of Soviet aid (even assuming the other countries have had independently shaped aid policies), or to the OPEC countries, whose aid is largely of Saudi (and, to a degree, Kuwaiti) origins and is—in countries other than those two, at least—of recent origin and subject to wild swings in volume. OECD aid also is channeled in considerable measure through multilateral institutions. Of this, some $2 billion, over four times the total to all broad-based multilaterals from other sources, goes to the largely recipient-controlled UN programs.[21] Its bilateral aid is not concentrated even nearly as narrowly as that of other groups of donors: French, Japanese, and American bilateral aid, perhaps historically of the worst quality in the OECD, is far more dispersed. Soviet and other CMEA bilateral aid was small to nonexistent, apart from alliance support, and was given mainly on nonconcessional terms; CMEA multilateral aid was utterly negligible. OPEC aid is fairly recent, narrowly concentrated, and heavily bilateral.

To restrict the focus to OECD aid omits from consideration only a very few donors that played a long-term role that involved something beyond alliance support. Further, the OECD donors are the core of the phenomenon, not only in terms of bulk and length of time but in terms of the development of standards that affected the shape of the whole aid process. There are also compelling reasons of feasibility to stick with OECD donors: only they have open political processes, and only they have published consistent statistics on the distribution of their aid. In short, the treatment here covers the bulk of what went on—the bulk of the time, the bulk of the aid, the bulk of the countries that were serious long-term participants, and the center of the action that defined the international processes involved in aid.

The other cases must be borne in mind, however, and indeed they provide interesting contrasts to OECD aid. In critiquing OECD aid, it is helpful to keep contrasting possibilities in mind. In this framework, the wide distribution of even the most concentrated OECD donors appears not in comparison to some hypothetical ideal but in comparison with strategies actually adhered to by others. The strategic and economic possibilities for aid appear as alternatives to the policies that actually were pursued, for the most part, by the DAC.

## Solidity of Support over Time

It is interesting to note, in considering the factors that sustained support for foreign aid over the long haul, that the few DAC donors that ever consistently *declined* in the percentage of GNP given to aid over several decades were ex-colonial powers (Britain, and earlier France and Italy) or two states, the United States and Australia, whose aid contained conspicuous elements of concentration on special relationships with Third World countries of possible security value to the donor. (France and Italy, whose aid turned upward in the 1980–84 period, had declined in aid,

TABLE 4.6

Trends in DAC Donors' Net Disbursed Aid: Five Year Intervals, 1950–1989
(Percentages of GNP)

| | 1950–1955 | 1956–1959 | 1960–1964 | 1965–1969 | 1970–1974 | 1975–1979 | 1980–1984 | 1985–1989 |
|---|---|---|---|---|---|---|---|---|
| Australia | — | — | .45 | .58 | .56 | .51 | .48 | .43 |
| Austria | — | — | .04 | .12 | .11 | .20 | .29 | .25 |
| Belgium | .11 | .34 | .64 | .48 | .50 | .54 | .56 | .47 |
| Canada | .10 | .17 | .15 | .29 | .43 | .50 | .44 | .47 |
| Denmark | — | .12 | .11 | .23 | .44 | .61 | .76 | .88 |
| Finland | — | — | .04 | .06 | .13 | .17 | .29 | .51 |
| France | | | | | | | | |
| (including DOM/TOM) | 1.24 | 1.44 | 1.17 | .70 | .65 | .60 | .72 | .74 |
| (excluding DOM/TOM) | — | — | — | — | .39 | .36 | .47 | .54 |
| Germany | .11 | .20 | .41 | .39 | .34 | .38 | .46 | .42 |
| Ireland | — | — | — | — | — | — | — | .22 |
| Italy | .23 | .22 | .16 | .16 | .13 | .11 | .23 | .36 |
| Japan | .04 | .49 | .18 | .28 | .23 | .23 | .31 | .31 |
| Netherlands | .27 | .43 | .36 | .46 | .60 | .81 | 1.01 | .96 |
| New Zealand | — | — | .19 | .19 | .25 | .40 | .28 | .26 |
| Norway | .04 | .12 | .14 | .22 | .42 | .81 | .97 | 1.09 |
| Sweden | .04 | .08 | .11 | .28 | .49 | .86 | .85 | .88 |
| Switzerland | .02 | .18 | .06 | .11 | .15 | .19 | .27 | .31 |
| United Kingdom | .42 | .42 | .54 | .44 | .40 | .44 | .37 | .31 |
| United States | .32 | .48 | .57 | .46 | .28 | .24 | .24 | .21 |
| DAC total | .34 | .48 | .51 | .42 | .33 | .34 | .36 | .35 |
| DAC median | .10 | .22 | .18 | .28 | .40 | .44 | .44 | .45 |

Sources: OECD, Development Cooperation, 1985, p. 335; and OECD, Development Cooperation, 1989, pp. 188, 211.

Note: The 1956–59 average for Norway assumes that a lack of reported aid in 1958 means that Norway gave no aid that year. Thus, the actual figure for this period may be slightly higher.

prior to that, since the late fifties.) By contrast, those donors whose aid rose furthest and most consistently were countries without significant strategic interests or possibilities, or colonial ties—Switzerland, Sweden, Norway, Finland, Denmark—except for the Netherlands. However, the share of Dutch aid going to former colonies had fallen off greatly by 1970, when the steep rise in the Dutch aid total began, and the colonial share continued to diminish through the seventies.

Very specifically, the two donors showing the most decline in their aid—the United States and France—were arguably the two whose rationales for aid were the most self-interested. French aid was, it is true, high as a percentage of GNP despite the decline, if one counts all aid. If one excludes the extremely doubtful aid to overseas dominions and territories (DOM/TOM), however, French aid was in the moderately high category only; and other examples of apparently self-serving French aid could be found as well. France's percentage of multilateral aid was the lowest in the DAC. The United States devoted about half its bilateral foreign aid to Security-Supporting Assistance, and domestic opponents of aid effectively demanded that aid be justified on grounds of serving U.S. vital interests. Japan, whose aid tended to be more focused on commercial targets, wobbled around an aid-to-GNP ratio that was low during the seventies, while all but two or three other DAC members increased their aid, as table 4.6 indicates. However, when Japan and particularly France started to improve the quality of their aid, giving more to multilateral organizations around 1980, for instance, the total quantity of aid also rose. Although all three countries did give substantial aid that served developmental goals, it is interesting to note how rationales for aid that emphasized narrow national interests tended to go with weak support for aid in the long term.

While there is no firm evidence on this point, a plausible conjecture would be that donors, even those starting with strong aid programs, which based their domestic advocacy of aid upon claims and concerns not cleanly connected to a simple rationale of helping the poor did not fare particularly well in their aid programs in the long run. The tempting strategy of billing aid programs as serving direct national interests, even if effective in the short run, was not able to sustain support for the programs. Rather, it was those countries which based their aid on a rationale that emphasized Third World development, rather than donor advantages, which were able to build strong, long-lasting aid programs.

## Conclusion

Chapter 3 argued that whatever end donors had in mind in giving aid should show up in where they spent the aid. The argument of this chapter is complementary. If the factors that motivated donors varied from donor to donor (or potential donor), then there should be corresponding variations in their aid programs. In both chapters it is possible to argue in two ways: on one hand, there is little evidence that economic and political factors greatly influenced aid spending *in most cases*, and on the other, there is a good deal of evidence that concern for the poverty of the recipients heavily influenced aid spending. The evidence of the preceding chapter is particularly helpful in examining whether aid was spent in a way that promoted donor economic interests most effectively. The evidence of this chapter helps in examining the influence of donor international political objectives on their aid programs. And here it appears that the strengthened longevity of the OECD countries' aid programs varied not with the varying incentives their strategic positions gave them but with the internal political climate, and the extent to which that disposed countries to policies favoring the poor at home and abroad.

The major line of analysis has been to examine differences in the aid spending of the DAC donor countries, which are this book's primary concern. Those donor countries with the widest global aspirations and interests, and the most possibility of global influence, have not been particularly vigorous aid donors, measured in the percentage of GNP allocated to foreign aid. Similarly, those which concentrated their aid upon states in their own region, as Japan and Australia did, have not had particularly strong aid records. Those donors with strong social democratic influence, high social spending at home, and more citizen voluntary contributions to overseas development, however, have tended to have the strongest aid programs. Most of these—the Netherlands, Norway, Sweden, Denmark—are countries with few overseas political interests that are of current importance to them or that figure in their aid programs, and have little or no possibility of building any. Also, it has appeared that those countries, such as the four just named, which have emphasized the humanitarian rationales for aid have maintained aid programs that grew stronger over time, while those—the United States in particular—which prominently included strategic rationales for aid in their initial discussions of foreign aid have fallen off in their aid spending.

Of course, not all foreign aid has been motivated by humanitarian considerations. Various kinds of national self-interest played strong roles, particularly in some of the donors' programs. France clearly was interested in promoting French influence in its former colonies. True, this may have included a kind of influence hard to fit into the Realist paradigm—the *besoin de rayonnement*, for instance—but French motives certainly involved a continued French presence in Africa and maintenance of colonial or quasi-colonial ties. This motivation showed up not only in where bilateral aid was spent but also in the low level multilateral aid spending. The United States, likewise, clearly was motivated in at least half of its bilateral spending by strategic considerations. And of course it is quite possible that other strategic rationales, not so easy to isolate, may have influenced other donors. At the same time, even in these cases that are the worst for my argument, there remains a good deal of aid spending that is hard to account for along national self-interest lines. And—the main point of this chapter—there is strong positive evidence that those donors which had self-interested rationales for aid on the whole had weak aid programs, while those which stressed humanitarian concerns and the need for international cooperation had very strong aid programs.

Also, noting the differences in the aid programs of the OECD donors in this way should not obscure the extraordinary similarities their aid programs shared. For this reason, contrast with CMEA and OPEC programs, as well as with the DAC donors' own past, is helpful in setting the DAC aid programs in proper perspective. One notes the third of DAC aid multilaterally channeled, the steadiness of the programs over time, the concessional terms on which they are offered, their availability to virtually any Third World country, and the relative absence of tying of aid. These features may not seem as striking as they really are until one sees that even where something superficially like OECD foreign aid—and originally developed as a rival to it—was initiated by the Soviet bloc, it retained none of these features but was concentrated on clear allies, was not at nearly such concessional terms, and primarily consisted of tied aid, that is, of goods and services provided by the donor. This only underscores the departure that OECD aid was from previous forms of international transactions, a massive fact not to be lost sight of amid discussions of the details of DAC donor differences.

## CHAPTER FIVE

# Who Advocated Aid:
## Supporters and Opponents of Development Assistance

> My own view has always been that the purpose of foreign aid is not just to fight a Cold War, but to build a better world. Our aid programs express the true voice of America, the spirit of our continuing revolution. We have only to look at the terse statistics of human need: 83% of the world's people underfed, more than 60% illiterate, 70% sick or poorly housed. The ancient adversaries of mankind—poverty, hunger, disease, and ignorance—are the allies of tyranny; they are the real enemies of mankind, more than the militancy of a Mao or a Khrushchev. They grip large portions of the world.
>
> —Hubert Humphrey[1]

> Has the Foreign Aid program . . . contribut[ed] toward winning the Cold War? . . . This test . . . is the only one under which the Foreign Aid program can be justified. It cannot, that is to say, be defended as a charity. The American government does not have the right, much less the obligation, to try to promote the economic and social welfare of foreign peoples. . . . We should eliminate all government-to-government capital assistance and encourage the substitution of American private investment. . . . [Aid] has not . . . made the free world stronger; it has made America weaker.
>
> —Barry Goldwater[2]

THERE IS direct as well as indirect evidence that aid was based on humanitarian principle and commitment to a world community. Evidence about motive is often pooh-poohed by Realists. Morgenthau says you cannot know anyone's motives, that even if you knew them, motives would not tell all, that philosophical differences do not affect policy, and so on. Structural Realists are apt to regard motive as epiphenomenal. Thus it was important to start by demonstrating consistent state behavior which gave evidence that actual policy responded to differences in domestic philosophy, as the previous chapters have done. Evidence about how aid money was spent and about which donors were more committed to aid showed DAC donors acted *as if* they sought recipient welfare. But we need not rest content with an *as if* argument. Detailed evidence about public opinion, political parties and leaders, domestic interest groups, leading advocates and critics of aid, and international groups that supported aid shows that the motives for giving aid were closely tied to the domestic political and personal moral philosophy of the advocates, and that humanitarian motives were the strongest basis of support for aid domestically. International norms exerted a growing influence on donors, too, which will be examined in this chapter as something that sustained aid and its expansion, in chapter 6, as creating the climate in which it was possible for aid to get started, and in chapters 7 and 8, as a factor that sustained aid and led to improvements in its quality and quantity.

Public opinion strongly supported aid in most DAC countries. But the variations in support suggest that public support was an important factor in sustaining aid programs and, also, that the basis of public support was strongly humanitarian and linked to domestic political views. Those countries with relatively weak public support were relatively slack aid donors, and countries with particularly high levels of support seem to have expanded their aid programs rapidly. The relatively few elite studies seem to line up with mass opinion data. The people who were most apt to support aid were not those particularly concerned with national security issues or those opposed to communism. Rather, people on the left, people concerned about reducing domestic inequality, and people concerned with remedying regional inequalities in Europe were the political groups most supportive of aid. In addition, wealthier people, young people, students especially, people from professional families and union families, and people with regular religious practice tended to support aid. There is specific support for the contentions made in the last chapter that those who favored strong social welfare spending favored aid, that those who were apt to contribute to private voluntary organizations helping the Third World favored aid, and that moderate left parties favored aid.

There was strong consensus that aid should serve humanitarian goals and that the right reasons for giving aid were the moral ones. Strong supporters of aid almost invariably expressed a strong moral basis for their support, and their intention that aid be directed to the poor and that it be divorced from national strategic or economic goals was much more pronounced than among those less in favor of aid. Most people felt aid should go to countries that needed aid and used it well: there was little support, in Europe at any rate, for the idea of directing aid toward countries which were of economic or strategic significance for the donor. Most people felt the best motive for giving aid was a humanitarian one—because of need, because poor countries needed help to get on their feet, or "because we have so much"—and the strongest single predictor of support for aid, itself accounting for 37% of the variance, was agreement with the proposition "it is our moral duty to help" poor countries. In one study, those who expressed egocentric values in personal life were far less prone to support aid. Moreover, those few who felt that aid should be given not for humane reasons but for strategic reasons did not really want aid to be given, anyhow; such people tended to be for cutting or decreasing aid. The strongest supporters of aid were particularly strong in opposing the use of aid for the advancement of particularistic national interests.

An interesting ambiguity emerges with respect to the idea of "national interest" however, which helps to clarify the relation between support of aid on the grounds that it will make a more prosperous, safer, stabler world and support of aid on the basis of compassion or of duty to help people in need. In the extensive ten-country Euro-Barometer study on aid to the Third World, those who thought it in the national interest to help poor countries tended to be those who thought it a moral duty. Those who thought it in the national interest to help poor countries were more likely than others to support increased aid but less likely than others to say aid should be given in a way that promoted specific national interests (security, trade, raw materials), however; and this effect remains when one controls for the association with belief that aid is a duty. The view that helping poor countries is "in our interest" appears, then, to amount to a belief that the national interest justifies a general commitment to making the world a better place, and decidedly not to the belief that pursuit of the national interest should consist in calculating the special advantages which accrue to one's own nation particularly. It appears to involve an expansion of national identity beyond national borders, the identification of the national interest with a wider global interest, a kind of world citizenship which says it is in my country's own interest to be a good citizen, for without a just and civic world, all will suffer.[3] Official statements of national aid policy were also in broad agreement that a just, prosperous world is in the national interest, and that both humanitarian concern and this interest in building a better world are good reasons for the country to support foreign aid.

The same patterns emerge when we look at parties, politicians, interest groups, intellectuals, and worldwide organizations that pushed for aid. Those that wanted more aid wanted aid divorced from national interests; they tended to be groups and persons with strong moral or religious principles and those on the moderate left. In country after country, the politicians and political parties that strongly advocated aid were those on the left, and factions within political parties that advocated aid were those which were concerned with idealistic causes. Aid supporters advocated increased aid, delinking aid from specific national interests, and aid more focused on the needy. There is considerable evidence, also, that in power they put their ideas into practice. Groups and individuals with strong laissez-faire principles tended to be opposed to aid, yet all but the most principled also sought to tie aid to national interests. Thus, business groups lobbied to tie aid to purchases in the donor country but usually were at best indifferent to having an aid program. The domestic groups that advocated aid tended to be unions, church groups, and charitable organizations; they were notable for wanting purer aid as well as more aid.

Similarly, prominent worldwide advocates and opponents of aid linked their views to their basic political and philosophical positions. The strongest institutional advocates of aid were church and labor groups and private voluntary groups concerned with the Third World, such as Oxfam. The voices raised against aid were long those on the right, and they opposed aid specifically because of its similarity to the welfare state: they felt that in a free market, poor countries would do well, and that aid only increased bureaucracy and created big government and dependence. Milton Friedman, P. T. Bauer, the American Enterprise Institute, taxpayers groups, Edward Banfield, and so on opposed aid. The voices in favor of aid were those of prominent social democrats like Gunnar Myrdal, Willi Brandt, and strong internationalists like Paul Hoffman and Barbara Ward. After the Vietnam War, there were also critics of aid on the extreme left—Frances Moore Lappe and Theresa Hayter, particularly— who felt that aid simply promoted the extension of capitalism in the Third World. There is no evidence whatever, though, of aid being advocated or strongly opposed on the basis of a strategic rationale unconnected with any strong ideological position.

In sum, domestic political and philosophical views seem to have shaped both the moral attitudes toward aid and the perception of the international system that made support for the welfare of poor countries seem either wasted money or an essential investment in world order. Countries seem to have been strongly influenced by their domestic political orientations, and those of the parties in power, in selecting their foreign aid policies. At the same time, the growing international consensus on aid among the DAC countries also seems to have shaped what countries thought, and what they thought their proper obligations were. Thus, both domestic society and international factors influenced what countries did about foreign aid. Yet in the mix of considerations, humanitarian motives clearly had the strongest influence, on the public at large and on strong advocates of aid.

PUBLIC OPINION DATA: STRENGTH OF PUBLIC SUPPORT FOR AID

Public support for foreign aid programs has been uniform and strong in the developed democracies in recent years, just as the programs themselves have been. The countries with stronger public support have tended to have stronger aid programs, and those with support for increasing aid have showed rapid increases, while countries with weak support have had stagnant or declining aid.

A sizable majority of respondents—61% to 80%—in each of ten EEC countries in a 1983 Euro-Barometer survey identified "helping poor countries" as an "important" or "very important" goal, and in no country did more than 11% identify this as "not important at all." In the ten countries taken together, 22% identified helping poor countries as a national goal that was very important and an additional 45% saw it as important.[4] The percentages of those favoring an increase in aid ranged from 20% to 48%, while only 4% to 20% in various countries favored a decrease in aid. Overall, 32% favored increasing aid, and a mere 10% wanted a decrease. In an earlier (1980) Euro-Barometer poll, most respondents wanted to keep aid at its current levels, while 24% favored an increase in aid, and 25% wanted to decrease it.[5] Earlier data for most European countries is consistent with this. The exception seems to be Austria, where a 1980 poll is reported to show "the public at large does not seem to be particularly interested in development issues" and where aid is among the weakest in the DAC in volume and quality.[6]

Scandinavian public support for aid has been consistently high. A 1968 poll in Sweden found that 33% of Swedes surveyed thought aid should be increased, and 49% thought it was "about right as it is," with only 11% in favor of reducing or eliminating aid. A survey of similar polls from the 1966 to 1969 period in Sweden shows similar results. In the 1980s, polls reported in *Development Cooperation* show a 50% to 60% majority in favor of maintaining aid at its current high levels, with 15% to 17% favoring an increase and 5% to 24% wanting a decrease. Forty-eight percent of Danes favored the 1% of GNP target for aid—a strong test of support—in 1960; this fell to 36% to 40% in the midsixties but rose to 54% in 1975 and 60% in 1983. Polls from Norway in the 1974 to 1983 period are reported as showing "steadily growing" support for aid, while more wanted an increase than a decrease in 1983, even after Norway attained the 1% of GNP target.

The cases of Japan, Italy, and Finland are particularly interesting because of the conjunction between high levels of public support for increasing aid and rapid increases in levels of aid. *Development Cooperation* reports the numbers of Japanese in favor of increasing aid as at 40% from 1977 through 1983, with only 3% to 7% in favor of a reduction. The Japanese started in the late seventies to strengthen their historically weak foreign aid program. Italians were particularly supportive of increasing aid in the 1983 and 1980 Euro-Barometer surveys, with fully 48% favoring an increase and only 8% favoring a decrease in 1983. Italian aid figures climbed rapidly in the early eighties, as well. A 1981 poll showed a staggering 80% of Finns in favor of increasing aid, with 55% still in favor in 1984 despite rapid increases in aid funding. Finnish aid increased by almost a factor of three in the course of the decade. Early results from the Netherlands, whose aid rose rapidly in the 1970s, also show strong percentages in favor of increases until (but not after) attaining the 1% target. Thirty-six percent of the Swiss in 1984 favored increasing aid, with only 8% wanting a reduction, and Switzerland, too, increased its aid substantially in the early eighties.

American public opinion, while substantially weaker, is nevertheless clearly in favor of having an aid program. An extensive 1974 survey by Laudicina finds 68% of Americans in favor of aid, with 28% opposed. But he finds many Americans, unlike Europeans, thinking their country was "doing more than it should" to combat world poverty (44%), while only 17% thought it was doing "less than it should," and only 8% favored an increase in foreign aid, while 47% favored a decrease.[7] Wittkopf traces American public opinion about aid in the late forties and early fifties and in the period from 1974 to 1986, and finds support hovering between 69% and 79% in the earlier period, and between 46% and 53% in more recent years, with 18% to 31% opposed in the fifties and 36% to 41% opposed in the later period. American aid rose until the midsixties but has fallen since then, falling steeply during the Reagan and Bush years;[8] aid behavior has thus been roughly parallel to aid opinion data. Other surveys from the period in between show 51% for and 33% opposed in 1958, and 58% for and 30% against in 1963, with 53% in 1961 favoring a decrease in aid.[9]

Some data from other English-speaking countries suggests intermediate levels of support. Only 12% of the Canadian public in a survey from the early 1960s favored increasing aid. A small 1979 poll in New Zealand showed 69.6% in favor of aid. A 1983 poll showed 65% of Australians in favor of helping Third World countries.[10] An earlier extensive poll in 1969 showed most Britons in favor of reducing aid (36%) or holding it constant (37%), although 81% of Britons favored giving aid.[11]

In sum, public support for aid was generally quite strong, with national policy often lined up with the degree of public support. Support was highest in the European countries with the strongest aid programs, intermediate in Britain, Canada, Australia, and New Zealand, and lowest in aid laggards like Austria and the United States. The lower levels of support in the United States—with the U.S. public alone more in favor of reducing than increasing aid, and with public support declining from a high point in the fifties to a lower level of support from the midseventies on—is particularly interesting in view of the decline of U.S. aid spending, starting in the midsixties, at the same time aid programs of other countries rose or remained constant. Rapid increases in aid occurred in countries with high levels of support for aid and in those where the public said it wanted increases; but aid declined where the public wanted declines.

Thus, the aid data suggest that public support played a substantial role and influenced changes in aid spending. The absence of systematic data makes any formal causal analysis difficult. Generally, scholars conclude that public policy and elite support influence mass public opinion as well as the reverse; and in the case of aid it is certainly the case that in countries with strong aid programs and strong public support there were government efforts to build support for vigorous aid policies.[12] Thus, it is impossible to say with certainty just what the causal relations between public opinion and aid spending are. But the data do create a strong presumption that public support was important; also, elite data, when available, indicate that elites had attitudes similar to those of the general public, although they were generally more favorable toward aid. Thus, the bases of public support for aid should yield important information about reasons that countries favored aid, both as causes and as effects of government policy.

*Bases of Support for Aid*

Chapter 4 argued, on the basis of evidence about differences in national spending patterns, that strategic influence, fear of communism, retention of colonial ties, and promotion of trade and investments did not seem to be important motives in providing aid. Positively, it argued that aid found support from the same values which expressed themselves domestically in concern about issues of poverty and in government action to overcome them, as expressed domestically in the strength of left and social-democratic parties, of social spending, and of private contributions to voluntary organizations concerned with overseas development. The public opinion data confirm each of these assertions.

In the 1983 Euro-Barometer study, when respondents from eight DAC countries are grouped by how they planned to vote in the next election, those on the right were least likely to support aid, and those voting communist in the next election were most likely. Those who placed themselves as on the left half of a left-right scale were more likely to support aid. There was an inverse relation between support for aid and concern about strengthening military defense. Those with positive affect for colonialism (agreeing "they were happier when they were colonies") were less likely to support aid, and those who agreed that Third World nations were "held back" in their development by colonialism were more likely to support aid. These results are statistically significant: they hold true for respondents in each country separately, as well as for all Europe. They are robust, holding up for each of six separate measures of support for aid, and for an index of the six together. And none of them seems to be explained by the others; they all persist and remain significant when put in a regression together, and stay significant, except for views on strengthening military defense, which become insignificant. In Europe fear of communism, strategic concerns, and support for colonialism appear to have led not to support of aid but to disinterest in it.[13]

The opinion results on positive sources of support for aid again confirm the presumptions made in the last chapter. Domestic and personal values seemed to play an important role in the international policies people wanted. Those who counted reducing domestic income inequality an important national goal were significantly more likely to favor foreign aid. Those who had made personal contributions to organizations that helped the Third World were more likely to favor aid. These results, too, were all significant, held for each country separately, and remained in competition with each other, even for people at the same point on left-right scales. The people who lived out concern for the poor in their own lives and favored it as a national goal favored it as an international goal, too.

This same principle is almost certainly at work in the tendency for those on the left to favor aid more than those on the right. In the Euro-Barometer studies of 1980 and 1983, those who place themselves on the left, and those who plan to vote for left parties in the next election are more apt to favor aid. In the United States, Laudicina notes that Democrats were more likely to favor aid than were Republicans, liberals than conservatives, and very religious people than the less religious. And, despite the general tendency for working-class people to be less sympathetic to aid than those of higher income, education, and professional status are, union households were more likely to favor aid than were non-union households.[14] Many of these characteristics are also observable in table 5.1 on page 146, using 1983 Euro-Barometer data, which show how support for aid wanes, on each of four measures, as one moves from left to right, from agreement that the Third World is exploited to disagreement, or from an assessment of domestic poverty issues as important to unimportant.

People with greater political involvement, younger people, students, the better educated, those from professional households, and those with higher income were all more favorable to aid, as well. These effects all show up in all the European countries in the 1983 Euro-Barometer survey. Rauta, in an earlier and more detailed study, shows that Britons who were better educated and who were more informed about aid were more apt to be interested in it, as were those more interested in politics and those more favorable to immigrants and to racial minorities. Laudicina notes the same for Americans. In general, this goes along with consistent findings that elites are more favorable toward aid than is the general public. Lindholm finds a strong correlation of support for increasing aid with university education, with knowledge of the problems of poor countries, and with desire for more information.[15]

In the United States, those who are concerned about international affairs are more apt to favor foreign aid than those who are not; but concerns about cooperation are much more important than opposition to communism. Wittkopf argues in a major book on American public opinion and foreign policy that there have consistently been two different elements in public concern about international affairs, which he terms "cooperative internationalism" (defined by support for international cooperation and détente) and "militant internationalism" (defined by support for sending troops abroad and opposition to communism). Support for foreign aid is greater as one moves toward more concern for foreign affairs along either axis. However, it should be noted that cooperative internationalism (CI) affected support for aid much more strongly than did militant internationalism (MI), as is shown in table 5.2, based on a table in Wittkopf's book. Wittkopf uses high and low placement on these two axes to divide the public into four groups, which he calls Internationalists (high CI, high MI), Accommodationists (high CI, low MI), Hardliners (low CI, high MI), and Isolationists (low CI, low MI). Differences in militant internationalism between Internationalists and Accommodationists made little difference in support for foreign aid, although Isolationists were noticeably less likely to favor aid than were Hardliners. Differences in cooperative internationalism made a very large difference in support for foreign aid in all cases.[16]

### Ideology and the Importance of Conviction

Strong moral and political convictions went with support for aid. People who described themselves as "religious" in the 1983 Euro-Barometer survey were slightly more likely to favor aid than were those who described themselves as not religious; however, the handful who considered themselves atheists were more likely to favor aid than were the merely a-religious, and the "don't knows" were least likely to favor aid. Again, people who did not place themselves on a left-right scale were less likely to favor aid than were those placing themselves anywhere on the scale, except those at the extreme right. The religion variable in the 1983 survey is not a terribly helpful predictor of support because it is divided between about two thirds religious and one third nonreligious, with no other significant groupings. The data from the 1980 Euro-Barometer survey are more helpful. There, a classification based on frequency of attendance at religious services (more than once a week, once a week, rarely or never) allows one to identify those of strong or moderately strong convictions. Regular attenders at services were substantially more likely to favor increases in

TABLE 5.1

Support for Aid Broken Down by Respondent Characteristics and Views (Percentages)

| Respondent Characteristics and Views | (158) Aid Should Be | | (159) In a Recession | |
|---|---|---|---|---|
| | Increased | Decreased | Keep Aid at Current Level | Cut out All Aid |
| Level of education (439) | | | | |
| (31%) High | 40 | 8 | 58 | 6 |
| (39%) Middle | 26 | 12 | 43 | 12 |
| (30%) Low | 25 | 14 | 36 | 13 |
| Is the respondent still in school? (439) | | | | |
| ( 7%) Yes | 52 | 5 | 57 | 11 |
| (93%) No | 29 | 12 | 45 | 5 |
| Left-right self-placement (432) | | | | |
| (26%) Left | 42 | 10 | 52 | 10 |
| (37%) Middle | 28 | 9 | 45 | 9 |
| (25%) Right | 25 | 14 | 45 | 10 |
| We have a moral duty to help Third World (121) | | | | |
| (30%) Agree strongly | 54 | 3 | 68 | 4 |
| (44%) Agree weakly | 26 | 7 | 45 | 7 |
| (20%) Disagree | 9 | 31 | 20 | 26 |
| It is in our interest to help Third World (123) | | | | |
| (28%) Agree strongly | 49 | 4 | 66 | 4 |
| (42%) Agree weakly | 29 | 7 | 47 | 7 |
| (20%) Disagree | 15 | 27 | 24 | 23 |
| What countries should we aid? (155) | | | | |
| (70%) Poorest countries | 36 | 6 | 53 | 6 |
| (22%) Those useful to us | 15 | 22 | 28 | 19 |
| Third World: exploited by countries like ours (114) | | | | |
| (26%) Agree strongly | 43 | 8 | 58 | 9 |
| (34%) Agree weakly | 31 | 10 | 49 | 9 |
| (31%) Disagree | 22 | 16 | 37 | 13 |
| Helping those most in need in our country is (043) | | | | |
| (23%) Very important | 42 | 9 | 53 | 10 |
| (51%) Fairly important | 30 | 9 | 47 | 9 |
| (20%) Less important | 21 | 18 | 40 | 15 |
| Gave time or money to PVO aiding Third World (157) | | | | |
| (60%) Yes | 37 | 6 | 55 | 6 |
| (36%) No | 22 | 19 | 32 | 18 |
| Strengthening military defense is important (051) | | | | |
| (22%) Agree strongly | 28 | 13 | 40 | 13 |
| (35%) Agree weakly | 27 | 11 | 44 | 10 |
| (37%) Disagree | 37 | 10 | 52 | 9 |
| Third World: do not really want to work (115) | | | | |
| (26%) Agree | 43 | 22 | 30 | 19 |
| (27%) Disagree weakly | 29 | 9 | 47 | 7 |
| (36%) Disagree strongly | 19 | 6 | 59 | 6 |
| Third World: happier when they were colonies (119) | | | | |
| (38%) Agree | 47 | 15 | 40 | 6 |
| (22%) Disagree weakly | 35 | 8 | 50 | 7 |
| (18%) Disagree strongly | 21 | 7 | 64 | 14 |

*Source*: Computed from the data of Rabier et al. 1985, *Euro-Barometer 20*, made available by the Inter-University Consortium for Political and Social Research. The data for *Euro-Barometer 20* and *Euro-Barometer 13* were originally collected by Jacques-René Rabier, Helene Riffault, and Ronald Inglehart. Neither the collectors of the original data nor the Consortium bear any responsibility for the analyses or interpretations made here or elsewhere in this book.

*Notes*: The numbers in parentheses by each question indicate the variable number; the full question wording is given in table 5.9, at the end of this chapter. The percentages in parentheses before the various responses to questions indicate the percentage of the sample that answered that way; percentages add to less than 100% in most cases because some respondents gave no answer. The percentages in the main body of the table indicate what percentage of respondents (in the category represented by a given line of the table) favored the response at the top of the column. Row percentages do not add to 100% for variables 158 or 159 because an intermediate response was also available (see table 5.9). The total sample size used here was 8,414, and included DAC countries only, excluding Greece and Luxembourg. The results are weighted to better represent the population of the DAC countries in question, using the Euro-Barometer European Weight (variable 009).

**TABLE 5.2**

U.S. Support for Aid Classified by Respondent Foreign Policy Views: Percentages of U.S. Mass Public Favoring Aid for Economic Development and Technical Assistance, in Four Groups by Attitudes toward Internationalism

| | Low | COOPERATIVE INTERNATIONALISM | | | High |
|---|---|---|---|---|---|
| **High** ↑ | | *Internationalist-* | | | |
| | *Hardliners* | *Hardliner* | | *Internationalists* | |
| | *MI High, CI Low* | *Differences* | | *MI High, CI High* | |
| I | 1974 | 46% | 1974 | 32% | 1974 | 78% |
| N | 1978 | 38% | 1978 | 27% | 1978 | 65% |
| T | 1982 | 54% | 1982 | 26% | 1982 | 70% |
| E | 1986 | 60% | 1986 | 15% | 1986 | 75% |
| R | | | | | |
| N | *Hardliner-* | | | *Internationalist-* | |
| A | *Isolationist* | | | *Accommodationist* | |
| T | *Differences* | | | *Differences* | |
| I | 1974 | 15% | | 1974 | 2% |
| O | 1978 | 6% | | 1978 | −4% |
| N | 1982 | 24% | | 1982 | 4% |
| A | 1986 | 22% | | 1986 | 12% |
| L | | | | | |
| I | | *Accommodationist-* | | | |
| S | *Isolationists* | *Isolationist* | | *Accommodationists* | |
| M | *MI Low, CI Low* | *Differences* | | *MI Low, CI Low* | |
| | 1974 | 31% | 1974 | 45% | 1974 | 76% |
| | 1978 | 32% | 1978 | 27% | 1978 | 69% |
| | 1982 | 28% | 1982 | 38% | 1982 | 66% |
| **Low** ↓ | 1986 | 38% | 1986 | 25% | 1986 | 63% |

*(Rows labeled down the left margin: M I L I T A N T   I N T E R N A T I O N A L I S M)*

*Source*: Computed and derived from Eugene Wittkopf, 1990, *Faces of Internationalism: Public Opinion and American Foreign Policy* (Durham, N.C.: Duke University Press), table 3.1, p. 54, with permission of the publisher. The classification of Americans into four groups displayed along these two dimensions is Wittkopf's also.

*Notes*: Table entries indicate either the percentage of the population that was favorable to aid, in four U.S. subgroups in each of four years, or the differences in those percentages between subgroups.

aid, and less likely to favor decreases, more likely to say aid should continue unabated, and less likely to say that it should be stopped, in a recession.

While religiosity is slightly anticorrelated with being on the left, both led to increased concern for aid, and together made a big difference in people's support for aid, as table 5.3 shows. Preferences for increasing aid, and for continuing aid uncut if there were a recession, are strongest for religious people on the left, intermediate for people who were religious but more to the right or people on the left but not religious, and weakest for a-religious people on the right. This is not surprising, in view of the strong emphasis on egalitarianism that is part of the defining ideology of the left and of the support for market rather than government interventions that characterizes the right. It is also unsurprising in view of the strong teaching of the Bible and the churches on concern for the poor. Those who did not express their political views and/or reveal their church attendance were generally less likely to support aid than were those who had any position whatever.[17] People without any convictions, bereft of any principled basis for seeking something other than national self-interest, were the weakest supporters of aid.

Views on international politics paralleled views on domestic politics and on interpersonal ethics: those inclined to help the poor themselves and those favoring domestic poverty measures favored aid as well. The Euro-Barometer survey shows that those with political commitments to parties concerned with poverty or with regular religious practice favored aid. Those without strong convictions were least favorable toward aid. A similar but more explicit finding by Lindholm correlates what he calls "egocentricity" with low support for aid: of Swedes who thought securing a good living for oneself and one's family to be life's most important goal, only 18% favored increasing aid; but 53% of those who strongly disagreed that this was life's main goal favored increased aid.[18] Wittkopf's findings that any convictions about the need for international involvement bolster aid, but that convictions about the need for international cooperation are the best predictors of support for aid, are similar again. These findings are just what is to be expected if aid is preferred not on self-interested grounds but out of moral conviction. If people regarded aid as a means to national gains, moral convictions should not have made a difference to support: they make a difference because support for funding poor people abroad requires some principled basis for policy. In fact, those completely without convictions had complete disinterest in aid; support for aid was more likely from those of just about any political or religious convictions whatever. But strong commitments to an egalitarian political philosophy or to religious practice or to international cooperation inclined people to favor aid strongly.

TABLE 5.3

Percentages Favoring Increasing, Decreasing, Maintaining, or Cutting Aid, Broken Down by Regularity of Religious Attendance and by Political Self-Placement

| Self-Placement on a Left-Right Political Scale (58) | Increase Aid (64) | | | Decrease Aid (64) | | | Maintain Aid in a Recession (65) | | | Cut out All Aid in a Recession (65) | | |
|---|---|---|---|---|---|---|---|---|---|---|---|---|
| | | | | | | Church Attendance (57) | | | | | | |
| | Regular | Rare | NA | Regular | Rare | NA | Regular | Rare | NA | Regular | Rare | NA |
| Left | 34 | 29 | 25 | 18 | 25 | 32 | 37 | 37 | 34 | 18 | 20 | 27 |
| Right | 25 | 17 | 13 | 18 | 30 | 41 | 37 | 30 | 28 | 19 | 21 | 28 |
| No answer | 22 | 18 | 9 | 17 | 29 | 32 | 35 | 23 | 22 | 18 | 25 | 31 |

*Source*: Computed from the data of Rabier et al. 1983, *Euro-Barometer 13*; see notes to table 5.1 for further information.

*Notes*: The numbers in parentheses by each question indicate the variable number; the full question wording is given in table 5.9. The total sample size used here was 8,827. The results are unweighted. The percentages in the table show the percentage of respondents in each classification that favored the response at the top of each set of three columns (Increase, Decrease, Maintain, or Cut Aid).

### Direct Evidence about Motives

The best evidence about support for aid, however, comes from questions that ask directly why aid should be given and what it should be used for. The general public decidedly, often overwhelmingly, felt that the most important reasons for supporting aid were humanitarian, and that the aid should be used not to promote national self-interests but to alleviate poverty and promote economic progress for those in poverty.

People show strong preference for directing aid to needy countries and to effective programs. Laudicina's survey of Americans does not ask specifically which types of countries should be assisted, but it does offer respondents a list of seventeen countries, from which respondents picked India (29%), Bangladesh (24%), and Pakistan (13%) first as desirable recipients. A question about which kinds of assistance were favored and disfavored indicates that "medical help, doctors, nurses," "train their students in our universities," "food, clothing," and "teachers and books" were the most favored categories, while the public thought "military training and equipment" was the worst idea, followed by "financial grants," and "investment of U.S. corporations." The American public strongly preferred channeling aid through private or international organizations, or the Peace Corps, rather than giving to recipient countries directly.[19] A similar result appears in the 1969 British study by Rauta, where respondents had a chance to say which countries should receive further aid. The most common answers were that aid should go to countries in great poverty (89%, with 58% "definite" in their views) and to countries that have used aid well in the past (90%, with 62% "definite"). Rauta also shows that the more strongly people supported aid, the more strongly they favored poverty as the criterion for where aid should go.[20] The 1983 ten-country Euro-Barometer study is particularly helpful in sorting out where people thought aid should go, not only because it is cross-national but also because respondents were given a clear choice between alternatives about where aid should go. An overwhelming 75% of those responding said that aid should go to "the poorest countries" rather than to "those on which we depend for raw materials" (13%), "those who buy a lot of products from us" (8%), or "those that are of strategic interest to us for political or defense reasons" (4%). Results were similar in each country, and were stronger for people strongly favorable to aid.[21]

Questions directly about motives for giving aid show a pattern similar to that revealed by questions about where aid should go. The Laudicina, Rauta, and Lindholm surveys all give respondents an opportunity to name and evaluate many disparate motives, and in each case humane motives are most favored, although other motives are also accepted. Laudicina finds 29% of Americans say aid should be given for "moral, humanitarian reasons," 18% say "to help them help themselves," 13% say "because we have so much, a disproportionate share," 8% say "to raise their living standards," 5% say "to teach them new methods, technology," and 4% give other poverty-related reasons—totaling 77 mentions of poverty-related reasons per 100 respondents in response to one open-ended question. There are only 31 mentions per 100 respondents that refer to self-interest or milieu goals such as "to have them as friends or allies some day" (10%), "to keep down world problems, peace" (6%), "to keep them from turning to communism" (6%), "to have access to their natural resources" (5%), or "to help improve trade relations" (4%). A second open-ended question elicited 73 mentions per 100 respondents of humane reasons or moral duty, as reasons why aid should be given, 30 mentions of cautions ("help them as long as we don't neglect our own," etc.), 5 mentions of making a better world, and 5 of "helping to keep ourselves strong."[22] Lindholm's survey instructed people to rate four motives for giving aid. He found 48% of Swedes absolutely agreeing that "we should help the developing countries because it is a matter of showing solidarity with other people," and 84% agreeing at least on the whole. Twenty-nine percent agreed absolutely, and 65% at least on the whole agreed, that Sweden should help "because it is partly the rich countries' fault that the developing countries are as poor as they are now." Only 12% agreed absolutely and only 35% at least on the whole to giving aid because the developments in the Third World "are a threat to our own standard of living." Only 19% agreed strongly (although 63% on the whole) that aid should be given because "we can get new countries to sell our goods to."[23] Rauta, asking Britons to rate reasons for giving aid as good or bad, also found the most preferred motives "that they are poor and need help" (84%) and that "we have more technical know-how than they do" (86%), although many also considered pursuit of raw materials a good motive (81%). However, the numbers of those who found the first two motives "quite good" motives (47% and 46%) were much higher than those who found pursuit of raw materials a quite good motive (32%). Many respondents in the three surveys were not averse to having aid help their own country as well as the recipients, but that appeared to be a secondary motive.

## Motive and Strength of Support for Aid

Most respondents, then, found humane and moral reasons the best motives for giving aid and wanted aid spent in a way that alleviated poverty rather than in a way that brought specific benefits to their own country. Equally important are data that show that those who were most motivated by concern for helping the needy countries were the strongest, most active supporters of aid.

Rauta found that strongly pro-aid Britons were much more likely than those strongly opposed to cite poverty as a factor which should definitely qualify a country for aid (78% versus 23%) and much more likely to state that "they are poor and need help" was a very good motive for aid (79% versus 10%). Fifty-one percent of those who chose "getting them on their feet" as a better motive for aid than "encouraging British investment" were strongly in favor of aid, as opposed to 35% of those who chose the other way. Strong aid supporters were also much less apt than those very unfavorable to agree that "Britain should never have given up the empire" and more inclined to think that on the whole Britain harmed the people of the colonies by colonialism.[24] Lindholm found 53% of Swedes who "experienced pangs of conscience" over the hunger in the Third World in favor of increasing aid, as opposed to 18% of those who never did.[25] In the 1983 Euro-Barometer survey of eight DAC countries, 56% of those who thought there was a moral duty to help poor countries wanted to increase aid, as opposed to 9% of those who saw no such duty; 68% (as opposed to 19%) thought aid should continue unreduced in a recession; 74% (as opposed to 21%) felt they would be willing to sacrifice 1% of their salary to this end if necessary.[26]

The 1983 Euro-Barometer data allow tests of the relative strength of different factors explaining aid and provide a strong, cross-nationally supported basis for concluding that such moral motivations undergirded aid. Testing a whole series of demographic and attitudinal variables which are individually correlated with support for aid shows that almost all come out as significant in the expected direction for Europe as a whole, but six items are consistently much stronger predictors than others. The results are more or less similar for different measures of support for aid. Table 5.4 focuses primarily on a four-item index of support, based on whether respondents felt aid should be increased, whether aid should be continued in a recession, whether they favored aid in general and whether they thought helping poor countries an important national goal. The table also gives bivariate correlations with two items on the index. The most important predictors of support for aid, in order, are the respondent's (1) agreement that there is a moral duty to help Third World countries, (2) agreement that aid is in the interest of the donor country, (3) agreement that aid should go to needy countries, (4) personal contribution of time or money to help Third World countries, (5) disagreement with the statement that people in Third World countries do not really want to work, and (6) emphasis on the importance of trying to assist the poorer regions in the respondent's own country. This is a very robust result, and is true in almost all the individual European countries and for other measures of support for aid. Other important explanatory variables were (7) degree to which the respondent perceived his or her own country as rich, (8) (leftward) self-placement on a left-right scale, (9) disagreement that Third World countries were happier as colonies, (10) disagreement that they are beginning to compete with us with their own products, and (11) agreement that we should try to reduce the number of very rich and poor people in our own society. Statistically significant predictors also included the respondent's (12) agreement that Third World countries are exploited by the developed countries such as our own, (13) religiosity, (14) student status, (15) level of education, (16) socioeconomic status, and (17) agreement that having been colonies held back Third World countries' development. The signs are all in the predicted direction. (The exact wording of the questions from Euro-Barometer 13 and Euro-Barometer 20 that are discussed here is given at the end of the chapter, in table 5.9.)

These rankings are roughly similar for different measures of support for aid. The various factors together explain about a quarter of the variance for the individual questions on support for aid and about half the variance (53%) for the index, which is very good for public opinion items. The most powerful predictor, the respondent's view of whether there is a moral duty to help Third World countries, by itself explains 37% of the variance in the index, and between 13% and 32% of the variance for the individual support items.

All the explanatory variables listed remain significant, at a .01 level, even in competition with one another, in Europe as a whole, for the index

TABLE 5.4
Best Predictors of Support for Aid, Tested against Each Other

| | | Multivariate Estimation | Bivariate Correlations[a] | | |
| | | Four-Item Index | Four-Item Index | Favor Aid (127) | Increase Aid (158) |
| Variable Number | Question | Beta | $R^2$ R | R | R |
|---|---|---|---|---|---|
| (121) | We have a moral duty to help | .338† | .37 .61 | .57 | .44 |
| (123) | It's in our own interest to help | .204† | .25 .50 | .47 | .36 |
| (155) | Aid needy countries, not those useful to us | .160† | .15 .38 | .30 | .32 |
| (157) | Respondent has given to help Third World | .123† | .08 .28 | .26 | .21 |
| (115) | Third World countries don't want to work | −.115† | .12 −.35 | −.31 | −.26 |
| (043) | Important to aid poor areas in our country | .090† | .08 .28 | .22 | .20 |
| (042) | Agree that our own country is rich | .064† | .01 .12 | .09 | .01 |
| (432) | Leftward self-placement on Left-Right scale | .053† | .02 .13 | .08 | .16 |
| (119) | Third World happier when colonies | −.047† | .05 −.22 | −.19 | −.20 |
| (120) | Third World countries competing with us | −.044† | .02 −.14 | −.13 | −.14 |
| (045) | Equalize rich and poor in our country | .044* | .02 .15 | .11 | .15 |
| (114) | Third World is exploited by countries like us | .039† | .05 .23 | .19 | .19 |
| (436) | Respondent is religious | .039† | .00[b] .05 | .06 | .03 |
| (STU) | Respondent is a student | .037† | .01 .12 | .10 | .12 |
| (EDU) | Respondent's level of education | .026† | .03 .18 | .14 | .14 |
| (SES) | Respondent's socioeconomic status | .024† | .01 .12 | .09 | .12 |
| (113) | Third World was held back by colonialism | .022† | .05 .22 | .20 | .19 |

*Multivariate Regression Model*

Index = $A + B_{121}*Var_{121} \ldots + B_i*Var_i \ldots + B_{113}*Var_{113}$ + Error term

Adjusted $R^2$ for entire model = .532     $F = 563$     Significance level = .0001

*Source*: Computed from Rabier, et al. 1985, *Euro-Barometer 20*. See table 5.1 for further information.

*Notes*: The index uses the all-Europe weighting. The index of support for aid includes answers to four questions: Whether we should increase aid (158); whether to continue aid even in a period of declining living standards (159); whether helping poor countries is rated an important national goal (047); and whether the respondent favors his country helping Third World Countries (127). Socioeconomic status (SES) is a sum of household income (quartiles), respondent's occupational status, and occupational status of head of household (452, 453, and 456). Level of education (EDU) and student status (STU) are both derived from variable 439. The N, the number of respondents, was 8,414 in the bivariate correlations, and 8,410 in the multivariate estimation.

[a] All the bivariate correlations were significant at a .01 level.

[b] $R^2$ for this variable was about .002.

* Significant at a .01 level.

† Significant at a .05 level (everything unmarked fails a .05 level significance test).

of aid support, except for variable 045, which is significant at a .05 level. Most remain significant for the individual support items, and many remain significant for the index in each of the DAC countries taken separately. The strongest predictors—a sense of moral duty to aid, belief that aid is in the national interest, desire that aid go to needy countries rather than to those advantageous to the donor, personal commitment to alleviate Third World poverty, disbelief that Third World people are lazy, and commitment to domestic egalitarianism—are significant and important for all indicators of support for aid and are significant in all the individual DAC countries, except that the "lazy" variable fails in one and the "egalitarianism" variable fails in two of the eight DAC countries surveyed individually. These six personal attitude and behavioral variables, by themselves, do almost as good a job of prediction as all seventeen variables. Two of these six variables directly support the hypotheses put forth in the last chapter to explain the association at the macro level between national support for foreign aid and for social spending and PVOs concerned with the Third World—concern about domestic inequality (which by itself explains 7.0% of variation in the index, $R = .264$), and reported personal almsgiving to causes concerned with Third World poverty (which by itself explains 7.9% of variation in the index, $R = .282$).

The results in table 5.4 suggest that demographic factors such as being on the left, religiosity, education and information, and various opinion variables are genuine causal factors, since none disappears in competition with the others. The findings in table 5.3, discussed above, that strong political and religious principles lead to support of aid, and that greater levels of awareness and information lead to greater support for aid receive additional confirmation from the Euro-Barometer regression. Each of the polls strongly suggests that the bases of support for aid lie in increased sensitivity to human need and not in calculations of strategic advantage. A similar picture emerges from the other variables that predict support or opposition to aid: none makes sense on the basis of a calculated pursuit of national interest. If aid is to be given to secure foreign policy advantages, or exports, or raw materials, it is irrelevant whether those to whom it is given are lazy. But if aid is justified in terms of aid to those in need, the belief that the recipients are undeserving would be relevant. If aid is favored by those who disapprove of colonialism, who do not take a romantic view of it, and who think their own countries still exploit Third World countries, it is not likely to be favored as a means of continuing exploitative links. If aid is given solely out of any kind of calculation of advantage, what one thinks of domestic inequality is not relevant.

In sum, all indicators suggest that sympathy with the Third World, moral conviction, and desire to help the poor of the less developed countries emerge consistently as the bases of support for aid.

*The Relationship between Milieu Goals and
Humanitarian and Moral Concerns*

The three most powerful explanators are a particularly interesting set, and it is helpful to look at their interrelationships. Strong support for aid went together with the belief that aid should be given to needy countries, the belief that aid is "in our own interest" and especially with the sense of a moral duty to help. The first and third variables clearly are indications of a moral concern that is not directed to self-interested objectives. The belief that "it is in our interest to help them [Third World countries]" is ambiguous, however. Does this expressed perception of the value of aid to the donor indicate a self-interested motive? I will argue that in the ordinary sense of the word, it does not.

The question of what is "in our own interests" depends on how widely one draws the boundaries of the personal or national self. "Our own" interest might mean, at one extreme, "that interest of our own nation which is inherently jeopardized by the success of others, since we fear not being relatively better off." It might mean "our narrow national interest, in indifference to how others fare." Or it might refer to a sense of national well-being that is hurt by the sense of human tragedy and deprivation around the globe. Thus, the view that aid is in our own interest might well express a concern with pressing human needs, involving a commitment to and a belief in the necessity of building a world more just and therefore more able to work well, or a sense of world citizenship that identifies one's own interest with important interests of others worldwide. What clues are there as to whether people thinking aid is "in our own interest" referred to direct benefits, or to a felt need to strengthen international order and an identification with peoples and problems on the basis of common human identity? There is no direct or certain way to tell, but the way this sentiment is associated with other opinions provides important clues.

Those strongly agreeing that "our own interest" was involved did not want aid to promote direct national advantage, for they were less likely than others to want aid spent to further any kind of narrow national interests. Almost 78% of those who saw a national interest in helping poor countries said that aid should go to the poorest countries rather than to those of strategic, trade, or raw materials importance to their own country, as opposed to 70% of all those surveyed and only 65% of those who did not see aid as in the national interest. Also, those who agreed strongly with the "our own interest" statement were more willing to take personal action to help poor people overseas than were those who saw no such interest: 72% said that they would be willing to withhold 1% of their own salary to help the world's poor if need be, and 66% said they had actually contributed themselves in the last couple of years, as opposed to 30% and 37% of those who did not agree that aid is "in our own interest."

The evidence of where those who saw "our own interest" in aid wanted money spent does not seem to have been based on a fearful competitiveness interpretations or on a nationalistic indifference to the fate of others. The expressed and enacted personal willingness to help the foreign poor rather suggests that those who felt "our own interest" involved had a stronger sense of identity with human beings in poverty around the world than did those who did not. Agreement that giving aid was a moral duty—the item best predicting support for aid and best predicting a desire for aid to reach the poor—was strongly associated with belief that giving aid was in the national interest, as table 5.5 shows. And even when one holds constant whether respondents thought aid was a moral duty, those who thought aid in the national interest were generally more likely to favor aid going to poor countries rather than to potentially useful ones, as table 5.6 shows, and were also more likely to state their willingness to make sacrifices themselves, and more likely to actually have done so.[27] Thus, the responses of those who thought aid was good for "our interests" are most consistent with the assumption that they perceived the "national interest" as including world citizenship and a responsibility to do one's part in building a world free from hunger, for both moral and prudential reasons.

### INDICATORS OF SUPPORT FOR AID OTHER THAN PUBLIC OPINION POLLS

In general, the same patterns that characterize the general public appear when we look at notable advocates (and opponents) of aid, political supporters (and nonsupporters) of aid, and the organized groups which championed aid. Church groups, charitable agencies, unions, relatively left parties, and persons committed to domestic reductions of poverty and inequality, championed aid; those with strong commitments to a laissez-faire philosophy and those on the extreme right were the usual opponents. In the case of these more articulate sources of support, the connections that are hypothesized from correlations in public opinion are often explicitly stated by supporters and opponents.

### Groups

The patterns of support for foreign aid in civil society are the same in country after country, and tally exactly with what the public opinion data indicated. Those who wanted tied aid gave no special effort to increasing the quantity of aid; those who were strong supporters of aid and advo-

TABLE 5.5
Perceptions of Moral Duty and of National Interest in Foreign Aid (Percentages)

| It Is in Our Own Interest to Help the Third World (Variable 123) | We Have a Moral Duty to Help (Variable 121) | | | | |
|---|---|---|---|---|---|
| | Agree Completely | Agree to Some Extent | Disagree to Some Extent | Disagree Completely | Don't Know |
| Agree completely | 61 | 18 | 8 | 7 | 4 |
| Agree to some extent | 26 | 60 | 34 | 22 | 21 |
| Disagree to some extent | 6 | 12 | 37 | 20 | 6 |
| Disagree completely | 3 | 4 | 11 | 44 | 5 |
| Don't Know | 4 | 7 | 10 | 7 | 64 |
| N = 9,718 | N = 3,128 | 4,150 | 1,091 | 756 | 593 |

Sources: Computed from Rabier et al. 1985, Euro-Barometer 20. See sources in table 5.1 for further information.

Notes: The results are unweighted. The numbers in parentheses by each question indicate the variable number; the full question wording is given in table 5.9. Percentages show the proportion of those agreeing or disagreeing with question 121 who agree or disagree with question 123. Column totals may not add to 100% due to rounding.

TABLE 5.6
Moral Duty, National Interest, and Support for Aiding Neediest Countries: Percentages in Favor of Directing Foreign Aid to Needy Rather than Useful Countries, Broken Down by Avowal of a Moral Duty and by Belief That Aid Is in Our Interest

| Giving Aid Is In Our Own Interest (123) | We Have a Duty to Give Aid (121) | | |
|---|---|---|---|
| | Agree | Disagree | All Respondents |
| Response of those who agree | 80.1 | 55.7 | 77.7 |
| Response of those who disagree | 77.7 | 52.9 | 65.4 |
| All respondents together | 79.8 | 54.1 | total sample 70.1 |

Source: Computed from Rabier et al. 1985, Euro-Barometer 20. See the notes to table 5.1 for further information.

Notes: The percentages listed in the table show what proportion of the respondents in each category that wanted aid to go to the poorest countries rather than to those supplying needed raw material, to those who might buy products from the respondent's country, or to those countries of political or defense importance (question 155). The percentage in favor of directing aid to needy countries is shown for each group of those agreeing or disagreeing with question 121 (moral duty) and question 123 (own interest). The margins of the four-fold table show percentages favoring aid to the poorest for answers to the two questions separately, and for all respondents in the sample. Only those who answered all three questions are included, an N of 8,069. The results are unweighted. The numbers in parentheses by each question indicate the variable number; the full question wording is given in table 5.9.

cates of increasing aid also wanted it purged of self-serving interests. Business groups rarely lobbied for more aid, and sometimes opposed it, but fairly consistently sought to have aid tied. Churches, charitable organizations, labor organizations, universities, and groups promoting internationalism supported aid, and sought to make it less an instrument of donor interests and more focused on the poorest countries and groups.

In Austria the Roman Catholic church advocated development that would address basic needs and help the poor and minority groups, while the Austrian Trade Union Congress in 1979 asked for increased Austrian aid, "based on . . . basic needs, stabilization of earnings from raw-material exports and an intensification of international trade."[28] German foreign aid finds support, despite "increasing hostility to foreign workers" in a difficult economic climate, Hofmeier and Schultz argue, due to "the patient activities of small but active groups within all political parties, in the Churches and among various movements, particularly those of the younger generation."[29] Forster notes the influence of the Swiss nongovernmental organizations (NGOs) in promoting aid more in line with poverty and developmental objectives.[30] Svendsen is not specific about groups in Denmark, but argues that "aid has come under growing pressure from . . . business interests seeking to tie aid," yet aid "has its roots in a . . . strong tradition of welfare considerations."[31] The tripling of Finnish aid has resulted from "significant mobilization" of Finnish public opinion, Kiljunen says, with "the predominant features of the mobilization of public opinion" being "the so-called 'percentage movement' in which individual participants commit themselves to giving 1% of their income to the humanitarian aid projects of different . . . NGOs."[32]

In the United States, there has been an agricultural lobby for food aid and a lobby for aid to Israel. However, while labor and internationalist associations have provided some support, most lobbying for foreign aid has fallen to the churches. Eugene Carson Blake, president of the National Council of Churches during the 1950s, argued that "Christian duty compels us to help other nations financially and technically," which Rippy characterizes as "typical of the attitude of [U.S.] religious groups, whether Protestant, Jewish or Roman Catholic." The American Friends Service Committee early saw the "heritage and tradition of our Nation" as giving the United States "a compelling moral and spiritual obligation adequately to respond to the needs and aspiration of peoples in the economically underdeveloped countries," while a statement by the Congregational churches drew the link between domestic poverty and aid in saying that "national wealth and power are . . . to be used in the service of human welfare, both within and beyond the nation; it is the particular responsibility of the nations that are strong to help bear the burdens of those that are weak."[33] Bread for the World, a "Christian citizens' lobby" that made influencing legislation on international hunger issues its main focus but also concerned itself with domestic poverty, hunger, and nutrition issues, has been a major voice for aid from the early seventies on.

In the United States there were also strong voices against aid from the beginning of the program. These tended to be conservatives, segments of the business community, or groups with strong cold war views. Eugene Castle, in support of his own argument against aid, usefully quotes from statements by the American Taxpayers' Association, an address to the New England Export Club, the American Coalition of Patriotic Societies, the National Federation of Independent Businesses, the Republican Committee of One Hundred, and other conservative patriotic and business groups against the "waste," "attempt at bribery" and buying friends, "giveaway," and "defense of Socialist-Communist governments around the world" that aid represents. Dan Daniel, the national commander of the American Legion, opposed aid in a 1956 speech because "we are citizens of the United States . . . not of the world" and "should look first to our own interests and safety." Daniel argued that we can "never rely upon an authority outside America for the protection of America's interest," that "the world's . . . only hope for peace is a militarily impregnable America," that allies should give more heed to our views, and that we should realize "that friends can't be bought."[34]

Business is part of "a broad societal consensus on aid" in Japan. Yet the Japanese have untied most of their aid, and this move has led to rapidly falling shares of procurement contracts from bilateral aid going to Japanese firms. While NGOs "have only recently been very active in Japan . . . they frequently criticize the program for not being more sensitive to basic human needs in developing countries," as Orr notes (see table 5.7).[35] Also, Japan's multilateral aid has more than doubled as a percentage of GNP, while bilateral aid has risen slowly, so that the multilateral share of Japan's aid has risen from 26% to 41% over the last decade, according to DAC figures (see table 5.8). Thus, aid has moved steadily toward a greater emphasis on recipient need over the last decade, and away from commercial usefulness to Japan, at the very time when levels of Japanese aid have risen, which suggests that the push for higher aid funding has come from sources which are concerned that Japan use its foreign aid as a means to development, not simply as a commercial tool.

In New Zealand, Hoadley lists eight church groups, three general development organizations, three university or youth groups, and several overseas volunteer corps advocating aid. Such "aid idealists" supported higher aid funding, multilateral aid, and poverty-oriented aid and criticized the government for providing aid to repressive regimes and for letting "political goodwill, diplomatic access, benign tutelage, and private sector economic stimulation" influence aid. Businessmen, listed as active

TABLE 5.7
Contracts for Japanese-Funded Aid Projects, by Nationality (Percentages)

| Nationality of Contractor | 1982 | 1983 | 1984 | 1985 | 1986 | 1987 | 1988 |
|---|---|---|---|---|---|---|---|
| Japan | 57 | 63 | 66 | 52 | 48 | 38 | 27 |
| Other OECD members | 15 | 9 | 10 | 15 | 17 | 16 | 22 |
| Less developed countries | 27 | 29 | 24 | 33 | 35 | 47 | 50 |

Source: Computed from Robert M. Orr, Jr., 1990, *The Emergence of Japan's Foreign Aid Power* (New York: Columbia University Press), table 3.2, p. 67, and used by permission.

Notes: Table entries show what percentages of contracts to work on Japanese aid projects go to Japanese contractors, to contractors from other OECD countries, and to contractors from LDCs, including local procurement in the aided country. The years given are Japanese fiscal years.

TABLE 5.8
Evolution of Japan's Aid Spending, 1974–1989

| | 1974–79 | 1978–81 | 1982–85 | 1986–89 |
|---|---|---|---|---|
| Aid totals as percentages of GNP | | | | |
|   All aid | .23 | .27 | .32 | .34 |
|     Bilateral aid | .17 | .19 | .21 | .20 |
|     Multilateral aid | .06 | .09 | .10 | .14 |
| Multilateral aid as a percentage of all aid | 26 | 33 | 31 | 41 |

Source: OECD, *Development Cooperation*, various years.

Note: Rounding error may cause Multilateral Aid and Bilateral Aid figures to total to more than All Aid.

lobbyists in other areas, tended, along with treasury officials and Maori leaders, to "see aid as already too generous, yielding too few concrete benefits to New Zealand," and to oppose multilateral aid.[36] Eldridge finds some Australian businessmen willing to accept the low level of tying, but business does not push for aid. Rather, "the official aid program draws on a wide range of professional, scientific, technical and educational groups and institutions, who cumulatively provide a broad base of support for its maintenance and expansion," as well as on "voluntary agency and church groups and sections of the labour movement and the media." However, there is no "effective counterweight to the Department of Foreign Affairs in shaping the aid program," and the unfortunate result is that "seeking to reform Australian aid programs in favor of poorer groups" is tough, and the current scheme at best "places little weight on benefits to the poor," although "some good projects [get] implemented."[37]

Edward Horesh notes that in Britain "the Report of the Brandt Commission was a best seller and there are a number of charities and other lobbies that keep the [aid] issue alive."[38] Elizabeth Stamp argues that

Oxfam, oriented to small-scale development for the poor, has had a measurable effect on British support for aid over the last twenty years, organizing the Freedom from Hunger Campaign in the early sixties, working in schools and training colleges, setting up a broadcasting trust and film unit, publishing, together with the group Christian Aid, a development magazine, the *New Internationalist*, and so on.[39] O'Neill sees an early influence of missions on Irish aid, and this apparently is carried on in the emphasis on moral purpose in Irish discussion of aid.[40] Sharp similarly observes, "Irish governments have claimed that their development assistance policies are rooted in fundamental national values. As citizens of a Catholic country, the Irish had a moral obligation to help the poor where they could, and a long and continuing 'missionary tradition' can be cited in this respect."[41] Pratt argues that groups such as Canadian University Service Overseas (CUSO), Oxfam (Canada), interchurch coalitions, and the Canadian Council for International Co-operation were effective in the middle to late seventies in promoting a "reform internationalism" with a "general ethical responsiveness to Third World needs with a recognition that the international economic system distributes the benefits of international trade and investment to the significant and persistent comparative disadvantage of the poorest countries, . . . argu[ing] for at the least major reforms . . . and . . . substantial resource and technology transfer[s]."[42] Bernard Wood notes that consumer and scientific groups and internationalists such as the United Nations Association of Canada were interested in aid.[43]

## Parties and Politicians

In example after example, it also appears that parties with strong socialist or domestic redistributive concerns advocated more and better aid and strengthened aid when in power, while conservative governments tended to retrench. Strong conservative leaders like Reagan and Thatcher were particularly powerful in reducing aid expenditures and in reducing the quality of aid, while strong internationalists strengthened aid in quality and quantity.

Harold Wilson was an early advocate of aid, writing a book supporting a better British aid program—*The War on World Poverty: An Appeal to the Conscience of Mankind*—in 1953. Vogler sees a large difference between British political parties and politicians with respect to aid. "Under the Wilson and Callaghan governments, official aid expenditure rose from .37 to .43 per cent of GNP between 1974 and 1979," and Labour claimed it as "the fastest growing part of the government's spending programme," he says.[44] Edward Horesh sees elements of a bipartisan consensus in British aid policy before Thatcher, although Labour governments have sought to keep the Overseas Development Administration a separate and autonomous agency, while Conservative governments have "incorporated it in the Foreign and Commonwealth Office."[45] Both authors agree, however, that the Thatcher government represented a sharp break. Vogler says the "Thatcher government's approach to North-South issues may justly be regarded as an extension of its domestic economic philosophy." Mrs. Thatcher was very outspoken, referring to aid expenditures as "hand-outs," and seems to have felt "antipathy" to the Brandt Report, which sold widely in Britain. Aid expenditures fell steadily, until by 1986–89 they were in the .28–.32% of GNP range. Fellow Tory Edward Heath, who had been on the Brandt Commission, like the opposition parties and other OECD countries, was critical of "cuts that appeared disproportionate relative to overall public expenditure reductions."[46] Horesh notes that British aid statistics which were set up in 1977 and 1978 to monitor attention to the poorest were discontinued in 1979 under the Thatcher government.[47]

While the Thatcher divide was particularly sharp and ideological, a similar, if less marked, pattern of party differences obtains in other English-speaking countries. Steve Hoadley notes that in New Zealand

> the Labour Government of 1972–1975 expressed its traditional internationalism by raising aid totals to nearly 0.6 per cent of GNP, increasing the multilateral proportion, and instituting projects in black Africa and Latin America. The National Government after 1975 allowed aid to fall in relative terms to around 0.25 per cent of GNP, stressed bilateral projects, and phased out African projects because they were difficult to administer. The next Labour Government after 1984 again stressed the importance of giving aid to black Africa, and then China, and pledged to raise aid to 0.51 per cent of GNP by 1991 and to stress regional programmes in the South Pacific.[48]

However, in Australia, Eldridge finds that though "Labor's aid policy is . . . somewhat more radical" on aid than other governments' have been and has emphasized "redistribution and basic needs of poorer groups more strongly than their conservative counterparts," in practice the government does not live up to its rhetoric under either party, and the differences are slight.[49]

Cranford Pratt observes that the Canadian International Development Agency (CIDA) had strong backing under Liberal prime ministers Lester Pearson and Pierre Trudeau, and that CIDA's budget grew prodigiously in the Trudeau period. Each "appointed prominent and independent individuals . . . who could be counted on to be vigorous champions of the aid programme both within and outside the bureaucracy." Mitchell Sharp, the secretary of state for external affairs, in 1971 argued that the "one good and sufficient reason for international aid . . . is that there are less fortunate people in the world who need our help," and a 1975 report,

*Strategy for International Development Cooperation, 1975–1980,* proposed that "assistance . . . be concentrated in those countries which are at the lower end of the development scale" and that "Canada . . . give the highest priority to development projects and programs aimed at improving the living and working conditions of the least privileged sections of the population . . . and at enabling these people to achieve a reasonable degree of self-reliance." But Pratt argues that there has been steady retrenchment both from volume targets and from attempts to orient aid toward developmental goals and the needs of the poor in succeeding Conservative administrations. Aid levels which rose through the sixties and seventies have declined during the Conservative administrations in the eighties,[50] with aid becoming a matter of "maximizing the advantages for Canadian interests," even though interest in humanitarian concerns remained strong in Canadian political culture.[51]

Party and ideological differences in the United States are particularly striking. Aid was instituted by the Truman administration, over the opposition of Senator Taft and other conservatives, downplayed by the Eisenhower administration, and reinvigorated by Kennedy, who raised aid spending levels to their high in 1963. Kennedy's Peace Corps for overseas voluntary service by American youth was emulated by almost every developed country government, and served as a model for Johnson's domestic service corps, Vista, as well. Kennedy also gave a worldwide boost to emphasis on development, calling for the 1960s to be the "development decade." The flavor of U.S. political debate appears in the contrast between books by Senator Goldwater, the 1964 Republican presidential contender, and Senator Hubert Humphrey, later the Democratic vice-presidential candidate. Just as he attacked the institutions of the American domestic welfare state, including even Social Security, Goldwater attacked foreign aid as unconstitutional, harmful to the taxpayer and the American economy, wasteful, a source of "anti-Americanism among proud peoples who, however irrationally, resent dependence on a foreign dole," and, above all, a hindrance to the cold war effort, strengthening socialism and "making it more difficult for free enterprise to take hold."[52] Humphrey, by contrast, wrote that the "ancient adversaries of mankind—poverty, hunger, disease, and ignorance—are the allies of tyranny" and listed the Marshall Plan, Point Four, Food for Peace, and the Peace Corps, all "meant to benefit people generally, not just an elite," as successes in the struggle against "grinding poverty and voiceless desperation." Humphrey did mention cold war and business benefits in replying to critics, but he advocated that "more of the capital-development lending should be shifted to the Inter-American Development Bank and other international finance institutions" and emphasized that "the purpose of foreign aid is not just to fight a Cold War, but to build a better world" in a way that shows "deference to smaller nations." America should not emulate those "older powers, hardened to international leadership, [which] have sneered at us for . . . 'do-goodism,'" but rather should use its "energies and resources outwardly, for the sharing of freedom and the good life, and not wholly inwardly for self-protection or self-satisfaction."[53]

The same general patterns of support show up in recent U.S. aid history. In the aftermath of the Vietnam War, Congress moved in the early seventies to "New Directions" legislation to assure that aid would reach the neediest people and to place human rights restrictions on aid and, as noted in chapter 3, from 1974 sent a higher-proportion of non-SSA U.S. bilateral aid to poorer countries. Aid was in moderate decline in the United States from the midsixties until President Reagan slashed the aid program deeply from .27% of GNP in 1980 to .21% in 1988 and .15% in 1989, with the percentage of aid going to least developed countries (LLDCs) and to other low income countries (LICs) falling most swiftly (from .04% and .10% of GNP in 1982–83 to .03% and .04% in 1989). The Reagan administration cut multilaterally channeled aid and negotiated smaller International Development Association (World Bank) replenishments, thus harming multilateral aid internationally. The rapid decay of aid in quality and quantity under Reagan paralleled the withdrawal of money from domestic programs for the poor and the buildup of military spending.

In France, a long-term decline in aid was turned around by the accession of a socialist government. Yves Berthelot and D. Besnaiou observe a consistent difference between the parties on foreign aid, with the socialists maintaining a long-term commitment to aid and "occasionally adopt[ing] aid to the Third World as a campaign theme when many considered it scarcely an electoral issue." Mitterand made French relations with "the Third World . . . a priority . . . from the first day of his seven-year term." He tried "to coordinate development policy with other policies, in areas of trade, for instance, . . . and appointed a strong deputy for Third World cooperation, Alain Vivien, who deplored 'generous talk . . . contradicted by a more sombre reality.'"[54] Hugon agrees that "since May 1981, the new cooperation and development policy has been set more in a Third-World perspective."[55] Mitterand committed himself to reach the .7% of GNP target by 1988, and sought to remove calculation of the subsidies given French Overseas Territories and Departments (TOM/DOM) from the calculation of aid.[56] Non-DOM/TOM aid had declined from about .42% of GNP in 1970 to .38% in 1980, while aid to DOM/TOM had remained constant or even risen a bit to comprise over 40% of the aid budget. Mitterand's goals were not fully met, but France's aid rose substantially at once, with the total above the .7% target after 1981, and non-DOM/TOM reaching .54% in 1989. French contributions to multi-lateral aid, historically low, also rose sharply.[57] He emphasized aid for LLDCs, particularly in Africa, and self-reliant development.[58] French aid to LLDCs did rise, reaching the .15% of GNP target by the end of the eighties, and aid to other lower income countries rose, too. In short, Mitterand substantially increased aid and improved dramatically its quality, in line with his own and his party's proclaimed views.

Hofmeier and Schultz note a similar change in German aid policy when the Social Democrats came to power. "Throughout the 1960s," they state (with a good deal of exaggeration), "aid policy was, by and large, regarded as being functional with respect to the self-interest of [West Germany]." The German Social Democrats had "always stated that the effects of aid projects were intended to be of a long-term nature and . . . quite [independent] of the regimes in power," while the Christian Democrats disagreed. The election of the Brandt (Social Democrat–Liberal) government in 1969 led to a deemphasis on foreign policy considerations and recipient ideology and eventually to a "long-standing consensus" on development policy in recent years, which stresses "protection of human rights, furthering of democratic behavior and a reduction of military expenditure in the developing countries." Brandt himself chaired the international Brandt Commission Report, which became the basis for "comprehensive reformulation" of German aid policy. The report emphasized alleviating absolute poverty and making "economic and social contribution[s] to development in the Third World" to "eas[e] tensions . . . [work to] assur[e] peace" and, by supporting nonaligned countries, strengthening "independence and self-reliance." A strong aid minister, Erhard Eppler, attempted to "focus German aid policy as much as possible . . . on the needs of the developing countries," and this was put in an official policy document in 1971, which was updated in 1973 and 1975. The provision of aid is expected to be on the principles of social progress and justice for the poorest population groups. The fight against absolute poverty is confirmed as "the overriding aim of German development policy" in a 1982 official document. Further, it was agreed under the Social Democrats that aid should grow at twice the rate of the federal budget. After Eppler's departure, however, his successor, Egon Bahr, stated in 1975 that "balance between the requirements of development policy and of our own other interests" was required.[59]

In the smaller Continental states, too, leftward parties have been more favorable to aid, and more concerned that it be poverty-oriented. There has never been any great enthusiasm for aid in Austria; however, Skuhra's analysis suggests that the Austrian socialists have been most supportive. Certainly Kreisky, leader of the Socialist party after 1967, was a vocal advocate of aid and, earlier, as foreign minister, had set up a commission recommending a 1% of GNP target for aid.[60] The OVP (Österreische Volks Portei), in power from 1966 to 1969, on the other hand, stressed bilateral aid and aid to the more advanced LDCs, and was criticized by the Socialist opposition on the basis of DAC criteria. Renard notes that in Belgium the Flemish Liberals are most hesitant about the .7% of GNP target, the Christian Democrats "more positive," and the Socialists "the most outspoken advocates" of stronger development policy, including a 1% target for ODA/GNP, while the Flemish Socialists also "have been most critical of the 'commercialization' of aid policies."[61] While Forster does not talk extensively about Swiss party differences on aid, he does note that "left-wing political parties" along with NGOs are the advocates of basing aid on humane criteria. The pressure for tying comes from "representatives of the export sector," who would like "ODA . . . to be put more directly to the service of Swiss enterprises."[62] In the Netherlands, the strong emphasis on social justice and greater equality as aims of aid and on the need to work for structural change in the world system as well to increase the aid target markedly were effectively advocated, starting in 1973, by the socialist aid minister Jan Pronk, a development economist much influenced by the New Left. Pronk sought to raise the ODA target to 1.5% of GNP and put forward (1) poverty, (2) need for foreign assistance, (3) policies directed toward the poorest in the country, and (4) compliance with human rights standards as criteria for selecting "concentration countries" for Dutch aid.[63]

Japan is something of an exception in that there are few party differences on aid. However, such party differences as there are are consistent with the finding elsewhere that aid tends to be supported by parties more to the left. Ronald Dore notes that the Democratic Socialist Party is a strong advocate of aid. The dominant Liberal Democratic Party (LDP) has supported aid but tends to view it as a tool of foreign policy. The Socialist Party is very anticapitalist and anti–United States, and thus tends, like extreme leftists in the United States, to see aid as a tool of an exploitative capitalist strategy of U.S. imperialism. There is also, he says, an Afro-Asian block in the LDP which sees the United States as unlikely ever to give Japan her due. The partisan differences do not seem particularly large in Japan, however, more interesting is the relation between strategic reasoning, international status, and domestic support for aid.[64]

Throughout Scandinavia there is a strong consensus in almost all parties on the general outlines of aid policy; the only party in Scandinavia opposed to aid altogether is a small right-wing tax-revolt party in Denmark. But within the consensus, parties to the left or with strong idealistic or religious roots held out for stronger aid, while center parties sought to promote business interests and to scale aid back.

In Norway parties on the left have sought higher aid targets and parties on the right, lower targets, although all support high levels of funding. In the early seventies Labour sought to raise the aid spending target from .75% to 1% of GNP, and in 1972 won approval for reaching the higher target by 1978 with the Conservatives alone disagreeing. In 1975 and 1978 Labour proposed further increases. During a later difficult time for the economy, parties agreed to retrench to the 1% target, except that the Christian People's party (CPP), which "gives prominence to questions involving values and norms" and has resisted attempts to depart from traditional altruistic principles for Norwegian aid, wanted a higher figure. The CPP now seeks a 1.7% target for aid, with any aid designed to affect business interests to be extra, beyond that, and the Left Socialists seek a 2% target. The Conservatives have tried to lower aid targets and tailor aid more to business interests. The small, right-wing Progress party wanted to "limit aid to humanitarian assistance and support for the Norwegian industrial and commercial interests."[65] In Sweden, "conservatives want more tied aid," and a non-Socialist government "stressed the need to increase the return flows of aid" as well as a system of investment guarantees and introduced new forms of aid such as "concessionary credits, directed . . . at middle- . . . and high-income countries" which were "clearly commercially motivated."[66] Södersten notes that the Liberals and the Center party attempted to get Sweden to the 1% target in 1975, while the Moderate (conservative) party resisted. A disguised reduction in 1982 by the Social Democrats was successfully opposed by the Liberal and Center parties, and especially by the three "most militant" wings within the Social Democrats, the Christian wing, the young socialists, and the women's groups.[67] In Finland, Kiljunen observes, while there was general agreement on the DAC targets, the Center party emphasized that "it is much more difficult for us to work for the achievement of such a percentage target than those countries which carry the sins of a colonial past." President Kekkonen by contrast emphasized that "the responsibility is also Finland's although we have never participated in carving up the colonies or exploiting them. Both the ethics of being a human being and our own direct interests oblige us to do as much as our resources and abilities permit to increase development cooperation with the peoples of other countries."[68]

## Idealism in Government Policies and Statements

Examination of the domestic bases of support for aid consistently shows that advocates of aid were not groups seeking some advantage for themselves or for the country but were idealists concerned with international order and poverty. They advocated that aid be severed, as far as possible, from the pursuit of particularistic national interests as well as that it be increased. They tended to advocate that aid be specifically directed to the needs of the poorest groups and countries. They tended to be groups either committed to the amelioration of poverty in domestic society, or to some sort of internationalism, or both, and often were groups with some sort of well-articulated moral, religious, or political philosophy that emphasized altruism and community spirit. These generalizations hold true whether one looks at public opinion, interest groups, individual politicians, or political parties; they parallel data on national differences; and the same is true of international groups and prominent intellectuals supporting aid.

Government policies often reflected this idealism to some considerable degree. Knud Erik Svendsen argues that a "remarkably high consensus" in Denmark has in fact focused aid on "low-income countries among the developing countries" and "the poor in these countries . . . [as] the main beneficiaries," with half of aid being multilateral, implementing "the poverty orientation" that 1961, 1970, and 1982 reports recommended, although "growing pressure from . . . business interests" seeking to tie Danish aid is a real problem.[69] Jacques Forster notes the humanitarian motive in Swiss aid as "the product of a tradition started by Henri Dunant with the foundation of the Red Cross in 1863. . . . This motive . . . is well understood and accepted by public opinion" and corresponds to Swiss law, which "gives priority to supporting the efforts of the most disadvantaged countries, regions and population groups."[70] Horesh observes that in Britain "all spokespersons at whatever level stress that this criterion [development] must be met before other interests are considered" and notes that the 1975 white paper, despite the difficult times for Britain, emphasized not trade advantages but that "a higher proportion of British aid should directly benefit not only the poorest countries but the poorest people in those countries." A memorandum of 1975 also "added the objective of strengthening the role of women in development."[71] Bertholet, de Clercq, and Janssen sum up by saying that "the motivation of Dutch development aid has a strong moral component, rooted in socialist and religious convictions. Socialist solidarity with the working class was widened to solidarity with the poor on a world-wide scale and the strong Dutch missionary tradition was deepened and broadened from charity to justice and from works of charity to development efforts. The moral conviction was, and still is, a countervailing power against political and economic considerations of self-interest, which are, of course, not alien to Dutch development aid."[72]

Sergio Alessandrini states that the "aims of the Italian development-cooperation policy had for a long time been charity and assistance," and were strengthened by a 1971 bill that "signaled a new trend . . . seeking to 'increase the technical, cultural, economic and social growth in the recipient countries.'" However, commercial aims were increasingly prominent in the midseventies, when a "switch from an ethical and altruistic approach to a more self-interested one" occurred "while the economic situation was worsening at the end of the seventies." But as the decade ended, "the 'world's hunger' issue was raised several times in the Italian Parliament by an active minority group," and appropriations, which had fallen throughout the seventies, were raised with "these resources . . . to be used for the satisfaction of fundamental human needs." At the start of the eighties a bill assigned priority "to the satisfaction of the most pressing needs of the least-developed countries and to the welfare of the poorest people of the developing countries," while the minister stated that "food and implementation of immediate projects for the struggle against poverty are the most important and the most urgent aspects of development cooperation. Italy must act for their achievement." Alessandrini notes that "the most commercial or self-interested aims, such as securing an export market . . . have . . . disappeared from the explicit official declarations" in the early eighties.[73]

Hofmeier and Schultz report a "long-standing consensus" on development policy in Germany in recent years, a consensus that, summarizing a 1982 official document, they characterize as stressing "protection of human rights, furthering of democratic behavior and a reduction of military expenditure in the developing countries. The provision of aid is expected to be on the principles of social progress and justice for the poorest population groups. The fight against absolute poverty is confirmed as the overriding aim of German development policy."[74]

Given the sources of support for aid in domestic society, it would be quite extraordinary if this were not the case. Popular sentiment, elite opinion, and specific lobbying groups were important constituencies; and policymakers were themselves drawn from the same population that held idealistic opinions about foreign aid. While in power, officials faced additional pressures which might make them swerve a bit, yet it is evident that many were strongly committed to assisting the poor.

The degree of idealism behind aid varied greatly, of course. Even in quite idealistic programs such as the Danish one, aid programs once in place were a target of opportunity for business lobbyists, just as military and other government contracts are. Parties varied in their orientation to aid, and government policy shifted as the parties shifted. De Gaulle's motivations for aid were not Mitterand's, and the spending patterns show it. Governments that faced a strong national idealistic consensus had stronger and more poverty-oriented programs than those which, like New Zealand's, had to keep a middle course between opposed factions. Even idealistic government policy usually had some interest in combining humanitarian motives with other factors. Smith shows nicely that even private charitable organizations set up explicitly to help the poor in the Third World inevitably were influenced by a variety of nonaltruistic motivations.[75]

Sometimes the statements of a government frankly reflected its mixed motives. Belgium's 1977 statement said, "The government takes as the starting point for its bilateral policy the fight against poverty," but a less idealistic statement, justified on the grounds of promoting "a new realism," was issued in 1981.[76] The Thatcher government was quite open about seeking to make aid serve direct British interests as well as about seeking to reduce the level of funding. And Britain has never made a secret of recognizing a special obligation to Commonwealth countries. Often, however, official government statements have an idealistic tone that the actual programs do not merit. Eldridge deplores the self-serving elements that lessen the quality of Australian aid, especially because of their contrast with official government and party statements.[77] Early French aid statements covered over the directly self-interested elements in aid without a mention. The current Austrian aid program "lays down . . . goals such as basic human needs, infrastructure, unemployment, agriculture, improvement of income distribution, rise of productivity in general and especially of weak, small-scale industries," but the program itself is small and has a high percentage of tied aid.[78] Inflated claims of what programs are like naturally produce a good deal of cynicism.

### Two Idealistic Motivations

Two basic arguments underlay the positions of most advocates of aid: response to human need and the creation of a more orderly world. Logically, as Robert Packenham points out, the two things are independent; we cannot assume that "all good things go together."[79] These distinct motives went together with surprising frequency, however: they are found intertwined too often, by too many sophisticated people aware of the distinction between them, for the juxtaposition to be a mere mistake. Even the advocates who were most intent on aid that would help the poor—Barbara Ward, or Gunnar Myrdal, say—could not refrain from linking the two ideas: we must help those who are poor because they are in need, *and* if we do not, we will reap the consequences of our hardheartedness; or we must build a peaceful world we can all live in or perish, and the first step toward building such a world is to make sure that the neediest persons are helped.

The Swiss law on development links these when it argues that "development cooperation supports the efforts of developing countries to improve the living conditions of their populations. It must contribute to enabling these countries to carry out their development by their own means. It seeks, in the long run, a better equilibrium within the international community" precisely by giving "priority to supporting the efforts of the most disadvantaged countries, regions and population groups."[80] Similarly, Chancellor Kreisky argued that increased Austrian aid would "contribute through solidarity, cooperation and friendship to the creation of a more just and stable international order."[81] A 1977 Belgian policy statement states that "cooperation policy is aimed at achieving more international justice" and that the policy is aimed at "the fight against poverty," including meeting basic needs and helping the poorest, but Belgian aid policy also makes "the achievement of political and economic stability in the world" an aim, along with establishing "the good-will and stability which aid may bring in the Third World . . . [which is] crucial for the long-term welfare of Belgium."[82] Anthony Clunies Ross advocated as fundamental Australian aid objectives "that we should play a significant role in contributing to the economic development of the underdeveloped part of the world. The aim in other words *is* economic development. The motive can be regarded as humanitarian or as one of enlightened self-interest. Both will in fact lie behind the policy in people's minds. I believe that it is widely assumed in Australia that a prosperous world is in our interest, and there seems to be some sense in their view."[83] British policy routinely expresses concern that "the increasing gap between rich and poor threatens the stability of the world," which Horesh sees as evidence that British aid is based on "enlightened self-interest as well as on moral considerations."[84] And Vogler, after stating that "the reaction to the Brandt report showed that there is a surprisingly large domestic constituency concerned with the direction of British policy on development aid and the broad issues of North-South inequality," goes on to remark, in an interesting phrase, that "Brandt's view of interdependence—that what is right just happens to be what is expedient as well—has been echoed in many quarters, not least among the opposition parties."[85]

The ideas of human dignity and interdependence were linked by the belief that only on a basis of just consideration for the weak was it possible to create international order. The idea of interdependence also removed condescending and humiliating overtones from aid by considering it an act of human solidarity in building a better world. Much of the interdependence rhetoric—such as changing the name of the DAC's annual report, from *Development Assistance* to *Development Cooperation*—clearly sought to present foreign aid on a basis of dignity and mutuality, as a common project among partners. Emphasis on the wrongs of the colonial past or the injustices of current trade relations often had a similar function: to show how the problems of the countries most obviously in trouble were not their problems alone and signs of their inferiority, but were common human problems to be tackled together.

A 1981 Irish statement, "while again reiterating 'our responsibility to play our part in the process of developing the Third World' emphasized that the motivation was based 'not on charity or altruism but on a realization that our future is inextricably bound up with the developing world.'"[86] The Dutch felt that "building a world of sovereign nations also meant that a common interest was at stake. Therefore, the word 'aid' should be dropped and be replaced by 'development cooperation.'"[87] Elements of compassion, self-preservation, justice, and human destiny are mixed together when Brandt argues over and over that assistance to those in dire poverty is "a question of common survival" and at the same time needed to remedy "glaring injustice," to respond to "appalling" want, and to "avert a great danger for mankind."[88] This mixing is not because those who think this way, a group including distinguished economists, are unaware of how it fails to make sense if pushed into the framework of a rational egoist calculus, but because the aim is precisely to develop a different way of thinking and acting that takes actors out of that self-defeating logic.

This move is not simply a rhetorical device, or tact, or a euphemism, or an attempt to avoid bragging about one's virtue, though it may in fact help smooth discussion in those ways. It emerges from a different analytic perspective that looks at international problems as human life together rather than simply as a calculus of costs and benefits; that sees different nations as different parts of the human family, who coinhere in one another, who are members of one another. A logic of loyal membership, friendship, or citizenship is different from a logic of calculated advantages, even if the cultivation of virtues and social virtues is a part of the calculation. We can understand in a more or less complete and analytic way how the logic of calculated advantage works; the logic of loyalty and common identity is probably less susceptible to analysis, and is certainly at present less well understood, but we know from experience that it works well.

Thus, when President Urho Kekkonen of Finland analyzed the problems of underdevelopment and elaborated the premises for development cooperation, his apparent emphasis on long-term self-interest involved an implicit appeal to the idea that we are and must be involved with all mankind:

> It would be short-sighted for us [in Europe] to believe that we could afford to withdraw into a citadel of peace and plenty, while the greater part of mankind sinks ever deeper into the miseries of underdevelopment and overpopula-

tion. . . . The strategy for the new United Nations Development Decade is an important expression of the emerging philosophy of international responsibility which recognizes that the concepts of social justice must have an universal application. . . . I wish to add my personal conviction that the problems of development must be tackled with the same urgency as the issues of war and peace.[89]

Elements of moral reflection, of urgent international need calling for good citizenship, of standing and falling together, and of self-definition with reference to prevailing international concepts of action are blended together in this 1970 statement to the UN.

Bo Södersten notes that Sweden's policy is based on "reform internationalism" of which "one element . . . is altruism," and that

behind reform internationalism lies the belief that countries have obligations that extend beyond their borders. These obligations may have a completely rational foundation but they also have a moral dimension. When the Swedish government launched its first major proposal to increase foreign aid in 1962, Prime Minister Tage Erlander expressed the sense of moral obligation very clearly when he said that "assistance was an expression of a feeling of moral duty and international solidarity" and that "peace, freedom and prosperity are not exclusively national, but something more universal and indivisible."[90]

The attempt to see foreign aid in terms of human interdependence was thus not simply a failure to understand the free-rider problem; and the juxtaposition of interdependence and compassionate or dutiful response to those in need was not simply a confusion between two distinct goals or an attempt to palliate the awkwardnesses of economic inequality. Rather, this approach expressed essential elements of an outlook in which the context for international politics was that of global society, human solidarity, and a recognition that we are all bound together in failure and success in the common human enterprise.

## INTERNATIONAL SOCIETY AND INTERNATIONAL PUBLIC OPINION

Just as the governments of developed countries responded in part to the growth of domestic political opinion that recognized aid both as a duty and as an opportunity to do good, so they responded in part to the international public opinion that recognized the same things. Countries came to see the necessity for a worldwide response to poverty as international voices increased awareness of the needs of the Third World. Countries began to accept that the developed countries had obligations as they saw other countries do so. Countries compared themselves with others, considering whether they were being good citizens or not, and were influenced by their perception of the behavior customary for states in their position or of what it was reasonable to expect them to do. Often they wanted a kind of moral prestige, wanting to appear worthy and responsible, and wanting international respect. They were, in fact, sensitive to international public opinion, especially in countries that served as their reference group. Such sensitivity sometimes took the form of a desire to play along with what others were doing: a conformist or a follower's mentality. But it could also involve trying to take a position of leadership: to define a role that expressed their distinctive national identity, or to exert constructive influence by setting standards of public-spirited and just behavior. Commentators on individual nations' aid policies instance both kinds of factors.

David Scott, arguing for the highest possible amount of Australian aid, not limited to 1% in grant form and free from neocolonialism, argued that "we must heed the warnings of U Thant, Barbara Ward, Gunnar Myrdal, Sen of F.A.O.A., [Arthur] Goldberg . . . , Julius Nyerere," and others who have called attention to Third World problems.[91] Stokke sees Norwegians as influenced by, and responding to, the impact of Third World NIEO demands as an "external impulse" that had an impact in conserving the relatively altruistic character of Norway's aid.[92] Similarly, the Irish sought to gain "moral authority" and "the intangible moral benefits which come from cooperation with our fellow men" while "satisfying the desire of the Irish people to play a constructive role" and "add to our moral authority in seeking to influence constructively the policies of other developed nations toward the Third World," as Irish politicians put it.[93] Sharp, arguing that Irish foreign policy "adopted a strategy of performing roles that emphasized their claim to represent a sovereign, independent state with particular virtues," claims that "Irish foreign policy was directed at acquiring and publicising a distinctive . . . role for Ireland in this [aid] process, both as an end in itself and as an instrument of other policies."[94] O'Neill also says that "the Department of Foreign Affairs, at least, perceived Ireland as a 'developed' country," and that establishing that identity may have been a motive in Irish aid.[95]

The Swiss, according to Forster, sought "to project" an "image" abroad: "that of a country which, while admittedly privileged, remains sensitive to world problems and generous to the victims of catastrophes of all sorts." Moreover, Forster sees relations with the developed countries, as well as with the Third World, as an "interest at stake" in Swiss development policy: "By our contribution, we collaborate in the equitable division between the industrialized states of the costs of the assistance necessary to Third World countries."[96] Bertholet, de Clercq, and Janssen note that a desire to "polish up" Holland's "image and acquir[e] some international influence" may have been a motive in improving Dutch aid.[97]

Concern over possible criticism also played a role. International (DAC) standards were used as a basis for Socialist opposition criticism of the Austrian OVP in its 1966–69 administration for emphasizing bilateral aid and aid to the more advanced LDCs.[98] Vogler says the Thatcher government "was heavily criticized domestically and by the OECD for cuts that appeared disproportionate relative to overall public expenditure reductions," and that "the government . . . soften[ed] its line a bit in 1981" as a result.[99] Cassen et al. say that "aid has not been a major issue in Australia and Japan; each is a follower in that it has sought to meet internationally agreed pledges, but has not come up with new initiatives." The "Japanese have been very concerned with their international image, and to a large extent have viewed aid as a way to prove that they are responsible members of the OECD." They state that "a country like Japan, whose international status is rising, but which still feels . . . a discrepancy between its international prestige and its real economic power, may be more punctilious than others about conforming to the more idealistic standards of international conduct, such as moving toward aid targets."[100]

There is widespread scholarly consensus that Japan's aid policies at first were heavily focused on improving Japanese trade, with "the desire to show good faith to Western Industrial Nations" a secondary motive, as Loutfi, summarizing White, puts it.[101] However, there is also agreement that Japanese aid policy has changed considerably. From about 1977 on the Japanese sought to appear as a responsible power and good neighbor, especially in the eyes of the developed countries. Farnsworth cites Prime Minister Fukuda's 1977 statement that "it is a matter of urgency for Japan diplomatically to present to foreign countries an image as a peaceful, culturally oriented nation" and argues that Japan seeks "friendship."[102] Ronald Dore argues that what weighs heaviest with the foreign ministry is "an obligation *vis à vis* the other *rich* countries to share the burden." He cites the Foreign Ministry's 1978 report, which "contains a strong statement of the need for foreign aid with emphasis on Japan's 'good neighbour' reputation, [and] her low standing in the DAC GNP ratio league ('if we look back on our reactions to North South problems, it can hardly be denied that—chiefly because of the unclarity of our basic beliefs on these matters—we have been lacking in consistency and not up to the standards of other advanced countries')."[103] Farnsworth and others also observe that the Japanese spoke of making Japan a "bridge between North and South." Yasutomo lists economic well-being, national prestige, domestic support, peace diplomacy, and national security as interrelated Japanese objectives, although the "quest for [great power] status" seems most prominent; he observes that Japanese aid "reflects the strong desire to play a more active role in international affairs . . . [along with] . . . external pressures to 'do more' in world affairs and national aspirations to do more as a nonmilitary power."[104] Orr says Japan's aid policy stems from a "combination of factors—concern over international status, fear of isolation, desire to conform to world trends, and the need for the Ministry of Foreign Affairs to strengthen its bargaining position by using outside pressure."[105] Fukui reports that "virtually all MOFA officials [that he interviewed] agree that Japan should promptly accept the full economic, political and possibly military burdens as an equal ally, pretty much as defined by American and European leaders."[106]

Japanese statements also reflected concern about poverty, however, and concern for a peaceful world order. Loutfi argues that "the motivation of Japanese foreign aid" was "a mix of various economic, political, and humanitarian considerations" even at an early period, citing Prime Minister Eisaku Sato's July 1965 speech to the Diet, which recognized "Japan's moral responsibility . . . to assist in . . . economic development," and Foreign Minister Miki's 1967 UN General Assembly remark that "it is not realistic to hope for peace and stability in Asia without first improving the sorry state of poverty there."[107] Farnsworth cites Professor Toru Yano's thesis that Prime Minister Fukuda's 1977 ASEAN speech was a crucial turn in Japanese foreign policy and "an implicit commitment for Japan to perform the role of bridge between North and South." Prime Minister Ohira emphasized human development in his speech to UNC-TAD in Manila and in his January 25, 1980, speech to the Diet.[108] Dore notes that Ministry of Foreign Affairs (but not MITI) discussions of aid now stress basic human needs and "long-term interests in a more secure and peaceful world."[109] Yasutomo notes a "favorable national consensus" for "the use of foreign aid for humanitarian and interdependence uses," and states that "while popular support for economic assistance remains steady, strategic aid conjures up a slightly different and less popular vision [which] . . . causes unease. . . . The leadership . . . attempts to dilute the strategic coloring of aid by utilizing the more popular rationales of humanitarianism and economic interdependence."[110] Brooks and Orr see Japanese aid moving from initial attempts to increase trade, to attempts to cultivate good relations, especially with raw material suppliers, to a greater focus on basic human needs.[111] And Orr observes that "public opinion in Japan was aroused significantly during the 1984–1985 period over the plight of drought-stricken countries" and that in September 1985 Foreign Minister Abe Shintaro proposed a "Green Revolution for Africa" plan at a conference of foreign ministers from the seven major industrial countries. A direct result of this proposal was the creation of a "Green Corps," under the direction of JICA, Japan's aid agency.[112]

The changed consensus has been reflected in changed aid spending. Japan has not only markedly increased its aid spending in the last decade, but it has at the same time markedly improved its quality, raising the percentage of multilateral aid and directing rising percentages of its bilateral aid to the least developed countries. (Bilateral aid to LLDCs as a percentage of all Japanese ODA rose from 5% in the early seventies to about 15% at the turn of the decade to around 20% by the late eighties.) In Japan, as elsewhere, domestic public opinion based in humane concern and the influence of world public opinion appears to lead not only to more aid spending but to spending focused more on need, even while it has to contend with other possible uses of aid that are attractive to national leaders with many conflicting responsibilities and bureaucratic missions.

Kiljunen sees growing Finnish support for aid as part of a growth in Finns' international consciousness. As Finland, which in 1960 had but five embassies outside Europe and North America, became less isolationist, Finnish concern for Third World development deepened in the early seventies, "reflecting partly domestic attitudes and partly those new approaches embraced at international forums." Finns understood foreign aid as an established and worthwhile practice that helped define proper international conduct and create international community. Thus a fledgling State Committee for International Development "emphasized the role of the U.N. system . . . [and] Nordic cooperation" in a 1963 report, and urged the necessity of participating in this "'form of activity in international cooperation which is becoming more and more important.' The Scandinavian countries were seen as the major reference group." Similarly, "mobilization of public opinion for a substantial increase in the volume of development aid" was based on "dissatisfaction with the Finnish aid performance, as compared with those of other Nordic countries" as well as on "the growing awareness and concern about the needs and problems of the developing world."[113]

The sense of being in an international community, with general obligations of taking a constructive part and repaying past kindnesses by some with present kindnesses to others in need—the sense of "diffuse reciprocity"—was clearly present in some countries' association of their aid programs with their having been recipients of Marshall Plan aid in the past. Raucher notes that Paul Hoffman's highly successful fund-raising as head of the UN Special Fund involved extensive travel with personal, carefully prepared appeals to national leaders, in part because "European leaders who appreciated what the Marshall Plan had done for their countries usually had difficulty refusing" Hoffman, who had earlier served as the Marshall Plan administrator.[114] Kreisky's proposal of an Austrian plan for development assistance specially included mention "of a 'Marshall Plan' for the Third World . . . a massive transfer of resources for the development of infrastructure" that would aid the economies of the industrialized countries and meet needs in the LDCs."[115] Similarly, Bertholet, de Clercq, and Janssen state that "in the early fifties, the Dutch reacted positively to President Harry Truman's Point Four Program. The success of the Marshall Plan enhanced their belief in Truman's 'bold new program.'"[116]

## CONCLUSION

The usual arguments against the possibility of moral influence on politics often rule out evidence about motives. Motives of statesmen are said to be hard to discern. Public opinion may not influence policy. Public statements may be hypocritical. And more fundamentally, structural factors may be more powerful than conscious motives, influencing leaders and bureaucracies charged with the national interest, selecting those leaders who—whatever their motives—will serve the national interest, and rewarding states that follow the dictates of realpolitik and causing others to decline. Thus it was important to start by establishing the case that foreign aid served humane interests oriented toward Third World development by looking at external state behavior.

In their actual foreign policy behavior, the developed democracies acted as if the thing that motivated them to give foreign aid was a humane internationalism. They provided aid monitored by development experts, and made sure it was used for development. They spent the aid mainly on needy countries, and not on countries of economic importance. Only a small amount of aid was spent on countries of strategic importance, except by the United States, which spent about a third of its aid that way. A sizable, and increasing, portion of aid was channeled through multilateral agencies which effectively buffered donor influence. The countries that had strong economic and strategic interests in the Third World were not particularly vigorous donors; the countries that had strong domestic commitments to helping the poor tended to be the committed aid donors. Countries with vigorous aid programs tended to provide aid in the least self-interested forms as previous chapters have shown.

But the argument that moral factors lay at the heart of support for foreign aid is not just an *as if* argument: this chapter has presented abundant evidence that the external behavior was accompanied by consciously humane motives. In general there was strong support for foreign aid among elites and among mass publics. When asked, people said the motives for aid were humane, not strategic ones. When asked what should be done with aid, people said it should be given to the countries that needed it and could profit by it. People and groups with special concerns for promoting trade and the advantages of capitalism, resisting communism, or advancing national interests evinced no special interest in foreign aid. Chapter 4 noted that countries with higher social spending and private donations to help the Third World had higher aid spending; public opinion data in this chapter showed that citizens favoring domestic equality and making personal contributions to the Third World tended to be strongly in support of aid; and that aid rose rapidly where public opinion favored it strongly. People and groups with strong moral and religious affiliations, those concerned with poverty and equality at home, those interested in international peace, and those who supported nongovernmental efforts to alleviate Third World poverty were stronger aid supporters. The relatively few people who felt aid should be used to promote trade or strategic interests tended to be negative toward aid in any case. People and groups that were consistent, strong advocates of aid always said aid should be governed by the interests of the recipients.

These results are extremely robust. They appear consistently in public opinion data from almost all the DAC countries, and they are consistent across time. They remain significant when various factors are controlled for in the mass opinion data. Elite opinion data are similar. The same results emerge when one looks at politicians' attitudes for (or against) aid. In almost every country, the parties (and factions within parties) that supported aid were those concerned with issues of equality and alleviation of poverty, not those concerned with the free market or with military and strategic issues. The groups in society that supported aid were churches, unions, private voluntary groups concerned with the Third World, and intellectuals. These groups invariably wanted more aid, but also aid that was freed from national interests and directed more toward the needs of recipients, especially the poorest. Most intellectuals who spoke out against aid were advocates of an unregulated free market, opponents of big government, and staunch anticommunists; the prominent advocates of aid tended to be long-time advocates of peace and alleviation of poverty. Advocates and opponents of aid drew analogies with domestic welfare programs. The international groups advocating aid, again, were the voluntary aid agencies, the ILO, the international trade union movement, and the churches. These in turn drew the connection to their religious and pro-labor principles explicitly.

In sum, there was strong, lasting support for expending major resources on aid, which people justified on idealistic grounds. There is very little evidence at any level that aid received support from people and groups seeking to advance particularistic national interests; there is substantial reason to think that people concerned with narrow national interests, or with ideological concerns such as spreading free markets and resisting communism, tended to oppose aid. Evidence of many kinds shows that those with strong moral principles, broad worldwide sympathies, and internationalist leanings supported aid, and that the supporters of aid wanted aid directed toward the needs of the poor and purged from self-interested conditions.

TABLE 5.9
(English) Wording of Questions on *Euro-Barometers 13* and *20*

### Questions from Euro-Barometer 13

(Variable 057) In political matters people talk of "the left" and "the right." How would you place your views on this scale? (Ten boxes are numbered, left to right, and respondents circle one box.)

(Variable 058) Do you go to religious services several times a week, once a week, a few times in the year, or never?

(Variable 064) Now I would like to ask you if you think our aid to the developing countries should be increased, remain the same, or be decreased?

(Variable 065) So far we have given aid to the developing countries in a period of rising living standards. If our own living standards ceased to increase, do you think we should go on giving, decrease, or stop our aid to developing countries?

### Questions from Euro-Barometer 20

(Variable 042) If you compared (our country) with all the other countries of the world in terms of how rich we are, at what level would you put us? (Show card: range of one [poor] to seven [rich])

Preface to Variables 043, 045, 047, and 051:
Here is a list of problems that people of [our country] are more or less interested in. (Show card 1) Could you please tell me for each one whether you personally consider it is a very important problem, of little importance, or not important at all? (9 questions)

(Variable 043) Reducing the differences between regions of our country by helping the less developed regions or those in most need.

(Variable 045) Try and reduce the number of very rich people and very poor people.

(Variable 047) Helping poor countries in Africa, South America, Asia, etc.

(Variable 051) Strengthen our military defense against possible enemies.

Preface to Variables 113, 114, 115, 119, 120, 121, and 123:
Many things are heard and said about Third World countries. For each of the following statements, would you like to tell me if you agree completely, agree to some extent, disagree to some extent, or disagree completely? (Show card)

(Variable 113) In former times the fact that they were colonies held back their development.

(Variable 114) They are exploited by the developed countries such as our own.

(Variable 115) They do not really want to work.

(Variable 119) They were happier when they were colonies.

(Variable 120) They are beginning to compete with us with their own products.

(Variable 121) We have a moral duty to help them.

(Variable 123) It is in our own interest to help them.

(Variable 127) Some people favour, others are against, helping the Third World countries. Are you personally (1) very much for, (2) for to some extent, (3) somewhat against, or (4) very much against?

(Variable 147) Talking about people from Third World countries living here, would you say that your country does too much, or too little, or about the right amount to help them?

(Variable 155) There are different kinds of countries in the Third World. (Show card) In your opinion which type of countries should we be helping most? (One response only) (1) The poorest countries; (2) Those on which we depend for raw materials; (3) Those who buy a lot of products from us; (4) Those that are of strategic interest to us for political or defense reasons.

(Variable 156) If you were told that in order to give more help to Third World countries it will be necessary to hold back 1% from your salary, would you agree to this idea or not?

(Variable 157) Have you, during the last couple of years, given help to an organization concerned with the Third World by giving money or help in any other way?

(Variable 158) Now [do] you think that our aid to the Third World countries should be increased, remain the same, or decrease?

(Variable 159) So far we have given aid to the Third World countries in a period of rising living standards. If our own standard of living stopped increasing, do you think we should go on helping Third World countries, decrease our help, or stop it altogether?

(Variable 432) In political matters, people talk of "the left" and "the right." How would you place your views on this scale? (Card shows boxes from one [left] to ten [right])

(Variable 436) Independently of whether you go to church or not, would you say you are (1) a religious person, (2) not a religious person, (3) a convinced atheist?

(Variable 439) How old were you when you finished your full-time education?

(Variable 451) We would like to analyze the survey results according to the income of persons interviewed. (Show income card) Here is a scale of incomes, and we would like to know in what group your family is, counting all wages, salaries, pensions and any other income that comes in. Just give me the number of the group your family falls into *before* tax and other deductions.

---

*Source*: Rabier et al. 1985, *Euro-Barometer 20*, and 1983, *Euro-Barometer 13*. See notes to table 5.1 for further information.

*Note*: The wording of the questions is as given in the published ICPSR codebooks to the *Euro-Barometer* studies.

## CHAPTER SIX

# What Prepared the Way:
## Historical Antecedents of Aid

> Men of goodwill in Britain—and particularly in the Labour
> movement—have prided themselves on the fifty years' march out
> of nineteenth-century industrialism and inequality towards so-
> cial justice and the welfare state. More than half a century ago the
> pioneers of this movement, seeing all around them the ugliness,
> the squalor, the misery, the want and poverty which Victorian
> capitalism had brought in its train, dedicated themselves and
> those who came after them to the creation of a new Britain in
> which hunger and poverty would be no more. Their dream has
> been very largely realized. Now those who honour their memory
> must look to wider horizons: their mission in the second half of
> this war-torn century must be to carry the war on poverty and
> want . . . to the uttermost ends of the earth. . . . The war on
> world poverty . . . is the only way in which we in the more fa-
> voured countries can fulfill our obligations to 1,500 million peo-
> ple all over the world; and, lifting our eyes above the tensions and
> struggles of world politics, we shall find that in fighting this war
> we are treading the way—the one way only—to peace and a more
> abundant life for all mankind.
>
> —Harold Wilson[1]

THE HUMANITARIAN and egalitarian ideas and movements shown to account for cross-national variations in aid giving and domestic support for
aid prepared the way for aid in the fifty to eighty years before aid programs were conceived of and governed their subsequent evolution. This
chapter examines how the growth of humane internationalism, social democracy, and concern for poverty made articulation of foreign aid programs possible, by fostering the general thinking that lay behind foreign
aid and the specific ideas and institutions from which it emerged. Early
private charitable movements provided experience and technical know-
how, historical and theoretical arguments, and analogous experiences
and commitments out of which foreign aid policies could be constructed.
Domestic government polices set in place from roughly 1890 until 1930

also provided examples. Powerful historical experiences in the thirties and forties, and the lessons that policymakers drew from them, were embodied in a series of concrete institutions and arrangements, which provided the foundation for foreign aid programs in 1949–51.

After this chapter's discussion of how the ground was prepared for the idea of foreign aid to take such deep and rapid root the subsequent chapter will look at how the initial aid plans did in fact take root and quickly ramified into a thicket of interconnected and mutually reinforcing programs. The final empirical chapter will trace the growth and modification of aid programs in quantitative terms, showing that many indicators point to a steady development of norm-governed change in aid.

## The Rise of the Welfare State and Its Roots of Support in Domestic Humanitarian, Labor, and Social-Democratic Movements

The growing strength of labor and labor-oriented parties, and of charitable concerns for the poor and disadvantaged in all segments of society, lay behind the rise of welfare state institutions and prepared the way for the growth of international humanitarianism. The adoption of domestic social welfare measures was more than just the result of specific interests or political strategies; it involved fundamental changes in philosophy and awareness about poverty in domestic society. Domestic labor and humanitarian movements were linked to growing support for internationalism and international institutions, opposition to war, and early international humanitarian efforts. Convictions about international justice and belief in a broadly participatory international order as the basis of peace and prosperity were counterparts of moral and intellectual developments in domestic society and politics, and both together prepared the way for international programs of development assistance.

### The Rise of the Welfare State

During the seventy-five or so years before aid started there was a steady movement toward domestic welfare institutions among the industrial democracies that later formed the core of the OECD. Welfare state outlays have increased relative to GNP in all Western countries since the turn of the century[2] and have transformed their polities.[3] The rise of the labor movement and social-democratic parties in Europe involved ideals and arguments, commitment to what Tawney called "the strategy of equality,"[4] as well as organized political pressure. Robert Goodin argues that both sociologically and morally, "the social assistance programs of the welfare state are best seen as devices to protect the vulnerable and dependent beneficiaries. That is at one and the same time their intention, their effect, and their justification." Also it was in fact "their advocates' principal (though not sole) argument for them, and it continues to be one of the most prominent arguments offered for their expansion." Robson says Lloyd George's welfare measures were intended as "tentative steps . . . to protect the weakest and most vulnerable elements in society such as the aged poor, the unemployed workman, the sweated worker." Titmuss sees the growth of the welfare state as a progressive acknowledgment of collective responsibility for those in "states of dependency."[5] As such, the development of economic assistance, welfare, and planning within the borders of the national state helped lay the foundations for international economic aid.

In country after country, the evolution of welfare state institutions was bound up with philosophies of social solidarity. By the turn of the twentieth century, there was consensus in France that the "state . . . had a responsibility to provide for the subsistence of the poor and those in need," as Freeman argues. A French Enlightenment "movement toward the humanization of poor relief" led the 1791 Declaration of the Rights of Man and 1793 Republican Constitution to recognize "that 'public relief is a sacred debt. Society owes subsistence to citizens in misfortune.'"[6] French Radicals like Prime Minister Leon Bourgeois invoked the idea of solidarity in "an organic and interdependent society," an idea originated by Catholic theologians and early adopted by socialists, as a basis "to unite the working and middle classes around a program of social progress for all."[7] Germany, the "institutional innovator" of the welfare state, tried to address growing "demands for socioeconomic equality in the context of the evolution of mass democracies" and to "the loss of 'security functions' by families and other communities."[8] In the years from 1883 to 1889, Germany enacted laws establishing accident, health, old-age, and invalidism insurance, providing unprecedentedly "comprehensive protection of the working man."[9] Although German welfare measures sought to "blunt the appeal of Marxism to the working class"[10] and "strengthen" and "unify" the country,[11] the very need to forestall socialist challenges to state legitimacy shows the power these ideals exercised. The Scandinavian countries began to enact comprehensive social welfare legislation in the late nineteenth century, drawing on ideas of British utopianism and utilitarianism, and the traditional role of the church and other charitable organizations. By the time the Great Depression fully gripped Scandinavia, there existed a safety net of basic, though by no means gap-free, social insurance.[12] And Bartholomew argues that Canadian conservative traditions, as well as socialist commitment to "social justice and equality," undergird Canadian support for the welfare state. In Canada as in Europe "the conservative tradition informs us that . . . those born to high stations are obliged to care for those born to low stations."[13]

The British government expanded state regulation and provision for working conditions, public education, health, and housing starting in the nineteenth century, and established social security measures starting with a Workmen's Compensation Act in 1897.[14] The best-selling 1942 Beveridge Report ushered in the ideal of "cradle-to-grave" benefits, and the rash of legislation passed under the Labour government from 1945 to 1948 remains the framework of the welfare state in Great Britain.[15] At the same time, the "welfare state" concept, coined in 1941 by Anglican Archbishop William Temple as a contrast to the "power" and "warfare" state against which the British were then locked in mortal combat, involved implicit reference to international affairs. As Flora and Heidenheimer state, "Thus launched to sustain morale and discipline during a period of wartime crisis, the term subsequently came to be more closely associated with the social benefits that democratic governments hoped to offer once the war was over."[16]

In sum, solidarity and commitment to equality and concern about poverty and justice clearly were important among the diverse motives involved in the development of the welfare state. Einhorn and Logue say, "Support for welfare programs in Western democracies rest on three basic motivations . . . *altruism*, an unselfish desire to help others, . . . *self-insurance*, . . . [and increasingly upon] *solidarity*," which they see as "a willingness to tie one's fate to that of others and . . . to share a sense of group identity."[17] Flora finds "the emergence of the European welfare state" linked to "the evolution of mass democracy" and deems it part of a "democratic struggle for a more equitable share [of a nation's] material wealth" and culture, as well as a "reaction to the problems of the industrial working class."[18] Myrdal argues that the "large-scale egalitarian reform policies . . . set in motion in all developed countries, and . . . escalating ever since World War I . . . were regularly argued simply in terms of achieving greater social justice. The importance of this valuation was gradually becoming so widely accepted that political conditions were created for the reforms to pass through the parliaments."[19]

These motives for the welfare state provide a basis for extension of its logic beyond national borders. Goodin argues that the logic of "protecting the vulnerable" involved in the welfare state justifies concern for poor nations through the provision of foreign aid, and his analysis of the growth of domestic social protection gives clues that help us understand how such an extension has come about. He notes that expansions of welfare services have usually started by identifying "a group in need and [showing] . . . there was nothing that they could have done to alleviate their own distress" as Beveridge did in complaining, in 1907, of the economy's cyclic nature and the state's lack of "control or supervision of the labour market." Programs are then adopted in a "sequence [that] proceeds from cases where the dependency is conspicuous to ones where it is less so."[20] The same logic, I would argue, led from national to international cases of dependency, and from international response to natural disasters and wars to attempts to end chronic states of poverty.

Nobel Prize-winning economist Gunnar Myrdal argues that the process of gaining concessions for poor countries was also like the establishment of the welfare state in its peculiar blend of moral suasion and political pressure from below. While holding that the really effective arguments for foreign aid, as for domestic social programs, appeal to humane concern rather than self-interest, he also stresses that in both arenas the rich usually make concessions only under compulsion: "To be induced to do so the rich and privileged must sense that demands are raised and forcefully pressed, and that power becomes assembled behind them. At that stage, moral ideals in the upper class are given their chance to play a supporting role."[21] Pressure from below, when linked to moral ideas, exacts concessions partly because of a sense of obligation and partly because of a recognition that the powerful moral ideas must be accommodated.

Moreover, Myrdal argues that the "request that rich nations should aid poor nations" would have been "impossible even to formulate" without the "doctrine of equality" and the development of the domestic welfare state. He lauds Alfred Marshall, in writing after World War I, for foreseeing that just as "every . . . Western country can now afford to make increased sacrifices . . . [to] rais[e] the quality of life throughout their whole populations," so "a time may come when such a matter will be treated as a cosmopolitan rather than national obligation." This is just what Myrdal thinks has happened as "the misery of those far away has been brought home to the peoples of the richer countries" in recent decades. "Before World War II hardly anyone saw a common responsibility on the part of all the developed nations to aid underdeveloped countries. Now such a responsibility is gradually becoming recognized as a general proposition."[22] This is "nothing else than the rapid spread over the globe of the old ideals of liberty, equality, and brotherhood, . . . increasingly . . . realized in the last two generations within the national Welfare States . . . of the Western World."[23] Hence Myrdal argues that "the welfare state is hesitantly and very slowly being widened to be conceived of as a welfare world."[24]

### Humanitarian, Charitable, and Religious Roots of the Welfare State

Havighurst argues that "widespread unemployment and great distress" in England troubled the Victorian conscience; he concludes that by "1900 it was generally recognized that state action, on a national level, was necessary to cope with the social evils which had developed with industrialization." Charles Booth's 1889 "Life and Labour" series, which concluded that 30.7% of Londoners lived below subsistence level, commanded wide attention and figured in parliamentary debate.[25] Studies of other cities likewise revealed a large "destitute and miserable" minority, as did a 1904 British Army report. The London *Times* argued in 1909 that laissez-faire policies had "left us the legacy of multitudes badly born, badly taught, badly fed, and finally robbed of employment" and required a "readjustment of values." Yet Havighurst argues "social service agencies and . . . social literature . . . sought not only to alleviate distress but to get at the causes." Leonard T. Hobhouse, prominent sociology professor and writer for the *Manchester Guardian* and the *Nation* inveighed against "a blunting of moral responsibility," arguing that "the political order must conform to the ethical idea of what is just" and that socialists and liberals must "make common cause against the growing power of wealth." The master of Balliol told his students, "when you have . . . learned all that Oxford can teach you, . . . go and discover why, with so much wealth in Britain, there continues to be so much poverty and how poverty can be cured."

Bremner likewise argues that in the United States a new view of poverty arose after about 1830 and formed the basis of the wave of humanitarian concern which swept the country. This both provoked and resulted from the increasing numbers of settlement house workers, clergy, artists, academics, and writers documenting deprivation in the cities. Jacob Riis's photo essay, *How the Other Half Lives* (1890), the well-known 1894 tract "If Christ Came to Chicago," novels by Stephen Crane and Theodore Dreiser, Robert Hunter's 1904 study of New York's poor, and Walter Rauschenbusch's 1907 *Christianity and the Social Crisis* were all well known and influential.[26]

The social crises of the late nineteenth century led proponents of a "Social Gospel," as May[27] argues, "to attack untrammeled individualism with the equally powerful notion of equality." Antonides says that "spokesmen for 'social Christianity' condemned . . . disregard for workers' rights and welfare." The influential Washington Gladden studied "low wages and dismal working conditions" of railways, mines, and factories, arguing in 1886 that "the Christian moralist is . . . bound to admonish the Christian employer that the wage-system, when it rests on competition as its sole basis, is anti-social and anti-Christian. The doctrine which bases all the relations of employer and employed upon self-interest is a doctrine of the pit."[28] Carter says that the Social Gospel movement began to revive in the thirties, sparked by the Depression and by fascism in Europe, and became much more international in its focus. Thus the Oxford [Missions] Conference of 1937 "came out for full employment, universal educational opportunity, social security, and conservation."[29]

Humane movements to alleviate poverty were not simply palliative or remedial in their focus, but sought to change underlying social and political conditions. Wade calls the settlement house movement the first war on poverty.[30] From its beginnings in the 1880s, the movement was concerned not only with salvaging individuals but also with transforming the social environment through fact finding, program development, and widened government responsibility. The deleterious effects of industrialism, rather than personal moral failures, were seen as the major cause of poverty; and changes in the social environment, rather than individual reform, were pushed as remedies for want—housing codes, child labor laws, legislation on women's hours and wages, workmen's insurance.[31] Charitable foundations established by Rockefeller, Carnegie, and other donors at the turn of the century, "attack[ed] misery at its source through the weapon of research." Such foundations permitted "greater intelligence and vision than the donors themselves could hope to possess." These systematic efforts at charity "climaxed the long effort to put large-scale giving on a businesslike basis" and also paved the way for state administration of welfare programs.[32]

Many figures involved in social work, domestic reform, philanthropy, and religious work also saw their concerns as strongly connected to questions of international peace and justice. The Rockefeller Foundation has had a special department dealing with international health from its beginnings. Andrew Carnegie, concerned with questions of poverty and charity in the United States, was also active in opposition to war and promoted peace research.[33] At the 1937 Oxford Missionary Conference, Carter observes, "Chinese and Japanese delegates made a special point of their fellowship together even though the China Incident was a week old when the conference convened."[34] Noted settlement house worker Jane Addams, a cofounder of the Women's International League for Peace and Freedom, "got much comfort" from John Hobson's "Toward International Government" and its account of the activity of international organizations.[35] Florence Nightingale's efforts at establishing a profession of nursing involved her in care of wounded soldiers amid the horrors of the Crimean War in 1854 that commanded worldwide recognition.

### Labor Movements and Social-Democratic Parties

The rise of the social welfare state also reflected the growing power of labor; and this involved a labor philosophy as well as a struggle for power. Labor organizations, earlier banned, were strengthened by British acts of 1871 and 1875 and French acts of 1864 and 1884. Trade union centers were set up in Scandinavia in 1898–99, and the Italian unions gained wide support around 1906.[36] Much of the power of labor came from the rise of parties strongly committed to labor demands: the British Labour party, social-democratic parties, labor parties, and even the U.S. Democratic party. Patterson and Thomas argue that "growth of parties identified with the complex of . . . social democratic" ideas has been central in Europe's twentieth-century political history. After World War II, growing concern for equality and social justice and the restoration of democracy may have made "Social Democratic parties . . . the strongest political force in Western Europe" by 1945.[37]

The rise of social democracy was based on a powerful set of ideas about the rights of the poor and disadvantaged and on an international solidarity among workers. Patterson and Thomas define social democracy as "a belief that social and economic reform designed to benefit the less privileged should be pursued within a framework of democracy, liberty and the parliamentary process." Crosland emphasizes "political liberalism, the mixed economy, the welfare state, Keynesian economics and a belief in equality."[38] Einhorn and Logue speak of the Scandinavian Social Democratic parties elevating "material discontents . . . into abstractions like justice, dignity, equality, and solidarity."[39] Minkin and Seyd see the British Labour party philosophy as a mixture of "collectivism . . . directed toward . . . humanitarian redistribution of income" and a "vague conception of the moral and social transformation of man."[40] The June 1918 constitution of the British Labour party speaks of seeking "a new social order based not on fighting but on fraternity—not on the competitive struggle for the bare means of life, but on deliberately planned cooperation in production and distribution for the benefit of all who participate by hand or brain."[41]

Socialist parties, based on universal ideals of solidarity, naturally showed particular interest in internationalism. May argues that socialists had "*lasting* interest" in "transnational links" and in "institutionalising their contacts," and claims that socialists correctly hold that "their comrades engage in unofficial or extra-party transnational contacts to a far greater degree than the adherents of any other ideology." Saul Rose "alleg[ed] that 'Socialism has always been an international movement because its principles are universal.'" May finds wide scholarly agreement that there is "an *inherent* relationship between Socialism and internationalism," because of "the universal relevance of its values and/or the universal applicability of its principles."[42] This internationalism made it natural for labor unions to support Third World concerns and foreign aid programs and, indeed, to anticipate the programs that were later proposed. British trade unions promoted and supported indigenous unions in the colonies in their demands for fair wages and working conditions. Ernest

Bevin, important in the trade union movement and Labour party, wrote in 1939 that "empires, as we have known them, must become a thing of the past" and be replaced by "a common contribution . . . towards the development of the Colonial Empire both in relation to defence, trade, and the recognition of equality" on a basis of democracy and human rights. Nicholson sees in this statement "the seed which blossomed in 1950 into the Colombo Plan" for foreign aid, at the Commonwealth Foreign Ministers' meeting which the ailing Bevin, foreign secretary in the Labour government, "insisted on attending."[43]

## THE GROWTH OF INTERNATIONALISM

The hundred years or so prior to the beginning of foreign aid also saw growing sentiments that war was an unacceptable method of settling international differences and increased recognition that people throughout the earth constitute a single human family. The growth of international consultation and international technical organizations, attempts at peace plans and the outlawing of war, the rise of internationalist thought, the creation of an international court and a League of Nations, the growth of international humanitarian movements and relief efforts, and forays by the churches, labor, and government into concern for poverty across borders all paved the way for the creation of foreign aid programs in the middle of this century.

### International Law, Collaboration, and Humanitarianism

The nineteenth century saw a steady increase in international collaboration. A steady development of international technical conferences and administration accompanied, and outlasted, the increase in cooperative high-level consultations among the major powers that followed the Congress of Vienna in 1815.[44] Participation in intergovernmental organizations doubled every couple of decades from about the 1860s onward, and international non-governmental organizations increased rapidly in this century.[45] Mangone traces the growing study and practice of international law in modern Europe, the establishment of tribunals and laws of war, efforts at arbitration and disarmament, and the steady humanitarian efforts that resulted in the progressive abolition of the slave trade.[46]

The history of the Red Cross illustrates how the growth of international law, codes of war, and efforts to secure peace were closely bound up with international humanitarian efforts. J. Henry Dunant, a young Swiss doctor on a trip to Italy, saw soldiers lying without medical care days after the Battle of Solferino in 1859 and was "seized by horror and pity." He began attending the wounded himself and organizing local women to help who, though initially reluctant, ended by crying to one another, "We are all brothers." Dunant's "prophetic" book, *A Memory of Solferino*, shook the Continent, profoundly affecting a "public opinion . . . increasingly receptive to humanitarian considerations."[47] His proposals for a volunteer organization to aid wounded soldiers and for an international convention to protect medics "led to the creation of the Red Cross . . . [and] the Geneva Convention," according to Pictet;[48] and Red Cross humanitarian concern since has taken step after step toward the creation of international humanitarian relief of suffering of all sorts, paying minimal attention to national borders in its response to changing world problems.[49] The 1919 League of Red Cross Societies (LRCS) was formed to provide aid in natural disasters.[50] Though mainly organized "for short term relief assistance in acute situations," the Red Cross movement found its ability to respond quickly "imposes a moral duty to accept tasks outside the movement's traditional field, as long as other solutions are lacking," so that "over the last two decades, Red Cross involvement in famine situations . . . has been regarded as . . . natural," even leading at times to "lengthy and large scale relief actions involving major feeding and supplementary nutrition programmes." According to Willemin and Heacock, this reflects the breadth of the initial aims, which "can be summed up in a single gesture, that of the Good Samaritan."[51] Thus, the "traditional humanitarian activities of the Red Cross fall within a framework of concern for world peace. . . . The original approach of Henry Dunant was not only to respond to human suffering and to mitigate the evils of warfare, but to put an end to war," as reflected in the (1961) motto of the League of Red Cross Societies, *per humanitatem ad pacem.*[52]

The increasing international responsibility for refugees also reflects the development of international humanitarian concern. Fridtjof Nansen, appointed Commissioner for Russian Refugees in 1921 by the League of Nations at Red Cross behest, worked tirelessly to create a new international attitude of responsibility toward refugees. Nansen's "active love of humanity" made him the only man "to whom the doors of every Chancery in Europe were open," as Lord Curzon put it in 1923.[53] After his death in 1931, the work was continued by the Nansen Office and the Intergovernmental Committee for Refugees, founded in 1938, which was merged into an International Refugee Organization, which was, in turn, replaced by the United Nations High Commissioner for Refugees (UNHCR) in 1951. Their work has effected a "continual broadening . . . of the definition of a refugee."[54] UNHCR Poul Hartling states that Nansen's "unique" example was "inspired . . . by a whole-hearted commitment to the dispossessed," yet his effectiveness depended upon states' willingness to respond to his appeals. Thus he provided a model of how to meet "urgent needs of refugees . . . and to seek durable solutions to their problems" by "arousing respect for the basic rights of every man" and mobilizing "goodwill on a global scale."[55]

Institutionalized war relief may also have laid foundations for later foreign aid efforts. The Committee for Relief in Belgium raised $52 million from private charities early in World War I, during the period of American neutrality. After the war, Herbert Hoover headed a European Relief Council, which raised $30 million in the winter of 1920–21. During two years of neutrality in World War II, some seven hundred U.S. organizations raised $90 million for civilian and refugee relief overseas, and Congress appropriated an additional $50 million for distribution by the Red Cross. The National War Fund raised $750 million in war fund drives, with almost half going to overseas war-related relief efforts. Between 1939 and 1945, American volunteer agencies sent approximately $500 million in goods and funds overseas to war sufferers; in the six years after the war, private philanthropy raised nearly $2 billion for relief reconstruction and social services abroad.[56]

Private international philanthropic efforts, which often foreshadowed later governmental development efforts, increased dramatically in the seventy-five years prior to the start of foreign aid. Curti and Birr discuss some of these in their book *Prelude to Point Four*.[57] Lyman White describes numerous international NGOs involved with social welfare in areas of health, social service, migration, the status of women, child welfare, relief, minorities, and migrants in the twentieth century.[58] Curti traces American philanthropy abroad back to 1793 earthquake assistance and nineteenth-century efforts to alleviate Irish and Russian famines. The Rockefeller Foundation worked to combat typhus abroad. Early missionaries supported vernacular public schools in India, education for women abroad, and health efforts throughout Asia.[59] Romanofsky observes that scores of American social service organizations founded international groups to work on the same problems abroad, and these broadened their focus in response to experience. The American Foundation for Overseas Blind, founded in 1915 to help blinded Allied soldiers, by 1950 was attacking vitamin A deficiency, which causes blindness in LDCs. The American Council of Voluntary Agencies for Foreign Service (ACVAFS), led by a social worker, Charlotte Owen, assisted the United Nations Relief and Rehabilitation Administration, fostered its 1946 child welfare conference, helped develop UNICEF, and organized CARE and the Licensed Agencies for Relief in Asia (LARA) in 1945. In the early fifties the ACVAFS focused on "technical assistance, as opposed to relief," providing a report, "The Moral Challenge of Abundance," and instrumental testimony in favor of foreign aid legislation that expressed "the basic humanitarian attitude that permeated the ACVAFS."[60]

Increasing religious and secular efforts to aid the needy around the world between World War I and World War II were, Curti says, "influenced by the ideal of brotherhood . . . basic in our Judeo-Christian culture."[61] Maddox notes that missionaries have "organiz[ed] and operat[ed] schools, hospitals, clinics, social service centers, and demonstration farms" to raise levels of living and increase productivity, including 137 well-established farm, agricultural, and miscellaneous projects in 66 agencies surveyed in 1953, as well as 119 medical and 1,363 educational projects.[62] Bremner observes that by the time Point Four started up, religious and other voluntary agencies operated "approximately 2,500 social service, medical, educational, agricultural, and even industrial projects" in all parts of the world.[63] Bock, as part of a series tracing the history of foreign assistance in the wake of the excitement caused by the Point Four program, interviewed fifty-five consultants with long experience in private overseas aid. Projects included farm credit, relocation, job training, community development, and literacy efforts. Workers emphasized "revitaliz[ing] local traditions" and "cultural life in the community," making life more rewarding "for the people in terms of their own values," "encouraging a sense of human equality and dignity," and "finding ways of imbedding improved practices . . . without [upsetting] existing spiritual, cultural, or social frameworks which give meaning, satisfaction, or security to the people."[64] Curti sums up the motives for American philanthropy in general, saying that

> two interrelated motives overarched all others. One was related to Judeo-Christian teachings about the duty of compassion and charity . . . sometimes expressed in the doctrine . . . that the holder [of wealth] is only God's steward and obligated to give to the poor, the distressed, and the needy. From many diaries, letters, and other evidence it is clear that this factor was a dominant one in a great deal of giving. A second motive was humanitarianism, embracing the same conception of the brotherhood of man and of the duty of those who can help the needy to do so, but secular in character. It reinforced and supplemented the closely related Hebraic-Christian values.[65]

## International Labor

From its inception, the labor movement had a strong international element; the explicit internationalism and concern for working people made it a natural base of support for international assistance in raising standards of living. As early as 1818, industrialist Robert Owen addressed concerns of the working class to the European powers assembled at Aix-la-Chapelle. Twenty years later, Jerome Adolphe Blanqui, professor of political economy at the University of Paris, remarked, "The Powers have often entered into treaties whereby they are committed to take human life. Why, then, should they not commit themselves today for the safeguard and the sweetening of human existence?"[66] Denis Le Grand, a French manufacturer, faced with a French government claim that "international competition" made workers' welfare legislation impossible, appealed to the governments of France, Germany, Switzerland, and the United Kingdom in 1855 for joint legislation "to protect the working classes."[67] Ghebali argues that the ideas behind international standards for labor had three motivations, all of which found voice in Le Grand's appeal: humanitarian or philanthropic principles; "a link between the protection of workers and social peace"; and an attempt to overcome competitive disadvantages that would accrue to a single country adopting labor standards. Ghebali states that "the social and humanitarian ideas of the European revolution of 1848" opened up space for the *Congrès international de bienfaisance* to fight for labor legislation; ideas about protection of labor spread though social-democratic and Catholic social circles, and among academics and "even . . . associations of industrialists."[68] In 1880, the Swiss government proposed a conference to draft a treaty on factory legislation. Pope Leo XIII commended the idea, and a conference was finally held in 1890, in Berlin. An 1897 informal conference in Brussels of civil servants and social scientists led to formation of the International Association for Workers' Legal Protection in 1900.[69]

In 1914, AFL president Samuel Gompers proposed that an international workers' conference "meet at the same time and in the same place as the future peace congress," and French trade union leader Leon Jouhaux argued "that the future peace treaty should contain special clauses relating to labour legislation," a proposal endorsed by "representatives of the trade unions in the allied countries . . . in 1916."[70] Building upon the work of the International Association for Labour Legislation set up in 1901 in Basel,[71] the conference led to formation of the International Labour Organization (ILO), which was recognized in the league covenant. The ILO saw its mission in strongly idealistic terms, and emphasized the connection between peace and justice. The preamble to the original ILO constitution of 1919 sees the elimination of unjust conditions for workers as a prerequisite for peace.[72] A scroll with a Latin inscription that translates "If you wish peace, cultivate justice" was sealed into the cornerstone of the ILO building in Geneva in 1919.[73] A widely circulated 1930 publication, *A Little Book of the ILO*, depicted the organization's function in terms of a broad humanitarian mission: "As a lighthouse throws its beam abroad into the darkness, searching out and illuminating obscure and hidden places, so does the ILO serve to explore and discover those parts of the earth where men work in hardship and privation, awaiting the day when principles of justice and humanity shall reign."[74]

The ILO argued for international cooperation to raise the standard of living of poorer countries from the forties on. The 1941 ILO conference in New York called for "the planning and application of measures of reconstruction,"[75] and the landmark Philadelphia Declaration of May 10, 1944, which advocated assisting less developed countries, was incorporated in the organization's charter, as a continuation of fundamental ILO principles. The Declaration states that "poverty anywhere constitutes a danger to prosperity everywhere" and that "the war against want requires to be carried on . . . within each nation, and by continuous and concerted international effort . . . with a view to the promotion of the common welfare." As "all human beings . . . have the right to . . . conditions of freedom and dignity, of economic security and equal opportunity," making this possible "must constitute the central aim of national and international policy." Its concluding paragraphs speak of the "fuller and broader utilisation of the world's productive resources" to be "secured by national and international action, including measures to expand production and consumption" and "to promote the economic and social advancement of the less developed regions of the world," which is "a matter of concern to the whole civilized world."[76]

## The Growth of Internationalist Sentiment

During the first half of the nineteenth century there was already "an ideological climate in which [the leading] states agreed, as never before, on the necessity of working together in the interest of avoiding further war," Hinsley argues, expressed in formulas such as "Each nation has its rights, but Europe also has its rights." Despite the failure of the Concert of Europe, the peace movement in 1856 wanted the Congress of Paris to find "some system of international arbitration" that would subject the "interest of nations" to "fixed rules of justice and right."[77] Beales says the various peace congresses held from 1843 on gained respect over time. Andrew Carnegie endowed a permanent foundation for the promotion of peace and wrote the Boston Congress of 1904 to propose "a union of the Great Powers to declare that there would be no more war and to *enforce* the declaration."[78] The Inter-Parliamentary Union was established in 1888 with members from different countries seeking to "study all questions of an international character" and secure cooperation for international peace. White argues that the International Peace Bureau of Geneva, set up in 1892, with "annual 'Universal Peace Congresses' attracted much attention and developed support for the idea that international problems should be settled peacefully." The Hague conferences of 1899 and 1907 reflected strong anti-war sentiment and received endorsement from the tsar, the U.S. secretary of state, and other leading figures.[79] Bertrand Russell in 1910 argued that "all hopes of freedom at home and humanity abroad, rest upon the creation of international good will" as a basis for "some international instrument of government" going beyond the Hague tribunal.[80]

The First World War provoked unprecedented anti-war sentiment. It was only as a "war to end all wars" that Wilson justified entering the Great War, and despite his failure to realize the far-seeing principles which he proposed for creating a peaceful world after the war, there was widespread support for those principles. The Inter-Parliamentary Union helped make "way for the creation of the League of Nations and its permanent Secretariat" during the war, according to Lange.[81] During the war, numerous organizations sought to prevent further conflicts. American, Belgian, British, Dutch, and German women founded the Women's International League for Peace and Freedom in 1915.[82] "Distinguished Americans . . . including former President Taft" founded a private League to Enforce the Peace, which called for a League of Nations; Lord Bryce headed a British branch.[83] The Dutch Anti-War Council organized representatives from forty nations into a Central Organization for a Durable Peace, which Beales says "influenced Wilson in propounding the 'Fourteen Points.'"[84] A Federation of League of Nations Societies was founded in 1919 to "promot[e] the understanding, approval and application of the principles embodied in the Covenant of the League of Nations."[85]

Internationalist sentiment also recognized economic obligations and, from the early twenties on, articulated a case for economic assistance to people abroad, and for the recognition of an interdependent world economic community with mutual duties. In 1923 Russell argued that "the reasons for desiring international government are two: first, the prevention of war; secondly, the securing of economic justice as between different nations and different populations," concluding "the rights of a nation against humanity are no more absolute than the rights of an individual as against the community."[86] The Catholic Association for International Peace, in discussing the Moral Law in Relation to States, argued that "states are . . . united by the . . . bonds of humanity. Men do not cease to be brothers in the human family when they become grouped into states, nor do they get rid of their obligations of universal charity when they take on the character of national citizens or national rulers. . . . Charity is as necessary for human welfare among states as among individuals."[87]

Early in the century, church interest in international social reform led to calls for what we would now term international programs of economic development. Peoples of non-European areas were full participants in the work of the 1910 Edinburgh World Missionary Conference, which began "the modern phase of missionary cooperation." The ongoing International Missionary Council (IMC) formed there listed "seeking justice in international and inter-racial relations" among the main objectives in its constitution, along with "leading souls to Christ" and "building the Church."[88] The IMC's "milestone" 1928 Jerusalem meeting, guided by "Christian experts like Professor R. H. Tawney of the London School of Economics, [and] Harold A. Grimshaw, Chief of the Native Labor Section, International Labor Office, Geneva,"[89] included concern for "problems such as . . . industrialism, . . . [and] the problems of the rural areas" among its evangelical concerns. "Human brotherhood under God's Fatherhood" entailed working "to remove race prejudice and adverse conditions due to it, . . . [and] to enable all alike to enjoy equality of social, political and economic opportunity."[90] The strong concern at the 1928 conference for promotion of international social justice as an essential part of the missionary endeavor was influenced by the Social Gospel movement but also by much longer-standing missionary concerns with the "Christianization of Society," Shivute argues.[91] Thus the "production of Christ-like character in individuals and societies and nations through faith in . . . Christ" meant Christian agencies should "undertake programs of rural reconstruction designed to transform rural life." A 1939 Episcopal missions booklet spelled out what these aims might mean, as raising the status of women, opposing the killing of girl babies, and resisting rigid caste rules, in addition to giving medical and technical help, since the gospel requires "recognizing the right of men of all races and classes to an equal chance of development of personality, a transvaluation of values in which a man is seen to be of more worth than a plantation or a mine."[92] A 1944 IMC pamphlet emphasized church concern for assisting people in "struggle for livelihood," "furthering individual and community health" and nutrition and that churches seek to overcome illiteracy, arguing that "Christians should identify . . . with every serious effort at human uplift and the relief of suffering."[93]

About one third of the official account of the First Assembly of the World Council of Churches, held in 1948, deals with issues of "The Church and the Disorder of Society," most of which is concerned with "The Church and the International Disorder," and "Christian Reconstruction and Interchurch Aid." Specifically reflecting concerns of African and Asian delegates, the report stressed the need to "lessen the burden of toil and alleviate poverty," and it argued that "in the face of international disorder" the "churches and all Christian people" are obliged to "make sacrifices for the hungry and homeless."[94] Particular attention is given to the needs of refugees.[95] The World Council and IMC also called a conference to found a Committee of the Churches on International Affairs,[96] which called for "development . . . of international law and . . . supranational institutions," "respect for human rights," "the furtherance of international economic cooperation," "the promotion of international . . . humanitarian enterprises," and recognition of "the obligation to promote to the utmost the well-being of dependent peoples including their advance toward self-government."[97]

## THE CONSOLIDATION OF INTERNATIONALISM IN THE THIRTIES AND FORTIES

The type of international order that emerged during and following the Second World War was not the product simply of the new distribution of power, the interests of the constituent states, or their internal needs and struggles; ideas about international and domestic politics and economics structured the way interests were perceived. The experiences of the twenties and thirties, and the significance they seemed to postwar policymakers to hold were decisive and created a clear presumption about the importance of cooperative, public-spirited policies, both in domestic and international affairs. That impression was strongly reinforced by the marked contrast the experience of the forties and fifties presented.

The deterioration of international and domestic economy and society that had taken place in the interwar period loomed large in people's minds. Beggar-thy-neighbor economic policies in the twenties and thirties, and vengeful and tightfisted attitudes toward reparations and war debts after the First World War were thought to have led to domestic chaos and international animosities, which had fostered a second war.[98] Difficult economic circumstances had led to the breakdown of democracy and to the rise of demagogic national regimes, whose destructiveness spilled over easily from domestic to international politics and was especially responsible for plunging Europe again into war. The attempt to cope with international problems, with chaos and wrong abroad, by turning one's head or minding one's own business—the attitude of the U.S. in failing to join the League or of Chamberlain in abandoning Czechoslovakia as a little-known, faraway land—was seen as an abdication also leading to disorder and ultimately war.

This understanding of the international lessons of the twenties and thirties was reinforced by the contrasting developments of the forties and (later) the fifties. It was evident to Americans that the U.S. support of Britain and participation in the war had been crucial to the defeat of Hitler. Moreover, the mood of the wartime period contrasted in every way among Americans with the malaise that preceded it: not only could Americans take pride in the leadership they had exerted during the war; they also felt optimism in working together to make a stronger and better world. Early in the Second World War, Britain and the United States had begun making plans for the construction of a generous peace, based as much upon reconstruction of democracy and a sound international economy as upon strong military preparedness and resistance to aggression. The establishment of the United Nations as a new and overarching framework of international organization, the economic institutions created at Bretton Woods, the attempts of the United States to establish democracies in Germany and Japan, the creation before the war was over of a Relief and Rehabilitation organization and the subsequent institution of the Marshall Plan—all were parts of a general outlook that saw peace and prosperity coming out of cooperation and a decent opportunity for the peoples of every land. The continuing prosperity and the political as well as economic recovery of Europe after the war, which owed much to the involvement of the United States in undertaking measures to promote European cooperation and unity, continued to attest to the wisdom of these policies. The increasingly amicable and cooperative relations that emerged in Europe had created a new era in European history, not only in a steady prosperity but also in the unprecedented peace and trust among European nations.

The wartime and postwar periods seemed to confirm lessons drawn from the unsatisfactory experience of the twenties and thirties in domestic as well as international politics. The immediate postwar period confirmed the trends of the preceding decades toward the creation of a welfare state. Faith in laissez-faire capitalism free of any state direction received a near-fatal blow in the Great Depression. In the United States, neither the efficacy nor the morality of an unregulated and unbuffered economy any longer seemed plausible. Britain, despite admiration of Churchill's wartime leadership, voted in a Labour government immediately after the war. Keynesian economics reigned not only because of its undoubtable intellectual power but also because of the success of policies of economic management, during the war and thereafter, which contrasted so strikingly with the economic failures of the Depression. The experience of the thirties did not leave the theory class in the United States with a permanent residue of Marxist intellectuals as the sixties did, but it did leave a strong bias in favor of egalitarian policies. Similarly, in Europe, the devastating experience of the thirties and forties left an atmosphere in which even conservative parties no longer seriously opposed the creation of measures to promote social welfare. The increasing social surplus and rapid economic growth, and the relative social peace and stability of the developed countries after the war and on into the early sixties naturally lent to the domestic, as to the international, policies that accompanied them extraordinary legitimacy, and even an aura of common-sense inevitability.

In sum, the failures of the interwar period and the success of the wartime collaboration against fascism and of postwar efforts at cooperation and reconstruction reinforced liberal-democratic presumptions, both in domestic and in international politics: the lesson seemed to be that cooperative and inclusive policies led to order and prosperity, and isolationism and intransigence alike, abroad, and abdication of social responsibility for the economy and for the needy at home led to chaos and breakdown. The experience and historical learning of the thirties and forties provided an atmosphere in which solutions based upon international cooperation and upon the promotion of prosperity and alleviation of poverty by government policy seemed plausible, natural ways of approaching problems.

### The Lessons of the Twenties and Thirties

The Depression and the general economic chaos of the interwar years left most observers with a sense of the need for stronger economic planning and for measures to deal with domestic economic breakdown; the breakdown of international cooperation of those years left observers with a sense of the need for international cooperation. Nobel Prize-winning economist Sir W. A. Lewis was struck in 1949 by

> the contrasting approaches of writers in the twenties and in the later thirties. In the twenties economists write of current events as meteorologists write of sun and rain . . . as . . . matter[s] beyond human control. . . . In the thirties, . . . this attitude disappears altogether; ıt comes to be regarded as the duty of governments to alter and control the course of economic events. . . . In twenty years the climate of economic opinion has changed completely.

Lewis himself thought the two "outstanding lessons of the interwar period" were

> that the economic system cannot just be left to look after itself . . . [but] it requires to be supplemented by positive and intelligent government action . . . [and] that without international cooperation we are lost. . . . Deflationary curtailment of international trade . . . debtor creditor muddles . . . competitive exchange depreciation . . . serve only to remind us that nations cannot prosper in isolation. National sovereignty in economic relations spells chaos.

Prompter and more generous "international assistance to the most needy countries" was, Lewis thought, a sign that "we are beginning to learn some of the lessons."[99]

H. W. Arndt's 1944 assessment, *The Economic Lessons of the Nineteen-Thirties*, is similar: international economic coordination cannot be left to "look after itself" or to "an 'automatic' international system." Rather, "correction of maladjustments in the world economy . . . will have to be carefully planned if we are to avoid the international economic chaos of the interwar period," first, through "conscious policy" to address "changes in the productive structure of the various national economies," second, through "a measure of control [over] . . . international trade and investment," and, third, through "international co-operation if not supranational economic authorities."[100]

Writings from the period tell the same tale: the depression and the chaos in Europe that resulted from the competitive nationalism of the twenties and thirties could only be averted in the future by setting aside narrow, greedy, selfish attitudes, and by making conscious, governmentally directed efforts to assure that individuals and peoples have reasonable prospects. G. D. H. Cole's 1932 *Guide Through World Chaos* stated that recovery, either through socialism or through a restored capitalism, would have to employ international measures and argued the need for "world unity" through international institutions, including a worldwide democratic assembly.[101] Lewis Lorwin, of the Brookings Institution, writing for the National Committee on the Cause and Cure of War in 1933 in preparation for the World Economic Conference, advocated a "world planning council" of people able to rise "above particularistic points of view and . . . work out policies based upon the assumption of a progressive and simultaneous rise in the standards of living and in the economic welfare of all the countries in the world" as a basis for world peace.[102] The board of the Carnegie Endowment for International Peace followed a report by a group of distinguished economic experts from six nations (including Bertil G. Ohlin and Charles Rist) in urging, in 1936, "the need for creditor nations to help debtor nations" and "cooperation of the nations to raise the standard of living of their several peoples and to assist in solving their pressing social problems."[103]

Green views President Roosevelt's January 1944 message to Congress proclaiming that "individual freedom cannot exist without economic security and independence" as a kind of "second Bill of Rights . . . for all regardless of station, race, or creed," which, though not greatly noted, marked a transition of great importance.[104] A 1950 ILO report, quoted by Asher in his account of the period, similarly observes that "a great transformation was taking place in economic thought. The economy was no longer regarded as being fundamentally self-directing and capable of maintaining continuous full employment except for periodic crises. Instead, the possibility of an equilibrium at a low level of employment for an indefinite period of time had been recognized." Asher connects this lesson with a concern for international interdependence, as the other authors do: "The abiding fear of large-scale unemployment and deflation which characterized the 1930's and to which the 'freedom from want' clause of the Atlantic Charter was a response, shaped postwar aims, aspirations, and programs of peoples and governments everywhere." Asher continues, "Because depression anywhere threatens prosperity everywhere, and because national antidepression policies also have international repercussions (the 'export of unemployment' is a tempting form of foreign trade in a depression), international discussion during the war inevitably became concerned with questions of employment and stability in the postwar world."[105]

These economic lessons from domestic and international life found natural reinforcement in the strategic security lessons of the interwar period. In retrospect, the U.S. failure to join the League, and the failure to stand up to Fascist and Nazi international aggression early on reflected a kind of uninvolved standing aside that was the counterpart of a lack of willingness to engage in international economic cooperation. The failure of responsible groups in Germany to stand up to Hitler's thuggery at home, again, was another kind of unwillingness to protect the weak and vulnerable that was seen as leading in the long run to disaster for everyone. Isolationism, the failure to stand up and be counted or to sacrifice for the public interest, appeared on every front, domestic and international, as selfish and also foolish: a short road to disaster for all.

These lessons were further reinforced as the war forced a reexamination of purpose, as Arndt argues. Cordell Hull, the U.S. secretary of state, set up a committee to deal with postwar problems almost as soon as the European war started. Also, the Allies needed "to formulate war aims . . . to counter Hitler's New Order and Japan's Co-Prosperity Sphere," and a "wave of idealism" responding to the war with "plans for a better postwar world" was a "characteristic" response of British and American public opinion. In addition, "by demonstrating the power of government action in mobilizing economic resources, the war itself generated a climate of optimism about what could be done to make a better world, abroad as much as at home." Thus, Harvey in 1942 observes that "the average citizen has been thinking a great deal about how to win the peace . . . [seeking] formulation of 'peace aims'. Groups and societies for the study of the problems of the peace sprang up like mushrooms overnight," with pamphlets and studies galore.[106]

Roosevelt linked issues of international peace and economic justice in putting "freedom from fear" and "freedom from want" in his influential "Four Freedoms" speech of January 1941. In saying that "millions in England and in China," in Norway, and even in Germany and Italy ask, "What does the future hold after this struggle is over?" and in answering that any lasting peace rests upon the "natural rights of all peoples to equal economic enjoyment" and that "security from want, disease, and starvation" goes along with "security from bombing from the air," it is doubtful that FDR thought in terms of the United States contributing to raising living standards in India or China.[107] But the war and depression, like the earlier struggles of labor, framed issues in terms of a discourse of universal human needs and rights which logically led in that direction. The rhetorical momentum of the Atlantic Charter, signed with Churchill in August 1941 as a statement of Allied war aims, was even greater. Its "assurance that all men in all the lands might live out their lives in freedom from fear and want" stirred comment worldwide, including reaction in poorer countries that probably took these strong statements a good deal more literally than the signers intended them.

These ideas provoked applause and further thought. U.S. Undersecretary of State Sumner Welles saw the Atlantic Charter as providing at last "a common purpose" for the wartime effort: "the general increase of the prosperity of the world, raising standards of living, access to raw materials, and increasing the volume of international trade." A 1941 publication by the World Citizens' Association associates the "importance of victory . . . in fighting Nazism" with "the immense effort of cooperation which is extending to all parts of the world"; some contributors argued that "the time is ripe for an international organization which would aid the undeveloped countries."[108] Vice President Henry Wallace argued in 1942 that "everybody in the world" should have "the privilege of drinking a quart of milk a day."[109] Wendell Willkie argued in his 1942 book *One World* that the end of colonialism was essential to the cause of freedom and, in pursuing his theme, that "there are no distant points in the world any longer" and that "our thinking in the future must be worldwide." Willkie surveys various areas of the world and argues the need of "more modern industry" in "technologically backward areas" and sees "provisions of the Atlantic Charter, and the enunciation of the Four Freedoms" as "signs of great progress" that "have aroused hopes around the world" and decries Churchill's statement limiting the Charter to Europe primarily, noting how people hoped for worldwide application. For he holds "the United Nations must become a common council, not only for the winning of the war but for the future welfare of mankind," and, in language reminiscent of Donne's famous statement that "any man's death diminishes me because I am involved in mankind," concludes that "to raise the standard of living of any man anywhere in the world is to raise the standard of living by some slight degree of every man."[110]

Lewis Lorwin, with considerable foresight into the later UN structure, calls in 1941 for a "World New Deal." Making democracy "more workable under modern economic systems without curtailing the basic freedoms of the individual" entails making individual freedoms "a real capacity and not a formal right . . . to do away with *disguised coercions* due . . . to economic and social exigencies, by guaranteeing a living minimum and by extending social protection to the weak and under-privileged." Though he gives no blueprint for the World New Deal, he sketches major institutions needed, including (1) an International Relief and Social Assistance Commission, "to promote common action to prevent starvation, alleviate distress, protect the welfare of children, organize public health services" with subsidiary Children's Fund, World Health Bureau, International Nutrition Council, and so forth; (2) a World Economic Development Organization—"to promote expansionist economic policies, to deal with trade and industrial problems, . . . organize technical aid, to advance agricultural commodity agreements, to help the industrialization of new countries, . . . promote the improvement of industrial conditions and social security provisions"—with an International Trade Commission, an Investment Bank, and Labor and Industrial Offices; and (3) an International Colonial Administration, to "develop plans for the economic development of colonies . . . and their eventual self-administration." Eventually these institutions would all become more closely related, and the World Assembly "would thus evolve into a World Federation representing the growing economic interdependence and political solidarity of all nations and countries of the world."[111]

Harvard professor Kirtley Mather, appraising "the resources of the whole earth in terms of the total demands of the entire human family," argues that "next . . . on the agenda of civilization is the invention and practice of satisfactory procedures for making [resources for a rich and full life] . . . available to all members of the human family." The Atlantic Charter and other international agreements "give to mankind a glimpse of a new world of international justice and democratic co-operation for all the peoples of the earth." This requires freedom for colonial peoples, an "international educational agency" to support them in their freedom, and "a program for self-development," which is foreshadowed in Britain's Colonial Development and Welfare Act of 1940. Urging that we "accept our own share of responsibility" for colonial people, he quotes Julian Huxley to the effect that "the United States [is not really repudiating the old imperialism if it fails] to co-operate actively in the effort to transform it into a campaign for the all-around development of backward areas and backward peoples." The essential is a "brotherly attitude," a "joy of community," which grows "as each improves his own skill in the art of co-operation" and "sympathetic consideration for the rights and needs of others." Yet he argues that it is also "in the long run the only way . . . to gain freedom and security in a world like ours," and that "efficient weapons of destruction" placed in our hands make this transformation a matter of survival.[112] Eugene Staley argues along similar lines for "planetary economics" as an alternative to world anarchy, since the modern world has become a community after "the rise of internationalism in many forms" in the nineteenth and twentieth centuries.[113]

Such ideas were widely disseminated and common currency. Harvard economist and Federal Reserve Board adviser Alvin H. Hansen, in a 1942 pamphlet, "Economic Problems of the Post-War World," circulated by two departments of the National Education Association—the National Council for the Social Studies and the National Association of Secondary School Principals—presents plans that border on the idea of foreign aid. Hansen mainly argues for government domestic policy to guarantee full employment by strong government planning, bold extensions of New Deal programs, and the like,[114] but one section, "The Economic Tasks of the Post-War World," presents an international agenda including "developmental projects in backward countries" and "international collaboration to . . . promote active employment." He states that

> capital and technical skill should both be made available under international governmental auspices. . . . The rates of interest, if any, should be low and payments should be asked for over extended periods of time. . . . A sort of international RFC [Reconstruction Finance Corporation] might prove a suitable device for stimulating foreign investment. On the one side, there will be need for an international public development corporation to promote large-scale projects in industrially backward countries and areas; on the other for an international authority under which private corporations seeking foreign-investment outlets could obtain minimum guarantees based on the principle of insurance.

Acknowledging that these measures might need subsidies, he argues that

> such a program constitutes an investment on behalf of international security. . . . Increases in the productivity of the [foreign] peasant . . . may seem of remote interest to many Americans; but they will contribute in the long run to both the economic and political security of the United States

and also "challenge the courage and creative genius of mankind." Despite a "heavy cost" to the United States, it is needed in order to avert

> new deep depressions and new world wars. *That* is something which we really cannot afford. In the past we have failed to recognize the great responsibility which goes with vast power, political and economic. We must be prepared to make a contribution in both fields. We must recognize our political responsibilities for maintaining world peace; and equally we must recognize our economic responsibilities for achieving and maintaining world prosperity.[115]

Conservatives as well as liberals shared in this idealism. Herbert Hoover argued that "acceptance of materialism and loss of spiritual standards" permitted "the growth of regimes based on brutality" and that "no political solutions, however realistic, will suffice to give us a peaceful world unless they are accompanied by a return to something better than a belief in material well-being—a return to faith in higher things." The Versailles peace provided "soil upon which . . . revolutions throve" by allowing "the destruction, the miseries, the disillusions and the moral degradation of the war" and left "legacies of selfish nationalism and imperialism and [of] hate, fear and revenge." Although opposed to managed economies, Hoover and Gibson concurred that "the economic aftermaths of that [1914] war were among the primary causes of the collapse of the world into this second World War." Thus the foundations of a lasting peace require "rebuilding prosperity in the world," with the United States combating "famine and pestilence . . . rampant over most of Europe and Asia," and allied governments bearing "the burdens of shipping, credit, and distribution of supplies . . . for the enemy as well as for liberated countries if there is to be peace and recovery" and providing sustained management of economic problems, though without compromising economic freedom. The "international economy must be a reflection of domestic economy." They go on to note all the nations and peoples of Europe and Asia, including here Koreans, Ethiopians, Persians, Arabs, Siamese, and Filipinos, will "insist upon their independence" and "their economic, boundary, and defense policies will present great problems."[116]

Sumner Welles, writing in his 1943 book, *The World of the Four Freedoms*, conceived of as a "Blueprint for Peace" states even more bluntly that tariff hikes in the early twenties led to a "withering blast of trade destruction," which "brought disaster and despair to countless people. The resultant misery, bewilderment, and resentment . . . paved the way for the rise of those very dictatorships which have plunged almost the entire world into war. When human beings see ahead of them nothing but a continuation of the distress of the present, they are not apt to analyze dispassionately" the claims of demagogues. Lowered world trade "dangerously reduced" the "standards of living everywhere," and "totalitarian governments then being set up seized avidly on the opportunity." Hence, "creation of an economic order in the post-war world which will . . . render security to men and women and provide for the progressive improvement of living standards is almost as essential to the preservation of free institutions as is the actual winning of this war." The "universal principles of the Atlantic Charter," which aim to promote the economic prosperity of all nations "great or small, victor or vanquished," are the basis for "the maintenance of a peaceful and prosperous world of the future." He quotes Roosevelt's instructions to Eisenhower that "no one will go hungry or without the other means of livelihood in any territory occupied by the United Nations, if it is humanly within our powers to make the necessary supplies available to them," and advocates letting the UNRRA "without a moment's delay . . . alleviate the suffering and misery of millions of homeless and starving human beings, if civilization is to be saved from years of social and moral collapse."[117] President Truman expressed a similar thought in 1946, saying that "at the threshold of every problem which confronts us today in international affairs is the appalling devastation, hunger, sickness, and pervasive human misery that mark so many areas of the world."[118]

## Institutionalizations of International Society

Throughout the interwar years there was a steady growth of international cooperation and of a sense of social responsibility for those at risk internationally that found institutional expression.

### EARLY EFFORTS AT ECONOMIC COLLABORATION AND ASSISTANCE

Early attempts at international economic and social cooperation were undertaken primarily through the League of Nations. The League was originally organized for collective security against aggression, but more than half its expenditures were in the social and economic field, and it left an enduring positive legacy in the foundations it laid for international economic cooperation and social justice. The League Mandates system moved toward recognizing the political rights of colonized peoples, and also linked international recognition of political sovereignty with attention to needs for social and economic development. League efforts on behalf of refugees laid the groundwork for later responses to emergency needs, such as the UNRRA. Its loans to economically troubled countries were a step toward aid efforts to assist countries with chronic economic difficulties. By setting up its Health Organization and the ILO, the League began a lasting process of technical and economic cooperation, for the organizations founded and the staff they developed continued through the forties, making studies and undertaking international advocacy on world health, nutrition, labor standards, and problems of underdevelopment. By its ostensive universal character and mission, the League also started people thinking in terms of world community and worldwide responsibilities. F. P. Walters argues that UN institutions, though "modified and magnified, . . . are in practically every case the direct and recognizable offspring of those of the League" and reminds us that "much of what is now taken for granted as the accepted and permanent background of international activities is, historically speaking, the consequence of changes introduced by the provisions of the Covenant and by the practice of the Council and the Assembly."[119]

As Brown says, "International cooperation on economic and social problems was both intensive and experimental during the interwar years" and constituted an "inheritance" for the United Nations.[120] Ludwik Rajchman, secretary of the League's Health Organization and head of its Epidemic Commission, directed efforts against cholera, typhus, and typhoid in Europe in 1920 and against epidemics in the Middle East.[121]

There were loans to Austria and Hungary for reconstruction and financial rehabilitation in 1921 and 1924, as well as loans to Estonia and Danzig, and other plans considered for Albania, Portugal, and Rumania.[122] The League labored to suppress the drug trade and prostitution, to improve statistical standardization, and also worked on social problems, sought to promote intellectual cooperation, and so on.[123] China tried to get it to supply "technical know-how and capital" in 1919, making the argument that "China could 'assist the League of Nations to prevent a most probable world war,'" according to Van Soest, an argument "repeated by all developing countries" later, and a 1931 agreement sent a group of experts to China to organize "post, telegraphs, and customs."[124] Boudreau argues that "the international food movement was born in the 1930's" in the League.[125] The Health Organization of the League of Nations "engaged in studies of the state of nutrition in different countries," and there was a European Conference on Rural Life and a comprehensive study of Agricultural Production.[126] Studies of living conditions worldwide helped bring questions of poverty to public view. With respect to "social and cultural cooperation," Brown says that "the objective of raising the standard of living was implicit in many forms of interwar 'economic' cooperation."[127] Van Soest notes that "in October 1937, the [League of Nations] Council invited the Economic and Financial Organization to investigate what international measures could be taken to raise the standards of living of the world population."[128]

The League cooperated with international relief efforts, such as the Belgian Relief drive that Hoover organized after the First World War, and other types of reconstruction efforts and summarized "principles and methods used in the League Reconstruction plans . . . in a special study published by the League Secretariat in 1930" that was reviewed again in a 1943 joint session of League Economic and Financial committees as an aid to the upcoming reconstruction.[129] The United States planned for relief of Europe after the war, initially in the U.S. government office planning for relief and reconstruction (OFRRO) and later in the United Nations Relief and Rehabilitation Administration (UNRRA).[130] Relief of war-caused suffering was certainly a step toward a more international approach to alleviating problems of want and human deprivation. The UNRRA concept went much further, however; many who favored responding to the devastation of World War II thought that the relief efforts organized after the First World War had failed specifically by not having provided for the regeneration of European productive capacity as well as for relief; and the UNRRA was explicitly planned to deal comprehensively with problems of reconstruction.[131]

Wilson's fifth point had insisted "the interest of the population concerned must have equal weight" with even justified colonial claims. The

Mandates system set up under the League ceded former overseas possessions of Germany and Turkey to the Allied powers, but the Mandatory powers had to submit annual reports to the League and were responsible for "protection of the interest of the natives," "regulations against usury," and "promotion of the material and moral well-being and social progress of the inhabitants."[132] Article 23(b) of the League Covenant "reflected the international concern for the welfare of people in *all* dependencies and not of the mandates alone" and required the trustee powers to "undertake a wide range of activities in promoting the general welfare" and specifically, in the language of the article, "to secure just treatment of the native inhabitants of territories under their control." The ILO particularly concerned itself with standards and conditions in the developing countries.[133]

British and French efforts to provide for colonial development and U.S. technical assistance missions laid something of an institutional grounding for later aid and may in part have reflected these League charges. Britain's Colonial Development Act of 1929 provided funds for promoting the economic development of the British colonies, although in amounts inconsequential compared to later foreign aid programs.[134] The initial act restricted spending to a million pounds per year, and less than £7 million was actually spent in 11 years. The 1940 Colonial Development and Welfare Act made £5 million available per year for education and research as well as for capital costs, and a new 1945 Act provided £120 million over ten years. A further 1948 Overseas Resources Development Act provided further funds for development lending at low rates, to profit-making enterprises.[135] The acts were directed to British colonies and were tiny compared to Britain's foreign aid in the fifties, which averaged $190 million spent per year in the period from 1950 to 1955.[136] They provided some advance preparation for later programs of aid, however. France began a small program of colonial assistance in 1935, which was expanded after the war. In 1947 France set up what later became its two main aid organs, the Fonds d'Investissement pour le Développement Économique et Social des Territoires d'Outre-Mer (FIDES) and the Caisse Centrale de Coopération Économique (CCCE).[137] FIDES spent about $73 million annually from 1947 to 1952,[138] as contrasted with the French foreign aid program, which spent around $500 million per year from 1950 to 1955.[139]

Episodic private and government-directed American missions to provide technical advice or scientific help overseas date to the early 1800s. Early missions went to Japan, Liberia and Persia, Cuba, and the Dominican Republic and Haiti. By the early part of this century, however, the U.S. government was involved regularly, though without any formal program, in supplying experts and technical personnel, as well as in staffing some military and financial missions, to countries requesting assistance from the United States, especially in Latin America. Experts were sometimes paid by the countries requesting assistance, but in other cases the United States footed the bill. The United States, seeing itself as an alternative to the corrupt European system and as an elder sister to other American republics, may have found it particularly natural to extend fraternal technical assistance to the Latin American republics.[140]

WARTIME COLLABORATION

U.S. technical assistance to Latin America was put on a systematic basis in 1938.[141] Congress authorized the president to detail any government employee to undertake short-term technical-assistance missions to other governments in the hemisphere, and also authorized use of government services in cooperative undertakings related to the Buenos Aires conference of 1936.[142] Glick suggests that these measures arose both from the increasingly regular stream of requests for technical assistance that were being received and from an increased concern for hemispheric affairs. Direct U.S. interests in countering German influence in Latin America was clearly a motive, too. The resulting Interdepartmental Committee on Scientific and Cultural Cooperation spent increasing amounts over the next decade, totaling about $17 million in all. After the war started, Roosevelt made Nelson Rockefeller coordinator of inter-American affairs, with an office which became a government-owned corporation in 1942, the Institute of Inter-American Affairs (IIAA), for undertaking public health and agricultural projects with Latin American governments.[143] Its activities had many characteristics in common with later development efforts, and appear to have served as Benjamin Hardy's models in the suggestions Truman used in proposing his Point Four program.[144] They are significant in understanding the evolution of foreign aid because they show the gradual growth of a climate in which overseas assistance was thought of as a logical activity in strengthening international cooperation.

The momentum of wartime collaboration and the determination to try to create a postwar world that would provide economic as well as political stability as a basis for a lasting peace established principles that facilitated later development efforts. Roosevelt's much-acclaimed Four Freedoms speech of January 1941 set out freedom from fear and freedom from want as linked goals. On June 12, the Inter-Allied Council in London defined the common aim of the war effort as including cooperation for "economic and social security" as well as safety from aggression as the "only true basis of enduring peace." The August 14, 1941, Atlantic Charter signed by Roosevelt and Churchill underlined the need for the "fullest collaboration" to secure "economic advancement and social security" for all and "peace . . . which will afford assurance that the men in all lands may live out their lives in freedom from fear and want." Twenty-six allies adopted the principles of the Atlantic Charter as the basis of their war aims on January 1, 1942, in a "Declaration of the United Nations."[145] The Lend-Lease program, provided goods on a concessional basis under Article VII of the February 1942 U.S.-British Mutual Aid Agreement, which again emphasized joint promotion of employment and better standards of living worldwide, elements that made agreement "mutually advantageous." The program and its principles, "open to . . . other countries of like mind," was subscribed to by sixteen other governments before the end of the war.[146]

Roosevelt surprised many by choosing a conference on food and nutrition as a starting point for postwar collaboration. The League's attempts at cooperation in nutrition had always appealed to him, and Brown argues that he saw in them an "opportunity to launch postwar cooperation . . . in an area in which conflicts would be less sharp than in the . . . difficult fields of trade and finance."[147] Whatever its intent, this conference naturally led to increased focus on the needs of poorer countries. The May 1943 United Nations Conference on Food and Agriculture at Hot Springs, Virginia, officially stated that it "met to consider the goal of freedom from want in relation to food and agriculture . . . [and] recognized that freedom from want means a secure, adequate, and suitable supply of food for every man" and concluded that "freedom from hunger" indeed "can be reached." The conference's final act states that after "winning . . . the war . . . to deliver millions of people from tyranny and from hunger . . . we must equally concert our efforts to win and maintain freedom from fear and freedom from want" and that "the first cause of hunger and malnutrition is poverty"; it calls particular attention to the needs of vulnerable groups, and observes that "freedom from want cannot be achieved without effective collaboration among nations." Other conference reports state "the diets consumed by the greater part of mankind are nutritionally unsatisfactory," noting the deficiency of Chinese and African diets, "undernutrition and malnutrition" in Egypt, and the fact that many in India do "not get *enough* to eat." "Narrowing the gap between consumption levels" of developed countries and "vast regions elsewhere" and "finding means for improving the purchasing power of lower-income groups" would advance the goal of "progressive expansion of the production of food . . . [and] fuller distribution to all people, particularly those in greatest need."[148]

Perhaps the most important movement toward "international social welfare" was the establishment of the United Nations Relief and Rehabilitation Administration (UNRRA), which Van Soest says "first manifested" the "change in the American attitude toward international cooperation"[149] and which Friedlander says "initiated the important role of the United Nations in the area of health, economic progress, education, cultural achievement, and social welfare," saving millions of lives.[150] A November 1943 Allied agreement established the UNRRA, which at once began to provide food, clothing, medicine, seeds, fertilizer, livestock, tractors and other supplies, attempted agricultural and industrial reconstruction, and rebuilt transportation systems, hospitals, and training institutes in war-ravaged and occupied lands in forty-two countries, including China, the Philippines, and Korea as well as Europe, the Soviet Union, and the Middle East, and aimed to help those in enemy as well as Allied and neutral lands. Some forty-four countries contributed, although the United States provided about 70% of the total. Donors responding to an appeal that "each member government . . . not occupied by the enemy . . . contribut[e] . . . one percent of the national income" included many countries which later were recipients of development assistance, as Brown notes. The appeals anticipated a frequent 1% target for foreign aid.[151]

The UNRRA was followed up by a good deal of further collaboration to assist the underdeveloped countries specifically, although the organization itself was terminated in December 1946 due to "political frictions."[152] UNRRA resources were transferred to a United Nations Children's Fund (UNICEF), and specialized agencies such as the IRO and WHO took over many of its functions.[153] Friedlander argues that "the UNRRA proved that an international organization is able to work at least as well as a national one," with its success shown "by the fact that after its termination, a number of international agencies were set up under the auspices of the United Nations to carry on its work."[154] And Asher observes that the initial activities of the UNRRA, "provid[ing] supplies and technical assistance to China, Greece, Korea, the Philippines, and Yugoslavia" as well as to war-torn advanced nations, "raised the hope—subsequently dashed—that large-scale relief programs might soon be undertaken within the United Nations System," in part by authorizing technical experts, training in social welfare, and so on. Partly for this reason, there was a great "expansion of services developed in the period 1946–1949," when "the term 'technical assistance' came into general use," even before the creation of the Expanded Programme of Technical Assistance (EPTA), which he rightly calls "the first major [UN] program of an operational character undertaken on a long-term basis . . . to meet the special needs of the underdeveloped countries."[155]

*The Formation of Postwar Institutions*

New international practices once instituted establish underlying principles that are extended as time goes on. This can be seen in the way that creation of a United Nations began a process that gradually committed the developed countries to providing help in development and overcoming the poverty of the poorer nations. By establishing a United Nations in which rich nations and poor, small nations and large, former colonies and colonial powers alike were represented, the victors of the Second World War created a symbolism by which it was to be expected that the concerns of all national groups were going to be taken into consideration. If all nations were to be represented, it was difficult to limit the organization to security issues when many members felt economic concerns were most important to them. A growing acceptance of the principle that prosperity of all countries is a matter of international concern made it difficult to argue against capital transfers to the neediest countries. Thus, as Baldwin says, the "United Nations [became] ... the primary channel through which the underdeveloped countries could exert pressure on the United States to make soft loans" with groundwork laid between 1943 and 1948 preparing the way for later developments, placing "pressure on the [World] Bank," which began operations in 1947, "and by implication on the United States" to offer developing countries concessional finance.[156]

THE UN AND THE ECOSOC

Early plans for the UN included "a powerful Economic and Social Council" (ECOSOC) along lines that had been suggested by the 1939 Bruce Committee, sponsored by the Specialized Agencies of the League.[157] The economic and social functions of the proposed UN were narrowed at the preliminary Dumbarton Oaks conference due to British and Russian misgivings. However, at the San Francisco conference, the Latin Americans and other less developed countries "vigorously attacked the draft" and, ultimately obtaining the support of the split U.S. delegation, successfully pressed for giving "economic and political development" an important place in the charter, "add[ing] an Economic and Social Council with broad functions, together with the Trusteeship Council, as principal organs."[158] The preamble listed "cooperation in solving international problems of an economic, social, cultural, or humanitarian character" as a major goal, and the charter contained chapters on international economic and social cooperation and on the Economic and Social Council. Article 55, supported by an implementing article 56, stated that to create "conditions of stability and well-being which are necessary for peaceful and friendly relations," the United Nations "shall promote ... higher standards of living, full employment, and conditions of economic and social progress and development."

Each attempt to focus on what the Western countries considered the pressing problems of European reconstruction led to attempts by LDCs to point out the seriousness of their problems; and each time those problems were deferred on grounds of urgency in Europe, a stronger implicit commitment was created to deal with the problems presently. The ECOSOC, convened as soon as the first UN General Assembly began in January 1946, at once set up a Nuclear [skeletal] Commission on Economic and Employment, which had concluded by May, in Van Soest's words, that "economic stability was dependent on both recovery and economic development," with a subcommission on economic development (starting in June) to advise "on long-term development of production and consumption throughout the world and in particular on . . . levels of consumption in the less developed regions."[159] The economically devastated nations of Europe wanted an Economic Commission for Europe (ECE), which was established in 1947 with Gunnar Myrdal as executive secretary, "to facilitate the reconstruction of Europe, to raise the level of economic activity." Western arguments that the war had left Europe in crisis enabled China to argue the same and India to argue its need for resources to deal with the crisis of a non-war-induced famine in part of its subcontinent, leading to establishment of an Economic Commission for Asia and the Far East (ECAFE) later that year. An Economic Commission for Latin America (ECLA) was set up in 1948.[160]

Thus, by the end of the forties there were repeated calls in the ECOSOC for assistance not just to Europe but to lands suffering chronic poverty. When the advanced countries that had created the UN sought to defer the problems of backward countries because of the pressing needs for reconstruction, the Soviet Union, the Philippines, some South American countries, and Lebanese delegate A. Malik argued the UN should provide grants for development of less developed countries as well as assist in repairing war damages.[161] General Assembly Resolution 58, which passed unanimously in 1948, said that in view of the need for expert advice for development, there was a "responsibility for assisting such development," and the ECOSOC provided experts to Haiti in the summer of 1948 and, in December, voted to "institut[e] a program of technical assistance for economic development."[162] While these early debates spoke of "short-term transitional problems of India and Pakistan and other countries which had just become independent," and did not foresee the "massive" resources needed to address the problems of underdevelopment, they established a UN Technical Assistance Programme, which served as a foundation for later expansions.[163]

THE WORLD BANK

The creation of an International Bank for Reconstruction and Development resurrected an old idea for an Inter-American Bank, first mooted by Harry Dexter White in 1940, and was included in the American version of proposals for a conference, finally held at Bretton Woods in June 1944, whose main purpose was to establish an International Monetary Fund for exchange rate and currency stabilization. The Russians and some of the smaller European powers supported the idea, but the main support came from the Latin American delegates, who saw in the Bank the possibility of an institution that would address their concerns for development, concerns shared by White, which lay in part behind his original proposal. The Latin American delegates to the Bretton Woods conference lobbied successfully for language that gave development equal priority with reconstruction. After a rocky start that kept the Bank from commencing lending operations until May 1947, loans were made almost exclusively for European reconstruction until January 1949. Nevertheless, it became clear in 1947 that the Bank's function in European reconstruction would come to a close quickly, as soon as the Marshall Plan began to operate and displaced that function from the Bank.

The Bank provided capital for development, which many borrowers could not obtain, as well as technical assistance and advice. As an institution from the first importantly, and soon exclusively, concerned with financing development, moreover, the Bank was a crucial step toward the kind of concessional finance for development which foreign aid later provided, although the Bank itself originally lent only at commercial rates of interest. Baldwin puts the matter nicely when he says "the Bank eventually played an important role in the process of legitimizing soft lending . . . but during the 1943–48 period it had to concentrate on establishing its own claim to legitimacy."[164] As James Morris says, "Today the World Bank seems as solid an institution as any on earth. In 1946, when it began work, its reputation was much less reassuring."[165] By establishing international lending for development as a credible business proposition, the Bank served as a lightning rod for objections from a conservative American business community and, as such, won many of the battles for credibility that foreign aid needed to fight in order to be accepted.

THE MARSHALL PLAN

The Marshall Plan, first discussed in the spring of 1947 and announced by Secretary of State George C. Marshall in June at the Harvard commencement, was important for the development of later foreign aid programs to LDCs in three major ways: it broke new ground by establishing the legitimacy of aid from one nation to another in peacetime; it provided a specific precedent for the new nations in the ECOSOC to refer to as a model of aid which was fully concessional; and (in the long run), by establishing the OEEC as an outgrowth of its workings, it created a basis for the later organization of the OECD and a precedent for the OECD's involvement in the business of development financing and, hence, for the role of the DAC.

The idea of international aid had been hard enough to sell during the war under the rubric of the Lend-Lease program; this itself was a substantial departure from the attitude toward the repayment of war debts by allies after the First World War. The move into concessional peacetime assistance, here on a temporary basis, for postwar reconstruction was another important transitional step that made the later adoption of longer-term programs of concessional assistance for development easier. This transitional character is evident, and indeed it is common to group the Marshall Plan and earlier wartime efforts such as the UNRRA together with later *development* assistance programs in discussions of foreign aid.[166] This is useful for some purposes, and underscores the important transition that the earlier programs, and the Marshall Plan, provided. The difference in character between the two must also be kept firmly in mind, however.[167]

In the long run, the Marshall Plan had a strong influence both because it promoted the general idea of economic cooperation and because it left an important organizational legacy. The Committee for European Economic Cooperation (CEEC), which organized Marshall Plan aid, became the Organization for European Economic Cooperation (OEEC), and finally the OEEC was reorganized in the early sixties as the OECD, with its new emphasis on promoting development epitomized by the creation of its Development Assistance Committee (DAC).[168]

## CONCLUSION

Why did foreign aid come into being when it did?

This book's investigations started from the striking fact that nearly all developed democracies adopted foreign aid policies in the decade after midcentury, and kept them steadily, although no policies of this kind had existed before. Previous chapters have indicated that aid, when it did come into being, was primarily directed to the poorest countries, often through multilateral institutions, in a way designed to promote economic development; that those countries with the strongest domestic commitments to eradicating poverty, and the strongest public interest in international poverty, were those which had the most vigorous foreign aid programs; and that ordinary citizens, elites, interest groups, and political parties who supported aid were those with concerns about moral issues of poverty and need at home and abroad, and supported aid more focused on poverty as well as increased aid. But that evidence does not, by itself, explain why foreign aid came into being when it did. This chapter has shown that the preconditions of aid were building for almost a hundred years before aid started. A growing understanding of international affairs as necessarily the affairs of the whole human family and an increasing acceptance of government management of the domestic economy and intervention on behalf of the economically disadvantaged provided the intellectual and moral foundations on which aid was built. These changed understandings took concrete form in public debate and its changing pre-suppositions, social movements, systematic humanitarian undertakings, the teaching of the churches, and the growth of organized labor and labor parties, as well as in the development of government social welfare institutions and increased international organization.

The willingness to consider government programs of assistance to peoples overseas clearly reflected the growth of the domestic social welfare state, and of labor unions and social-democratic parties, which had been growing in influence throughout the century and particularly after the end of the war. The rise of the welfare state involved measures to promote equality and reduce poverty, including the creation of government-run programs of assistance to the poor; in practice, also, there was increasing acceptance during the thirties and forties of broader government action to manage the economy in the public good. The labor movements and social-democratic parties that pressed for welfare state measures were from the first committed to a set of values which emphasized the dignity of labor and the needs of the poor on the basis of an ethic universal in scope; perhaps in consequence, labor and labor parties were consciously internationalist in their rhetoric and development of contacts from the beginning. Thus it was natural for such parties after they came to power to press for measures of concern for the poor and for the improvement of the economic situation of workers across borders. It was no accident that the first strong foreign response to Truman's Point Four proposal came in a commitment to the Colombo Plan by Labour Foreign Secretary Ernest Bevin, who as a councillor of the Trade Union Council in the thirties had championed British responsibility for colonial welfare and rights to self-determination, or that the ILO made raising living standards worldwide an important goal as early as 1944.

The welfare state and the rise of internationalism both drew strength from humanitarian movements throughout the century. The settlement house movement, the rise of the Social Gospel, the increased and increasingly professional role of charitable foundations and professional associations of social workers and groups concerned with domestic poverty and social problems, and investigations into the condition of the domestic poor all helped pave the way for public concern supporting government measures to alleviate domestic poverty. Often the groups that were concerned with meeting needs also maintained an interest in addressing the structural causes of poverty. There was also a growth of institutions and individuals interested in ending war and promoting international solutions to problems. Often, such groups—such as the Carnegie Foundation, The World Citizens Association, the League of Nations Societies in various countries and their international association—were explicitly interested in international economic cooperation. Activities of assistance to poor people overseas were also pioneered by the work of American churches in overseas medical and technical assistance, voluntary efforts on behalf of Belgian Relief and Refugees, the growing role of the Red Cross, and the formation of groups like CARE and Oxfam. Domestic groups concerned with particular aspects of social welfare often later became involved in similar problems overseas, and many international humanitarian groups, like domestic ones, were concerned with institutionalized—often governmental—solutions to structural problems as well as with alleviating immediate distress. Groups such as the Red Cross, the International Missionary Council, and the World Council of Churches also called for efforts to raise standards of living around the world.

The interwar period saw a steady development of humane internationalism in theory and in practice. The Belgian Relief of the twenties, the creation of a Commissioner for Refugees, League efforts at loans to countries in need, the Mandates system and the recognition of responsibilities (especially by Britain) to the welfare of people in the colonies, the work of League economic and social agencies,[169] especially including the ILO, led to further institutional innovations, along with a growing public commitment to a goal of freedom from want in the 1940s, which specifically prepared the way for aid. Green observes that "the Second World War marked a turning point in the development of international concern for human rights. The excesses of the Fascists in Italy and the Nazis in Germany . . . shocked public opinion throughout the world," so that Roosevelt's proclamation of the Four Freedoms and the Atlantic Charter affirmation of "the right of all peoples to choose the form of government under which they will live" became clearly articulated as Allied war aims.[170] Regular U.S. technical assistance to American Republics starting in 1939, the UNRRA, Lend-Lease, the formation of the FAO at the Hot Springs conference and the World Bank at Bretton Woods, the definition of the UN as concerned with economic and social matters, the formation of a permanent UN Children's Emergency Fund, and the Marshall Plan form a chain of successively more extensive commitments to international assistance, especially to those in need. These actions were accompanied by increasing rhetorical commitment to a world that was united, and governed by principles of self-determination, not only in matters of formal sovereignty, but also in economic matters. The Four Freedoms speech, the Atlantic Charter and its endorsement in the 1942 Declaration of the United Nations, the commitment to the goal of "freedom from want" in the Hot Springs conference, the Philadelphia Declaration of the ILO, the language of the UN Charter, and the Universal Declaration of Human Rights (which included a Charter of Economic and Social Rights) articulated commitments to worldwide efforts to help those in need and to raise the standard of living.

The links between these efforts to set up international institutions and domestic commitments to welfare, and to a broad liberal international-ism, are clear. The official U.S. advocates of international relief and eco-nomic cooperation were confirmed New Dealers and Wilsonian interna-tionalists like Cordell Hull, Henry Wallace, Harry Dexter White, and Roosevelt and Truman themselves. British advocates included prominent Labour party members and Keynes himself. While rationales for provid-ing international assistance certainly contained a strong argument that assistance to those in need was the basis for building a secure and pros-perous world, isolationists and those opposed to the domestic welfare state did not see the rationale for international measures of economic cooperation and assistance which antedated the provision of regular for-eign aid to less developed countries; the calls and support for prototypical measures came, as later support for aid did, from humanitarian, social democratic, prolabor groups, and from those concerned with world peace and international law.

Worldwide response to declarations such as the Atlantic Charter showed that Latin American and other less developed countries saw in the articulation of general principles of international cooperation and free-dom from want implications that the originators did not, to be sure. However, it illustrates nicely the way in which states are placed in an international society in which the principles they articulate and the prac-tices they undertake define the character of the society in a way that leads to ongoing change. The evolving rhetoric of principled Allied war aims, and the evolution of international organizations and international relief operations, followed the pattern set by welfare institutions before, in which measures are taken first to help those to whom some obvious un-preventable catastrophe has happened, and assistance is then progres-sively extended to broader categories of people in need. As previously ignored persons come into view as members of a society founded on a recognition (in principle) of the human rights of all, it becomes more and more difficult to find a rationale for ignoring their needs and demands. This process found a kind of culmination in the debates of the United Nations Economic and Social Council in the late forties.

Certainly there was nothing inevitable about Truman's proclamation of a general program of U.S. support for development (initially by means of technical assistance) in the poor countries, and nothing inevitable about the response that led to the clear institutionalization of foreign aid programs over the following dozen years. But the way for the program was clearly prepared by the development of a set of institutions and the articulation of a philosophy that recognized freedom from want as an important international goal in which the leading world countries took an interest, and in behalf of which they undertook serious commitments of resources. Both the institutions and the philosophy presupposed looking at world problems from a point of view of world citizenship and universal human kinship, and presupposed, also, governmental response to alleviate human need in domestic society. The institutionalization of concern for human need and an expansion of people's identification beyond national borders lay behind almost every move that prepared the way for aid throughout the first half of the twentieth century.

## CHAPTER SEVEN

# How Aid Grew:
## Development of Regular Aid Programs

> Only by helping the least fortunate of its members to help them-
> selves can the human family achieve the decent, satisfying life
> that is the right of all people. Democracy alone can supply the
> vitalizing force to stir the peoples of the world into triumphant
> action, not only against their human oppressors, but also against
> their ancient enemies—hunger, misery, and despair.
>
> —Harry S Truman

WHY DID foreign aid occur at all? The sudden discontinuity with past
practice began with Truman's call in his inaugural address of January 16,
1949, for a "bold new program" of technical assistance to less developed
countries that would help them to attain higher standards of living. The
fourth point of the speech, in which he set out his proposal, is worth
quoting in full.

> Fourth, we must embark on a bold new program for making the benefits of our
> scientific advances and industrial progress available for the improvement and
> growth of underdeveloped areas. More than half the people of the world are
> living in conditions approaching misery. Their food is inadequate. They are
> victims of disease. Their economic life is primitive and stagnant. Their poverty
> is a handicap and a threat both to them and to more prosperous areas. For the
> first time in history, humanity possesses the knowledge and skill to relieve the
> suffering of these people. The United States is pre-eminent among nations in
> the development of industrial and scientific techniques. The material resources
> which we can afford to use for the assistance of other peoples are limited. But
> our imponderable resources in technical knowledge are constantly growing
> and are inexhaustible. I believe that we should make available to peace-loving
> peoples the benefits of our store of technical knowledge in order to help them
> realize their aspirations for a better life. And, in cooperation with other na-
> tions, we should foster capital investment in areas needing development. Our
> aim should be to help the free peoples of the world, through their own efforts,
> to produce more food, more clothing, more materials for housing and more
> mechanical power to lighten their burdens. We invite other countries to pool
> their technological resources in this undertaking. Their contributions will be
> warmly welcomed. This should be a cooperative enterprise in which all nations

work together through the United Nations and its specialized agencies wherever practicable. It must be a worldwide effort for the achievement of peace, plenty, and freedom. With the cooperation of business, private capital, agriculture, and labor in this country, this program can greatly increase the industrial activity in other nations and can raise substantially their standards of living. Such new economic developments must be devised and controlled to benefit the peoples of the areas in which they are established. Guaranties to the investor must be balanced by guaranties in the interest of the people whose resources and whose labor go into these developments. The old imperialism—exploitation for foreign profit—has no place in our plans. What we envisage is a program of development based on concepts of democratic fair-dealing. All countries, including our own, will greatly benefit from a constructive program for the better use of the world's human and natural resources. Experience shows that our commerce with other nations expands as they progress industrially and economically. Greater production is the key to prosperity and peace. And the key to greater production is a wider and more vigorous application of modern scientific and technical knowledge. Only by helping the least fortunate of its members to help themselves can the human family achieve the decent, satisfying life that is the right of all people. Democracy alone can supply the vitalizing force to stir the peoples of the world into triumphant action, not only against their human oppressors, but also against their ancient enemies—hunger, misery and despair.[1]

Truman's call was a surprising one. His inaugural address provided him an opportunity to put his own distinctive stamp on administration policy. The address dealt with the main points of U.S. foreign policy, and the first three points simply recapitulated existing commitments. The fourth, the "bold new program," took everyone off guard. The speech was at once widely acclaimed, in the United States and abroad; it was also much criticized. And Truman's idea of foreign aid did not remain his own possession for long. It at once touched off an upsurge of interest in development, calls for development, and new programs by other countries and by the United Nations.[2] Within the next three years, three other important programs of international assistance had been initiated not under U.S. auspices: the development lending of the World Bank; the Colombo Plan for South Asian countries; and the Expanded Programme of Technical Assistance (EPTA) of the United Nations. The rapid imitation of the Point Four plan by others, as well as the reaction it received, suggests that Truman's judgment had correctly descried an option that could command wide support, despite its novelty. Truman's Point Four speech forms a clear divide between the foreign policy of developed democracies before and after it, and raises again the question with which the book's investigation of aid started: whether aid's appearance and growth was a response to human need in which moral factors played an important part, or whether it can be explained on the basis of donor self-interest.

The last chapter argued that the ground was well prepared for this kind of suggestion to take such deep and rapid root. The values and the strategy of liberal internationalism that formed the inherent logic around which aid policies and practices grew was rooted historically in a set of overlapping and interrelated movements that had developed particularly in the preceding fifty to eighty years as well as in the more recent events in the decade immediately preceding the beginnings of foreign aid programs in 1949–51. Two main developments were essential to the later development of foreign aid: a growing commitment to an egalitarian and humane society in which the elimination of needless poverty was a social and governmental priority; and a similar commitment to a cooperative and peaceful international order, in which all peoples received a just share, and had hope for the future, and in which all were able to get along, in consequence. The gradual development of internationalism and of domestic social responsibility for poverty in the first half of the century found newly strengthened articulation and institutional embodiment in the forties. The increasing disorder and chaos of that period underscored the importance of finding policies that would bring about a better world, domestically and internationally. The proclamation of an Allied consensus on war aims included self-determination, freedom from want, and freedom from fear, and these goals found institutional expression in programs like Lend-Lease, the UNRRA, the FAO and the World Bank, and the United Nations and its Economic and Social Council (ECOSOC).

These major changes, both domestic and international, altered the character of the international system prior to and irrespective of any major shifts in the balance of power, and hence prepared the way for that further alteration that foreign aid constituted. Running through them were common threads of interpretation of the international order, summed up perhaps in the maxims that "poverty anywhere is a threat to prosperity everywhere" and that a secure international order must be based on "freedom from want, freedom from fear." This interpretive framework did not consist simply of the statements policymakers or others made about the international system and its institutions, however, much less of their private intentions. It was present in their actions, in the new postwar institutions themselves. Those actions and institutions had a positive force, a dynamic thrust, because they organized behavior around social forms with a natural social meaning.

By setting up a domestic order in which the lower classes were assumed to have equal rights with upper classes, and in which those at the bottom of the social heap were to be helped; by setting up institutions for cooperation that, at least potentially, included all countries; by setting up programs of international transfers to assist countries laid low by war to recover; by setting up an international forum for debate, and debate on economic and social issues as well as those of international security—by all these things the dominant powers not only continued the development of certain social trends and expressed their interpretation of what had gone wrong in the interwar period but also provided a basis for defining what sort of ongoing processes were to be regarded as legitimate. The major institutions and actions of the postwar order that were in place by 1949 in their very form clearly expressed implicitly what had also been stated explicitly, that is, a new definition of the relations between nations, in which cooperative processes that included the weak as well as the strong were to serve as the basis of lasting prosperity and peace.

How does such an explanation play out against competing explanations which lay the emphasis on factors of national self-interest? I will first look at various explanations of the sudden institutionalization of foreign aid at midcentury, then examine the history of the growth of foreign aid in detail.

## WEIGHING ALTERNATIVE EXPLANATIONS FOR THE EMERGENCE OF AID

Looking at any of these explanatory factors—at economic or political self-interest and at international humanitarian and civic considerations—the crucial question in examining the historical trajectory of aid programs is that of change: What change in these factors accounts for the sudden origin and spread of aid programs and for their subsequent persistence and evolution? Humanitarianism and civic-mindedness are presumably enduring human traits, though they may vary from time to time or culture to culture. To explain the abrupt changes in international practice that foreign aid comprised then requires showing what changes in these traits occurred or what other factors changed to cause these traits to operate in a new way. I will discuss factors of both sorts, but first it is important to point out that the same kind of requirement affects an attempt to explain foreign aid in terms of political and economic interests of donor states. The factors of political and economic interest had been around a long, long time; foreign assistance policies had not. An explanatory account of the origins of foreign aid in terms of political and economic interest needs to show how the changes in interests of the donor states in general corresponded to their adoption of foreign aid policies.

One explanation of this type would rest on the decolonization that occurred after the Second World War. Foreign aid as a means of influence became possible, this line of argument would go, only after there were less developed states not bound to a colonizing power. More generally, the vast disparities of wealth and power between sovereign states that existed after decolonization created a new situation in which this sort of policy became available as a means of influence. While it is true that a great many new states, some of them very poor and very tiny, appeared as decolonization proceeded in the fifties and sixties, the overall contrast which emphasis on this fact suggests is false. There were underdeveloped countries, many of them of direct interest to major powers, in Europe for centuries. In the nineteenth century there were former colonies in Latin America that were in fact the object of a certain amount of trade rivalry between Europeans, and especially between England and the United States. There is no record of any systematic use of economic transfers, apart from payments to secure some specific objective or treaty, in that period, however.

Furthermore, the appearance of the new African nations mostly dated from 1957 on, well after the basic principle of foreign aid and the programs of the United States, the United Nations, France, England, and some others had been established. Advocacy of aid to less developed regions began in the late thirties and early forties, and was associated with peace and labor groups, churches and New Dealers in the United States. The same people had begun calling for decolonization at about the same time. Further, there was an outpouring of support for Truman's bold new program by such groups after it was announced, but little support elsewhere. The timing suggests that the new aid program and the appearance of the new nations drew upon the same values of self-determination and support for human dignity, but not that the shift in power that the existence of these nations constituted was a main cause of aid.

A second type of explanation would fix the new aid policies on the changed political incentives created by a bipolar world, and the East-West rivalry that accompanied it. It is not to be denied that this factor had influence, particularly in the United States, and particularly in the fifties and early sixties. As a structural explanation of aid, however, this has two empirical problems: it does not account for why the bipolar world affected similar powers differently, and it does not account for why the bipolar world affected differently placed states similarly.

The Soviet Union and the United States both found themselves in a major rivalry from the late forties onward. But though the United States maintained a program of bilateral and multilateral aid to LDCs, the Russians did not. The relatively small-scale, though well-publicized, Soviet effort at aid in the late fifties and thereafter never approached the magnitude of efforts by the United States or other Western states, as chapter 4 showed. The Eastern bloc countries, principally the Soviets, did have a program of aid, so-called; but it was quite unlike Western foreign aid. First, it was much smaller, absolutely and as a percentage of GNP. More significantly, it was not available to LDCs in general; some 90% went to a few close allies—Vietnam, Cuba, and later Afghanistan—and most of the remainder to other states bordering the Soviet Union. Almost none of the aid was channeled through multilateral aid institutions. Aid that was given to LDCs other than the three client states just mentioned was fully tied—a provision of Soviet and East European goods—and had so small a grant element that it was essentially a loan at commercial terms. The net flow of resources from Soviet and East European "aid" in later years other than to close allies was actually negative.[3] States such as East Germany and the Soviet Union had standards of living substantially higher than those of the poorest of the DAC donors but did not undertake similar programs.

An additional problem with the bipolar world or East-West rivalry explanation is that it does not square with the behavior of the various other OECD countries that undertook aid programs. The problem here is not just that these countries were not themselves engaged in a rivalry for influence with the Soviet Union. It would have been possible for some U.S. allies to have seen themselves as doing their part in retaining Western influence in former colonies, for instance, or in contiguous areas of the Third World. Indeed, there is no doubt that this was sometimes the case. The problem is that virtually all the advanced democratic states undertook aid programs, including neutrals like Sweden and Austria, and including latecomers like Finland and Ireland. Their aid included assistance to U.S. foes, like Vietnam and Nicaragua. And, even apart from these anomalous cases, from the declared motives of the neutral (and some of the nonneutral) donors, and from the universality of participation by democratic advanced states, the level of participation does not seem to vary with the susceptibility to cold war threat at all, or with susceptibility to U.S. influence. Countries with strongly independent foreign policies—France, Sweden, the Netherlands—had strong aid programs; countries that usually followed the United States more closely did not.

The timing of aid and its antecedents also is unfavorable to the hypothesis that the bipolar world lay behind aid. As U.S. interest in aid and U.S. hegemony weakened, for the time being at least, in the seventies and eighties, other OECD countries increased their aid commitments. Aid from most OECD countries grew particularly fast in the era of détente. Furthermore, the antecedents of aid—the UNRRA, the establishment of the World Bank and of the ECOSOC in the United Nations, and calls for achieving freedom from want and for assistance in raising standards of living—were well under way before there was a widespread realization, in the late forties, that there would be a bipolar world or a cold war. And there is every reason to suppose that aid will continue now that the cold war is over.

Cold war considerations did play an important part in establishing foreign aid programs, particularly in the United States; but they did so primarily in a negative way. As has been shown in previous chapters, there was no real foreign affairs constituency to press for aid except among liberal internationalists and those with humane interests in economic assistance (and except, in the United States particularly after 1973, for a lobby for aid to Israel). Concerns about communism were real, and played the role of gaining swing votes for foreign aid and diffusing criticism by an appeal to the centerpiece of U.S. foreign policy in the early cold war. They do not account for the bases of support for aid, however, or account for the patterns of aid giving among OECD countries. It would be a mistake indeed to neglect the ways in which foreign aid was influenced by cold war considerations, or even by the new economic possibilities open to the donor states. However, as just argued, the economic incentives and the structural changes such as decolonization and the U.S.-Soviet rivalry that accompanied the end of World War II do not explain the origin and growth of foreign aid. They do not even tally with the pattern of variation of aid between countires and over time. Structural changes obviously are relevant to a full understanding of the aid process. But one must look elsewhere for underlying variables which changed in ways that can account for the major changes which the appearance of foreign aid as a regular part of foreign policy represents.

## Humane and Civic Internationalist Convictions

On the hypothesis that aid arose largely from humanitarian and cooperative-internationalist convictions, what changes in these convictions, or in the milieu in which they operated, account for their efficacy in the postwar period in engendering this new pattern of international transfers? Why did these factors have this effect in the postwar period and not before? Why did aid practices spread and develop, and maintain their place in DAC countries?

I have shown that although the development of foreign aid programs was not an inevitable thing, it was the logical culmination of innovations in social thought and practice that had been growing in Western societies, in the previous fifty to a hundred years particularly. The argument is *not* that earlier events conclusively determined the direction that would be taken later but that later events, subject to contemporary choices, also drew upon the heritage of possibilities which the social and intellectual creations of the previous periods provided. Such creations also had certain dynamic tendencies for development, though the choice about how, or whether, to follow these up lay open. The crucial preconditions of aid were two: the development of domestic social welfare policies and the rise of a belief in the importance of international cooperation. Both changes represented not simply particular political developments in scattered countries but the rise of coherent social and political outlooks, political traditions, and shared values amongst a group of countries that were increasingly closely associated with one another.

The spread and timing of calls for international aid closely followed changes in attitudes toward poverty, and in the domestic social welfare institutions designed to deal with economic needs of the domestic population. The Western democratic welfare state developed over five to ten decades before the war, and by the end of the war was widely accepted as a part of the government's proper role in providing for the citizenry. The growth of aid also roughly tallies with the growth of the welfare state: welfare state institutions and expenditures continued to grow throughout the postwar period, and particularly in the late sixties and seventies, which was also the period of the most rapid rise in aid spending. Acceptance of the welfare state came relatively late in the United States; only after the war did the general outlines of social spending come to be accepted, and there was conservative opposition to the whole apparatus (for instance, Goldwater's objection to the Social Security system) until the midsixties. The economic stagnation, and serious U.S. cuts in aid spending in the late eighties and early nineties come at a time of increasing domestic disaffection with welfare state institutions throughout the developed democracies. Thus, the development of the welfare state prepared the way for foreign aid, and the later success of aid roughly has reflected the extent of acceptence of welfare-state concepts.

In fact, convictions that there should be public assistance to the poor, and the varying strength of those convictions, help account for four observed patterns of aid outcomes. They explain the initial timing of aid: why the policies were widely adopted after World War II but not at all before. They explain the participating countries, that is, predominantly those in the Western, democratic bloc of advanced countries. They explain the continuing growth of aid norms: the surprising development over the years of standards for foreign aid in stricter conformity to the developmental and humanitarian purposes for which aid was supposed to be given—standards well adhered to by a number of OECD donors and, at least in part, by most, even the large, lax ones. They also help explain the reasons why those aid norms have continued to exert a stronger influence in some OECD countries than in others and have slackened some in the last decade.

At the same time, the origins of foreign aid represented part of a different long-term development, that of international institutions, as documented in the last chapter. Over a similar period of time, from the late nineteenth century on, there was increasing interest in institutions of international law and in the establishment of cooperative relations among nations. This led to the formation of international peace conferences, and of various bodies for international economic cooperation, as well. Although most of these were of little or no help in promoting international cooperation in the short run, they provided a climate in which the devising of instruments of international cooperation became more and more a possibility. In addition to these general movements, the development of economic science and government planning enabled, and the influence of radical groups and states spurred, the development of institutions of international economic cooperation.

Aid policies were the natural, though not the inevitable, fruit of trends toward social justice and international cooperation. One can see how these trends might logically eventuate in aid, while it is obscure why structural incentives would lead to policies of this kind. In particular, they suggest how foreign aid policies came to be thought of, why they took the institutional forms they did, and why support and opposition came from the quarters it did. If foreign aid was but the instrument of power politics and mercantilist strategy, one needs to ask how such an instrument was chosen, or even conceived of. But if the development of social welfare institutions and an ethos of international cooperation was of increasing importance in the twentieth century, especially in the democratic countries, and was a factor in the way those countries approached international relations, then the devising of instruments of economic assistance, both as ends in themselves and as means to the attainment of other ends, such as international stability, becomes understandable. If foreign aid was only or mainly set up to garner wealth and influence to the donors, then it is necessary to explain why policies were devised that gave a large part to international institutions, technicians, and economists, and that were in various ways isolated from influence by working diplomats and the central state machinery. But these emphases are perfectly logical if foreign aid arose out of conviction that it was desirable to assist the needy and promote international cooperation. Similarly, if foreign aid served primarily national or subnational interests in the donor countries, it is difficult to understand why aid found support mainly from groups and individuals concerned with social justice and with a cooperative international order, and was opposed by conservative groups, by and large. But if changes in internationalism and the welfare state lay behind the interest in foreign aid, the patterns of enthusiasm and disaffection for aid are as expected, and the whole development becomes meaningful and intelligible.

The historical developments in question provide, in short, a pattern that not only accounts for the time and the countries in which aid programs arose in the sense of tallying with it, but also an explanation in the sense that the creation of aid policies is a natural, though certainly not foregone, conclusion of these historical trends.

*Major Periods of Development of Foreign Aid*

It was argued earlier that ideas and basic values have an effect in structuring dynamic change, to produce ongoing reform. In the remainder of this chapter I will argue that just such a process of structuring has continued throughout the whole foreign aid era: the essential ideas of the foreign aid regime were not only the basis on which new plans were developed, but were the basis of the political strength on which that regime grew. In each of the three major periods of aid institutionalization, the strengthening of support for aid (measured in terms of donor commitment of scarce resources) went along with the provision of an understanding of aid (and institutions that enforced that understanding), which placed the emphasis more squarely upon impartial commitment to cooperation and development, as opposed to particularistic donor interests. That new definition of international relationships which comprised foreign aid gathered strength over time: foreign aid was made more development oriented, more professional, more poverty oriented, more subject to international control and scrutiny. And this strengthening of the definition, away from particularistic donor interests and toward a cooperative systemwide concept, seems to have been not an impediment to the generation of donor support but the very thing that led to such support.

Foreign aid proper, as defined in this study, essentially began in January 1949, with the announcement of the Point Four program and the beginning of the shift in World Bank lending from European reconstruction to development loans to the Third World. It will be convenient to think of three main periods in which aid institutions developed, starting with 1949. *An initial institutionalization* began with vigor in 1949–51 and continued in slackened form through the midfifties. *A reinstitutionalization*, marked by a revival of interest in aid in the late fifties, resulted in a spate of important new institutions and commitments in the period from 1958 to 1961, and continued in slackened form through the mid-to-late sixties. A more diffuse *series of reforms* commenced at the end of the sixties and continued through the beginning of the seventies and beyond. Each of these will be discussed in turn.

## INITIAL INSTITUTIONALIZATION OF FOREIGN AID

In the initial period of institutionalization, four particularly important programs were set up: the Point Four program, announced by President Truman in his inaugural address in January 1949; the reorientation of World Bank lending that took effect in 1949 and 1950; the Colombo Plan, originated in January 1950 at the Commonwealth Foreign Ministers' meeting in South Asia and formally launched in July 1951;[4] and the creation of a United Nations Expanded Programme of Technical Assistance. Each of these emphasized, to some extent, the nature of the program as technical assistance rather than as ongoing support involving a transfer of resources. Each of them, and especially the latter two, involved a compromise and a debate between the developed and the less developed countries. Despite some disagreements and disappointments, each involved a recognition by all parties of the importance of international cooperation to promote development. These four initiatives laid the groundwork for the development of at least rudimentary programs of foreign aid throughout most of the countries of the Western alliance during the early and midfifties.

## Point Four

In one way, the Point Four program is both the most important and the most obscure of these four major initiatives of 1949–50. Its import resides not just in its size—though it was, in fact, much larger than any of the other three in cash volume of resources provided[5]—but in the role it played in putting the foreign aid idea on the agenda of the developed countries as a legitimate and worthwhile activity. It is no accident that two other programs followed it, and that in the wake of Truman's announcement it was fully possible for the World Bank to follow through a shift to lending to the less developed countries. Its origins are obscure, however, in that although the idea was not entirely novel, its acceptance by the United States was a surprise move resulting from an unusual presidential judgment.

The address itself had, and has continued to have, an enormous impact. The first three points of the address—support of the United Nations, continuation of the Marshall Plan, and a strengthening "of the free countries to resist armed attack"—were relatively expected. The fourth point was quite unexpected, and was the influential innovation: "a bold new program for making the benefits of our scientific advances and industrial progress available for the improvement of the underdeveloped areas."[6]

How did the Point Four plan come about? Truman had originally planned a low-key inaugural address, probably focused on domestic policy, but advisers convinced him that he should not neglect the platform this unique occasion would provide him.[7] Truman's attention was caught particularly by a suggestion, which some senior aides thought foolish,[8] to expand the program of technical assistance to Latin America which had been institutionalized on a very small scale ten years before[9] into a general program of technical assistance to poorer countries. This he made the innovative final point in his outline of the principles of American foreign policy, the "bold new program" to which he chose to devote his unique policy platform. Why?

Probably it is impossible to know just what prompted President Truman to set out his Point Four plan. Even had Truman later stated what his motives were, there could be no guarantee that these reported retrospective feelings reflect the motives which were uppermost at the time. And although in one way his surprise move—one that might well, had circumstances been only very slightly different, never have come about—represented a supreme instance of personal decision and the influence of chance, in another way the (ultimately) favorable reception the announcement received (for a variety of reasons) at home and abroad indicated that Truman's choice was a shrewd judgment which articulated a path that was politically viable—a choice, that is, which had generalizable bases of support.[10] After all, the plan—no matter why Truman conceived it—could not have been realized without congressional support. And no matter what opinion was in the United States, its favorable reception and imitation abroad must have reflected factors of yet more general appeal.[11]

Certainly, the plan was affected by security concerns. It followed in the steps of the Marshall Plan, which had been so successful in stabilizing a Europe on the brink of collapse, and a prey, as it seemed to the administration, to communism. Attempts (albeit of a somewhat different sort) to shore up with economic and military support regimes that seemed about to collapse had been extended to China (unsuccessfully, as it turned out) and then to Greece and Turkey. And the passage of these measures in Congress was much affected by perception of the Soviet threat—as evidenced in the Czechoslovakian coup, for instance. At the same time, the justification of the plan to the public plainly rested not just on perception of the communist threat but upon humanitarian concerns as well.

The nature of the plan as formulated also is an important aspect of the *way* in which these various concerns entered into the program. The Point Four plan drew upon the previous, smaller-scale, U.S. experience of IIAA *technical* assistance (a kind of aid Truman had emphasized, probably to avert criticism of a "giveaway" program); and a series of specific projects building economic infrastructure was the plan's mainstay. Thus, whatever the mixture of *motives* that entered into the plan, the *execution* consisted of projects focused on economic criteria. This in turn then led to the development of staff and organization whose professional orientation, and whose ostensible purpose and recruitment, directed them to issues of development, not of political influence. The specifically technical orientation of the program's conception imparted a particular bias to the consideration of development issues, to be sure. The same was true of the IBRD, which relied heavily on economists (and, initially, on bankers). But this technical and economic orientation embedded the experts of whatever kind in a debate about the purposes of development rather than about the influence of the donor countries; indeed, a debate about the latter considerations would have seemed to *all* concerned completely out of place. And insofar as security concerns motivated programs of assistance at all, a significant transformation had occurred in concepts of security. While there is no doubt that foreign aid funds were at one time or another used for purposes of political influence, the sort of security interest that was being urged here was one that referred not to influence on the direction or alliances of other governments but to the role that internal prosperity, stability, and hope had in producing stable governments.

Truman clearly chose in the Point Four speech to make Third World development a major agenda item for the United States (and thus for the West)—the taking of some such move was not at all a necessary consequence of previous commitments but indeed a "bold" step, and a political risk. Yet in fact, though the move was not inevitable and though it gained power through the dramatic timing of the speech, Truman's decision was an extension of a logic implicit in much earlier decisions to establish inclusive international institutions.

### The Changed Direction of the World Bank

The World Bank's shift of its lending from European reconstruction to development finance, largely outside of the European areas, was a second important decision in the origination of international commitments to foreign aid. This decision, which could not have been undertaken without the acquiescence of the U.S. director, seems to have preceded Truman's speech in a certain sense: beginning with the first loans of 1949, announced weeks before Truman's inaugural and thus prepared months in advance, the Bank lent almost exclusively for development projects in the developing countries; in its first two years of operations, it had lent almost exclusively for European reconstruction. The change need not have taken the form of a systematic policy or even a conscious choice by the end of January 1949, of course. Moreover, in one sense it may be seen as the consequence not of any policy objective at all but as an imperative of institutional survival. The Bank, which had originally been conceived as the instrument of European reconstruction, had proved, as constituted, inadequate for that task. When the need for greater resources became apparent, the United States had undertaken the Marshall Plan, at a scale unmatchable by the Bank. European reconstruction was, in any case, a project with a sure if perhaps indefinite time horizon. The shift to financing development was necessary if the Bank was to stay in business.

However, the Bank's staying in business was not a foregone conclusion. An early president of the Bank had questioned that idea, stating that the Bank should stay in business only until capital markets began to work more efficiently. It is questionable whether that intention could really have led the institution to seek to disband itself. But the international support the Bank needed to continue and to expand operations could easily have flagged as it switched from European reconstruction to development lending in Africa, Asia, and Latin America. Truman's endorsement supported the Bank's almost exclusive switch from 1949 on, providing legitimation to the Bank's course. And the Bank's specialization in development projects became a major force in the promotion of development economics, and in support of aid, in the following decade.

## Origins of the United Nations EPTA

From the start, the less developed members had pressed in the UN, particularly in the Economic and Social Council (ECOSOC), for measures that would address their felt needs for economic development. The less developed ECOSOC members had, at the time that an Economic Commission for Europe was set up, insisted on matching it with commissions for developing areas. The Economic Commission for Latin America (ECLA), under the brilliant leadership of the Argentinian economist Raul Prebisch, was particularly active in advancing arguments, such as that of declining terms of trade, for making provisions for the advancement of the less developed countries. There were additional calls in the ECOSOC for action to help the less developed countries; and the General Assembly had adopted various resolutions about development and provision of social welfare designed to fulfill some of the Charter obligations to "promote higher standards of living, full employment, and conditions of social and economic progress and development."[12]

Within a few months of Truman's speech calling for a new emphasis on technical assistance to poorer countries, discussion began in the ECOSOC of expanded UN programs along the same lines. Specialized United Nations agencies such as WHO, FAO, and so on had already undertaken developmental activities or small projects at the behests of member states since their foundation. But more concerted programs, aimed not at specific problems or conditions but at overall problems of development, were beyond the scope of the specialized agencies. A practical harbinger of later efforts was the comprehensive report on economic development in Haiti, prepared that summer.

A more controversial, explicit exploration of policy was the July speech of the chairman of the Sub-Commission on Economic Development, V. K. R. V. Rao (of India), which called for a United Nations Economic Development Administration. Rao's plan was for an organization financed through contributions of member governments that would provide loans at a nominal rate of interest for projects which were not bankable. The projects would be financed partly by the governments of the recipient countries, and could be regional projects covering several countries. And, crucially, the aid provided, though still termed "technical assistance," could also include the procurement of materials.[13] This proposal was important as a forerunner of later calls for a United Nations program that would provide for capital resources—variously termed, as the debate continued, an Economic Development Administration, a Special UN Fund, a Capital Development Fund, or a Development Program. At the time, however, it drew strong opposition—from the U.S. representative to the Sub-Commission, Emiliano G. Collado, and from the president of the World Bank, Eugene Black, particularly. Black's objections in part seem to have come from concern about the reputation of the Bank and the need not to duplicate its work (or steal its thunder); but both sets of objections also deemed the idea of providing capital at a nominal rate of interest unsound financially. Since essentially the same proposal, with many of the same details, was incorporated in the plans for the IDA ten years later, it may truly be said, as Rao himself later put it, that the proposal was "ahead of its time." The concept of capital transfers—even if the principal was ultimately to be repaid—was not yet legitimate, especially under international auspices.

Rao's proposal was but one idea aired in the Sub-Commission, however. The more modest proposal of a program to coordinate and expand the technical assistance projects that the United Nations was already undertaking was adopted in the ECOSOC in August, in its Resolution 222 (IX), and approved by the General Assembly in November as the Expanded Programme of Technical Assistance (EPTA). Like the UNEDA of the Rao proposal, the EPTA was financed by voluntary member contributions; but its emphasis was on technical assistance, and its scale more limited, and its language also stressed that "increased services undertaken by [a] government can be maintained, in the long run, only out of national production."[14]

Despite the language that carefully limited the idea of the EPTA to terms and dimensions which would not antagonize the major nations that would have to fund the program, especially the United States, and their financial communities, the EPTA constituted a third big step toward the establishment of regular and multilateral foreign aid, for three reasons. First, it was a further public step, following Truman's agenda-setting call, toward aid programs. Second, it was multilateral, and as such not only established a development assistance program in which the developing nations had a voice but also provided a place for other potential donor countries without bilateral programs of their own to make contributions. And third, it was a first step forward in initiation of UN programs for development—and thus began a line of steady movement toward a much more comprehensive UN program that assumed something like final form in the late sixties.

The ongoing UN pressure for more comprehensive development measures did not stop with the creation of the EPTA. The secretary-general, Trygve Lie, at the request again of the Economic and Social Council, (Resolution 290 [XI], 1950) appointed a group of experts to report on what could be done to assist the developing countries. The experts, A. B. Cortez, D. R. Gadgil, W. A. Lewis, Theodore W. Schultz, and George Hakim, chair, submitted their report in May 1951.[15] The essential finding of the "Experts' Report" was that a large influx of public capital was needed by the developing countries—perhaps some $5 billion per year. Their reasoning was as follows: the developing countries should be growing at a rate of at least 2% per year in GNP per capita. This would require capital inputs of some $10 billion per year beyond what could be raised in the countries themselves. Of that, only about half could be expected to be forthcoming in private capital markets. Therefore the remainder needed to be publicly provided. Of course, there were many other recommendations in the Experts' Report, dealing with measures to be taken by the developing as well as by the developed countries. The really powerful, and controversial, conclusion, however—and that which moved the debate that was going on between the developed and underdeveloped countries along—was the claimed need for large influxes of public capital.

## The Colombo Plan

A fourth important element in the establishment of an aid regime was the Colombo Plan. The plan was a scheme for providing aid to the countries of South and Southeast Asia, first definitely formulated at the Commonwealth Foreign Ministers' meeting in January 1950 in Colombo, the capital of Sri Lanka (then called Ceylon). A Consultative Commission was formed at that meeting, which began drawing up a six-year plan the following May, and produced a report after a London meeting in September.[16] The plan was formally launched in July 1951.[17]

The Colombo Plan was not really a plan in the sense of a blueprint for definite economic developments, but more nearly a consultative arrangement, facilitating the negotiation of requests for economic and technical assistance between the nations involved. The intention was not that the plan should be limited to Commonwealth donors; and after the United States joined, it became the largest contributor. Most of the aid that was provided by the United States, and perhaps by any of the donors after the initial years of the program, might have been provided under other auspices had the plan ceased after a short tenure in existence;[18] although there were characteristic emphases to Colombo Plan aid, such as an emphasis on training.[19]

What was significant about the Colombo Plan was the way in which, at an early critical juncture, it broadened the idea of participation in foreign aid programs, including not only the United States and former colonial powers like Britain, but Canada, Australia, and New Zealand, as well. Britain, indeed, heavily concerned with her own financial problems at the time the idea was proposed, was rather reluctant to get involved in what apparently had been proposed, by Ceylon's finance minister, J. R. Jayawardene, as what Singh calls a kind of "Commonwealth 'Marshall Plan.'" Nehru, on the other hand, would have preferred a more international solution, through the UN, to a semibilateral Commonwealth instrument.[20]

In part this was because of the slightly anticommunist tone that the Conference had, and imparted, to the Plan. The Australian minister of External Affairs, Sir Percy Spender, who finally pushed the plan through the conference, for instance, talked and had thought out his ideas in the context of concern about communist expansion. While without this tone, the plan might not have been adopted, what was accepted as a common focus was the emphasis on economic development; and it was this that is mentioned in subsequent public discussions of the plan. Most sources, in fact, except Singh, whose interest is scholarly and historical, omit mention of the concern about communism.[21] Official Colombo Plan literature tends to speak of the plan in terms that focus exclusively on the concern for economic development. For instance, a 1964 British government publication on the Colombo Plan, which is one of the fullest official expositions, blandly states,

> The purpose of the meeting was to exchange views on World Problems and particularly on the needs of the countries of south and south-east Asia. At this meeting the Colombo plan was born. A Consultative Committee was set up "to survey the needs, to assess the resources available . . . and to provide a framework within which an international co-operative effort could be promoted to assist the countries of the area to raise their living standards." These terms of reference constitute the sole mandate of the Consultative Committee.[22]

What is particularly interesting is that while various countries and statesmen had motives that included neutralism, opposition to communism, retention of Commonwealth ties, and so forth, only the promotion of international development and the reduction of poverty were goals that could be acknowledged as legitimate. Those who, for whatever reason, subscribed to the consensus proclaimed their support for development, which functioned as the only acceptable public channel for pursuing their countries' diverse purposes. This strengthened the grip of development aid norms both through the immediate expansion of programs and by a gradual modification of other sources of support.

Under the rubric of the Colombo Plan, then, national participation in programs of foreign aid, outside the then tiny amount of required UN assessments, was extended to a series of donor countries that previously had not been involved in foreign aid. Also, the plan, while the recipients were regionally limited, was structured as a joint initiative of the developing and developed countries, and, despite its rather loose organizational structure, thus furthered a multilateral conception of aid. The timing of the Colombo Plan, coming right after the Point Four proposal, also strengthened the sense of widening participation in a common aid effort.

### Additional European Efforts in the Fifties

In spite of the importance in principle of the Colombo Plan and the EPTA as representatives of an ongoing commitment to aid by a variety of developed nations, there was a quite small volume of aid given by countries other than the United States during the fifties. Most of what was given consisted of aid by the European colonial powers to colonies or recent former colonies. It is probable that this new provision of colonial development aid represented a sense of responsibility on the part of the colonial powers, as well as a desire to maintain relationships with the territories as they became independent. Nevertheless, this colonially linked aid did not unambiguously show a commitment to development as a goal on the part of the European powers.

Other European aid programs were extremely small. The Swedish government did not have an aid program at all until 1962. Nevertheless, a council of church and civic organizations formed, which coordinated private voluntary assistance from Sweden to the poorer nations. Finland likewise had no regular program of bilateral aid but experimented with a few individual projects: a hospital in Korea, for instance, and a health and agricultural project in India. The existence of these projects was, in itself, a new area of public policy. Other countries contributed to the EPTA. But major funding of aid except through colonial channels did not begin until the end of the fifties.

The United States retrenched from policies of foreign assistance during the Eisenhower administration.[23] Eisenhower appointed a committee to look into foreign economic policy, headed by steel executive Clarence Randall, which suggested that aid—other than technical assistance—should in general be cut out. Eisenhower moved in this direction, saying in a summary of his May 1954 message to Congress that aid should be "curtailed."[24] Eisenhower's appointee as director of the foreign aid program was not enthusiastic about the program. The program itself was administratively reorganized four times in five years. Congress, likewise, was unenthusiastic.

Nevertheless, the idea of foreign assistance gained adherents of several kinds. In the United States, a strong group of intellectuals, centered largely in Boston, advocated the expansion of an aid program and generally argued the humanity and the long-term wisdom for the interests of world peace of an approach that would pay attention to the needs of the developing areas. In Europe, Labour party members like Harold Wilson argued a similar case. The Swedish economist Gunnar Myrdal, an institutionalist whose (later Nobel Prize–winning) work focused on ethical problems in society, basing his case for aid essentially on the ethics of humane and egalitarian considerations rather than on the alleged advantages to stability, was also particularly influential on European opinion.

### REINSTITUTIONALIZATION OF AID

A decisive shift took place in the organization of foreign aid and in attitudes toward it in the late fifties and early sixties. At this time there was a strong increase in U.S. support for aid programs, an upsurge of support by the other industrial democracies, and a reform and proliferation of aid institutions that moved aid significantly in the direction of concern for the poor as a guiding force and removed aid significantly from political pressures. These changes were not, of course, total. But they were marked enough to constitute a second period of foundation, which, like the first, was in line with previous developments but not inevitable and had a crucial effect on the later history of foreign aid.

There were a great many institutional innovations in this period: the institution of the Development Loan Fund (DLF) in the United States as the first positive step toward aid made by the Eisenhower administration; the creation of the International Finance Corporation (IFC) as an affiliate of the World Bank; the creation with U.S. support of the first regional development institution, the Inter-American Development Bank (IDB); the proclamation of the 1960s as the Development Decade; the U.S. proclamation of a hemispheric Alliance for Progress; the founding of a U.S. Peace Corps for international development service; major policy statements by several European nations on foreign aid; the cooperation of donors in a consortium (organized by the IBRD) to assist India with its second, failing, five-year plan; and so on. Two of these were crucial, however, and stand as major landmarks. One was the creation of the soft-loan affiliate of the World Bank, the International Development Association (the IDA). The other was the creation or reformulation of the OECD—the Organization for Economic Cooperation and Development, an association of the economically advanced democracies, more or less—out of the old OEEC, which had grown out of joint European administration of Marshall Plan aid to Europe, and with it, the creation of the OECD's Development Assistance Committee, or DAC.

The IDA was a crucial step forward for three reasons, all important. First, it represented acquiescence to the idea of truly concessional finance as a major international instrument of development, the essential thing that the less developed countries had been calling for at least since the V. K. R. V. Rao speech of July 1949; that is, it accepted the principle of major ongoing (interest-free) capital transfers from rich nations to poor for purposes of development. The provision of interest-free finance, with a fifty-year payback period and ten-year grace period, meant that capital was being loaned almost indefinitely at (even in 1960) a negative real rate of interest; and that implied a continual process of replenishment by the donor nations that supported the IDA. Second, it was a commitment to providing a major portion of aid through multilateral channels, and also, thus, from a variety of donor countries. Countries providing aid were implicitly understood to include virtually all the developed countries in the Western alliance, with the U.S. share (and thus voting power) in a minority. The financial base was expanded, and U.S. influence was buffered and moderated. Third, the plan for the IDA involved dividing less developed nations into two groups, with the poorest eligible to receive the interest-free finance it provided. Thus it represented an acknowledgment that the focus of aid should be the alleviation of poverty, with an emphasis on those most in need.

The organization of the OECD and its Development Assistance Committee was important to the development of foreign aid practices primarily because it represented an acknowledgment by all the industrial democracies of an obligation to assist the less developed countries in their development and also because the DAC, serving as a monitor of aid and constituted in a way that emphasized expertise and led to a good deal of political independence, provided a continual influence on the donors toward accepting standards for aid that would make it more useful to the development of recipients, in quality and quantity.

The OECD served other important functions in economic coordination among the industrialized countries, of course; it was not *primarily*, though it was *importantly*, directed toward the problems of the developing countries. However, the choice of this instrument for partnership among the developed countries represented an emphasis upon the cooperative aspects of the relationship both among those countries themselves and between them and the developed countries.

Together with these two far-reaching institutional innovations, important both for their concrete character and their symbolic implications, were two more general movements in the character of aid: an important reorientation and resurgence of American support for aid, symbolized and greatly furthered by the Kennedy administration; and a dramatic rise, and a reorientation, in support for aid by the other OECD nations.

The change in the American political climate was crucial, for without that it would not have been possible to create an IDA or an OECD. That change, like the Truman decision of 1949, is not fully explicable. Had things fallen out differently, it might not have occurred, for it rested on a series of chancy events: personnel changes in the Eisenhower administration, a hotly contested decision whether to try to strengthen democracy by the OECD or by an expanded military alliance, the unexpected introduction of an odd but important resolution by Senator Monroney and its passage, and the political success—and experiences—of John Kennedy. Nevertheless, in these events it is possible to see consistent intellectual and moral currents at work in the pressures for a fuller realization of a strong and recipient-oriented aid regime.

The major institutional changes at the end of the fifties were followed by a revitalization and extension of aid in the early sixties. One factor in this revitalization was the early commitment of the Kennedy administration to foreign aid. Kennedy's concern about problems of world poverty went back to his Senate days and was particularly influenced by his trip to the Third World in the early fifties; this seems permanently to have affected his outlook on foreign aid, which changed from mild opposition to strong support at the time of this trip.[25] During the presidential campaign, Kennedy voiced the theme of increased concern about U.S. programs to deal with poverty in the Third World and mooted the idea of a volunteer corps of Americans, which later was institutionalized as the Peace Corps.

As president, Kennedy supported aid in several ways. First, his inaugural speech gave prominent attention to the plight of people in villages around the globe and to what help the United States would seek to undertake for them. Kennedy did set up a Peace Corps of U.S. volunteers, and took special pains to see that it was administered in a way that would be less influenced by U.S. strategic objectives. Kennedy also reorganized the U.S. foreign aid program as a whole, making AID—the Agency for International Development—independent of other U.S. foreign policy objectives, both in name and organizational aegis. At the same time, foreign aid funding was increased. Kennedy also put forward the idea of the United Nations proclaiming the sixties as the Development Decade. Specifically with respect to Latin America, Kennedy proposed the concept of an "Alliance for Progress," based on promoting economic growth as an answer to the social problems of Latin America. Despite the problems some of the initiatives, such as the Alliance for Progress, ultimately ran into, these actions resulted in wider interest in foreign aid in the early sixties, both in the United States and abroad.[26]

The prominence given to foreign aid by the Kennedy administration may, however, have been more important in the worldwide influence it had than in any long-run effect it may have had on U.S. aid policy. During the Johnson administration—due perhaps to the financial difficulties arising from the Vietnam War, the domestic programs of social spending, and Johnson's reluctance to raise taxes—U.S. foreign aid began a long-term decline as a percentage of GNP, which has continued to the present. Where large commitments of funds were not involved, the Johnson administration continued to support foreign aid. The UN at last, in the midsixties, got U.S. approval for establishing a development agency with concessional capital funding for projects, the UNDP, or United Nations Development Program. The Asian Development Bank was started with U.S. approval and subscription. And the role of the World Bank, and especially the IDA, grew and was further enhanced by the appointment of Robert McNamara in 1968. Nevertheless, the U.S. commitment did not seem to be sustained in the long term. The increased commitment to issues of international poverty, like the domestic poverty programs of the Great Society, seems to have been among the casualties of the Vietnam War.

However, the prominence aid received encouraged efforts both on the part of the other DAC countries and on the part of the potential recipients. The Development Decade concept, which sought to give symbolic recognition to the importance of economic development, became part of the UN consensus, so that the next two decades were voted "second" and "third" development decades. There were other Third World initiatives, some, such as the UNDP, resulting in definite action; others, such as UNCTAD, resulting in general principles and further calls.

More important for the future of aid, perhaps, during the sixties and, also, the seventies, foreign aid became a matter of increasing interest to the other developed countries. At first, this was an issue pushed by the United States, which advocated fairer "sharing" of the aid "burden" and institutionalized the OECD, and the DAC, to encourage the other advanced democracies to participate more vigorously on worldwide issues of cooperation. The DAC did indeed serve as a prod to such wider participation. However, increasingly this became a prod powered not by the energies of the United States, which was a laggard in the aid process from the early seventies onward, but by the mutual criticism of international aid professionals and of representatives of the various countries operating within the DAC.

The European programs that geared up in the sixties were started on a clear basis of idealistic appeal. The British 1961 white paper on aid emphasized that aid was to be conducted not to promote the particular economic or security goals of Britain but to foster Third World development. The French Jeanneny Report of 1963 made similar recommendations about French aid, though it also touted *besoin de rayonnement,* that is, the responsibility of France to promote French culture and language, as a rationale. Jeanneny, a friend of Jean Monnet, is said to have won de Gaulle's approval for these cooperation-oriented principles partly through Monnet's advocacy although the report seems to have had only slight immediate effect on actual French aid policy. Sweden delayed joining the DAC until 1964 on the grounds that aid policies were too much geared to ulterior purposes, and made it clear at the time of joining that Swedish participation was undertaken in a spirit of reforming aid. The Netherlands and other northern European donors also emphasized the developmental rationale for aid and sought vigorously to educate the public about the needs of the Third World and the responsibility of the developed countries.

The developments from the late sixties onward showed no major breaks in DAC aid as a whole, but a steady development based on already well established principles, which will be traced in detail in chapter 8. The inclusion of other advanced democracies and the institutionalization of agencies with independent judgment about development helped strengthen and broaden the regime that the United States had set up. In addition, once there was a forum for criticism by the LDCs, there were pressures for establishing an aid regime more multilateral and more geared toward the transfer of capital. Such pressure involved not just the making of demands or threats but the presentation of the forceful reasons why further efforts and changes were necessary, reasoning that was often supported by the smaller European states. Once it was established that aid—a practice of regularly providing development assistance to poorer nations—was recognized as a legitimate and worthwhile goal of policy, the natural logic of that goal meant that support came heavily from those who were genuinely concerned about Third World poverty and/or genuinely believed in interdependence among different nations and classes; such people readily supported changes to purify and strengthen aid.

Such successive changes could be resisted but, once in place, were hard to roll back without denying the whole rationale for aid. This meant that changes undertaken from a variety of motives tended to endure and to find further support in other quarters, when they extended the logic of a focus on development, and not otherwise. While some of the major changes—including the Point Four program itself, the decision to fund aid more heavily at the end of the Eisenhower administration to counteract U.S. unpopularity abroad, and the attempt to reformulate the OEEC as the OECD—reflected particular crises and interests of the donors, the changes that were made moved the regime steadily in a direction more oriented in fact toward its ostensible purposes.

## FURTHER INSTITUTIONALIZATION AND CHANGES FROM THE MIDSIXTIES ONWARD

The changes that took place after what I have called the period of "reinstitutionalization" of aid were less concentrated in time and less dramatic in the ways in which they created a changed institutional setup for foreign assistance. They were, nevertheless, substantial in scope. Again, I will focus on three kinds of changes, which affected both the programs of the DAC countries and the multilateral institutions through which, increasingly, much DAC foreign aid was channeled. One was just this great increase in aid funding through multilateral organizations and proliferation of multilateral programs of various kinds. Another was the increasing adoption of fairly strict DAC standards, including wide acknowledgment of the 1% of GNP standard for giving foreign aid as a goal. The third was the increasing focus on poverty as a criterion for aid, both in selection of recipient states and in attention to the impact of foreign aid projects on poor groups in recipient states. These changes took place from the period after the "reinstitutionalization" through the late seventies.

### The Increasingly Multilateral Character of Foreign Assistance

At the end of the fifties concern about Latin American affairs helped secure U.S. support for the creation of an Inter-American Development Bank (and associated Fund). As the sixties progressed, the concept of regional development institutions was extended to Asian and African Development Banks and Funds. These were slightly different in character; the African Development Bank, in particular, emphasized its independence from the developed countries, especially at first in a way that made it difficult to raise funds for the institution.

Along with these there was a great proliferation of United Nations programs. Most important here was the establishment of a capital-funded United Nations Development Program. This had been a goal of the Third World countries ever since the announcement of the Point Four program. Rao, the Indian representative to and chairman of the ECOSOC, had called for such an institution in the summer of 1949; at that time, the call had been regarded as preposterous by the West. Repeated demands for a capital development fund—usually debated under the acronym of a

SUNFED, or Special United Nations Fund for Economic Development—had been increasing throughout the fifties. Indeed, it was partly in hopes of parrying calls for a development fund controlled by the United Nations, and thus by the developing countries themselves, that the United States accepted the idea of a capital fund for grants and soft loans as part of the World Bank, despite claims that the establishment of the IDA was independent of the question of a UN agency with a large capital budget for development.

The Special Fund for Development was in fact set up in 1959, the same year in which the IDA was established, and development funding through UN agencies by the OECD countries doubled in two years, as table 7.1 shows. After 1965, when the Special Fund and the old Expanded Programme of Technical Assistance were consolidated in a United Nations Development Program, DAC contributions to UN programs again doubled in real terms. (The approximate quadrupling of disbursements in the decade following 1965 was offset by a fall in the value of the aid dollar to about 55% of its 1965 value.) The World Food Program, created by the UN FAO (Food and Agricultural Organization) in 1963; the African Development Bank, in 1964; Asian Development Bank, in 1966; United Nations Industrial Development Organization (UNIDO) in 1967; the World Employment Program, begun by the ILO in 1969; the African Development Fund, in 1972; and the Asian Development Fund, in 1974, were thus parts of a general organizational expansion in the late sixties and seventies that accompanied increased multilateral funding both for the IBRD and other development banks and for UN-associated development agencies.

## The Increasing Influence of DAC Standards

The defining characteristics of aid set out in chapter 2—its developmental orientation, its concessional character, its openness to public scrutiny and international monitoring and channeling, the wide range of donors and recipients, and the orientation of aid toward poorer recipient countries and sectors within the Third World—grew more pronounced through the years, and particularly from the midsixties on. Particular aspects of aid often improved in the years after the DAC targeted these as goals. Chapter 8 gives detailed figures showing a variety of ways in which foreign aid moved steadily over several decades in a direction that reduced the leverage, benefits, and control of the donors and increased benefits and freedom of action to the recipient countries. Thus, for instance, it appears that the setting of standards on the percentage of aid going to the least developed countries, and on the terms and conditions of aid, had an effect on donor performance. Certainly the shift toward more multilateral aid

TABLE 7.1
DAC Net Total Disbursements to UN Development Programs (Millions of Dollars)

| Net DAC Disbursements | | | |
|---|---|---|---|
| 1956 | 68 | 1965 | 187 |
| 1957 | 84 | 1966 | 225 |
| 1958 | 78 | 1967 | 261 |
| 1959 | 92 | 1968 | 281 |
| 1960 | 156 | 1969 | 308 |
| 1961 | 174 | 1970 | 368 |
| 1962 | 214 | 1971 | 431 |
| 1963 | 188 | 1972 | 641 |
| 1964 | 229 | 1973 | 662 |
| | | 1974 | 831 |

Sources: Disbursement figures through 1965 are from OECD, *Flow of Financial Resources to Countries in the Course of Development, 1961–1965*, p. 201; figures for 1965 to 1968 are from OECD, *Resources for the Developing World, 1962–1968*; figures for 1968 to 1971 are from OECD, *Development Cooperation, 1972*, pp. 222–23; figures for 1972 to 1974 are from OECD, *Development Cooperation, 1975*, p. 217. Inflation figures in text come from GNP deflator table in OECD, *Development Cooperation, 1972*, p. 336.

Note: There is a discrepancy between sources in 1968, suggesting that *Development Cooperation* may have used a different method of calculation. The *Development Cooperation* figures for 1968 are $264 million.

accompanied discussion of this issue in the DAC reports, although no specific standard was set. And the whole definition of foreign aid, as involving a certain standard of concessionality, was instrumental in keeping aid programs concessional and moving them toward greater concessionality. Much of the progress in these areas was in the late sixties and the seventies, and all this constituted part of the change in that period.

In fact, the pattern here is again familiar. Once it was decided to evoke wider participation in aid by the establishment of an OECD to work on issues of economic cooperation and strengthen the "free world," and in particular to set up a DAC to work on the development burden, it was hard to constitute a DAC except defined in terms that emphasized its technical competences. The DAC *could* have been set up otherwise, but it is doubtful that it could have worked to foster aid on any other terms. Once the DAC was given a professional staff and the power to collect statistics and conduct confidential reviews of the members' programs, there was necessarily the possibility of pressure among the members that could find its basis only in standards deemed relevant to the stated, the only commonly agreed-upon purpose, of aid: the promotion of development and alleviation of poverty. The adoption of a practice that implied a goal of development, especially when combined with the creation of an institution charged with a high calling and with a responsibility agreed upon among the constituent members, created ongoing pressure in the direction of the stated goal in terms of which the practice itself was, in any case, constituted. A certain set of ideas and values, not only publicly articulated in the chartering of certain activities but also implicit in their whole logic, made the activities and institutions instruments of that goal, imparting a continuing impetus to the members to change.

One particularly clear example of this was goals with respect to the volume of aid. While the overall *need* for development aid in the Third World was first articulated publicly in 1951, in the UN's Experts' Report, which did give targets for total official investment in LDCs,[27] the first suggested goals for development aid for individual donors came later. Interestingly, the first suggested 1% target was proposed for consideration by the World Council of Churches, in 1958.[28] Although the definition of numerator and denominator changed from time to time, and the percentage required sometimes did also, the idea of a fixed percentage of earning or production of each of the developed countries going to assist in development in the LDCs remained. In the early targets, the numerator was usually the total financial flow (aid plus private flows), sometimes net of reverse flows and sometimes not explicitly so; in many early versions the denominator was national income (usually less than GNP). Targets or hopes of this sort were put forth with increasing specificity by the UN General Assembly in 1960, by the first UNCTAD in 1964 and the second UNCTAD in 1968, and by the high-level meeting of the DAC countries in October 1968. The documents for the Second UN Development Decade in 1970 and for the third UNCTAD conference in 1972 suggested dates by which the goals should be achieved.

The second UNCTAD conference and later the Pearson Commission Report (in 1969) as well as resolutions for the Second and Third Development Decades adopted targets of about .7% of GNP for foreign aid (ODA) alone. The 1985 DAC report comments: "While reservations of one kind or another were expressed at the adoption of the International Development Strategy in 1970 on the 0.7 per cent ODA target by twelve developed countries, the target has received increasing acceptance and at the present time all DAC members except Switzerland and the United States have accepted the target either with or without a date."[29] Willard Thorp, DAC chairman from 1963 to 1967, writing in 1985 on the DAC's expanding influence states that "whatever the merits of the target" of 1%, which he regards as "of course, an entirely arbitrary figure based on no calculations of need or capacity to pay," it was necessary to have a uniform statistical basis "to discourage retrogression in the total volume and quality of aid and to encourage increased effort."[30] And he reports, "The one percent target did exert an influence. It gave the DAC Chairman effective arguments to the general public, the news media and government officials during his visits to the Member countries. Aid authorities in the countries below the one percent level found the simple numbers very helpful in their internal efforts to raise aid budgets."[31] Indeed, a number of European countries came up with stricter targets and have adhered to or surpassed their goals. And particular parties in some European countries set aid goals as part of their platforms, as chapter 5 discussed.

### Increasing Focus on Poverty as a Criterion for Aid

One consequence of the increased role of the World Bank in development finance was an increased focus on the need of large, very poor recipient nations. This was so despite the emphasis the Bank placed on projects that could be reckoned as providing a high return on investment (whether or not the return was recouped by the Bank). The distinctions that had been made in setting up the IDA between relatively more and relatively less developed Third World countries supported this emphasis.

But the most important role was played by Robert McNamara, who increasingly called for a priority on alleviating absolute poverty. McNamara's influence included the public advocacy of policies directed toward poorer groups, such as his 1973 appeal in Nairobi, and also was exerted behind the scenes at the Bank.[32] The Bank's research department, and especially Paul Streeten, also gave prominence to ideas such as that of a so-called Basic Human Needs strategy as criteria for foreign aid programs. The United Nations defined groups of "most seriously affected" and "least developed" countries as priorities for development. The general set of standards, and the shift in selecting recipients on the basis of need is documented, using quantitative indicators, in chapter 8. It is significant that the shift was prompted by efforts—of Streeten, McNamara, and others—to place an emphasis on the needs of the poorest groups, and also resulted in an explicit policy focus on poverty in many of the donor countries.

The United States Congress, reacting against disillusioning Vietnam War and Watergate experiences, prompted by influence from church-based lobbyists, also passed "New Directions" foreign aid legislation in 1973, which had a similar thrust, both in recommending choice of countries and in fostering programs that would reach the poorest sectors within the developing countries. The British Ministry of Overseas Development worked out a greater emphasis on reaching "the poorest," which was presented to Parliament in 1975 and targeted both poorest countries and poorest sectors within developing countries in British aid programs thenceforth.[33]

## THE AID REGIME IN THE EIGHTIES

The record of the eighties was rather different, and less encouraging for those concerned about sustaining and improving norms and practices of the aid regime. The internationally influential leadership of the World Bank, which in practice is set by its president, who is appointed by the U.S. president, muted somewhat the emphasis on alleviating extreme poverty it had set in the McNamara years. Overall aid levels were stagnant, with increases by some donors balancing decreases by others. The U.S. level of funding has continued to fall under presidents Reagan and Bush, and the United States weakened its commitment to multilateral aid, and made some moves to use its aid to improve its trade position. Margaret Thatcher decreased British aid funding by about 30%, making Britain one of the laggards of the DAC countries, and a 1980 white paper reversed long-standing policy on aid purposes, stating that aid policy would henceforth give more attention to furthering Britain's direct interests, including commercial interests. This amounts to a palpable lowering of earlier British standards for aid quality and quantity. Sweden declined somewhat in its aid giving, and there was increased pressure by the business community in the Scandinavian countries to use aid as an instrument to promote national economic interests.

On the other hand, other donors increased their aid quality and quantity. France, under Mitterand's leadership, increased its overall aid, and the multilateral share of its aid, markedly, and reduced the share going to DOM and TOM. Japan's foreign aid increased markedly as a percentage of GNP, which, together with its continued growth of GNP, made Japan the largest single aid donor by the end of the decade. Moreover, the increased funding was accompanied by improved Japanese aid quality, with a reduced share of aid ultimately buying the services of Japanese firms. Ireland joined the DAC in 1985, and committed itself to reaching a 1% of GNP target ultimately; and other relatively poorer non-DAC European countries have started or increased aid programs which may later result in DAC membership. Finland and Italy both dramatically increased their aid funding, with Finland retaining high aid quality and Italy improving its aid quality. Norway, though already the most vigorous donor, increased its aid yet further.

The mixed aid performance of the eighties, while ethically and humanly discouraging, does lend further support to this book's hypotheses.

If, as has been argued, foreign aid drew its strength in part from the domestic political values of the donor countries, then it is not surprising that aid commitments have tended to falter in recent years. Throughout the Western world there has been some disillusionment with social-welfare programs, and cutbacks in domestic programs have resulted. There has been a general swing toward laissez-faire, individualistic conceptions, and a growing tolerance for previously unacceptable poverty and homelessness within the developed countries. This seems to represent not just the pressure of less auspicious circumstances in recent years but also a certain lack of confidence in, or commitment to, welfare-state measures; and this has tended to go together with a debunking and challenging of foreign aid efforts. The countries where strong market conservatives have triumphed have retrenched on domestic social spending and on foreign aid together; while France, with strong social-democratic leadership, strengthened its aid programs.

Domestic political norms were not the only factor affecting aid in the eighties. Earlier targets and standards for foreign aid that were developed in the sixties and seventies seem to have worked to shore up and strengthen aid programs despite the difficult times. Such standards, and the conviction among many citizens in the developed countries that there is an obligation to assist less developed countries, helped many donors resist temptations to lower aid quality and quantity despite the pressures of world economic conditions.

## CONCLUSION

Chapter 6 showed how the gradual development of a set of ideas and institutions prepared the way for the formation of an aid regime, particularly over the half century before aid started, and how these trends were consolidated in the forties especially. This chapter has traced a corresponding pattern—the growth and development of the institutions and programs of foreign aid throughout the aid era—and has argued that there was a steady growth in the extent to which aid practices conformed to the underlying logic of working to overcome poverty. The next chapter will demonstrate that the existence of steady, ongoing change in the provision of foreign aid is not an artifact of the way I describe the developments of the aid era, and will do so by providing quantitative indicators that show a steady evolution of aid practices in the direction of making programs more geared to the needs of poor people and poor countries.

The Point Four program was soon joined by the Colombo Plan of the Commonwealth nations and by a reoriented World Bank and an Expanded Programme of Technical Assistance at the UN. Then throughout the sixties, more multilateral institutions were added, and the programs of the European donors became strong and substantial. In all this, a pivotal role was played by two international institutions: the World Bank and the DAC, and its parent OECD. That could not have happened, of course, without substantial U.S. support; but once the DAC was in place and operation of the World Bank well underway and receiving vigorous leadership, the course that events took was one that was not shaped, and was even sometimes resisted, by the United States. If international institutions embodying agreed-upon principles were nothing different from closely held instruments of national power, it is hard to see why they would be devised. It is because they develop a certain momentum and impetus of their own that they can command broader support, and have wider influence, than purely national policies. But by the same token, a decision to invest in such institutions is a decision to hand control over to the principles and rules that the institutions embody.

These institutions were crucial. But it is incorrect to see the account given here as essentially an institutional argument. For the international institutions had, actually, very little power: dependent for most of their funding upon the choices of the individual DAC donor states, all they could do was to propose goals and principles and get a hearing for their case. Further, these institutions were effective not so much in the sense of promoting themselves *as* institutions, as in the sense of furthering certain ideas or forms of international interaction that were their raison d'être. The DAC, especially, remained small, and is certainly not a widely discussed body. The IBRD sought to expand its own role, but also sought, under McNamara's leadership, to change standards for foreign aid and to emphasize assistance to poorer countries. Even if this was a move undertaken for institutionally strategic reasons—and there is no evidence that it was—it could not have succeeded unless the basis of support to which it appealed in donor countries was one that was founded in concern about questions of international poverty. And that is true of the aid institutions as a whole. Whether or not they sought to enhance their own status as organizations, the crucial element was their appeal to ideas that found support and resonance in the thought of the donor countries.

In discussing this process, the emphasis here has been upon the progress and the continuities. Of course, many of the changes that occurred were sharply contested. There was a good deal of demanding from the Third World countries, whose interests were very much tied up in the resolution of foreign aid questions. And there was considerable dissension within some of the donor countries, both at first and later, among those that wanted more aid programs and those that wanted fewer. Indeed, there is today more basis—if the argument here is correct—for renewed dissensus about aid in the donor countries than there has been in a long time, because some of the momentum in expansion of the welfare state, and some of the untroubled enthusiasm for it in the advanced countries, has begun to flag. And also, there is increased criticism of the effects of aid upon recipients. While the welfare state is not about to disappear, and aid programs are not either, a period of rethinking about both seems to have set in. What will be essential to a renewed aid commitment, if the general thrust of the analysis here is correct, is not a mere strengthening of institutions and programs by itself but a rethinking of the fundamental objectives and values on the basis of which foreign aid was advocated. The last chapter will turn to that task.

## CHAPTER EIGHT

# How Aid Changed:
## Ongoing Reform in the Foreign Aid Regime

> What we have done so far has been on the margin of the real difficulties. . . . Our ultimate aim must be to level off the dangerous and unacceptable differences between the standard of living and of economic development in various countries. . . . In the international field we must rely exclusively on measures to promote and accelerate the advancement of the poorest.
> —Dag Hammarskjöld[1]

THE ONGOING change and reform in the practice of foreign aid reflected the continued influence of ideas and ideals that gave birth to the practice of foreign aid in the first place. These were humanitarian and egalitarian ideals or commitments, on the one hand, and beliefs in (and commitment to) a cooperative international order as the only possible basis for lasting peace and prosperity in world affairs, on the other, and emerged out of the domestic political structures and values, and the common ethical heritage, of the Western countries. Chapter 7 outlined the history of aid from the Point Four speech through the 1980s. Both the beginning of foreign aid in 1949 and the evolution of aid practices afterward occurred in a way which presupposed that the aim of aid was development, and which involved norm-governed changes in international practices designed to deal with countries in one or another kind of need. This chapter shows how the steady growth of aid norms found expression in aid practices that are unmistakable in the dollar amounts spent on various activities. This specific argument, about ongoing change and reform in foreign aid and its basis in other-directed and public-spirited ideas and ideals, illustrates the thesis that cooperation involves more than simply a set of mutually beneficial deals or bargains, but shows ongoing development on the basis of underlying norms.

In the first part of this chapter I detail five or six ways in which foreign aid has exhibited steady change over the last several decades. Then I discuss why such ongoing change is not well explained by theories of regimes and cooperation under anarchy that focus on finding pareto-improving deals (mutually advantageous bargains), and why such change was to be expected if the impetus for aid came not from detailed calculations of national self-interest but instead from the application of certain domestic values and political ideas in the international context.

## ONGOING REFORM IN FOREIGN AID

There are several dimensions in which the aid regime has moved in a consistent direction over its lifetime. I will focus on five of these: (1) the increasing number of countries with a growing volume of aid (or increasing amount of resources devoted to aid) as a percentage of GNP; (2) the growing diversity of supply in the provision of aid, which left recipients less dependent and donors with less leverage; (3) the increasing role of multilateral aid; (4) the improving terms and conditions of aid, both with respect to financial concessionality and with respect to conditions on procurement; and (5) the resurgent emphasis on alleviating poverty and on directing aid so that it reaches poorer nations and groups.

### The Volume of Foreign Aid

The commitment of most donors to foreign aid has grown over time, as measured by the fraction of GNP devoted to aid. The overall DAC figures do not reflect this, because the United States has been the group's laggard and has steadily reduced its per GNP aid. A look at the numbers of DAC countries contributing at given levels relative to GNP charted over time tells a clear story, however (see table 8.1). There has been a very consistent rise over time in committed participation in funding aid. At the beginning, many donors had only very slight aid programs; now none funds at a level below .1% of GNP, even in spite of a slight decline in the last five years. At the beginning, almost no countries funded above .5% of GNP; now, a third of the DAC donors do, with a fair number of them above .75% of GNP.

Of course, this movement has not been uniform, and closer inspection will reveal subpatterns within it. The United States has declined in its level of funding. The former colonial powers have tended to decline at first, and then pick up. The noncolonial states, especially the small ones, have (in general) shown the steepest rise, as was shown in table 4.6. There it was noted that the pattern of these differences is quite consistent with this book's overall hypothesis. In his writings, the Swedish economist Gunnar Myrdal complained about attempts to sell foreign aid as redounding to the donor's benefit: this was unworthy, and also, he felt, unreliable as a tactic. Better to rely on people's sense of human solidarity and their principles for a more equal distribution, Myrdal argued. A rationale appealing to humane and egalitarian convictions would be likely to stand the

TABLE 8.1
Number of Donors at Various Levels of Aid Disbursements over Time

| Level of Aid Funding (Percentage of GNP) | 1950–55 | 1956–59 | 1960–64 | 1965–69 | 1970–74 | 1975–79 | 1980–84 | 1985–89 |
|---|---|---|---|---|---|---|---|---|
| over 1.00 | 1 | 1 | 1 | | | | 1 | 1 |
| .90 to .99 | | | | | | | 1 | 1 |
| .80 to .89 | | | | | | 3 | 1 | 2 |
| .70 to .79 | | | | 1 | | | 2 | 1 |
| .60 to .69 | | | 1 | | 2 | 2 | | |
| .50 to .59 | | | 2 | 1 | 2 | 3 | 1 | 1 |
| .40 to .49 | 1 | 4 | 2 | 4 | 5 | 2 | 3 | 4 |
| .30 to .39 | 1 | 1 | 1 | 1 | 2 | 2 | 3 | 4 |
| .20 to .29 | 2 | 2 | | 5 | 3 | 3 | 6 | 3 |
| .10 to .19 | 3 | 4 | 7 | 4 | 3 | 2 | | |
| .00 to .09 | 4 | 1 | 3 | 1 | | | | |
| DAC countries not included | 6 | 4 | 3 | 1 | 1 | 1 | 1 | 0 |
| DAC overall percentage | | | .51 | .42 | .33 | .34 | .36 | .35 |
| DAC median percentage | | | .19 | .29 | .42 | .50 | .46 | .43 |

Source: OECD, Development Cooperation, various years.

Notes: Table entries are numbers of countries in each percentage range; cells with zero cases have been left empty. In early years countries that later joined the DAC are not included; while data is not available, generally the countries had no aid programs in these years.

test of time; one appealing to donor self-interest, based neither on firm moral beliefs nor on solid logic, would not.[2] His argument is certainly consistent with the patterns of countries that showed the most long-term support of aid. The colonial countries declined after an initial burst of enthusiasm for aid, and began to increase their support again only as their programs were put on a less self-serving basis. The United States, which has most consistently mixed a security rationale with a humanitarian rationale for aid, has showed long-term decline in percentage of GNP contributed. But small donors without obvious ulterior motives, and which have shunned such rationales, have maintained and strengthened their programs most.

My own hypothesis suggests exactly the same thing. The power of ideals and broad interpretations of principles of conduct lies in their long-term staying power, as well as in their long-term effectiveness. Therefore, appeals based on more parochial interests—on national influence in international affairs, or on colonial ties—are less likely to be lastingly effective; but appeals to basic principles tap sources of long-term strength. Principled justifications for aid last longer, although they may take longer to get going. An aid coalition built around transient interests is apt to pay for its immediate successes with long-term disillusionment and lack of commitment to the aid project.

*Diversity of Supply and Reduced Concentration of Aid*

Under this heading I am referring to several related trends, but all have to do with moving further and further away from a situation in which a single patron provides aid to a few clients. From the beginning there was some of this diversity. But there were important increases over time. One of the defining features of aid from the start had to do with its openness as a regime or as an activity. Rather than being an option offered by one state to a few particular other states, aid was, in principle, presumed to be available to a poor country not by virtue of its relationship to a particular donor, but because of its needs for assistance in development. And while this was not the case in practice, over time patron-client relationships declined sharply. There are several aspects to the deconcentration of aid over time. One is the diversification of ultimate funding sources, as the United States, originally the preponderant source of foreign aid, came to provide only 20% to 25% of Western aid to the Third World. A second was the deconcentration of aid from particular donors. As time went on, donor countries that at first had directed much of their aid to a few recipients directed aid to many more recipients. Third, there was a decline of the dependency of recipients on any single donor.

Concerning the diversification of funding sources, simply the change in the percentage of foreign aid funding supplied by the United States over the years tells much of the story (see table 8.2). In the early years of foreign aid, the United States supplied up to two thirds of foreign aid; now the share has fallen to not much more than a quarter. Moreover, the smaller aid donors—Australia, Austria, Belgium, Canada, Denmark, Finland, Ireland, the Netherlands, New Zealand, Norway, Sweden, and Switzerland—rose from providing a small share to about a quarter of OECD aid. It was in part to attain this diversification, or burden sharing, that the United States set up the OECD in the first place; early discussions emphasized burden sharing. However, as time went on, the emphasis upon a higher level of funding may have taken over as a prompt to this diversification: the attempt in recent years by a good many of the European countries to attain a goal of 1% of GNP in aid has been a big factor, especially as United States aid funding has dropped.

A second area of deconcentration—one even more the outcome of similar decisions in each country separately—has been a decrease in the direction of national aid programs to a few important recipients. Whereas in the early sixties many donors directed 40% or more of their aid to two main recipients, by the end of the eighties none directed that much of their aid even to five main recipients. While in the early sixties almost all main donors directed at least 40% of their aid to ten recipients or less, by the end of the eighties only three did (see table 8.3).

TABLE 8.2
Percentages of Total OECD Aid Contributed Classified by Donor Grouping

| | 1950–55 | 1956 | 1960 | 1965 | 1970 | 1975 | 1980 | 1985 | 1989 |
|---|---|---|---|---|---|---|---|---|---|
| Percentages from each type of donor | | | | | | | | | |
| United States | 57 | 63 | 59 | 62 | 45 | 30 | 24 | 32 | 16 |
| Middle[a] | 38 | 32 | 33 | 30 | 36 | 42 | 49 | 42 | 51 |
| Small[b] | 5 | 5 | 8 | 8 | 18 | 28 | 27 | 26 | 32 |
| Aid total (billions of dollars) | 1.9 | 3.2 | 4.7 | 6.5 | 6.9 | 13.8 | 25.0 | 29.4 | 46.7 |

Source: OECD, Development Cooperation, 1985, p. 335; and Development Cooperation, 1990, p. 221.

Notes: Ireland is included in 1985 and 1989 only.

[a] Britain, France, Germany, and Japan are classed as middle donors.

[b] All other DAC donors except the United States are classed as small donors.

There was an accompanying decrease in recipient dependency on any one donor. Whereas in the early sixties most recipients had a primary donor state on whose patronage most of their aid depended, by the late seventies this was far from the case. Many recipients received more from international organizations than from bilateral donors—and usually from several such organizations, and not only those controlled primarily by the West as a bloc. But even of those which relied mainly on bilateral aid, few received most of their aid funding from a single donor. The marked change that has occurred is displayed in tables 8.4 and 8.5, which show the number of countries receiving given maximum percentages of aid from a single OECD donor in 1978 and 1964.

## Multilateral Aid

Multilaterally channeled aid has become a major part of foreign aid, though it was not so originally. At the start of the period there was some multilateral aid, but most of the financial resources multilaterally supplied to LDCs were at near-market terms, and were not what would now be defined as aid, in the strict sense, at all. Multilateral aid has been supplied almost exclusively by OECD countries, so that to use multilateral figures is effectively to consider aid multilaterally channeled from OECD countries for the most part. Multilateral aid from communist nations has been absolutely negligible, amounting to only about $9 million yearly at its height. Only a quite small percentage of OPEC aid has been multilateral, and this is more the case if multilateral aid is not taken to include the specifically Arab agencies and the OPEC fund.

At the beginning of the period about 7% of aid was multilaterally channeled; by the end almost one third of all OECD aid was; this is

TABLE 8.3
Number of Donors Concentrating Aid on a Few Countries

*Number of Donors Concentrating Various Percentages on Only Two Recipients*

| Percentage of Aid | 1960–61 | 1970–71 | 1980–81 | 1988–89 |
|---|---|---|---|---|
| 60–100 | 3 | 1 | | |
| 40–59.9 | 2 | 3 | 1 | |
| 20–39.9 | 2 | 5 | 5 | 4 |
| 15–19.9 | 2 | 4 | 6 | 2 |
| 10–14.9 | 1 | 2 | 3 | 8 |
| 0–9.9 | | 1 | 3 | 4 |
| DAC countries not included | 8 | 2 | 0 | 0 |

*Number of Donors Concentrating Various Percentages on Only Five Recipients*

| Percentage of Aid | 1960–61 | 1970–71 | 1980–81 | 1988–89 |
|---|---|---|---|---|
| 60–100 | 6 | 3 | | |
| 40–59.9 | 1 | 5 | 3 | |
| 20–39.9 | 1 | 7 | 12 | 13 |
| 15–19.9 | | | 2 | 4 |
| 10–14.9 | | 1 | 1 | 1 |
| 0–9.9 | | | | |
| DAC countries not included | 10 | 2 | 0 | 0 |

*Number of Donors Concentrating Various Percentages on Only Ten Recipients*

| Percentage of Aid | 1960–61 | 1970–71 | 1980–81 | 1988–89 |
|---|---|---|---|---|
| 60–100 | 6 | 3 | 2 | |
| 40–59.9 | 2 | 8 | 7 | 3 |
| 20–39.9 | | 4 | 8 | 14 |
| 15–19.9 | | | | 1 |
| 10–14.9 | | 1 | 1 | |
| 0–9.9 | | | | |
| DAC countries not included | 10 | 2 | 0 | 0 |

*Sources*: OECD, *Development Cooperation, 1985*, p. 306–14; and OECD, *Development Cooperation, 1990*, p. 233–42.

*Notes*: Table entries are numbers of countries in each percentage range; cells with zero cases have been left empty. In early years countries that later joined the DAC are not included; while data are not available, generally the countries had no aid programs in these years. The countries counted in the 1960–61 period are Belgium, Canada, Germany, Italy, Japan, Netherlands, United Kingdom, United States, and, in the case of concentrating on two recipients, Denmark and Sweden, also.

TABLE 8.4
Number of Recipients Receiving Various Percentages of Their Aid from a Single Donor, 1964

| | Highest Percentage of Aid Received from a Single DAC Donor | | | | | | | | | |
|---|---|---|---|---|---|---|---|---|---|---|
| | 0–9% | 10–19% | 20–29% | 30–39% | 40–49% | 50–59% | 60–69% | 70–79% | 80–89% | 90–100% |
| All recipients | 1 | | 4 | 7 | 5 | 13 | 11 | 16 | 11 | 13 |
| Major aid recipients[a] | | | 1 | 1 | 2 | 5 | 5 | 6 | 7 | 4 |
| Recipients of very large aid flows[b] | | | | | 2 | 2 | | 4 | 3 | 2 |

Source: Computed from OECD, Development Cooperation, various years.
Notes: Table is limited to cases where the data permit clear identification.
Table entries are numbers of countries in each percentage range; cells with zero cases have been left empty.
[a] Those receiving over $100 million in aid from multilateral and DAC bilateral sources.
[b] Those receiving over $400 million in aid from these sources.

TABLE 8.5
Number of Recipients Receiving Various Percentages of Their Aid from a Single Donor, 1978

| | Highest Percentage of Aid Received from a Single DAC Donor | | | | | | | | | |
|---|---|---|---|---|---|---|---|---|---|---|
| | 0–9% | 10–19% | 20–29% | 30–39% | 40–49% | 50–59% | 60–69% | 70–79% | 80–89% | 90–100% |
| All recipients | 7 | 25 | 26 | 16 | 8 | 5 | 8 | 3 | 2 | 3 |
| Major aid recipients[a] | 2 | 8 | 12 | 8 | 5 | | 1 | 1 | 1 | 2 |
| Recipients of very large aid flows[b] | 1 | 3 | 1 | 1 | | | | | | 1 |

Source: See sources in table 8.4.
Notes: Table is limited to cases where the data permit clear identification.
Table entries are numbers of countries in each percentage range; cells with zero cases have been left empty.
[a] Those receiving over $100 million in aid from multilateral and DAC bilateral sources.
[b] Those receiving over $400 million in aid from these sources.

shown in table 8.6. The steady move to multilateral aid was particularly pronounced in the midsixties to midseventies, and has leveled off since then. However, there is movement throughout the aid period; France, for instance, in the past an almost exclusively bilateral donor, began giving more of its aid multilaterally in the eighties. The United States, however, has decreased the multilateral share of its aid markedly in the eighties also.

The increase in multilaterally channeled aid reflected a shift in the OECD donor community as a whole. In early years most donors channeled at least 75% of aid bilaterally, and a number 90% or more. In recent years the latter is unheard of, and many donors have given upward of 35% of aid multilaterally. Again, table 8.7, showing the number of countries in each category of multilateral support, illustrates the movement.

In one way this table overstates the case. The earlier high-percentage-multilateral donors (those in the over 40% category) provided a very high percentage of their aid multilaterally indeed: over 50%, and sometimes over 75%. The later high-percentage-multilateral donors were mainly in the 40–50% category. However, there is a reason for this, and taking it into account, the table may, on the whole, even understate the case. When countries began foreign aid programs, they often started with multilateral contributions before they acquired the administrative capacity for bilateral aid programs. Their total foreign aid at this point, multilateral and bilateral, usually consisted of a tiny program, as a percentage of GNP and absolutely. There are sound reasons for having a national, that is, a bilateral, aid program: a national program helps generate support for aid, serves as a basis for involving citizens in problems of development, and allows countries to bring distinctive skills and perspectives into the worldwide aid business. As the bilateral program grows, initial very high percentages (amounting to fairly small cash amounts) in multilateral programs decline. The high multilateral percentages in later years tend to reflect instead a commitment to multilaterally channeled aid as an effective tool of development.

## Terms and Conditions of Aid

Since the midsixties, there has been steady movement on what is known as the terms and conditions of aid, that is, on its concessionality or financial terms, and on the extent to which aid is tied to purchases in the donor countries. Terms of aid have been consistently softened, and aid has become much more untied. These things have been the more true for aid to least developed countries, for since about 1970 there has been an

TABLE 8.6
Multilateral Percentages of DAC Aid, 1950–1989 (with Total Official Flows [TOF] as a Proxy for Aid [ODA] before 1970)

| Multilateral Aid as a Percentage of | 1956 | 1960 | 1965 | 1970 | 1975 | 1980–84 | 1985–89 |
|---|---|---|---|---|---|---|---|
| **Flows from all DAC countries** | | | | | | | |
| Foreign aid (ODA) | — | — | — | 17 | 28 | 31 | 28 |
| Total official flows (TOF) | 7 | 13 | 7 | 14 | — | — | — |
| **Flows from the United States** | | | | | | | |
| Foreign aid (ODA) | — | — | — | 13 | 27 | 31 | 20 |
| Total official flows (TOF) | 4 | 8 | 4 | 12 | — | — | — |
| **Flows from non-U.S. DAC countries** | | | | | | | |
| Foreign aid (ODA) | — | — | — | — | 28 | 30 | 30 |

*Sources:* OECD, *Development Cooperation*, 1976 and 1981–90 editions, and OECD, *Financial Flows to Developing Countries, 1956–1963.*

*Notes:* Figures before 1970 are based on percentages of net total official flows (TOF), rather than on foreign aid proper, since separate ODA data are not available before then. Comparison of the 1970 figures, given in both forms here, tends to indicate that the figures using TOF for ODA are roughly comparable in the early period.

TABLE 8.7
Number of Donors with Various Levels of Support for Multilateral Aid

| Percentage of Each Donor's Foreign Aid Channeled through Multilateral Agencies | 1965 | 1970–71 | 1980–81 | 1988–89 |
|---|---|---|---|---|
| over 40 | 5 | 4 | 5 | 4 |
| 35–39 | | | 1 | 3 |
| 30–34 | 1 | 1 | 4 | 5 |
| 25–29 | 1 | 3 | 4 | 2 |
| 20–24 | | 4 | 3 | 2 |
| 15–19 | | 1 | 1 | 1 |
| 10–14 | 1 | 4 | | 1 |
| under 10 | 7 | | | |
| DAC countries not included | 3 | 1 | 0 | 0 |
| Overall DAC multilateral percentage | 5.9 | 16.1 | 28.9 | 27.0 |
| Median DAC multilateral percentage | 11.2 | 22.6 | 30.4 | 31.3 |

*Source:* OECD, *Development Cooperation*, various years.

*Notes:* Table entries are numbers of countries in each percentage range; cells with zero cases have been left empty. In early years countries that later joined the DAC are not included; while data are not available, generally the countries had no aid programs in these years.

effort—in this area as in others—to give special consideration to these countries.

Before 1965 the picture is less clear, partly because there are not published data that are clearly comparable to later figures. However, it appears there was some deterioration in the terms on which aid was offered in the late fifties and early sixties as donors began to supplement their grants with more loans. The movement to improve terms from 1965 on was in part an effort to reform—or counteract—this deterioration. Probably the earlier retrogression in terms reflected the effort to get donors to increase the flow of financial resources of all types to the Third World, which was a main emphasis in the early years of the aid regime, and the absence of clear distinctions in those years between aid as such—ODA as it was later clearly defined by the DAC—and official flows of other sorts. Just such distinctions, based on a setting apart of foreign aid as an activity to be defined in terms of the assistance donors provided to recipients, that is, in eleemosynary terms, were instrumental in shaping and maintaining aid programs and policies that were directed to recipient welfare.

I will first examine the evolution of conditions on aid, that is, the degree to which aid was tied, and then the progress made in the financial terms of aid.

CONDITIONS OF AID

(TYING OF AID TO PURCHASES IN THE DONOR COUNTRY)

As is the case with the terms of aid, less satisfactory data are available earlier on. The later, more specific, data reflect both the increasing data collections of the DAC in general and the fact that collection of data on tying of aid became a tool in an effort to raise awareness of the problem tying presented. Very specific data on tying before the midsixties are unavailable, but OEEC and OECD reports state that "much" early aid is tied, or that about "two thirds" of the aid before 1963 or 1965 was tied (see table 8.8 and its notes). A later report that seems to be based on more detailed calculations suggests that in the years 1966 to 1968 some 22% to 26% of all official flows, or 24% to 29% of ODA (excluding export credits), was *un*tied. Almost all the reports, written at various dates, indicate that the degree of tying held quite constant before 1968. In that year there is a fairly precise account that reports 25% of all DAC aid is untied, and 56% fully tied (with the remainder partially tied), which seems quite consistent with the previous accounts. This is broken down as 91% of U.S. aid tied, while French, German, Japanese, and British aid come out 62%, 56%, 86%, and 44% tied, which tallies approximately with earlier (rougher) country estimates in a 1965 report. There is quite specific information given on years from 1972 on, largely because of an agreement reached—as part of the October 1973 agreement on terms and condi-

Table 8.8

Degree of Tying in Aid: All DAC Countries and United States (Percentages)

| | Before 1965[a] | 1966–68[b] | 1968[c] | 1972 | 1975 | 1980 | 1985 | 1988 |
|---|---|---|---|---|---|---|---|---|
| Untied | | | | | | | | |
|    Entire DAC | 24–29 | — | 25 | 35 | 40 | 56 | 54 | 57 |
|    United States only | — | — | 9 | 21 | 25 | 51 | 47 | 48 |
| Fully Tied | | | | | | | | |
|    Entire DAC | 67 | — | 56 | 35 | 29 | 32 | 36 | 31 |
|    United States only | — | 91 | 75 | 49 | 46 | 39 | 45 | 37 |

Source: OECD, Development Cooperation, various years.

Notes: The figures for the entire DAC include the United States in the average. Untied aid, partially tied aid (not shown here), and fully tied aid add to 100%. All figures are based on gross disbursements.

[a] Tying figures for years before 1965 are hard to get and are conjectural.

[b] Figures for 1966–68 are also very approximate.

[c] Figures for 1968 are more approximate than those for subsequent years.

tions—that members would supply such information for monitoring purposes. This indicates that starting from the late sixties there was steady movement toward untying aid.

The real movement in the percentage of tied aid from 1968 or so on does *not* indicate that there had been no movement earlier. What appears to have happened was that earlier discussions of tying that resulted in several resolutions (which were not very fully implemented) finally began to bear fruit in the resolutions of 1968 and of 1973–74.

There had been general approval of untying aid as early as a 1960 Bonn agreement, and the subject was reported as "kept under regular review" throughout the early sixties at the mutual accountability sessions, or Annual Aid Review, which the DAC has traditionally held. Resolutions on terms and conditions of aid recommended the reduction of tying in 1963 and suggested specific steps to that end in 1964. These had little effect on bilateral aid at the time, although there was success in keeping multilateral aid contributions essentially untied, despite some pressure that seems to have existed to try to increase donor contributions by compromising the principle of untied multilateral aid. What does appear to have changed during these years was an awareness of the problem that tying represented, and the undertaking of steps by donors to mitigate these effects. The 1968 resolution seems to have had an effect in the period immediately following, especially on the United States.

However, probably most important was the July 1974 Memorandum of Understanding on terms and conditions, along with the preceding October 1973 interim agreement which committed the DAC to collecting and publishing data on tying. There has been continued progress on untying since the memorandum, and the progress has been concentrated in the countries signatory to the agreement, while the five nonsignatories on which there are baseline (1972) data actually worsened in their tying performance, on the whole, from 1972 to 1982–83 (see table 8.9).

FINANCIAL TERMS OF AID

Even more central to the concern of effective development aid than the issue of tying has been that of the financial terms on which development aid was offered. From the early days of the DAC and before, this has been a central arena of contention over foreign aid. Indeed, in the early days of the World Bank, a great point was made of the fact that aid was a sound *business* proposition: the need was to legitimate the soundness of the enterprise to a skeptical audience of businessmen. The mixing of grants and commercial-type loans was sedulously avoided, because "soft loans" were seen as utterly unsound business practice. However, a fairly high percentage of early aid funding *was* in the form of grants. The early aid statistics, furthermore, sometimes lumped together loans at near-commercial terms and development assistance at concessional terms. Much of the earliest U.S. assistance *was* in the form of grants, as the Marshall Plan had been. In the fifties, increased financial flows to the Third World were argued to be an essential requisite of development; a push to increase the total flows and an actual increase in foreign aid from other OECD countries resulted, but the terms of aid deteriorated slightly. At any rate, starting in the early sixties there was growing concern over, and focused attention on, improving the terms of aid—and on reducing the associated problems of Third World debt burdens.

Such figures as there are (which are summed up in table 8.10) show a slight decrease in the percentage of grants in bilateral lending in the late fifties, which continued on into the early sixties, fluctuated for a bit, and then reversed in the seventies, when the grant percentage of bilateral lending turned upward decisively and (to date) permanently. Throughout the entire period from the early sixties on, however, the grant element of loans increased, as average interest rates first fell and then held constant in the face of inflation.

The change that table 8.10 reflects was not simply the result of changes on the part of one or two large countries but a shift in the behavior of all OECD donors over time, as the count of donors in various "grant element of ODA" categories in succeeding years in table 8.11 shows. There is a levitation toward higher grant percentages, which continued after donors reached the 95% bracket, as a more detailed breakdown would show. (Exact computations of the grant element are harder to get in earlier years.)

TABLE 8.9

Change In Tying Behavior between 1972 and 1982–1983 (Percentage of Aid that Was Fully Untied)

| | Number of Countries | 1972 | | 1982–83 | | Change | |
|---|---|---|---|---|---|---|---|
| | | Mean | Median | Mean | Median | Mean | Median |
| **1974 DAC Members** | | | | | | | |
| signatory | 10 | 56.7 | 62.7 | 68.1 | 69.0 | +13.4 | +6.3 |
| nonsignatory | 5 | 45.2 | 45.1 | 38.7 | 36.2 | −6.5 | −8.9 |
| **Non-1974 Members (omitted)**[a] | 3 | | | | | | |

Sources: OECD, *Development Cooperation*, 1976, p. 159, and statistical appendix; and OECD, *Development Cooperation*, 1985.

[a] Finland, Ireland and New Zealand were not yet DAC members in 1974.

TABLE 8.10

Grants, Grant Element, and Interest Rate in Bilateral ODA, 1950–1988

| | 1950–55 | 1956–59 | 1962 | 1964 | 1966 | 1968 | 1970 | 1974 | 1979 | 1983 | 1988 |
|---|---|---|---|---|---|---|---|---|---|---|---|
| **Percentage of grants** | 66 | 64 | 60 | 54 | 59 | 51 | 58 | 64 | 71 | 76 | 73 |
| **Grant element** | — | — | — | — | — | 58 | 63 | 65 | 76 | 80 | 89 |
| **Loan interest rate** | — | — | 3.6 | 3.4 | 2.7 | 2.9 | 2.8 | 2.6 | 2.6 | 2.9 | 2.7 |

Sources: OECD, *Development Cooperation*, 1965, p. 136ff.; OECD, *Development Cooperation*, 1967, p. 81; OECD, *Development Cooperation*, 1969, p. 77; OECD, *Development Cooperation*, 1970, p. 48; OECD, *Development Cooperation*, 1971, p. 62; OECD, *Development Cooperation*, 1976, p. 231; OECD, *Development Cooperation*, 1981, p. 197; OECD, *Development Cooperation*, 1985, p. 108; OECD, *Development Cooperation*, 1990, p. 218–19; and OECD, *Flow of Financial Resources to Countries in the Course of Development, 1956–1959*, p. 10.

Notes: The grants percentage is the percentage of bilateral foreign aid given as pure grants. The grant element adds to that the grant element of loans given at concessional rates; it is the best comprehensive measure of the degree of financial concessionality. The grant element of a concessional loan is the percentage of a loan that would be a grant if the loan at a given concessional rate were decomposed into a commercial-rate loan combined with a pure grant. The loan interest rate shown is the nominal rate; the real interest rate on ODA loans fell starting in the late sixties, because of increasing inflation, and was often negative.

In short, there was a progressive softening of the financial terms offered by most OECD donors, after a brief retrogression that occurred with the expansion of aid flows (broadly defined) in the late fifties and early sixties. This softening of terms, like the easing of conditions of procurement, was a result of an effort on the part of donors to promote aid more conducive to Third World development. And like efforts to untie, it

TABLE 8.11
Number of DAC Donors with Various Levels of Grant Elements over Time

| Grant Element (Percentage) | 1964 | 1965–66 | 1970–71 | 1975–76 | 1980–81 | 1983–84 | 1988–89 |
|---|---|---|---|---|---|---|---|
| 95–100 | 3 | 4 | 5 | 10 | 10 | 10 | 11 |
| 90–94.9 | 1 | 1 | 3 | 3 | 3 | 3 | 2 |
| 85–89.9 | 3 | 3 | 2 | 3 | 2 | 2 | 2 |
| 80–84.9 | 1 | 1 | 4 | | | | 1 |
| 75–79.9 | | 2 | | | | 1 | |
| 70–74.9 | 2 | | | 1 | 1 | | |
| 60–69.9 | 2 | 1 | 2 | | 1 | 1 | 1 |
| 50–59.9 | 1 | 1 | 1 | | | | |
| Below 50 | 2 | 2 | | | | | |
| DAC countries not included | 3 | 3 | 1 | 1 | 1 | 1 | 1 |
| *Grant Element (Percentage): Figures for Entire DAC* | | | | | | | |
| DAC total | 82 | 84.0 | 83.1 | 89.7 | 89.7 | 90.7 | 91.6 |
| DAC median | 74 | 83.6 | 86.0 | 96.9 | 96.6 | 97.2 | 98.7 |

Sources: OECD, *Development Cooperation*, 1985, p. 106; OECD, *Development Assistance*, 1967, p. 77; OECD, *Development Assistance*, 1990, p. 191.

Note: See notes to table 8.10 for definition of the concept of grant element. Table entries are numbers of countries in each percentage range; cells with zero cases have been left empty. In early years countries that later joined the DAC are not included; while data are not available, generally the countries had no aid programs in these years.

was accompanied by more specific efforts to improve the situation for the neediest recipients. Starting in the early seventies, there were special efforts and special targets set for eliminating tying and easing financial terms for least developed countries (LLDCs). These efforts, too, show up in the statistics of aid flows, where terms for LLDCs began to be consistently more lenient, even in bilateral aid, than terms in aid as a whole. In multilateral institutions, and above all in the World Bank, the distinction between the terms offered richer and poorer Third World countries was even more marked.

### Aid Oriented to Poverty

A fifth major trend in aid throughout the postwar period has been a shift toward focusing aid more on the poorest countries, as table 8.12 shows. The percentage of foreign aid (or ODA) given to low income countries as a whole rose substantially in the sixties and, the percentage disbursed to least developed countries rose during the sixties and, dramatically, during the seventies, while the percentage to newly industrializing and other so-

TABLE 8.12
Net Disbursed Foreign Aid, Classified by Recipient Income Level: Importance in the Donor Aid Burden and in the Recipient Countries

| | In Terms of Cost to the Donor (As a Percentage of Total ODA Given) | | | |
|---|---|---|---|---|
| Recipient Type | 1960–61 | 1970–71 | 1982–83 | 1986–87 |
| Upper middle income | 41.5 | 26.2 | 23.5 | 21.1 |
| Lower middle income | 11.8 | 17.4 | 17.3 | 16.3 |
| Low income | 46.5 | 56.2 | 59.3 | 62.5 |
| Memo item: Least developed | 6.5 | 10.2 | 24.6 | 28.2 |

| | In Terms of Importance to the Economy of the Recipient (As a Percentage of Recipient GNP) | | | |
|---|---|---|---|---|
| Recipient Type | 1960–61 | 1970–71 | 1982–83 | 1986–87 |
| Upper middle income | 1.5 | .7 | .5 | .4 |
| Lower middle income | 1.3 | 1.6 | 1.4 | 1.5 |
| Low income | 2.8 | 2.9 | 3.3 | 2.1 |
| Memo item: Least developed | 2.1 | 3.1 | 10.5 | 11.4 |

Sources: OECD, *Development Cooperation, 1985*, p. 122; and, for the eighties, OECD, *Geographical Distribution of Financial Flows*, various years.

Notes: By definition: upper middle + lower middle + low income = 100% in the upper table; but in some cases rounding leads to totals slightly different. Least developed countries are a subcategory of low income countries.

called upper middle income countries declined. The movement in bilateral aid was one that was reflected in the bilateral aid of most OECD donors, too, not just that of a few large donors.

Table 8.13 shows that the multilateral agencies, funded almost exclusively by the OECD donors, moved even more markedly than did the individual donor countries in their bilateral aid, toward a policy of support for the neediest countries, even as the donors moved toward channeling more of their aid through multilateral channels.

This was a result of a conscious policy effort by many people in the aid profession, and by the DAC particularly, to set standards encouraging donors to raise the percentage they gave to those LDCs most in need of assistance. Together with this effort, and with the efforts to provide aid to the poorest countries on more than usually concessional terms, which were mentioned earlier, went a concern for promoting types of aid apt to reach the poorest segments of the population within a given recipient country. Such efforts included more "social lending" for health, water-supply, nutritional, and educational projects, and emphasized "produc-

TABLE 8.13
Net Disbursed Foreign Aid, Classified by Recipient Income Level (Percentages)

| | DAC Bilateral Aid | | | Multilateral Aid | | |
|---|---|---|---|---|---|---|
| Recipient type | 1971 | 1981 | 1988 | 1971 | 1981 | 1988 |
| Upper middle income | 13 | 4 | 20 | 20 | 2 | 6 |
| Lower middle income | 27 | 38 | 14 | 25 | 19 | 9 |
| Low income | 59 | 57 | 66 | 54 | 79 | 85 |
| Memo item: Least developed | 9 | 20 | 27 | 17 | 32 | 42 |

Sources: OECD, Geographical Distribution of Financial Flows, editions for 1971–77, 1979–82, and 1985–88.
Notes: By definition: upper middle + lower middle + low income = 100%; but in some cases rounding leads to totals slightly different. Least developed countries are a subcategory of low income countries.

tive" projects such as provision of inputs for small-scale agriculture, which were believed to reach disadvantaged sectors. The movement toward funding poverty sectors was presented in tables 2.15 and 2.16.

### Summary of Facts of Steady Change in Foreign Aid

There is clear evidence that the OECD countries as a whole, and also most of the individual countries within the OECD, made steady progress toward: (1) more aid as a percentage of GNP (despite the U.S. decline in this area, which made the OECD total sink during the late sixties and most of the seventies); (2) aid less tightly linked to special, exclusive relationships between a particular donor and recipient; (3) aid more channeled and buffered by multilateral agencies; (4) aid offered at more concessional terms and with fewer conditions on procurement in the donor country; (5) and aid directed more to the poorer nations—particularly the least developed nations of Africa and Asia—and more consciously designed to reach poorer sectors within those (and other) countries.

On each of these dimensions there are actually two types of consistency across time. There was covariation among donors over time—the different nations tended to do the same things at the same time—and there was also a consistent direction of motion: rather than weaving back and forth, the donor community attempted to sustain or augment past gains on the dimension in question, and usually succeeded.

There was also a third kind of consistency. One example of this is found in the fact that these directions were sometimes explicitly linked in goals and targets, for instance, when there were special efforts to improve concessionality especially to the least developed nations. Even apart from such links, however, it must be observed that the five directions of movement are not a random set: they are all ones that work together to increase the quality and quantity of resources available for recipient development and that benefit the poorest recipients in particular. These trends also reduce the direct benefits to or leverage of the donors. This movement, both in its results and in the arguments advanced for it in goal-setting and monitoring forums, was geared to the interests of recipients and not to those of donors (at least as interests are ordinarily defined)—and were perceived as such by recipients that favored such changes and by donors that often needed specific encouragement to adopt them. That kind of consistent movement is hard to explain on structural grounds, and much easier to explain by assuming that some process of moral suasion was at work on the donors.

## THE GENERAL PROBLEM: EXPLAINING STEADY CHANGE IN THE INTERNATIONAL SYSTEM

The larger theoretical point that is at issue here concerns the idea of purposive change in the international system. I have argued that the steady change in the foreign aid regime making it more accommodating to the interests of recipients is attributable to donor country commitments to international cooperation and development and to a humane response to poverty.

Particularly at issue is the question of how it is possible to attain cooperation in the "anarchic" international realm. A good deal of recent work has been done on how various incentive structures might make cooperative bargains between rational egoists possible. But that valuable work must be supplemented with an appreciation of the role of shared values that modify the sense in which nations act as rational egoists. More specifically, I shall argue three things: (1) that it is difficult to explain consistent movement—such as that observed in foreign aid—on the basis of a regime based mainly on incentives to rational egoists; (2) that there are some theoretical reasons to expect humane values and beliefs going far beyond the available evidence to play a strong role in shaping foreign policies; and (3) that for these two reasons, a pattern of outcomes and processes of change is to be expected which is very much like that actually observed in the case of the evolution of foreign aid practices.

### The Theoretical Puzzle of Consistent Change

The dominant way of looking at international relations in scholarly work has been the realpolitik, or Realist, view that nations act first to preserve or extend their power position and then perhaps also to attain various secondary interests related directly to the welfare or concrete benefits of their own people (or some class thereof). I emphasize the idea of concrete benefits because if one is to construe the idea of "interests" so broadly that any desire whatever is included, for instance, a concern for the welfare of foreigners, then the term "interest" is just a synonym for what nations choose to do. Of course, nations choose to do what they choose to do. If Realism has any content, it is saying that what they choose is of direct, tangible benefit to the country, and especially as regards building the state's own power.

It is possible to base cooperation upon the pursuit of power and interest by states. Discussion of international coordination among states often looks to the way in which a bargain of some sort among the coordinating states could enhance the position of each participating state. A regime can then emerge as a set of principles, norms, rules, and decision-making procedures around which actors' expectations converge. Regimes are often theorized in terms of Realist or other explanations based on the self-interest of the participants. Some regimes are instituted or sustained by powerful actors who seek to establish a set of rules that favors their interest. In other cases, regimes may be the result of a bargain among states to overcome a "political market failure." Such regimes create norms that, when adhered to by parties to the regime, make them all better off, but that would not be observed in the absence of a bargain, since adherence involves costs borne by the individual state which obeys them and provides benefits which are shared by a wider group of states. Such regimes assume value of their own by defining rights, reducing transactions costs, and providing monitoring and high-quality information. By the use of negotiated agreements or implicit understandings, parties to a regime are able to improve their situation by their joint agreement to act in their collective interest rather than on the basis of a myopic self-interest.

International cooperation of this kind can often be useful, but there is no guarantee that it serves any interest larger than that of the parties to the deal. While it is pareto-improving for them, it can impose net costs on states not party to the deal, and there is no reason to expect that regimes based on the self-interest of the contracting parties will be any more sensitive to the needs of noncontracting parties than is the unnegotiated behavior of states. Also, there is no necessary reason why regimes based simply on self-interest should move, over time, in any particular direction. As times change, and as the parties to the original regime experience changes of interests, the regime may prove "sticky": it may be hard to change because renegotiation is costly and poses dangers that the regime may collapse; and states may continue their adherence to regime rules even when they would prefer not to, because they do not want to be seen as defecting, or dishonoring commitments. Renegotiation that reflects the interests of the parties sometimes may be possible, but if renegotiation takes place on the basis of changed participant interests, the direction of movement will generally be based on shifts that do not reflect any larger principle or sense of purpose, and should not display any particular pattern.

The type of change just observed in foreign aid over time is quite different. Change was consistent, in two ways: there was steady movement over time, and there was change in five or six dimensions, all of which reflected an allied set of goals. Moreover, the consistent direction of change was governed by the underlying norm of seeking to make aid more useful for purposes of development and more oriented toward the needs of impoverished members of the international system. Thus, change in aid was responsive not to the interests of contracting donor states but to the larger needs of the poor countries and to the attempt to construct a juster international system. In neither respect are the changes in the aid regime easy to explain on the basis of a mutually improving deal among the donor states.

The consistent change in aid is also hard to explain in terms of a bargain among the donor states because there were no binding rules that states undertook to obey. In each dimension of change, at any given point of time, the level of compliance with a standard—such as multilateral funding, financial concessionality, tying, percentage of aid going to the neediest countries, and so on—was highly variable. There was steady movement among members of the group over time, but there were rarely explicit international commitments to adhere to a rule or meet a standard. Standards that were set were essentially general guidelines. Thus, monitoring played a role only in shaming states whose aid was not particularly generous: it did not reveal noncompliance to agreements or undermine a state's reputation for living up to its bargains. Also, some states set and achieved higher standards for themselves than DAC guidelines called for, and continued to toughen their own standards even when they were doing better than other states. Such states could not have been criticized for not doing their part, since they were already performing better than most others; yet these states continued to set higher targets for themselves.

Change in foreign aid is hard to explain on the basis of donor state interest because it has been consistent in character, because it reflected the needs of the recipient states more than those of the donors, and because the change occurred not as compliance to an agreed-upon set of standards but on a voluntary basis, with most states steadily improving their performance despite the wide range of compliance with any particular standard at any one time. It suggests another basis for regime change, based on the effect of beliefs and moral values implicit in the practices of the regime.

For the directions of change in foreign aid were precisely aligned with the defining characteristics of the regime itself. Aid was, as noted in chapter 2, substantial, public, concessional, and developmentally oriented in a way that set it apart from any previous international capital transfers. And the steady movement in aid improved it in just these ways. The concept of aid itself implied a goal of assisting the poor and promoting development. Once aid programs existed, they proclaimed the essential validity of the concept. At that point, it was possible to criticize aid, as aid, for failure to seek the welfare of the recipients, but criticism of aid for failing to serve the interests of the donors was criticism of aid simply for being aid.

Thus the regime theory that has developed does not provide specially good ways of understanding progressing change, steady regime change in the same direction. That kind of change is better explained by a quite different sort of logic, as I will try to show: a logic of common ends rather than of common fears. An argument based upon incentives to members not to withdraw for fear of fostering the regime's collapse—or one based upon fixed rules and procedures sustained by a hegemon—can be very useful in explaining situations where fixed regimes stay in place, and perhaps are renegotiated periodically, and where expected levels of participation are more or less uniform or are defined according to some agreed-upon or well-understood formula. But such an agreement is less helpful in explaining movement in regimes, movement in a uniform direction but at somewhat erratic rates, by different regime participants without any well-set necessary level of participation.

On existing theories of regimes, or of international cooperation, one might expect to see quite a great deal of cooperation from time to time; but not steady motion. So where there is such steady motion, as here in the case of foreign aid, it is a puzzle, on the basis of these arguments.

### Beliefs and Values as a Basis for Regimes

There are, however, other possible bases for regimes. I shall explore the possibilities of explaining change in foreign aid as norm-governed change, that is, in the ways in which regimes might rest on shared convictions among regime adherents: both upon broad shared normative outlooks and upon beliefs or principles of action of a general tenor. One would expect change of this kind to be governed by the normative principles implicit in the regime. How can international regimes develop based on shared adherence to cooperative and inclusive values and to beliefs about the efficacy of cooperative, inclusive strategies? I have argued, specifically, that the aid policies of OECD nations were influenced persistently over a period of thirty-five years by ideas and values drawn from the general ethical traditions and the domestic political experience of these countries. Is there any more general theoretical basis for expecting such things to occur? I argue that there is.

Nations are faced by a need to anticipate a future that is filled with uncertainty. Even the possible contingencies and courses of action are unknown; knowing the probabilities of various kinds of future outcomes is, for the most part, out of the question. In this kind of a situation, basing a policy on detailed calculations of what will work out to the national advantage is a strategy of limited usefulness. Its usefulness is limited not only because of the difficulty of even guessing how a policy will turn out in detail but also because much of the need is not to choose among already existing alternatives but to generate new options, plans, and ways of doing things. In such a situation, general principles of wise action are likely to provide some of this vague guidance. And deeply held convictions that are general enough to be shared are likely to provide some of the vision and impetus needed to forge creative solutions to problems of long-term structuring in an unpredictable environment.

At the same time, the uncertainty of the long-term future means that there is not necessarily an obvious or overwhelming need to pursue a policy governed only by realpolitik considerations. There is ambiguity among policymakers as to what long-term course will work out best, and the constraints of the international system no more compel nations to devote full attention to short-term pressures to thrive than they compel them to structure their production solely around economic growth and military might to the exclusion of private or government luxury consumption. In such a situation, policy can be influenced by plausible arguments about a long-term future, and plausibility will be based in part upon a policy's affinity to a broad base of domestic political experience and interpretation, and upon generally accepted principles of practical reasoning, including a society's ethical traditions.

This is, in a general way, what happened in the postwar period as a whole, which led, among other things, to the creation of a foreign aid regime. During the fifty or seventy-five years before the start of foreign aid, there had been great changes in the degree of responsibility the states of Europe and North America took for poor people within their own societies. And there had been wider advocacy of the idea that only on the basis of a cooperative international order could peace be assured. The experience of the thirties and early forties served widely to confirm this point of view: domestic laissez-faire policies that ignored the plight of those in poverty were both inhumane and inefficient; and the chaos that developed in Europe was interpreted as the outcome of competitive policies that undermined international stability by creating economic troubles and consequent domestic political chaos. By contrast, those who planned for a postwar international order sought to put it on a footing that would promote peace and prosperity, and that would be more just, by conforming it to the pattern of domestic democracy and encouraging the development of institutions of international economic cooperation, democratic international forums open to all nations equally, assistance for those in need. Such policies antedated the start of foreign aid. The Bretton Woods institutions, the United Nations and, in particular, its Economic and Social Council (ECOSOC), the Marshall Plan, and the earlier effort to promote technical cooperation with Latin American countries, the Institute for Inter-American Affairs, were all steps toward working out international policies based on patterns of cooperation and inclusion that had deep roots in the democratic values and experience of the West.

It was in this context that foreign aid policies were conceived and implemented. That is not to say that such policies were determined by the tendencies of the times; they were not. To come up with innovative policies—even ones that are rooted in previous international and domestic experience—is not easy or inevitable. A look at the history of Truman's inaugural address, at the origins of the ECOSOC, at the early years of the World Bank, at aid to India in the fifties, or at the institution of the OECD and its DAC, at the Colombo Plan, at the development of very soft international lending, or at the rise of expanded multilateral funding of aid would clearly reveal that none of these developments was an obvious or foregone conclusion, and that each was contested at the time. Nevertheless, these policies spread because they had such roots. The arguments for the policies made sense, and found support, in a variety of OECD polities because those countries' domestic political discourse and structure made the policies seem sensible, and provided links between the societies' ethical and religious traditions and public policies designed to assist those in need.

But once such policies have been authored, they have some momentum. The rhetoric and arguments used to support the policies, the formal institutions, the professionals involved in the policies, and the public opinion generated all have a life of their own and, once set in motion, may be a source of ongoing advocacy for the continuation and reform of the policies. These institutionalities often act not only to advance their own status—as professionals, organizations, or interest groups, for instance—but also out of conviction about the issues that are their formal raison d'être. I conclude the discussion of the causes of the ongoing change in the foreign aid regime by examining some of the generalizable ways in which this seems to have worked.

*Processes of Steady Change*

What kinds of processes underlay the steady changes observed so far? Some type of explanation is needed to account for these regular progressions. The steady motion in five distinct (though conceptually related) areas, in directions favorable to the economic development of the recipients and unfavorable to the use of aid for leverage by the donors, is good evidence that concerns for economic development affected the overall evolution of the regime.

I have argued that there is a distance between interests of countries, interests, that is, in any discoverable or calculable sense, and values and commitments and beliefs that those countries hold; and that these values will influence their policies, through perception and definition of interests, and in other ways. This "distance" or "looseness of coupling" is located partly in certain mediating structures: in institutions, in lines of thought, and in stylistic affinities that hold across different levels of analysis and issue areas. If values play this kind of a role, mediated by institutions, intellectuals, and domestic political patterns, the outcome and process just observed in the development of foreign aid is just what should be expected.

We want to note a series of processes that can be observed in the ongoing reform of aid policies.

1. The initial definitions of foreign assistance programs created a *rhetorical momentum*. There was a clear commitment to development as an end in itself in Truman's articulation of the Point Four program in 1949, and in the other aid institutions that followed, such as the Colombo Plan or the United Nations Expanded Programme for Technical Assistance. Truman made sure to stress the benefits to the United States of a program of foreign assistance, but he also made sure to state that such a program to help others with U.S. technical skills should be undertaken, even if there were no benefit to the United States, simply because it was right to do so. The same rhetorical ambiguity has run through most advocacy of aid in the developed countries ever since. In some ways, the fact that aid was put on such a rhetorical footing was, politically, more important than whether or not such words were sincere (even if the latter issue is meaningfully definable, and ascertainable). Once aid had been placed on such a footing, it could be criticized on such a footing. Ever afterward it became politically difficult to set up aid practices—especially international ones—except on a basis that had to be defensible as appropriate to programs with primarily developmental intent. Foreign aid became embedded in a context of debate that made it easiest for those who wanted to have aid geared to developmental and antipoverty purposes to argue their case.

2. A related element in the process of reforming aid, then, was the *commitment to public scrutiny and criticism* that was structured into the way institutions were set up. The commitment to extend foreign aid throughout the OECD implicated it in an international process of scrutiny. This international cooperation, by itself or in the face of threats of chaos and subversion abroad, was part of a larger United States strategy, of course. Whether the commitment to this sort of a strategy was sincerely valued as an end in itself or merely as a means to other ends, however, making it work involved the United States and others in a process of having to defend their policies in terms of agreed-upon goals, in the UN ECOSOC, for instance, and also in the deliberations of Western-dominated bodies like the DAC and the World Bank. In either type of forum, it was easier to find common ground on the basis of general principles than on the basis of particularistic interests. Moreover, there were particular choices made—such as the setting up of the DAC as a body with independent professional staff and holding candid mutual review sessions in which the members' policies were commended and criticized—which led to pressures upon donors to conform to international standards.

3. These pressures were informal and (in a sense) voluntary: there were no sanctions, and members adhered to the guidelines, agreements, and targets that were set with differential strictness. Nevertheless, the practice of *setting targets* for volume, concessionality, untying, focus on LLDCs, and so on seems to have played a large part in the movement of donors toward policies more geared to recipients' development and in the prevention or stemming of backsliding on goals, as well. The setting of a target often led to reform in a particular area—especially if accompanied by better statistics on donors' adherence. DAC chairmen reported, too, that the targets—however arbitrarily arrived at—also were helpful in compliance because they gave internal advocates of more progressive aid policies leverage within the donor governments and societies.[3]

4. Thus, another factor in the steady movements of aid was the growth of *a corps of aid professionals* and others within the donor countries *committed to the goals* of Third World development. If there were to be aid programs at all, those drawn to staffing them tended to be those sympathetic to goals of development—both at the lowest and the highest level of staff. These then were further strengthened by the development of professional canons and pride. Particularly at the highest levels, to obtain men of high caliber for leadership—such as Robert McNamara at the World Bank—meant to appoint people with independent judgment and broad influence. This independent judgment often meant a commitment to humane, international public goals—such as the eradication of poverty—rather than only those that were national.

5. What is true of professionals was true of *institutions*, mutatis mutandis. Institutions that were to be effective and prestigious had to develop high standards that did not simply revolve around their own growth but around evident expertise and commitment to generally esteemed goals—and, in particular, the economic-developmental goals that were their raisons d'être.

6. The consensus rested too upon the existence of *groups in society concerned with development*. These typically were groups of intellectuals, churches, and labor or labor-oriented parties with commitments to issues of equality and/or helping the poor. One reason that these groups had influence was their more intense and more long-term involvement with developmental and aid issues. In the short term, it was often possible for agricultural or business or specific diplomatic interests to carry special clout on a particular aid-related issue. In the long term, however, the shaping of agreements and standards, and the community of reference for aid professionals, was more apt to be that created by those with long-term interests based around principles directly related to issues of Third World development.

7. Finally, the *power of principles* of equality, beneficence, and cooperation *rested upon* their connection to *wider spheres of moral and political reasoning*, especially in the OECD countries. In practice this was apt to occur, in the case of aid, in three or four specific ways. The existence of groups (church, labor, and intellectual) concerned with issues of poverty and development and international cooperation attested to the fact that these issues found roots in the broader moral and political traditions of the societies. Similarly, the independent commitments of professionals and the ease with which various sorts of positions could be justified also depended on the fact that their practical reasoning on this issue was rooted in broader ethical and religious and political traditions of practical reason. Ultimately, the whole plausibility and, indeed, conceivability of international cooperation and economic assistance rested upon the broad legitimacy that attached in domestic political affairs, and in everyday ethical life, to cooperative solutions, to aid to the disadvantaged, and to inclusionary, democratic relations.

Each of these factors contributed to a certain momentum or logic, by which, once certain commitments were acknowledged, they naturally tended to be extended. Thus there were a variety of ways in which rhetoric, formal institutions, professions, intellectual analysis, and public opinion allowed the extension of the principles of international assistance. They did so in large part because of their affinity to domestic values and because their analysis was governed by the kinds of presuppositions about cooperation that those values work well with.

CONCLUSION

The foregoing remarks finish my empirical and theoretical analysis of the causes of ongoing change in the foreign aid regime. However, it may not be amiss to conclude with some admittedly much more speculative remarks on possible policy-relevant implications of the analysis. In fact, I want briefly to make two kinds of comments: on the theoretical questions that arise about the wisdom of this sort of influence of domestic and ethical values and ideas on international politics, and on the specific set of institutions that arose after the Second World War, of which aid was a part. The last chapter will discuss where further reform is desirable, in foreign aid and in cognate areas of North-South relations.

### Are Domestic Political Values a Limit to Rationality in International Politics?

The discussion above deferred the question of whether the hypothesized process of extending ideas and values from domestic politics and general human moral discourse into international relations is a factor for rationality or for irrationality. It is common to talk about the influence of domestic political factors and values on international politics as a factor "limiting rationality," where rationality is understood as policies furthering the national interest. And more widely in social science it is common to talk about rationality in terms of means-ends rationality, or instrumental rationality, in such a way that anything that deviates from the calculated pursuit of an actor's goals is seen as a factor "limiting" rationality. In such a context, it seems that nothing can improve upon the calculated pursuit of an actor's ends. It is difficult to know what to term such an improvement in that vocabulary, for it is hard to do better than "rationality." Yet the force of the analysis is to suggest that it may be possible for factors that sway nations from looking too exclusively at a nice balance of self-interest to improve even individual national performance, or at least the overall capacity of a group of nations to all get along well.

That is because there may not be any obviously "optimal" course of self-interest, deviation from which is an error, or a partial failure of rationality. Instead of this picture in which there is some preset best position for actors of every type leading to some equilibrium balance of selfishness, there may be, I have suggested, a more entrepreneurial situation—a situation in which creative initiative is likely to arise out of vigorous national values, and in which a loose coupling between the pressures of survival in the international system and national behavior may make commitments to an international rationality, rather than to an individual national rationality alone, a possible and rewarding course for intellectually vigorous statesmen and nations.

I said that there was a "need" for broader insight and vision in planning long-term national policy, and I showed ways in which such vision, based on domestic and other broad values, might influence policy. But I have not argued yet for a match between the "need" and the type of influence exerted. In fact, there is no sure basis for knowing that they will match. In the case of foreign aid particularly it is difficult to ascertain for certain what the effects were. Indeed, conclusive evidence for these may never be available, for the question deals with the overall effects on the international system of policies implemented throughout the system, and there is no basis for historical comparisons on these systemic effects. Nevertheless, it is possible to speculate: to reason about the kind of broad domestic effects we might expect aid to have. I would like to conclude this section by doing so. In the next section, I will make some remarks about the specific case of foreign aid.

One kind of argument is somewhat irrespective of the specific national values that find their way into thinking about international relations. At this most abstract level, I could argue that there is at least a presumption that the basic principles which work well in domestic society may offer some guide to what will work well in another, less-well-understood environment of international affairs. In addition to any general wisdom which may be encoded in a country's domestic political system, there is a fair chance that the technique or style of rule which works well at home is one which that society has the experience to apply effectively abroad. This argument would suggest that there are structural reasons, as well as tendencies, for democratic societies to try to set up an international order using democratic principles and for authoritarian societies to structure their international dealings more on the basis of a raw pursuit of power.

### Foreign Aid and Postwar Institutions

Those who began to think about the structuring of a postwar world in the forties were faced with a powerful object lesson, as it seemed to them, in the failure of policies of narrow national self-interest. The policies that followed World War I had, at best, not been primarily designed to help each nation do well. Beggar-thy-neighbor devaluations, punitive reparations, exaction of war debts, and the like had fostered, as it seemed in hindsight, economic chaos and desperation which led to political chaos and madness, at first within nations, then in international affairs. Those who planned a post–World War II order were determined to try to avoid these consequences.

In fact, in a certain sense, the postwar period was a vindication of the Wilsonian vision. The creation of a group of democratic and prosperous nations in Western Europe led to a worldwide prosperity and a degree of peace and unity in Western Europe that was historically unprecedented. The creation of international economic institutions set up a level of cooperation among the major Western powers that avoided economic rivalries like those that had beset world affairs before the war, and that cooperation continued, in moderation, even as the specific arrangements altered or decayed. And similarly, the United States's push to promote decolonization, and to include the new nations in an international order in which there was some promise of their interests receiving at least some consideration, was an important factor in preserving a world order relatively peaceful and relatively favorable to continued cooperation between richer and poorer nations, despite their differences.

These arrangements were not ideally suited to the interests of the Third World—and, in my view, are to be faulted morally and politically for their insufficient attention to problems of poverty—but they were extraordinarily generous by historical standards. They were, in some important ways, rooted in the best traditions of Western democracies, though imperfectly; but that did not make them obvious choices for the Western countries. It is, in some ways, surprising that such farsighted policies were adopted and strengthened.

# PART III

# Conclusion

## CHAPTER NINE

# How Shall We Then Live?

> I have the audacity to believe that people everywhere can have
> three meals a day for their bodies, education and culture for their
> minds, and dignity, equality, and freedom for their spirits. I be-
> lieve that what self-centered men have torn down, other-centered
> men can build up.
>
> —Martin Luther King, Jr.[1]

CAN MORAL factors make a difference in international politics? Can conviction and compassion change the way states behave, or even modify the
quality of international affairs? Yes, at times. Despite the ever-present
flaws of human character and the pressures of the international system, it
is sometimes possible for moral principle and human fellow-feeling to
have a consistent effect on foreign policy. And so, limited as our powers
are, we have a responsibility to try to shape an international system on the
basis not merely of power but of justice and mercy.

Over a period of forty years, developed countries provided foreign aid
mainly because of their belief that they had a humane responsibility to do
so. And foreign aid has been the largest net financial flow to the Third
World, several times larger than net investment by multinational firms,
and has involved a score of developed country donors, a score of international agencies primarily funded by them, and over a hundred less developed countries. Foreign aid was imperfect, and at times compromised,
and certainly the poor countries pressed for aid as hard as they could. Yet
many convergent lines of evidence indicate that this wholly novel development in world political economy cannot be accounted for on the basis
of the economic and political interests of the donor states, and that their
concern for the economic development of the recipients was the prime
motive behind aid. The strongest source of support for promoting the
economic development of the poor countries has been a sense of justice
and compassion. Donors were also affected by their belief that an unjust
world was an unstable world, and by their consequent commitment to
building a just and generous international order as the basis for long-term
international peace and prosperity. Highly imperfect though it of course
was,[2] foreign aid made the international environment for poor nations
significantly different from any that had gone before it. We have, in con-

sequence, a much stronger international society and a more morally sensitive global order.

The larger argument of the book is that moral vision shapes international politics. How states act often reflects the values and principles they hold. While we are not in full control of events, our choices accumulate and help shape the kind of world we live in, and for which we then bear responsibility. We can choose to make the organization of international society reflect respect for the rights of others, or the rule of the strong; the world economy can incorporate concern for the economic and social needs of the weak, or it can be swept by the tides of unbuffered market forces. Ultimately, we live with the consequences of these choices, but those consequences take some while to become manifest. Thus, choices about what principles to adopt are simultaneously choices about what we value, about what we think the world is like, and about what to trust in.

In this chapter, then, I seek not to sum up the arguments of the book, as chapters 1 and 2 do, but to sketch their human consequences. Reflecting on the vision that shaped foreign aid over the past forty years, and that moved its advocates as they labored to build a better world, leads me to try to understand afresh the implications of the worldwide, human needs which aid, at its best, sought to address. Since, as I have argued, analytical insights and ethical perspectives are often closely bound together, I set out here, for any whom it may interest, my own understanding of the morally pressing issues that the rest of the book addresses indirectly, the vision which has motivated my analysis and informed my thinking.

The accumulation of technical capacity in the twentieth century makes it possible, as never before, to assure that each person on earth is able to earn a decent living, one which will support families free from hunger and despair. But the power of technology, set to work through the mechanism of the market, does not by itself suffice to provide economic opportunities even for the impoverished in the world's wealthiest societies. At the same time, technological progress makes advanced means of destruction more and more widely available. The ability to make nuclear weapons, once available only to the most advanced countries, may soon be available to petty tyrants or even terrorist groups and criminal syndicates. Chemical and biological engineering techniques, even less tightly controlled, offer other destructive possibilities. Even without deliberate attempts at destruction, the uncontrolled use of more and more powerful technologies is apt to wreak havoc upon the environment. In light of the past record of human destructiveness, this is surely a very chastening fact. Who that has read human history, or his own heart, can see the power which we increasingly have at our disposal as human beings and not tremble? So technological progress comes upon human beings as a kind of judgment—a terrible and just judgment that assays what we as a world human community have in our hearts, and imposes that result upon us.

It is important to understand the role of moral values in the construction of the international system because we are at a critical historical juncture. Response to human need is always a matter of urgency, whether or not anything else depends upon it. The unsatisfied needs of the poor constitute the gravest possible kind of catastrophe for those who are poor. But the unfolding of human scientific accomplishment gives a second kind of urgency to the question of building a more just society: in a world that is increasingly an interlinked whole, unmet human need will undermine the urgent necessity of creating a world at peace. The nineties are a transitional moment in which it is possible to set the tenor of the post-cold-war era. Patterns of international interaction, once established, often last a long time. We must choose between defining a course of costly self-denying commitment to human dignity and solidarity and the temporarily light costs of a withdrawal from international affairs which will ultimately wreak a much costlier havoc.

The aid regime has benefited the world in many ways; it has been a bright spot of concern for human need in the second half of the twentieth century. The best evidence indicates that aid has been successful, both at helping poor countries to develop and at improving the living standards of the poorer people within those countries.[3] The claim that aid to Europe worked but aid to less developed countries cannot has little basis in fact. The per capita GNP of Third World countries has, on the whole, risen quite rapidly in the postwar era, by historical standards. Aid has also helped establish worldwide norms that development ought to benefit the poor. Foreign aid has played a positive role in sustaining hope, and in keeping the world community together, too. Commitment to justice and to addressing human need, and especially the needs of the powerless and poor, is a linchpin holding society together, internationally as it is domestically.

Yet aid has not been adequate to the challenges of world poverty. The facts of human hunger and misery, as well as the need to establish a cooperative world, make it imperative to see the need for a more substantial effort, even while recognizing past positive achievements. While GNP has risen and poverty has been reduced from what it would have been, probably a greater absolute number of people now live in crushing poverty worldwide than did so forty years ago. Growth in GNP has slowed or stopped in many Third World countries. Most seriously, the least developed countries, and the African countries especially, are in increasingly perilous condition and are at risk of economic and ecological collapse. And in this world of misery, aid has been stagnant. While there has been a concern for aid to reach the poorest people, more emphasis on that concern is needed; for concern for human waste and suffering is the most important reason for foreign aid, and at its moral core. Aid shows signs of deteriorating in quality and quantity, in considerable measure because of the disinterest of the United States in sustaining a poverty-oriented aid regime.

Over the past twenty years the United States has consistently been the laggard of the DAC in the volume of aid provided, and the quality of its aid has been mixed. About 30% of U.S. aid has been provided to multilateral institutions, but as much as half of U.S. bilateral aid has been given as Security-Supporting Assistance, rather than primarily for purposes of economic development. The United States, almost alone in the DAC, has failed to make a commitment to provide .15% of GNP going for aid to the least developed countries. U.S. footdragging in supplying its fair share has held down the level of World Bank concessional loan (IDA) replenishments, lowering the contributions other nations were willing to make as well its own. Leadership is needed to maintain and improve the quality and quantity of aid and to develop the principle of concern for the weak in a world where many suffer. The United States could exercise leadership by supporting DAC standards and by placing a focus on poverty-oriented lending, if it were willing to participate in aid even at what is by DAC standards a low to moderate level of funding. Instead, it shows utter disinterest in aid—an unconcern with international poverty that matches its unconcern with domestic poverty.

The argument that the United States cannot afford a program of foreign aid or assistance to countries in the process of recovery from communism is untenable. U.S. aid expenditures as a percentage of GNP have fallen to a third what they were in the early sixties, when the cold war was at a high pitch, while U.S. per capita income has doubled. The percentage of GNP the United States spends on aid is less than that of any other developed country, less than a half of the average of the other developed countries. Ireland, with less than a quarter of our per capita GNP, spends almost as great a proportion of its national income on aid as we do. Moreover, the United States spends thirty to fifty times its foreign aid budget on military expenditures. The notion that aid is a bankrupting element of U.S. foreign affairs expenditures is utterly implausible. The United States could double its foreign aid expenditures and keep its foreign policy expenditures constant by a 3% cut in military spending. The United States has spent 5–9% of GNP for many years to maintain itself against military threats that are now largely abated. What we cannot afford to do is to create a divided and bitter world by failing to take seriously the problems of poverty that afflict most of the world's people and to which we are now contributing as little as one fifth of a percent of GNP.

The international institutions and regimes devised in the wake of World War II have served the United States and the world well over the past half century because they were founded on the sound principle of devising just and generous solutions, for conscience's sake and because those who devised them knew that without a just and generous social order, peace and prosperity were impossible. The UN and the World Bank ended up functioning quite differently from the way their founders anticipated. Yet they served the world community well because the Wilsonian principles of inclusion of all nations, and attention to their economic as well as security needs, were far-seeing ones. However, such institutions cannot last, unrenewed, forever. At this moment when the world has changed dramatically, we can work for international community to hold the world together for the next fifty years only by again seeking to make human dignity and justice the costly but effective cornerstone of world community.

One reason why it is important to understand accurately the character of the pressures and forces at work in international politics is that a false understanding leads us away from ideas of security based on justice and compassion, and toward an international politics based on the inevitability of self-interest. If the character of an anarchic international system requires states to prefer their national self-interest above every other goal, or suffer decline, then the recognition of human need and international crisis can make little difference. If states have no significant ability to build a different kind of international system, no effective choice is possible, there is little moral responsibility, and no point in struggling for a better world. Thus the larger theoretical point implicit in the argument about foreign aid is that important, consistent choice is possible: that it is possible to reform international relations in accord with conceptions of fairness and compassion, human dignity and human sympathy, justice and mercy. We need to be wary, for international life is full of perils; and for just this reason any kind of fatalism, or presumption that states have to act selfishly in their international policy, is as dangerous as it is unscientific. Though our control over events is limited, we exercise significant choice which affects the way the international system goes, and bear responsibility for the results.

There are purely intellectual reasons for trying to develop theory that helps us understand the role of ideas, values, and national self-conceptions in setting the tenor of international life. The view that what happens in world politics is governed essentially by factors of power and interest seems less and less plausible, as the commitment of reformers in the Soviet Union transformed world politics (and *before* the loss of Soviet power and the breakup of the Soviet Union) and ideas of freedom and self-determination swept across Eastern Europe like a powerful wind. Western Europe, too, transformed by ideas of democracy and European unity, makes clear the need for theories of international politics which explore the structuring and transforming power of ideas and values. Indeed, the twentieth century could be said to be, in international as well as domestic politics, the century of ideas. Ideologies and creeds, more than the fluctuations of power, have been the most powerful determinants of the history of the international relations of the twentieth century, as colonialism, national self-determination, communism, democracy, an international league, fascism, nazism, national liberation, resurgent Islam, and the collapse of communism and resurgent democratic ideals have chased each other across the face of the globe.

There are strong reasons to suppose that moral and political principles should affect countries' foreign policy, and may set an atmosphere that affects the way the international system works. I have argued that in general the principles and convictions which peoples and statesmen have are among the main determinants of their foreign policy, because there is no single, obviously best, uniquely rational course of action for a state which can be calculated independent of general beliefs about the character of the international system. The best course of action for a state (even given a particular set of ends) cannot be ascertained simply by imagining oneself in the situation of a particular state or statesman: it depends just as much upon the general outlook, the intellectual optic, with which things are surveyed from that physical vantage point. There is no neutral, colorless, subjectless process of observation by which sound policy can be logically derived from a state's structural position: peoples and leaders determine state interests and policies on the basis of their convictions and understandings of the world as well as on the basis of relatively uncontested facts about it. Thus, the way in which countries respond to their international political situation is inherently affected by their values and principles, for reasoned outlooks on life and politics are necessarily value laden.

For this reason there should tend to be systematic affinities between a country's domestic political values and practices and those of its international policies.[4] This is clearly observable in the case of foreign aid. Those countries with the strongest domestic welfare states tended to be those with strong foreign aid programs. The groups, parties, politicians, and intellectuals who advocated more attention to poor people at home usually advocated foreign aid. The same link shows up in public opinion data. Administrations and writers that sought cutbacks in domestic social spending also sought cuts in foreign aid. Those who originated the idea of foreign aid advanced the idea as a generalization of compassionate state response to domestic poverty, and made both moral and prudential arguments for it which paralleled justifications of the domestic welfare state.[5]

The same phenomenon—basic social principles influencing domestic and international politics in tandem—could be traced out in many other issue areas: in attitudes toward race and colonialism, in attempts to suppress dissenters and minorities domestically and tendencies to dominate neighboring countries, and in attitudes toward management of the domestic and international economies, for instance. The social principles we bring to international life may be prosocial or antisocial, but they involve important moral choices, in international as in domestic politics. The choices and principles of reasoning are closely related in the two arenas.

Values and principles with which people interpret international politics are not acquired only from life within their own country; we are influenced by our membership in world society as well. An awareness of international society played a role in sustaining and modifying foreign aid programs, and a foreign aid regime. As developed countries became formal equals with less developed countries in the United Nations and other international forums, people in developed countries found themselves forced to think through their relationship to the LDCs. Many people in developed countries came to agree both that Western colonialism had been an unjustifiable and deleterious infringement upon the Third World and that the ongoing international economic system placed Third World countries at a disadvantage. Some European countries that had themselves been recipients of Marshall Plan aid felt an obligation to reciprocate by reaching out to other states in trouble. The countries of the Third World pressed hard to try to establish such a sense of obligation to assist poor countries. Once aid became established as a regular practice, developed countries saw it as an important expression of their place in the international system, and countries having or desiring close cultural links to strong aid-giving states perceived themselves as missing the mark if they, too, did not have a strong aid program.

International influences that supported aid were not always purehearted and selfless ones. Pressure from the LDCs, fear of seeming stingy, a desire to be part of the group, and a need to assuage troubled consciences jostled with more humane and ethical concerns, as they do in every situation of moral and social suasion. Motives were mixed, and results were mixed, as they always are. But this complex influence arising from countries' sense of their place in international society was not a matter of calculating behavior required to ensure relative power or optimize incentives: it is a process of social influence such as occurs in domestic society and personal life. That the international system is shaped by beliefs and values established in international society is in itself neither good nor bad: a collective sense of racial superiority, or ideological intolerance, or hostile fear, or the idolization of power can shape international society, just as justice and mercy and humble awareness of our own limitations can. But in the case of foreign aid, the essential pressure of conscientious concern was transmitted through mixed motives as well as pure motives. Even when states gave aid to satisfy international opinion, the fact that that was what world sentiment required shows the power that humane principles had come to have. And in the end, the results amounted to a significant concession to the needs of the weak on the part of the strong, which the weak could not by force alone have compelled.

The essential moral vision that undergirded foreign aid programs was a recognition of the need for affluent countries to respond to crippling poverty, wherever it was found in the human family, a sense that, as Robert McNamara put it, "among our century's most urgent problems is the wholly unacceptable poverty that blights the lives of some 2,000 million people in the more than 100 countries of the developing world."[6] The growing awareness of world poverty, and the development of a sense of responsibility to those in need abroad, constituted a transformation of moral imagination in the developed countries. This newly perceived moral responsibility led to a completely novel set of policies toward less developed nations becoming the standard in all the developed democracies: the institution of concessional assistance was the primary financial flow to most poor countries. Aid both reflected and furthered the recognition of human solidarity, of international community and worldwide moral responsibilities. Response to dire human need worldwide became a principle which is acknowledged by almost all powerful states, and significantly influences their cash outlays. It forms a focus for the idealism of many young people in the developed countries. Foreign aid constitutes a pivotal, systematic change in the relations between rich and poor countries; a significant revision of the international system on the basis of the recognition of a moral obligation to the weak.

Such a moral vision included many elements: a greater awareness of the problems of people in poor countries and greater understanding of their perspectives; development of compassion for those in need and knowledge of their suffering; belief that it was possible to help raise standards of living abroad; and a felt obligation to assist the less fortunate people abroad irrespective of the benefits to one's own country. It also consistently included a belief that only by creating a just and generous international order was it possible to secure a peaceful and prosperous world. After comparing the need for assistance to poor countries to the parable of the Good Samaritan, Barbara Ward adds, "We reap what we sow," warning that "if freedom for us is no more than the right to pursue our own interest—personal or national," then "without vision, we—like other peoples—will perish."[7] Gunnar Myrdal, while admonishing against making aid an instrument of Western interests, and against justifying it on that basis, cannot refrain from warning about the "powder kegs" which are waiting if we do not respond to desperate human need.[8] The Pearson report, while emphasizing that the moral reason for foreign aid— "that it is only right for those who have to share with those who have not"—is "valid and compelling in itself," stresses that if we ignore "international development" as the "great challenge of our age," we shall "delude ourselves" in supposing "that the poverty and deprivation of the great majority of mankind can be ignored without tragic consequences for all."[9]

Moral vision is more than a set of goals or preferences; it includes an understanding of how the world works, an analytic and prudential element. Yet the understanding that concern for the weak and for the common needs of the human family must be at the heart of any sustainable world order is not simply a theorem in a calculus of long-term benefits either. Recognizing the destructive quality of greed and indifference and oppression is likely to prove compelling only to those alive to issues of justice, compassion, and human dignity. Rather, in an ambiguous world, in which it is difficult to trace cause and effect, one must choose among visions which offer different interpretations of history and of good policy, as well as different value emphases. Emphasizing the dangers of selfishness and indifference to human misery, and the constructive benefits of interdependence, involves an analytic stance, which implies a kind of moral influence and moral causation in international affairs, as well as a sense of justice and compassion.

To hold that the social order should show special sensitivity to the weak, internationally as domestically, inverts the principle of the dominance of the powerful, in its value emphasis, its analysis, and its choice of what to risk and what to trust. The central values involved in foreign aid—concern for the welfare and empowerment of the poor and for human solidarity across national borders—are the direct antithesis of any idea that power and self-interest must govern international affairs. The view that just, merciful, humble conduct is the foundation of order and that oppression and degrading poverty generate destructive contradictions also represents a line of analysis that reverses the widely held belief that economic or international order emerges when each individual, firm, or state pursues self-interest. Choosing to trust in one's own power and cunning skill involves one kind of analysis about what can prove efficacious in an uncertain world; choosing to trust in the hidden power of acting with genuine concern for others, and for the poor particularly, involves a different analysis as well as a different set of priorities.

International politics, like all politics, is a matter of moral choice and moral struggle. Whatever the immediate issues in international politics, the ultimate results depend in large part upon the fundamental moral vision by which states operate. Domestic and international politics are but different manifestations of the same phenomenon of moral choice. Of course, universal moral principles do not provide blanket prescriptions that can be applied blindly: they must be accurately applied to the concrete circumstances of time and place. But there can be no political prudence without morality, that is without consideration of the moral consequences of seemingly prudent action. The state that sets fundamental moral principle aside for the sake of successful political action builds upon sand, for it builds a destructive identity and a destructive world in which it is itself likely to perish. Statesmen who forsake conscience for the sake of public responsibilities lead their country by the short route to ruin.[10]

The test of our human solidarity is our solidarity with those who seem to have nothing to offer us. Concern for the weak, the poor, the powerless, the unattractive, the wrongdoer is concern for the human person as such. It involves our respect for their dignity, our conviction that they do in fact have something to offer, as well as our willingness to help them in their need whether or not they can repay us in any way. It is by choosing to respect the value of those without power that we put our trust not in the power of our material advantages, our cleverness, our self-control, and the furtherance of our own self-interests, but in the value of doing what is good and right (an act that sometimes has a power of its own, but a power which is often hidden and not subject to our control). To do so is wise. For we are out of control, as a human family, and cannot solve our own problems. We wish to hide the broken character of human life from ourselves and pretend there is real security in the acquisition of wealth and power. Disasters that come our way may remind us that we need to face up to fundamental lacks and problems. The terrible tragedy of Hiroshima and Nagasaki is a sign that should remind us that we do not have the wisdom to control ourselves, that we need to live in sober recollection of our human brokenness and failures, that if we cannot find peaceful resolutions to our problems, the destructive side of human nature may be allowed to put an end to us and the problems together. Yet we do not have the goodness or the power to build a world in which the power of destructiveness is wholly overcome. To think we can triumphantly construct a truly adequate world social order—or even rescue ourselves from our own destructiveness—would be to deceive ourselves.

The possibility of a final outworking of human destructiveness underlines the value of fragile human life; it not only ought to turn us to earnest attempts to work out a stabler international society, but also ought to turn our attention to those who lead hurt and wrecked lives here and now. The grand spectacle of human self-destructiveness ought to focus our gaze upon the needs of those who live and die in poverty. If it is uncertain whether we can overcome the problems of the future, it is certain that we can and should assist those now in dire need, at home and abroad. Doing so may be a requisite for being able to restrain the destructive tendencies in world society; it is also worthwhile, simply for the sake of those who are poor.

Compassion, generosity, justice are the things for which our life finally exists, in any case. It is by a life of love, of community, of reaching out to others whether we find them useful or attractive or not, that we come to open our hearts to what it truly means for us to be human. We are not very good at doing it; but, as with every task which requires inspiration, we can but work away at what we can do while we wait and hope. We cannot command our human destiny, but perhaps events will turn out graciously for us if, aware of our weakness and limitations, we set our sights on what is good. We must do what we can to control human destructiveness, even if we do not have the full strength to restrain powers which, now that we have grasped them, have us in their grip. Yet perhaps if we hear the cry of the destitute, those truly powerless in this world, it may help us present the desperate cry of the whole human family as an appeal to heaven.

# Notes

CHAPTER ONE

1. Keynes 1935, *The General Theory of Employment, Interest, and Money*, pp. 383–84.

2. See chapter 2, n. 16. However, much even of this would have been impossible apart from humanitarian support for other aid programs.

3. Beitz 1988, "Recent International Thought," and M. Hoffman 1985, "Normative Approaches," review this growing literature.

4. S. Hoffmann 1981, *Duties Beyond Borders*, p. 2; Beitz 1979 *Political Theory and International Relations*, first section; Walzer 1977, *Just and Unjust Wars*, chap. 1; and Keohane 1984, *After Hegemony*, chap. 7, discuss how moral considerations may affect international affairs.

5. Carr [1946] 1964, *The Twenty Years' Crisis, 1919–1939*, p. 168. Keohane 1986b, "Realism, Neorealism and the Study of World Politics," says this "realist" viewpoint became "the new orthodoxy in Anglo-American thinking on international affairs" after World War II (p. 8).

6. S. Hoffmann 1977, "An American Social Science," p. 44, quoted in Keohane, 1986b, "Realism, Neorealism and the Study of World Politics," p. 10.

7. Morgenthau 1954, *Politics Among Nations*, p. 4, and 1946, *Scientific Man vs. Power Politics*, pp. 191–92 and following discussion.

8. Morgenthau 1954, *Politics Among Nations*, pp. 27, 31.

9. Ibid., pp. 5–7.

10. Spykman 1942, *America's Strategy in World Politics*, p. 18.

11. The phrase is Jack Donnelly's, in his 1991 article, "Thucydides and Realism," p. 11, but the idea is common. Michael Walzer 1977, *Just and Unjust Wars*, defends concern with justice in warfare in chap. 1, entitled "Against Realism." Mark J. Hoffman, 1985, "Normative Approaches," p. 30 and discussion following argues Realists see irreconcilable conflict "between morality and the *raison d'être* of the state."

12. In Morgenthau's thought this is part of his larger doctrine of the autonomy of the political.

> Intellectually, the political realist maintains the autonomy of the political sphere. . . . He thinks in terms of interest defined in terms of power. . . . The economist asks: "How does this policy affect the welfare of society. . . ?" The lawyer asks: "Is this policy in accord with the rules of law?" The moralist asks: "Is this policy in accord with moral principles?" And the political realist asks: "How does this policy affect the power of the nation? (Or of the federal government, of Congress, of the party, of agriculture, as the case may be.)" (1954, *Politics Among Nations*, pp. 10–11)

13. Ibid., pp. 29–34, 5.

14. Kohn 1989, *The Brighter Side of Human Nature*, esp. chap. 3.

15. Hornstein et al. 1968, "Influence of a Model's Feelings," pp. 10, 222–26. Cited in Rushton 1980, *Altruism, Socialization and Society*, p. 4.

16. Rushton 1980, *Altruism, Socialization and Society*, pp. 2–3.

17. Fellner and Marshall 1968, "Twelve Kidney Donors," cited in Rushton 1980, *Altruism, Socialization and Society*, p. 6.

18. Staub 1978, *Positive Social Behavior and Morality*, p. 4.

19. Krebs 1982, "Prosocial Behavior, Equity, and Justice," p. 300, summing up pp. 261–308.

20. Hallie 1979, *Lest Innocent Blood Be Shed*.

21. Titmuss 1971, *The Gift Relationship*.

22. Mooney 1982, *Inequality and the American Conscience*, pp. 105 (citing historian J. R. Pole), 107.

23. Zarjevski 1988, *A Future Preserved*.

24. Waltz 1959, *Man, the State and War*, pp. 1, 238.

25. Waltz 1979, *Theory of International Politics*.

26. Ibid., pp. 107, 109. Waltz usually claims "a self-help system is one in which those who do not help themselves, or who do so less effectively than others, will fail to prosper, will lay themselves open to dangers, will suffer" (p. 118). He sometimes allows that states "at a minimum seek their own preservation" but may "pursue many goals," which "fluctuate with the changing currents of domestic politics" (pp. 118–19). But the logic of his position requires the former formulation. The self-help character of international politics is a "strong structural effect" (p. 109 re-emphasized p. 111) only if "no one can take care of the system" (p. 109). Where states are free to pursue various goals, they may elect to build a just and peaceful system.

27. M. Taylor 1976, *Anarchy and Cooperation*; 1982, *Community, Anarchy and Liberty*, esp. pp. 33–38; 1987, *The Possibility of Cooperation*. North 1976, *The World That Could Be*, pp. 145–47, cites other literature on cohesion and mutual assistance under anarchy.

28. Royce [1886] 1970, *California*, pp. 214–96, "The Struggle for Order."

29. Krasner 1988, "Sovereignty," cites, inter alia, Arthur 1985, "Competing Technologies and Lock-in by Historical Small Events." See also David 1985, "Clio and the Economics of QWERTY"; and Puffert 1991, "The Economics of Spatial Network Externalities."

30. Gould 1985, *The Flamingo's Smile*, p. 53; also Gould and Eldredge 1977, "Punctuated Equilibria," cited in Krasner 1988, "Sovereignty," p. 66.

31. Krasner 1988, "Sovereignty," pp. 66–94.

32. Waltz 1979, *Theory of International Politics*, pp. 110–11.

33. Axelrod 1984, *The Evolution of Cooperation*. The power of each unit is equal in Axelrod's model system; but the system is nevertheless a counterexample that directly refutes the claim of Waltz (1979) as formulated in *Theory of International Politics*.

34. Axelrod's system is not an isolated case. John Ferejohn 1990, "Rationality and Interpretation," notes the "folk theorem" that shows most interesting systems with many actors have multiple equilibria.

35. Jean-Jacques Rousseau, "Judgment on Saint-Pierre's Project for Perpetual Peace," and Immanuel Kant, "Perpetual Peace," in Forsythe et al. 1970, *The Theory of International Relations*.

36. Waltz 1979, *Theory of International Politics*, pp. 105, 117.

37. Axelrod 1984, *The Evolution of Cooperation*.

38. Schelling 1960, *The Strategy of Conflict*.

39. Keohane 1986a, *Neorealism and Its Critics*.

40. Keohane 1984, *After Hegemony*, p. 101.

41. Krasner 1983, *International Regimes*, p. 1; Oye 1986, *Cooperation under Anarchy*.

42. Coase 1980, "The Problem of Social Cost"; Keohane 1984, *After Hegemony*.

43. Keohane 1984, *After Hegemony*.

44. Axelrod and Keohane 1986, "Achieving Cooperation under Anarchy." For a critical review, see Haggard and Simmons 1987, "Theories of International Regimes."

45. See Osgood 1953, *Ideals and Self-Interest in America's Foreign Relations*; Donnelly 1991, "Thucydides and Realism," discussed below.

46. Joseph Grieco objects that this will not be true, because concern for relative gains dominates states' thinking, since their safety in an international anarchy depends on their relative position (1988, "Anarchy and the Limits of Cooperation," pp. 485–507; and 1990, *Cooperation among Nations*). But this is not necessarily so where there are more than two actors. An actor concerned with gains relative to a variety of other actors has incentives to seek joint gains in an interaction with any one of them, since this strengthens him relative to all the rest, as I argue in "Relative Gains and the Pursuit of Cooperation under Anarchy" (1992, mimeo).

47. Goldstein and Keohane 1990, "Ideas and Foreign Policy."

48. Donnelly 1991, "Thucydides and Realism," pp. 25–26. Donnelly's words span three paragraphs. He does not capitalize "Realist." He quotes Osgood 1953, *Ideals and Self-Interest in America's Foreign Relations*, p. 446.

49. Jean-Jacques Rousseau, "Abstract of the Abbé de Saint-Pierre's Project for Perpetual Peace," and "Judgment on Saint-Pierre's Project for Perpetual Peace," in Forsythe et al. 1970, *The Theory of International Relations*, pp. 158, 159.

50. Immanuel Kant, "Perpetual Peace," in Forsythe et al. 1970.

51. Waltz 1979, *Theory of International Politics*.

52. Thomas C. Schelling noted in 1960 in *The Strategy of Conflict* that saliencies—prominent features which focus interaction—are strategically crucial and depend on cultural idiosyncrasies as well as objectively identifiable strategic properties.

53. Wendt 1987, "The Agent-Structure Problem in International Relations Theory."

54. These helpful terms were coined by Waltz 1979, *Theory of International Politics*, pp. 63ff.

55. Keohane 1988, "International Institutions: Two Approaches," uses this term to refer to works such as Kratochwil 1986, "Of Systems Boundaries and

Territoriality"; Kratochwil and Ruggie 1986, "International Organization: A State of the Art on the Art of the State"; and Wendt 1987, "The Agent-Structure Problem in International Relations Theory."

56. Also, it is hard for a democratic polity to object without discrediting its sincerity and its own principles when other countries want a world democratic assembly (perhaps because they think they will do well in the voting). It is hard for a country that considers domestic national resources the property of the state to object if other countries press for world allocation of natural resources (cf. Russell 1923, *The Prospects of Industrial Civilization*, on the Soviet state and its claim to the natural resources of its republics).

57. See Russett 1990, *Controlling the Sword*.

58. This approach is elaborated with new sophistication by Putnam 1988, "Diplomacy and International Politics: The Logic of Two-Level Games."

59. Liss 1983, *Atlantic Empires*.

60. See, for instance, Todorov 1984, *The Conquest of America*; and Lauren 1988, *Power and Prejudice*.

61. Hanke 1949, *The Spanish Struggle for Justice in the New World*; and 1974, *All Mankind Is One*; Victoria [1696] 1917, *De Indis et De Juri Belli Relectiones*; Suarez [ca. 1611] 1944, *Selections from Three Works*.

62. Frank 1988, *Passions within Reason*, e.g., argues that people feel anger, care how they are regarded, etc., because (though they may not be aware of it), such emotions are useful to their survival. Even if true, this would not affect the argument here. International politics is a distinctive, anarchic realm only if the complex social considerations, emotions, and conscientious factors which affect interpersonal relations in civil society are absent. To acknowledge that states are sensitive to moral and social disapproval, whether for Frank's reasons or others, is to abandon the Realist position.

63. Waltz 1979, *Theory of International Politics*, treats emulation as evidence that the international system and pressures of anarchy are effective (despite his own methodological principles, which rule out evaluating system-level theories with evidence about foreign policy formation). But emulation of successful states is not evidence of system pressures, unless the behaviors emulated confer survival advantages upon those who engage in them.

64. See chap. 5.

65. See chaps. 5, 7, and 8.

66. Thomson 1988, "The State, Sovereignty, and International Violence."

67. Rawls 1953, "Two Concepts of Rules."

68. Ferejohn 1990, "Rationality and Interpretation."

69. Walzer 1977, *Just and Unjust Wars*, pp. 3–20. On the other hand, Clausewitz argues that warfare has nonethical imperatives—toward total conflict—which also influence its development.

70. See, for instance, Ruggie 1983, "International Regimes, Transactions, and Change"; Kratochwil 1986, "Of Systems, Boundaries, and Territoriality"; Kratochwil and Ruggie 1986, "International Organization: A State of the Art on the Art of the State"; Wendt, 1992, "Anarchy Is What States Make of It," *International Organization* 46, 2.

71. These factors are discussed in more detail in chap. 8.

72. This is related to Walzer's point in *Just and Unjust Wars* (1977, chap. 1).

73. This is documented in chaps. 6, 7, and 8.

74. The role of shared ideology is discussed by Goldstein 1988, "Ideas, Institutions, and Trade Policy"; and 1989, "The Impact of Ideas on Trade Policy," who argues that belief in free and fair trade influenced foreign policy in the United States. Similarly, Krasner 1985, *Structural Conflict*, discusses how the articulation of the ideas of dependency theory was important in unifying the Third World, helping to secure costly adherence to shared norms, and also how such an ideology created arguments which influenced developed countries, which felt a need to respond to the criticisms implicit in it.

75. In this regard, Peter Haas (1989, "Do Regimes Matter: Epistemic Communities"; and 1990, *Saving the Mediterranean*) has helpfully developed the idea of Epistemic Communities of experts, whose shared understanding of an international task to be done strongly shapes the actions that nations undertake. See also E. Haas 1990, *When Knowledge Is Power*.

CHAPTER TWO

1. Myrdal 1970, *The Challenge of World Poverty*, p. 275, original emphasis.

2. Summaries of the arguments of critics of aid, on the right and left, and of those who argue the case for self-interest, can be found in Riddell 1987, *Foreign Aid Reconsidered*.

3. Brian Smith 1990, *More than Altruism*.

4. Balanced, thoughtful, and critical accounts of the complexity of donor-recipient interactions can be found in chaps. 5 and 6 in Kreuger et al. 1989, *Aid and Development*; and chap. 4 in Cassen et al. 1986, *Does Aid Work?* Judith Tendler 1975, *Inside Foreign Aid*, has a useful account of how aid is influenced by bureaucratic interests. R. May et al. 1989, *Overseas Aid*; Mosley 1987, *Foreign Aid: Its Defense and Reform*; several chapters in Malek 1991, *Contemporary Issues in European Development Aid*; and chap. 5 of Kreuger et al. 1989, *Aid and Development*, discuss the effects of aid upon donor interests. The role of concern about communism in the early years of American aid programs is helpfully discussed in Rostow 1985, *Eisenhower, Kennedy, and Foreign Aid*; and in D. Baldwin 1966, *Economic Development and American Foreign Policy, 1943–1962*, among other places. The general mixture of motives in the United States is also discussed in an interesting way in Packenham 1971, *Liberal America and the Third World*. Robert Wood 1986, *From Marshall Plan to Debt Crisis*, argues that aid was largely a means of promoting world and U.S. prosperity by promoting a worldwide economy. Discussion of aid policies for other countries is widely scattered; see chaps. 4 and 5 in this book for references.

5. The one-third figure is, of course, a rough and conjectural estimate. See n. 16 below for more detailed discussion.

6. Multilateral organizations principally include (1) the United Nations Development Program (UNDP), its predecessors such as the Expanded Programme of Technical Assistance (EPTA), and other UN agencies that give development assistance, (2) the highly concessional lending of the World Bank's soft-loan window, the International Development Association (IDA), and (3) the highly concessional

lending by the regional development banks, the Inter-American Development Bank (IDB), the Asian Development Bank (ADB), the African Development Bank (AfDB), and so on.

7. The DAC definition of ODA (Official Development Assistance) is as follows:

> Official development assistance (ODA) is defined as those flows to developing countries and multilateral institutions provided by official agencies, including state and local governments or by their executive agencies, each transaction of which meets the following tests: a) it is administered with the promotion of the economic development and welfare of developing countries as its main objective and, b) it is concessional in character and contains a grant element of at least 25 per cent. (OECD, *Development Cooperation, 1974*, p. 115)

Use of DAC figures does not presuppose what the "main objective" of ODA is: that would of course be to beg the central question at issue here. With respect to the 25% standard, it should be borne in mind that (*a*) grants form a larger part of total ODA, net *or* gross, than do loans, and this has been true at least since the early sixties (Figures from *Geographical Distribution of Financial Flows*, various years); (*b*) the total amortization of ODA loans has usually been around 10% of new lending (net disbursements); (*c*) the proportion of "less concessional ODA loans" (grant element less than 50%) has been less than 10% of aid in recent years (see OECD, *Development Cooperation, 1984*, p. 112, for instance, compared with figures on total aid from tables at the back of the same volume); and (*d*) the total grant element in recent years has been over 80% on ODA loans and grants taken together. Indeed, for most donors, including the United States, the grant element has been above 95% in recent years (OECD, *Geographical Distribution of Financial Flows*, various years).

8. These goals, first articulated by President Roosevelt in 1941, were quickly adopted as war aims by Churchill and Roosevelt in the Atlantic Charter, and then by twenty-six nations in a Declaration of the United Nations. See chap. 6.

9. These widely quoted words are from the International Labour Organization's (ILO) Philadelphia Declaration of 1944, which was incorporated into the ILO charter. The Philadelphia Declaration was one of the first statements that "economic security and equal opportunity" and "rising standards of living" worldwide should be a "central aim of . . . international policy." See International Labour Organization 1969, *The ILO in the Service of Social Progress*, esp. pp. 207–9, and chap. 6, below.

10. OECD, *Development Cooperation, 1985*, p. 93, figures for 1975–76 and 1983–84.

11. The aid policies of the OECD donors are notable not only for their multiple and simultaneous appearance and for the sudden departure from all past practice which they constituted, but also for the remarkable similarity and continuity of OECD aid policies, and for the steady change in aid policies strengthening the essential defining characteristics of aid as a tool for promoting economic development.

The addition of new multilateral channels for aid in the UN system, the regional development banks, and the soft-loan window of the World Bank furthered and diversified the pattern of foreign aid without essentially reorienting or disturbing it. The rise in multilateral funding may, indeed, have strengthened impartiality and professionalism in the aid process; similarly, the development of many bilateral aid programs and, especially, their monitoring by the OECD may have done so. Again, after the initial establishment of aid programs bilaterally funded from many sources, the addition of participants like Finland, or much heightened participation from relative noncontributors like Italy and from regular stalwarts like the Scandinavians, may have done much to strengthen the international practice of aid giving. The regular development of aid practices that occurred is very important to understanding the aid process, as I shall argue in chapters 7 and 8. But the development cannot be said to have altered aid giving fundamentally, and this is also significant.

12. However, aid sometimes consisted of gifts of commodities, and other aid was sometimes tied to purchases in donor countries.

13. These properties did not apply perfectly to all programs at all times, of course: a single country's policy at a given time—say, Dutch aid in 1975—could be characterized as being more or less robustly funded, multilaterally channeled, untied, or small-farm oriented than that of New Zealand or than Dutch aid five years earlier or later.

14. In recent years, most DAC donors have given 75–80% of their aid in the form of grants, and the grant element of loans has generally been over 70%. Thus, the grant element in all OECD aid together has been close to 90%. However, the total grant element has been in the mid-80% range or above as far as the records go back. See, for instance, OECD, *Development Cooperation, 1985*, p. 106, which gives the 1965–66 grant element in ODA as 84%.

15. The absence of an international quid pro quo contrasts with the presence of conditions restricting the use of aid to developmentally relevant projects. A bribe generally has just the opposite structure: there are conditions about what its recipient will do for the other party but not on how the recipient uses the money gained, which is thought of as a payment. Thus, in the case of aid, the clear intent is that it be used to promote economic development.

16. Any such estimate is a guess, of course. In the early eighties, the United States provided about 22% of total aid, France, Germany, Britain, and Japan another 31%, and the smaller donors the other 47%. At most, 40% of U.S. multilateral aid served direct U.S. interests; for about a third went to UN organizations like UNDP, in which the United States had very little control, and the development banks where the United States had substantial influence were by no means mainly controlled by the United States. If one classes all U.S. Security-Supporting Assistance as directly self-interested, and about 20% of the rest of U.S. aid as directly self-interested, then a bit under half of the U.S. total (bilateral and multilateral) comes out as directly self-interested. Other donors had very little control over multilateral aid. One might reckon a bit over half of bilateral aid from the four major donors above as directly self-serving (more for Japan and France, less for England and Germany), and reckon about a quarter of the bilateral aid of the smaller donors as self-serving (with somewhat higher percentages for the commonwealth donors, Belgium, and especially Austria, and somewhat lower percentages for the Scandinavian countries and the Netherlands). This would sum to

about 34% of aid directly serving donor interests. In fact, this figure makes stronger assumptions of self-interest than I think warranted: very little of that third of aid that was multilaterally channeled served donor interests, in my view; and most bilateral aid was given to promote recipient needs. The common view that aid was self-serving comes from focus upon French, Japanese, and U.S. bilateral aid, which makes up well under a third of the total, and which, though more self-interested than most aid, is by no means wholly self-interested. However, all such estimates are at best very conjectural, and the terms change over time. For instance, as Japanese aid rose as a percentage of the total in the eighties, the quality of Japanese aid rose sharply: it became more multilateral, less tied, and in fact fell sharply in terms of the share of Japanese procurement. French aid also improved in quality and increased slightly, while U.S. aid declined in quality and quantity in the eighties.

17. Krasner 1983, *International Regimes*.

18. Keohane 1984, *After Hegemony*.

19. Axelrod and Keohane 1986, "Achieving Cooperation under Anarchy."

20. Oye 1986, *Cooperation under Anarchy*.

21. Keohane 1988, "International Institutions: Two Approaches."

22. In speaking of moral choice, it must be understood that there is no implication that states generally behave well or morally: they do not. Policies of enslavement and needless brutality are moral choices; policies of calculating selfishness are moral choices. The idea of moral choice certainly includes the possibility of genuine goodness, love of justice, and love of humanity, which can influence international politics not only here and there but also in systematic ways; and the specific study of foreign aid is designed to bring this neglected truth out. However, the domestic and international savagery of a Hitler or Stalin also reflects moral choice: the destructive and self-destructive choice of moral depravity into which societies, as individuals, are ever liable to fall.

23. Lindholm 1971, *The Image of the Developing Countries*.

CHAPTER THREE

1. Robert S. McNamara, Preface, in World Bank 1975, *The Assault on World Poverty*, p.v.

2. Robert Gilpin asserts that "the primary motives for official aid by individual governments have been political, military, and commercial," largely on the basis of U.S. aid to Israel and Egypt, and on the basis that "commercial motives explain a larger portion of Japan's aid" than it "cares to admit" (1987, *The Political Economy of International Relations*, p. 312). Hayter 1971, *Aid as Imperialism*; Hayter and Watson 1985, *Aid: Rhetoric and Reality*; and others (well summarized in Riddell 1987, *Foreign Aid Reconsidered*) argue that aid was a form of "imperialism" designed to render the developing countries dependent. The more sophisticated dependency arguments, such as that of R. Wood 1986, *From Marshall Plan to Debt Crisis*, claim that aid was used to discipline Third World countries to bring them into a market system.

3. Mexico's net aid receipts from 1984 to 1987 were $636 million; Bolivia's, $1,014 million; the differences were consistent, both for bilateral and multilateral

aid, although in one year, 1986, Mexico received more bilateral aid than Bolivia did (OECD, *Geographical Distribution of Financial Flows, 1984–1987*, pp. 64–65, 192–93). Nigeria's aid receipts were $193 million; Botswana's, $649 million, with the difference consistent year by year, for bilateral and multilateral aid (ibid., pp. 210–11).

4. The special ties of Australia, the United States, and Japan with states near them, sometimes based on a colonial or near-colonial relationship, will be discussed later in the chapter.

5. The idea that the pursuit of global goals of order and peace, or even resistance to communism, was self-interested is not self-evident. In some cases, an ideological obsession may have lain behind U.S. policy; in others, attempts to create peace in the Middle East, to support Israel, or to resist communism may have been idealistic objectives for which the United States was willing to sacrifice. In other cases, strategic rivalry and preservation of the U.S. way of life may have been the goals. In still other cases, the existence of a domestic constituency concerned about Israel or Poland played a part. The facile assumption that U.S. opposition to communism or support for Israel and Egypt in an attempt to secure peace in the Middle East simply reflected pursuit of strategic interests needs reexamination. However, such support was not based on concern about economic development or poverty, and for the purposes of the argument here, I treat it as simply self-interested, realpolitik behavior.

6. DAC reports have often included two lines for French aid figures, one including DOM and TOM, the other excluding them.

7. McKinlay, for instance, reports that around 94% of French aid went to former colonies in 1964–66, the years immediately following the end of France's colonial empire. As he details, there was certainly also a French trade interest in these former colonies. However, the percentage of French aid to former colonies began to fall sharply in the late sixties, reaching 73% by 1970 according to his figures (1979, "The Aid Relationship," p. 428).

8. This is discussed in more detail in chap. 5.

9. Martha Loufti 1973, *The Net Cost of Japanese Foreign Aid*, argues this, noting Prime Minister Sato's talk of Japanese "moral responsibility" in the area of aid. This and other elements of Japanese aid are discussed further in chap. 5.

10. See discussion in Yasutomo 1986, *The Manner of Giving*, pp. 9–10.

11. Orr 1990, *The Emergence of Japan's Foreign Aid Power*.

12. Figures from OECD, *Development Cooperation*, various years.

13. Orr 1990, *The Emergence of Japan's Foreign Aid Power*, table 3.2, p. 67.

14. McKinlay and Mughan 1984, *Aid and Arms to the Third World*, tables, pp. 42 and 46, and discussion, pp. 34ff., 42–46.

15. Israel's GNP per capita was reckoned as $3,923 in 1976, according to OECD statistics (*Geographical Distribution of Financial Flows 1971–1977*, p. 109). It is classed as an LDC but is really in an intermediate range, closer to Italy than to Brazil, say. To say Israel is supported *as an ally* because of the military threats it faces is not to say anything about *why* the United States chooses such an ally, nor to deny nor assert whether such a move is laudable or self-interested.

16. McKinlay and Mughan 1984, *Aid and Arms to the Third World*; Maizels and Nissanke 1984, "Motivations for Aid to Developing Countries"; Poe 1991,

"U.S. Economic Aid Allocation"; Bencivenga 1984, "An Econometric Model of the Geographical Distribution of Foreign Aid."

17. McKinlay and Mughan's (1984) chapters on power capabilities, competition with communism, economic structure and performance, and political structure and performance include eleven, twenty-nine, thirty-five, and thirteen possible variables, respectively. Their book is concerned with arms transfers and military assistance, which I do not discuss, as much as with economic foreign aid.

18. A positive correlation with poverty here means a positive correlation with the reciprocal of per capita GNP, or a negative correlation with per capita GNP or its log. One gets similar results with all three measures. Because one expects aid to rise more for very poor countries, if need is the criterion, and to lessen gradually as recipient income rises without some special crossover point to "negative poverty," curvilinear measures such as log GNPC or 1/GNPC should be expected to fit better than a negative correlation with untransformed GNPC, and they do. Again, in constructing a measure of need as poverty times population, the measure –GNPC times population simply comes out as –GNP, which ignores the population whose needs the income must meet, while 1/GNPC times population makes more sense. A strong case can be made for a suitable constant minus log GNPC as an even better measure, but the determination of the constant would involve long and questionable calculation, so I have stayed with the easier and more intuitive inverse of per capita income.

19. The figures are taken from Sanford 1989, "The World Bank and Poverty."

20. McKinlay and Mughan 1984, *Aid and Arms to the Third World*, p. 42.

21. The same thing emerges from the interesting analysis of McGillivray 1989, "The Allocation of Aid," pp. 561–68. McGillivray develops an index for each donor in each year from 1969 to 1984, weighting the per capita aid to a recipient as a fraction of that donor's overall aid per capita to the Third World by the poverty of the recipient, calculated as the place where its GNP per capita falls between that of the poorest and that of the wealthiest recipient in that year. A donor that concentrated all its aid on the poorest recipient would score 100 on McGillivray's index; a donor that concentrated all its aid on the recipient with the highest per capita GNP would score 0. McGillivray is interested in evaluating the relative aid-giving performance of the donors; but it is interesting that the DAC countries generally score very high, with four in the 90s and seven in the 80s for the period as a whole. Only the United States is under 70, and it scores 63. Multilateral aid from all agencies scores 86.

22. Auerbach 1976, "The Distribution of Multilateral Assistance," pp. 644–59. Auerbach studies three UN programs—WHO, EPTA, and the UN Special Fund—and also the aid from the IDA and the IBRD. The IBRD gives more loans to more advanced LDCs, but its loans are not counted as aid by the criteria of this book, since they are not concessional lending.

23. The 1969–70 figures are computed from OECD *Geographic Distribution of Financial Flows, 1969–1975*. The later figures are taken from Sanford 1988, "The World Bank and Poverty." The whole article is most relevant, as is the 1989 follow-up article, "The World Bank and Poverty."

24. Dowling and Hiemenz 1985, "Biases in the Allocation of Foreign Aid."

25. Maizels and Nissanke 1984, "Motivations for Aid to Developing Countries."

26. Bencivenga 1985b, "Motives for Bilateral OECD Aid," summarizing her 1984 dissertation, "An Econometric Model of the Geographical Distribution of Foreign Aid." Bencivenga's results are also developed in a different way in another paper, 1985a, "Explaining the Foreign Aid Policies of the OECD Donors." I draw here only on the "Motives" paper.

27. Bencivenga does not discuss the relative size of grants and loans in the aid of the donors; I put these figures, computed from the Overall Total tables from *Geographical Distribution of Financial Flows*, various years, into the discussion, which otherwise follows pp. 14–35 of her 1985b, "Motives for Bilateral OECD Aid." In discussing her work, I also lay substantially more stress than she does upon the extent to which poverty was a motivation. She explores many other factors.

28. It is impossible to sum up in detail the already very compressed fifteen to twenty page summary Bencivenga gives of her most interesting results, which test population, GNP, GNP growth rate, foreign exchange as a proportion of imports, exchange rates, economic ties with the communist bloc, borders on the communist bloc, trade, party legitimacy, historic ties with the donor, production of strategic commodities, and percentage of the population that is Muslim. The latter two factors were rarely of any importance.

29. Little 1982, Economic Development, p. 329.

CHAPTER FOUR

1. Goodin 1985, *Protecting the Vulnerable*, p. 154.

2. It is possible to take issue with this contention. One might argue that states with *less* trade and investment in the Third World had more to gain in the sense that they had more room to develop these things, to grow in trade and investment. However, the relative levels of trade and investment have not changed fast enough, over the last forty years, to make that a very plausible argument.

3. Swiss aid was less than .1% of GNP until 1968, and less than .2% of GNP until 1978, lowest in all the DAC except for Finland.

4. Spain and Portugal had had vast colonial empires but lost most of their possessions in the nineteenth century; these two countries were not long-term donor members of an aid regime. Portugal began an aid program to its colonies and former colonies and was originally a member of the DAC, but soon dropped out.

5. This presumes that French aid to its overseas dominions and territories (DOM and TOM) is not counted as aid. If the money spent on these overseas parts of France is included, French aid was fairly high as a percentage of GNP, although not at the top.

6. Other small states were less supportive of aid, however; size alone did not seem to be a good predictor.

7. The data for France, Belgium, the Netherlands, Germany, Italy, Luxembourg, Denmark, Ireland, and the United Kingdom are from the work of Rabier et al. 1983, *Euro-Barometer 20: Aid to Developing Nations*, codebook. The

codebook comes as part of a data tape made available through the Inter-University Consortium for Political and Social Research, Ann Arbor, Michigan. The ICPSR edition of the data is from 1984, ICPSR no. 8234. The data for the United States, Australia, and New Zealand, and the vague report about data from Austria, are from OECD, *Development Cooperation, 1984*, pp. 125ff. The question in the Euro-Barometer survey is whether respondents favor giving aid to Third World countries (variable 127); the *Development Cooperation* review of public opinion does not give the wording of the questions but question wording appears to have been roughly comparable. One British survey mentioned there gives percentages almost identical to those of the Euro-Barometer survey.

8. Mosley 1985, "The Political Economy of Foreign Aid." There are additional useful observations in chap. 3 of Mosley's 1987 book, *Foreign Aid*, which also summarizes the results of the article.

9. Robertson 1984, "Foreign Aid and Political-Economic Change in Advanced Industrial States," finds that the level of aid funding for eleven donors tends to increase in response to economic growth and budget surpluses and to decrease in response to higher levels of donor unemployment; however, aid to poorer LDCs shows less fluctuation than does aid to higher income LDCs. Robertson uses a pooled time-series analysis, and uses a transformation of gross ODA transfers as his dependent variable.

10. See the detailed discussion of party support for aid in chap. 5, which gives further indications that parties associated with labor and commitment to domestic alleviation of poverty tend to increase the quantity and improve the quality of foreign economic assistance.

11. OECD, *Development Cooperation, 1985*, p. 131. Accurate figures on social spending are difficult to get. The figures given in *Development Cooperation* appear to be somewhat at variance with those given in OECD 1988, *The Future of Social Protection*; these in turn are somewhat different from the figures in OECD 1985, *Social Expenditure, 1960–1990*.

12. As discussed later in the chapter, France's participation as a donor depends a great deal on what you count. If "aid" to DOM and TOM, really parts of France in effect, are excluded, the French level of contribution goes down markedly.

13. This point is discussed in OECD, *Development Cooperation, 1984*, pp. 135–40.

14. *R*-squared values are sometimes higher, sometimes lower, if one uses a dependent variable that includes aid to DOM and TOM for France. In years prior to 1978 other than 1970 and 1975 there are not good figures available for French aid spending excluding DOM and TOM, but it is possible to make a fairly good guess for years going back to 1970.

15. See OECD, *Development Cooperation, 1985*, p. 295.

16. See, for instance, Forsythe 1977, *Humanitarian Politics*.

17. The United States was completely exceptional in substantially decreasing its aid as a share of GNP by as much as 50%. The colonial powers initially gave a great deal of aid, largely directed to their former colonies, and then decreased their aid; subsequently, they have reincreased their aid without such a strong colonial focus.

18. See the discussion and figures in OECD, *Development Cooperation, 1984*, pp. 113–22.

19. Specifically, 44.7% in 1970, 49.2% in 1975, and 59.6% in 1980 (OECD, *Development Cooperation, 1990*, p. 243).

20. These are mid-1980s figures.

21. Figures are primarily from OECD, *Development Cooperation*, 1984 and 1990 tables, and OECD, *Geographical Distribution of Financial Flows*, various years, ending with the 1984–87 edition. Useful historical data in the 1990 edition of *Development Cooperation* are on pp. 186–87 and 242–45, and in the 1984 edition, pp. 235–39.

## CHAPTER FIVE

1. Humphrey [1963] 1964, *The Cause is Mankind*, pp. 83–84.

2. Goldwater [1960] 1961, *Conscience of a Conservative*, pp. 97–98, 101–2.

3. This topic is discussed further in chaps. 1 and 9. Construing "national interest" in this way seems logically incompatible with Realist or rational-egoist logic. To think of states as calculating, hard-shelled actors is to presume that they perceive interests in terms of what enhances their own strength and prosperity, not in terms of some general worldwide interest or compassion for the needy.

Similarly, a general concern for the esteem of other nations does not make sense in terms of a logic of Realist calculations or rational egoism. If the esteem of other countries could be translated into concrete advantages, then nations would be justified on self-interested grounds in seeking such esteem, to be sure; but there is no reason, if nations behave as rational egoists, why they would respond more favorably toward a nation that had garnered general, or ethical, esteem. This is a matter quite different from the advantages to be gotten from a reputation for, say, military and diplomatic toughness, or from a reputation as a cooperative, reliable, and reasonable partner in joint ventures. These reputations should affect the calculation that another self-interested state makes about dealing with one's own state; a reputation as a compassionate country, or as a good citizen, should not, for it will not make one a better partner with or a fiercer antagonist to the state that contemplates dealings with it. Yet the evidence suggests that countries cared about their general image, and wanted to conform to behavior expected of developed states and of other sets of countries they considered reference groups.

It can be argued, of course, that concern with social esteem, altruism, and so on arise in human beings either as a way of securing interests in a complex interaction situation or as a result of evolutionary selection that rewards intragroup altruism. Or one can argue that various emotions not directed toward doing well in the immediate situation provide, in the long term, resources for surviving better (Frank 1988, *Passions within Reason*). Actually, I am skeptical, but the issue is not of great relevance to the question of whether moral and social factors matter in international relations. The claim that the international realm is one unlike the domestic and interpersonal realm of relationships, social consciousness, broad norms, diffuse reciprocity, and moral values, but is instead a realm of naked, though perhaps carefully negotiated, calculating egoism cannot be defended by saying that there is, after all, a self-interested basis, prospective or evolutionary, for moral and social conscience in domestic society. The crucial claim about self-interest that Realist theories of international politics make is not that, ultimately, all the things that appear as moral arose in an obscure way from self-interest, but that the international realm is unlike domestic society precisely in that all elements of moral and social conscience which are at work in the latter are not at work in international politics. To hold that countries are concerned about their image as good citizens is to acknowledge that they are, however selfishly, swayed by moral considerations: it is to recognize that virtue is capable of levying tribute from countries in the international system, tribute that affects behavior in a way not too much compromised by the degree of sincerity of the tribute. And this, not that nations are saintly in motivation, is what I claim and what Realism, and what claims that states are only rational egoists, deny.

4. Rabier et al. 1985, *Euro-Barometer 20*, p. 35. All figures in this paragraph, unless specified, are unweighted averages for all respondents in the survey. Support was high in each of the eight DAC countries in the survey: Germany, France, Britain, Italy, the Netherlands, Belgium, Denmark, and Ireland.

5. Ibid., p. 34.

6. For this and the next two paragraphs, OECD, *Development Cooperation, 1984*, pp. 127–31. Austria is the weakest European donor except that Ireland, a DAC member only since 1985 and itself near Third World levels of GNP per capita, has lower aid volume as a percentage of GNP.

7. Laudicina 1973, *World Poverty and Development*.

8. Wittkopf 1990, *Faces of Internationalism*, pp. 70–76.

9. OECD, *Development Cooperation, 1984*, p. 131.

10. Ibid., pp. 128–31.

11. Rauta 1971, *Aid and Overseas Development*.

12. OECD, *Development Cooperation, 1984*, pp. 135–40.

13. Computations from Rabier et al. 1985, *Euro-Barometer 20*, and 1983, *Euro-Barometer 13*, are discussed more fully below. The countries surveyed in 1983 included two non-DAC countries, Greece and Luxembourg.

14. Laudicina 1973, *World Poverty and Development*, pp. 68–77. This result is particularly interesting since respondents from lower socioeconomic status backgrounds tend, in survey after survey, to be less favorable to aid than are those with higher income, higher status jobs, and more education; and union households were, generally in the lower status group. Thus, it appears that labor solidarity in a domestic context overcame other factors which might predispose people against aid.

15. Rauta 1971, *Aid and Overseas Development*, pp. 55–63; Laudicina 1973, *World Poverty and Development*, pp. 10, 21; Lindholm 1971, *The Image of the Developing Countries*, pp. 95–100.

16. These strong findings by Wittkopf 1990, *Faces of Internationalism*, are consistent with those in a brief report by Reilly 1983, *American Public Opinion and U.S. Foreign Policy*, and with surveys noted in OECD, *Development Cooperation*. These finding, as well as confirming evidence in Everts 1983, *Public Opinion, the Churches, and Foreign Policy*, also suggest that elites are consistently stronger supporters of aid than is the general public.

17. The only exception was that nonreligious people on the right were inclined to decrease aid more than those without stated political convictions.

18. Lindholm 1971, *The Image of the Developing Countries*, pp. 98–100.

19. Laudicina 1973, *World Poverty and Development*, pp. 44, 42–43, 48.

20. Rauta 1971, *Aid and Overseas Development*, pp. 31–32.

21. Computed from Rabier 1985, *Euro-Barometer 20*.

22. The data from Wittkopf 1990, *Faces of Internationalism*, tables A.5.3 and A.5.4 provide a very doubtful basis for arguing that anticommunism was a strong motive in public support for aid. It is true that the questions in A.5.3 that mention communism as a motive get slightly stronger approval ratings on aid than those in A.5.4 which do not. The questions from the fifties not mentioning communism get a favorable response of 63% to 79%, averaging 71%; those which mention resisting communism get a favorable response rates of 69% to 90%, averaging 81%. But these questions with higher response rates also are far more specific, mentioning not just "economic aid" but "machinery and supplies," which might allay public concern lest the aid go to build palaces instead. The source of the difference is unclear. It is true that later questions from the seventies and eighties, not mentioning communism or machinery, receive lower favorable responses, but this appears to be a difference between the two time periods. It is also true that in the fifties a follow-up to the question that asks about aid to "friendly countries" asks about aid to countries "which have not joined us as allies against the Communists," and finds support for aid to these latter countries in the 40% to 53% range, with a 46% average, which is some 44% lower. But the follow-up of helping "friendly" countries with those said to fail to oppose communism presents both a misleading picture and a highly leading question. One cannot know whether the difference is due to a desire not to appear procommunist, due to confusion about whether the latter question refers to helping countries that will oppress their own people, or due to people's basing their support for foreign aid on resistance to communism rather than on humane concern.

23. Lindholm 1971, *The Image of the Developing Countries*, pp. 56–59.

24. Rauta 1971, *Aid and Overseas Development*, pp. 32–34.

25. Lindholm 1971, *The Image of the Developing Countries*, pp. 98–100.

26. This and the following discussion in the next several paragraphs are computed from the data of Rabier et al. 1985, *Euro-Barometer 20*.

27. That was most markedly true for those who did not see aid as a moral duty; and for those most inclined to see aid as a duty, there is some fluctuation as one moves from those more to those less inclined to see aid as in the national interest. Most interestingly, the "don't knows" on national interest, among those who most strongly saw aid as a duty, were the strongest group in saying aid should go to the poor nations and to the poor within recipient nations; this group may have been ambivalent about the own-interest statement, as I myself would be, because of a belief that aid was needed for world stability and peace conflicting with a wording that made the motive seem self-interested rather than principled.

28. Skuhra 1984, "Austrian Aid," p. 69.

29. Hofmeier and Schultz 1984, "German Aid," p. 235.

30. Forster 1984, "Swiss Aid," pp. 411–12.

31. Svendsen 1984, "Danish Aid," pp. 130, 135.

32. Kiljunen 1984, "Finnish Development Cooperation," p. 159.

33. Rippy 1958, "Historical Perspective," pp. 1–2. Rippy's quotations of church groups are from the Senate Special Committee to Study the Foreign Aid Program, 85th Cong., 1st sess., Hearings 1957: "The Foreign Aid Program," pp. 555–56, 656, and 710.

34. Castle 1957, *The Great Giveaway*, pp. 157–58, 164–65, 167–68.

35. Orr 1990, *The Emergence of Japan's Foreign Aid Power*, p. 42.

36. Hoadley 1989, *The New Zealand Foreign Affairs Handbook*, pp. 60–61.

37. Eldridge 1980, "Diplomacy, Development and 'Small Government,' " pp. 20–24, 47–48, 50, 51.

38. Horesh 1984, "British Aid," p. 112.

39. Stamp 1982, "Oxfam and Development," pp. 100–101.

40. O'Neill 1984, "Irish Aid," p. 239.

41. Sharp 1990, *Irish Foreign Policy and the European Community*, p. 171.

42. Pratt 1989b, "Canada," p. 50.

43. B. Wood 1982, "Canada and Third World Development," p. 108.

44. Vogler 1988, "Britain and North-South Relations," pp. 199–200.

45. Horesh 1984, "British Aid," pp. 113–14.

46. Vogler 1988, "Britain and North-South Relations," pp. 197, 200–201.

47. Horesh 1984, "British Aid," pp. 125–26.

48. Hoadley 1989, *The New Zealand Foreign Affairs Handbook*, p. 60.

49. Eldridge 1980, "Diplomacy, Development and 'Small Government,' " p. 19.

50. The DAC figures for Canadian aid are found in table 4.6.

51. Pratt 1989b, "Canada," pp. 38, 44, 39, 59.

52. Goldwater [1960] 1961, *Conscience of a Conservative*, pp. 97, 101.

53. Humphrey [1964] 1965, *The Cause is Mankind*, pp. 83–84, 85, 86, 91, 83, 82, 83.

54. Berthelot and Besnaiou 1983, "France's New Third World Policy," pp. 33–34.

55. Hugon 1984, "French Development Cooperation," p. 200. Vivien's comment is not surprising in view of the colonial motives behind early French aid, such as the observation from de Gaulle's *Memoires* quoted by Hugon: "I resolved to clear away the obligations . . . imposed on her by her empire, but in order to avoid a foreign (American or Soviet) influence replacing that of France, so that the African peoples should speak our language and share our culture, we should help them," or the remark of G. Pompidou to the French assembly in 1964 defining development cooperation as "the follow-up to Europe's expansionist policy of the 19th century, which is marked by the creation or expansion of vast, colonial empires" (p. 202, n. 4).

56. Berthelot and Besnaiou 1983, "France's New Third World Policy," pp. 28–29.

57. OECD, *Development Cooperation, 1990*, p. 188.

58. Berthelot and Besnaiou 1983, "France's New Third World Policy," pp. 35, 38.

59. Hofmeier and Schultz 1984, "German Aid," pp. 208–9, 232, 211, 214, 234. The quotations are not from the 1982 document or the Brandt Report but from the authors' summaries. The Brandt Commission Report is Brandt Commission 1980, *North-South*.

60. Skuhra 1984, "Austrian Aid," pp. 67–68.

61. Renard 1984, "Belgian Aid," p. 93.

62. Forster 1984, "Swiss Aid," pp. 411–12.

63. Bertholet et al. 1984, "Dutch Development Cooperation," pp. 304ff.

64. Dore 1982, "Japan and the Third World," pp. 132–33. However, as Orr notes, Japanese aid has been improving in quality and quantity since 1979 (1990, *The Emergence of Japan's Foreign Aid Power*, pp. 55–57).

65. Stokke 1984, "Norwegian Aid," pp. 351, 353 n. 6, 353 n. 9.

66. Jellinek et al. 1984, "Swedish Aid," pp. 390, 387, 389.

67. Södersten 1989, "Sweden," pp. 175, 188–89.

68. Kiljunen 1984, "Finnish Development Cooperation," pp. 161–62.

69. Svendsen 1984, "Danish Aid," pp. 129–30.

70. Forster 1984, "Swiss Aid," pp. 397, 399; the latter quote taken from Swiss legislation enacted March 19, 1976.

71. Horesh 1984, "British Aid," pp. 113, 123–24 (quoting the government white paper of 1975, *More Help for the Poorest*), 125.

72. Bertholet et al. 1984, "Dutch Development Cooperation," pp. 313–14.

73. Alessandrini 1984, "Italian Aid," pp. 267, 265–66, 264, 267, 266.

74. Hofmeier and Schultz 1984, "German Aid," p. 214.

75. B. Smith 1990, *More than Altruism*.

76. Renard 1984, "Belgian Aid," pp. 90–91.

77. Eldridge 1980, "Diplomacy, Development and 'Small Government,'" pp. 17–20.

78. Skuhra 1984, "Austrian Aid," p. 67.

79. Packenham 1971, *Liberal America and the Third World*, p. 288.

80. Quoted in Forster 1984, "Swiss Aid," p. 399.

81. Skuhra 1984, "Austrian Aid," pp. 65–66.

82. Renard 1984, "Belgian Aid," pp. 90–91.

83. Clunies Ross 1969, "Economic Responses and the Question of Foreign Aid," p. 100.

84. Horesh 1984, "British Aid," p. 112.

85. Vogler 1988, "Britain and North-South Relations," p. 211.

86. O'Neill 1984, "Irish Aid," p. 244.

87. Bertholet et al. 1984, "Dutch Development Cooperation," p. 290.

88. Brandt 1986, *World Armament and World Hunger*, p. 16.

89. Kiljunen 1984, "Finnish Development Cooperation," pp. 155–56.

90. Södersten 1989, "Sweden," pp. 155, 157.

91. Scott 1969, "Some Aspects of Overseas Aid," pp. 117–19.

92. Stokke 1984, "Norwegian Aid," pp. 318–19, 349.

93. O'Neill 1984, "Irish Aid," pp. 243–44, 241.

94. Sharp 1990, *Irish Foreign Policy and the European Community*, pp. 169, 172. Sharp is sarcastic and cynical in general, and sees Irish aid as a manipulative ploy. His arguments are extremely unconvincing. First, he contradicts himself: he

is cynical because the program was so initially multilateral, the bilateral segment increased, and the multilateral segment was kept when the bilateral had to be cut back. Second, he gives no evidence, save noting that there seem to have been rare but occasional references to the possibility of trade gains from aid. Most importantly, he has no consistent argument to account for the aid, or for the great values that Ireland was to have gained from it. The whole view presupposes that a "distinctive position" matters; but this seems incompatible with the view that nations act cynically, which Sharp appears, at least in Ireland's case, to hold.

95. O'Neill 1984, "Irish Aid," p. 240.

96. Forster 1984, "Swiss Aid," pp. 397, 398.

97. Bertholet et al. 1984, "Dutch Development Cooperation," p. 288.

98. Skuhra 1984, "Austrian Aid," p. 68.

99. Vogler 1988, "Britain and North-South Relations," p. 200.

100. Cassen et al. 1982, "Overview," pp. 13–14, 18.

101. Loufti 1973, *The Net Cost of Japanese Foreign Aid*, pp. 49–50.

102. Farnsworth 1981, "Japan and the Third World," p. 176.

103. Dore 1982, "Japan and the Third World," pp. 130, 135.

104. Yasutomo 1986, *The Manner of Giving*, pp. 112–13, 124, 14.

105. Orr 1990, *The Emergence of Japan's Foreign Aid Power*, pp. 145–46.

106. Haruhiro Fukui 1987, "Too Many Captains in Japan's Internationalization," *Journal of Japanese Studies* 13, 1, p. 361, quoted by Orr 1990, *The Emergence of Japan's Foreign Aid Power*, p. 137.

107. Loufti 1973, *The Net Cost of Japanese Foreign Aid*, pp. 47–49.

108. Farnsworth 1981, "Japan and the Third World," p. 177–78.

109. Dore 1982, "Japan and the Third World," p. 135.

110. Yasutomo 1986, *The Manner of Giving*, pp. 113, 14.

111. William L. Brooks and Robert M. Orr, Jr., 1985, "Japan's Foreign Economic Assistance," *Asian Survey* 25 (March), cited by Yasutomo 1986, *The Manner of Giving*, p. 10.

112. Orr 1990, *The Emergence of Japan's Foreign Aid Power*, p. 95.

113. Kiljunen 1984, "Finnish Development Cooperation," pp. 151, 162.

114. Raucher 1985, *Paul G. Hoffman*, p. 136. The passage about the arguments Hoffman felt and used, starting p. 137, is also most interesting.

115. Skuhra 1984, "Austrian Aid," p. 67.

116. Bertholet et al. 1984, "Dutch Development Cooperation," p. 288.

CHAPTER SIX

1. H. Wilson 1953, *The War on World Poverty: An Appeal to the Conscience of Mankind*, p. 203.

2. T. Wilson and D. Wilson 1982, *The Political Economy of the Welfare State*, pp. 43–44. In Britain, for example, welfare costs in 1900 were 2.6% of GNP; in 1979, 20.4% of GDP, excluding education.

3. Some surveys and analyses of these developments can be found in Flora and Heidenheimer 1981, *The Development of Welfare States in Europe and America*; Hage et al. 1989, *State Responsiveness and State Activism*; P. Baldwin 1990, *The Politics of Social Solidarity*; Einhorn and Logue 1988, *Modern Welfare States*;

and DeSario 1989, *International Public Policy Sourcebook*. Dixon and Scheurell 1989, *Social Welfare in Developed Market Countries*, give timelines and summaries of the development of social welfare in ten developed countries. For developments since 1945, see Flora 1986, *Growth to Limits*.

4. The phrase is the title of the fourth chapter in Tawney [1931] 1965, *Equality*. Tawney, in the work just mentioned, and Richard M. Titmuss in his introduction to the 1965 edition of Tawney's book, pp. 9–24, see the extension of social services as reflecting an egalitarian, pro-Labour, democratic ideology and as opposed by what Tawney termed the "religion of inequality."

5. Goodin 1985, *Protecting the Vulnerable*, especially p. 147. Goodin quotes Robson 1976, *Welfare State and Welfare Society*, p. 21, and Titmuss, 1958b, "The Social Division of Welfare," pp. 42–43.

6. The paragraph follows and quotes from Freeman 1989, "Social Welfare Policy: France," pp. 220–21.

7. Hayward 1959, "Solidarity: The History of an Idea in Nineteenth-Century France," p. 277, quoted by Freeman 1989, "Social Welfare Policy: France," p. 220.

8. Flora and Heidenheimer 1981, *The Development of Welfare States in Europe and America*, pp. 18, 9, 9.

9. Rich 1977, *The Age of Nationalism and Reform*, pp. 224–25. See also Flora and Heidenheimer 1981, *The Development of Welfare States in Europe and America*, p. 19.

10. Holland 1989, "Social Welfare Policy: Germany," p. 201.

11. Stone 1984, *The Disabled State*, p. 56., in Holland 1989, "Social Welfare Policy: Germany," p. 202.

12. Einhorn and Logue 1988, *Modern Welfare States*, pp. 132–33; and Dixon and Scheurell 1989, *Social Welfare in Developed Market Countries*, pp. 347–48.

13. Bartholomew 1989, "Social Welfare Policy: Canada," pp. 186ff.

14. Dixon and Scheurell 1989, *Social Welfare in Developed Market Countries*, p. 311. Also, see Gilbert 1984, *The End of the European Era*, p. 48; and Havighurst 1979, *Britain in Transition*, pp. 90–104.

15. Dixon and Scheurell 1989, *Social Welfare in Developed Market Countries*, pp. 311–12.

16. Flora and Heidenheimer 1981, *The Development of Welfare States in Europe and America*, p. 19.

17. Einhorn and Logue 1988, *Modern Welfare States*, pp. 140–42.

18. Flora 1986, *Growth to Limits*, p. xv.

19. Myrdal 1973, *Against the Stream*, p. 40.

20. Goodin 1985, *Protecting the Vulnerable*, pp. 147, 149, 150.

21. Myrdal [1958] 1960, *Beyond the Welfare State*, pp. 227–28.

22. Myrdal 1973, *Against the Stream*, pp. 45–47 and 50.

23. Myrdal [1958] 1960, *Beyond the Welfare State*, p. 227

24. Myrdal 1973, *Against the Stream*, p. 47.

25. Havighurst 1979, *Britain in Transition*, p. 14. See also Seebohm Rowntree's 1901 study of York, *Poverty: A Study of Town Life*, cited ibid., p. 47. Other quotations and figures in the order they appear, ibid., pp. 13, 49, 52, 13, 34, 51.

26. Bremner 1956, *From the Depths*, pp. 16–30, 86–120, 123–39, 140–63.

27. Henry May 1949, *Protestant Churches and Industrial America*.

28. Antonides 1985, *Stones for Bread*, p. 24.

29. Carter 1954, *The Decline and Revival of the Social Gospel*, pp. 220ff., 189.

30. A. Davis 1967, *Spearheads for Reform*, from foreword by Richard Wade; cf. p. 14.

31. Bremner 1956, *From the Depths*, pp. 204–29, 230–43, 244–59.

32. Bremner 1960, *American Philanthropy*, pp. 117, 121.

33. For example, Carnegie 1909, *Armaments and Their Results*.

34. Carter 1954, *Decline and Revival of the Social Gospel*, p. 189.

35. In Addams 1922, "Peace and Bread in Time of War," pp. 243–44.

36. International Labour Organization 1969, *The ILO in the Service of Social Progress*, pp. 2, 22–24. The book quotes figures from the *International Labour Review* of 1921 for trade union membership in 1913.

37. Patterson and Thomas 1977, *Social Democratic Parties in Western Europe*, p. 12.

38. Crosland 1975, "Social Democracy in Europe," ibid., p. 11.

39. Einhorn and Logue 1988, *Modern Welfare States*, p. 74.

40. Minkin and Seyd 1977, "The British Labour Party," pp. 107–8.

41. Havighurst 1977, *Britain in Transition*, p. 139.

42. J. May 1977, "Cooperation between Socialist Parties," pp. 408–11, 423, with original emphasis. May cites the "doctrine of fellowship" idea from Beer 1964, *Modern British Politics*, p. 238, as well as an undated tract by Rose, *The Socialist International*, p. 5.

43. Nicholson 1986, *The TUC Overseas*, pp. 215–53; quotes from p. 262.

44. Mangone 1954, *A Short History of International Organization*, pp. 34–66, 67–97. A much larger number of conferences than Mangone cites on p. 93 is cited by White 1951, *International Non-Governmental Organizations*, p. 214, drawing on Shenton, 1933, *Cosmopolitan Conversation*, who in turn draws on *Annuaire de la vie Internationale*, Brussels, 1908–11.

45. Judge 1978, "International Institutions," pp. 81–83. Judge's tables are drawn from J. David Singer and Michael Wallace 1970, "Intergovernmental Organizations and the Preservation of Peace, 1816–1964: Some Bivariate Relationships," *International Organization* 24, 3; Michael Wallace and J. David Singer 1970, "Intergovernmental Organizations in the Global System, 1815–1964: A Quantitative Description," *International Organization* 24, 2; Kjell Skjelsbaek 1970, "Development of the Systems of International Organizations: A Diachronic Study," in *Proceedings of the International Peace Research Association Third General Conference*, vol. 2, *The International System*, IPRA Studies in Peace Research, no. 4, Assen, Netherlands: van Gorcum and Co.; Edwin H. Fedder, ed., 1971, *The United Nations: Problems and Prospects*, St. Louis: Center for International Studies, University of Missouri; and from various issues of the *Yearbook of International Organizations*.

46. Mangone 1954, *A Short History of International Organization*, pp. 98–125. White 1951, *International Non-Governmental Organizations*, notes the role

of various peace conferences held from 1843 on, and especially of the Inter-Parliamentary Union of 1888 and the International Peace Bureau of 1892, in preparing the way for the Hague Conferences of 1899 and 1907.

47. Pictet [1982], *Development and Principles on International Humanitarian Assistance*, p. 25. Pictet seems largely to follow Bossier 1953, *Histoire du comité international de la Croix-Rouge*, Paris, vol. 1; but he also notes Dunant [1862] 1939, *A Memory of Solferino*.

48. Pictet [1982] *Development and Principles on International Humanitarian Assistance*, pp. 17, 25–26. A similar account is given in Draper 1988, "The Development of International Humanitarian Law," pp. 67–90. Draper sets his account in a movement of development of laws of warfare in which Grotius and Rousseau were both important.

49. International Committee of the Red Cross and League of Red Cross Societies, 1983, *International Red Cross Handbook*, annex 1, p. 711.

50. The current Red Cross movement has a rather complex structure, detailed in "Red Cross and Humanitarian Assistance" in Macalister-Smith 1985b, *International Humanitarian Assistance*. There is a separate chapter on wartime relief efforts of the Red Cross. He states that "broadly, the ICRC has responsibility for international assistance during armed conflict while the League is concerned with peacetime relief" (p. 78).

51. Willemin and Heacock 1984, *The International Committee of the Red Cross*, p. 19. Non-European nations have always been free to join, and many have done so, starting with Ottoman Turkey in 1868, Peru in 1879, and Japan in 1886. See also Kalshoven 1988, *Assisting the Victims of Armed Conflict and Other Disasters*, and Pakistan Red Crescent Society (Punjab Provincial Branch, Lahore), [1981] *Dissemination of International Humanitarian Law*.

52. Pictet [1982], *Development and Principles on International Humanitarian Assistance*, pp. 87–88. In view of the early restrictions placed on the Office of the UN High Commissioner for Refugees, the ICRC made a statement in 1951 considering the refugee problem in strictly humanitarian terms and opening a great field of potential involvement for the movement. The motto *per humanitatem ad pacem* means "through humanitarianism to peace" or "through recognition of our common humanity to peace."

53. Jones 1939, *The Scandinavian States and the League of Nations*, p. 273.

54. Zarjevsky 1988, *A Future Preserved*, pp. 8, 17.

55. Ibid., pp. xi–xiii. Hartling makes reference here, also, to *Fridtjof Nansen*, by Fritz Wartenweiler.

56. Bremner 1960, *American Philanthropy*, pp. 127, 134, 167, 169–70, 172.

57. Curti and Birr 1954, *Prelude to Point Four*. There is also a brief discussion in Glick 1957, *The Administration of Technical Assistance*.

58. White 1951, *International Non-Governmental Organizations*.

59. Curti 1963, *American Philanthropy Abroad*, pp. 9–13, 22–64, 99, 148–71, 224–58.

60. Romanofsky 1978, *Social Service Organizations*, pp. 63ff., 56–57.

61. Curti 1963, *American Philanthropy Abroad*, p. 301.

62. Maddox 1956, *Technical Assistance by Religious Agencies in Latin America*, pp. 1, 27.

63. Bremner 1960, *American Philanthropy*, p. 182.

64. Bock 1954, *Fifty Years of Technical Assistance*, p. 3.

65. Curti 1963, *American Philanthropy Abroad*, p. 625. Also, pp. 575–76 document the reevaluation and rededication of American and European missionaries after World Wars I and II, learning to tailor programs to the needs of indigenous peoples. Chap. 11, "Searches for International Peace and Progress," pp. 301–38, reviews the increasing efforts in this direction.

66. Mangone 1954, *A Short History of International Organization*, p. 224, taken from Perigord 1926, *The International Labor Organization*.

67. International Labour Organization 1969, *The ILO in the Service of Social Progress*, p. 30.

68. Ghebali 1989, *The International Labour Organization*, pp. 2–4.

69. Mangone 1954, *A Short History of International Organization*, p. 224.

70. International Labour Organization 1969, *The ILO in the Service of Social Progress*, pp. 33 and 35.

71. Ghebali 1989, *The International Labour Organization*.

72. Ibid.

73. International Labour Organization 1969, *The ILO in the Service of Social Progress*, p. 2.

74. Ibid.

75. Ghebali 1989, *The International Labour Organization*, p. 11. The second quotation is from the 1941 conference itself.

76. The Philadelphia Declaration is reprinted in full in the appendix of International Labour Organization 1969, *The ILO in the Service of Social Progress*, pp. 207–9.

77. Hinsley 1973, *Nationalism and the International System*, pp. 107–9. The second quotation is from a protocol to an 1831 conference on the future of Belgium.

78. White 1951, *International Non-Governmental Organizations*, pp. 214–15. The quotation is from A. C. F. Beales 1931, *History of Peace*, pp. 259–62, whom White cites, and not from Carnegie's letter itself. See also, Tarlton 1964, *Internationalism, War, and Politics in American Thought*.

79. *Statutes of the Inter-Parliamentary Union*, article 1, quoted in White 1951, *International Non-Governmental Organizations*, pp. 214–17.

80. Russell 1917, "National Independence and Internationalism," in *Political Ideals*, pp. 169, 155.

81. Christian L. Lange 1937, "Introduction, Part I," in *Resolutions Adopted by Interparliamentary Conferences and Principal Decisions of the Council, 1911–1936*, p. 13, quoted in White 1951, *International Non-Governmental Organizations*, p. 217.

82. Beales 1931, *History of Peace*, pp. 281–82, quoted in White 1951, *International Non-Governmental Organizations*, p. 219.

83. Mangone 1954, *A Short History of International Organization*, p. 129.

84. Beales 1931, *History of Peace*, p. 299, quoted in White 1951, *International Non-Governmental Organizations*, p. 219.

85. Mangone 1954, *A Short History of International Organization*, pp. 220ff. Further information about these can be found in a box of International Federa-

tion of League of Nations Societies Bulletins, Ozd 844 In 8d, Mudd Library, Yale University and a folder with a booklet of Proceedings and Resolutions from the Plenary Congress of the International Federation of League of Nations Societies, Ozd 844 In 8a, ibid.

86. Russell and Russell 1923, *The Prospects of Industrial Civilization*, pp. 77, 97.

87. Roemer 1929, *The Ethical Basis of International Law*, p. 163.

88. International Missionary Council 1934, *The International Missionary Council*, pp. 11, 7. National (i.e., indigenous) church councils from China, India, Burma, Ceylon, Japan, Korea, the Philippines, and Siam attended, as did as eight or ten missionary councils of the Western countries.

89. Ibid., pp. 5–7.

90. Shivute 1980, *The Theology of Mission and Evangelism*, pp. 52–53ff.

91. Ibid., pp. 52, 55. The phrases quoted here only are Shivute's own.

92. Forward Movement Commission [1938] *"Into All The World."* The pamphlet itself is here quoting "Shaping the Future," by Basil Matthews.

93. J. Davis 1944, *The Preparation of Missionaries for Work in the Post-War Era*, pp. 8–9, 11.

94. World Council of Churches 1948a, *First Assembly of the World Council of Churches*, pp. 36, 59.

95. Ibid., pp. 60–61, 80–82. See also World Council of Churches, n.d. [early to middle fifties], "Refugees."

96. World Council of Churches 1948b, *The Ten Formative Years*, pp. 57–58.

97. World Council of Churches [1954], *Commission of the Churches on International Affairs*.

98. The rivalry between different commercial blocs, too, was a kind of division of the world that seemed to recapitulate in a different sphere the division of the world into blocs that had led to the first war.

99. Lewis 1949, *Economic Survey, 1919–1939*, pp. 199–201. The book follows lectures he had given from 1944 to 1947.

100. Arndt [1944] 1965, *The Economic Lessons of the Nineteen-Thirties*, pp. 295–98.

101. Cole 1932, *A Guide through World Chaos*, pp. 545–48.

102. Lorwin 1933, *The World Economic Conference and World Organization*, p. 14.

103. Carnegie Endowment for International Peace 1936, *World Economic Progress*.

104. Green 1957, "Expanding International Concern with Human Rights," p. 654. Both quotations are from the speech.

105. International Labour Organization 1950, *Fourth Report of the International Labour Organization to the United Nations*, pp. 25–26, quoted in Asher 1957, "Full Employment and Economic Stability," pp. 371–72.

106. Arndt 1987, *Economic Development*, pp. 43–44, who cites Harvey 1942, "War-Time Research in Great Britain on International Problems of Reconstruction," p. 164.

107. Hoover and Gibson 1942, "The Problems of Lasting Peace," p. 215; Welles 1943, "Blue-print for Peace," pp. 419ff.

108. World Citizens' Association 1941, *The World's Destiny and The United States*, p. 184.

109. This much-referred-to comment is discussed in Alcalde 1987, *The Idea of Third World Development*, pp. 141–142.

110. Willkie 1943, *One World*, pp. 11, 12, 126–27, 129, 148.

111. Lorwin 1941, *Economic Consequences of the Second World War*, pp. 484–85, 494–97.

112. Mather, 1944, *Enough and to Spare*, pp. 71, 83, 131, 137, 138–39, 143, 144, 143, 149.

113. Staley [1940] 1941, *This Shrinking World*, pp. 2, 54.

114. Hansen 1942, *Economic Problems of the Post-War World*, pp. 22–23. The pamphlet, designed for social studies teachers, sold for 30 cents.

115. The section begins "The elimination of large-scale unemployment must be undertaken through international collaboration and not alone by the separate action of individual countries. . . . If we do not deliberately adopt a wholly new attitude toward the problem of employment, economic frustration will again lead to chaos and war. International security will not be achieved merely by the defeat of the Axis powers, and it will not be maintained solely by the establishment and maintenance of an international police force. A well-rounded plan for international security needs also to contain a co-ordinated program of internal economic expansion in the major industrial countries for the purpose of promoting and maintaining full employment" (ibid., pp. 27–32).

116. Hoover and Gibson 1942, "The Problems of Lasting Peace," pp. 155, 239, 295, 296, 299, 313.

117. Welles 1943, "Blue-print for Peace," in *Prefaces to Peace*, pp. 428–29, 431, 433.

118. Quoted in Alcalde 1987, *The Idea of Third World Development*, p. 147.

119. Walters 1966, "The League of Nations," p. 39. See also articles in H. Davis 1944, *Pioneers in World Order*; and Kotshnig 1957, "Organizational Setting."

120. Brown 1957, "The Inheritance of the United Nations," pp. 153–99.

121. Yoder 1989, *The Evolution of the United Nations System*, pp. 14–15.

122. Brown 1957, "The Inheritance of the United Nations," pp. 153–99, esp. 159.

123. See Herbert May 1944, "Dangerous Drugs." Drug abuse control starting in 1912 and taken up by the League in 1925 is also described in Yoder 1989, *The Evolution of the United Nations System*, pp. 147–48.

124. Wellington Koo 1919, *China and the League of Nations*, pp. 7-16, cited in Van Soest 1978, *The Start of International Development Cooperation in the United Nations*, p. 4.

125. Boudreau 1945, "The International Food Movement," p. 15.

126. Grady 1944, "World Economics," pp. 162–63.

127. Brown 1957, "The Inheritance of the United Nations," p. 163.

128. Van Soest 1978, *The Start of International Development Cooperation in the United Nations*, p. 4.

129. Grady 1944, "World Economics," pp. 161–62.

130. The UNRRA was, of course, partly superseded by the larger American efforts at relief and reconstruction in the Marshall Plan. However, some of the functions specific to the relief of suffering were regrouped in UNICEF and in the office of the UN High Commissioner for Refugees, after the demise of the UNRRA.

131. Thus Grady writes: "The main task confronting national governments at the close of the present war will be to provide productive employment and high living standards for their people. It will be impossible to be secure unless means are devised for 'preventing or mitigating economic depressions'" (1944, "World Economics," pp. 163–64).

132. Gilchrist 1944, "Dependent Peoples and Mandates," pp. 135–38, 123.

133. Sady 1957, "Colonial Setting of the United Nations Charter," p. 831.

134. Facts and discussion here are drawn in part from the discussion in chap. 1 of Little and Clifford 1966, International Aid.

135. Ibid., pp. 31–32; and Van Soest 1978, The Start of International Development Cooperation in the United Nations, p. 31.

136. OECD, Development Cooperation, 1985, p. 334. This particular issue of Development Cooperation is also titled Twenty-Five Years of Development Cooperation: A Review.

137. There is a brief discussion in Arnold 1962, Aid for Developing Countries, pp. 88–89.

138. Van Soest 1978, The Start of International Development Cooperation in the United Nations, p. 31.

139. OECD, Development Cooperation, 1985, p. 334. See also Esman and Cheever 1967, The Common Aid Effort, p. 80; and Little and Clifford 1966, International Aid, p. 38f.

140. Curti and Kendall 1954, Prelude to Point Four, pp. 140–58ff., 209ff.

141. Glick 1957, The Administration of Technical Assistance, pp. 6–30.

142. Ibid., pp. 7–8. Public Law 63, 76th Congress, May 3, 1939, and Public Law 355 (76th Congress), August 9, 1939.

143. Glick 1957, The Administration of Technical Assistance, pp. 14ff.

144. Ibid., pp. 30ff. See also Bingham 1954, Shirt-Sleeve Diplomacy, p. 10.

145. Van Soest 1978, The Start of International Development Cooperation in the United Nations, p. 5, quoting texts in McClure 1933, World Prosperity as Sought through the Economic Work of the League of Nations, p. 259.

146. Brown 1957, "The Inheritance of the United Nations," pp. 178–79.

147. Ibid., pp. 181.

148. United Nations Conference on Food and Agriculture 1943, The Final Act of the United Nations Conference on Food and Agriculture, pp. 2, 16, 33; and 1943, Section Reports of the Conference, pp. 2, 5, 21, 26. More comprehensive 1945 technical reports from the Food and Agriculture Organization (FAO), which emerged from the Hot Springs conference, "emphasize the urgency of the problems of malnutrition and undernutrition throughout the world" and suggest that "wartime experiences" with management "be applied after the war to achieve freedom from want of food in Western countries and . . . substantial progress toward this goal in underdeveloped countries" (United Nations 1945, Five Technical Reports on Food and Agriculture, p. 11).

149. Van Soest 1978, *The Start of International Development Cooperation in the United Nations*, p. 35.

150. Friedlander 1975, *International Social Welfare*, p. 24.

151. Brown 1957, "The Inheritance of the United Nations," pp. 168–70. Friedlander 1975, *International Social Welfare*, pp. 18–24, gives slightly different figures.

152. Friedlander 1975, *International Social Welfare*, p. 24.

153. Yoder 1989, *The Evolution of the United Nations System*, p. 144.

154. Friedlander 1975, *International Social Welfare*, p. 25.

155. Asher 1957, "Problems of the Underdeveloped Countries," pp. 582–83.

156. Baldwin 1966, *Economic Development and American Foreign Policy*, p. 28.

157. Van Soest 1978, *The Start of International Development Cooperation in the United Nations*, p. 3.

158. Townley 1966, "The Economic Organs of the United Nations," p. 249; see also Keenleyside 1966, *International Aid*, pp. 115–16.

159. Van Soest 1978, *The Start of International Development Cooperation in the United Nations*, pp. 38–39, 40.

160. Townley 1966, "The Economic Organs of the United Nations," pp. 253, 254; cf. Asher 1957, "Problems of the Underdeveloped Countries," pp. 584–85.

161. Van Soest 1978, *The Start of International Development Cooperation in the United Nations*, pp. 41–43.

162. Asher 1957, "Problems of the Underdeveloped Countries," pp. 586–87, cites Economic and Social Council resolutions 200(III), 246(III), and 198(III) of December 1948, and records a $288,000 appropriation for the first year.

163. Townley 1966, "The Economic Organs of the United Nations," pp. 260–73.

164. Baldwin 1966, *Economic Development and Foreign Aid Policy*, p. 29.

165. Morris 1963, *The Road to Huddersfield*, p. 50, cited by D. Baldwin 1966, *Economic Development and Foreign Aid Policy*, p. 29, who calls Morris the "semi-official Bank Biographer."

166. For instance, Packenham 1971, *Liberal America and the Third World*.

167. Truman, in his memoirs, comments that the Marshall Plan and other aid programs previous to Point Four "gave notice to the world" of America's purpose to lead the free nations in building the strength to "preserve their freedoms" and "hinted at" the concept of the Point Four program. He sharply distinguishes the two plans, however, noting that the former was "emergency aid only" with a limited period of usefulness, while the latter was conceived of as "a continuing and self-perpetuating world" program of technical assistance to the underdeveloped nations (1956, *Memoirs* 2:244ff).

168. Franks 1978, "The Lessons of the Marshall Plan Experience," pp. 18ff. Lord Franks discusses the powerful impact the way in which the Marshall Plan was organized had upon the idea of European unity.

169. Green argues that despite the fact that "the concept of economic and social rights did not appear in the Covenant . . . and did not often arise in the work of the League" except "the Geneva Declaration of the Rights of the Child,

which was endorsed by the Assembly of the League in 1925. However, international action to eliminate the worst social evils . . . was greatly strengthened under the League. . . . The development of conventions and recommendations by the International Labour Organization emphasized a new international concern in labor questions . . . that traditionally had been regarded as a matter for national action alone," while the Mandates system was a "revolutionary . . . development of international affairs" in proclaiming "the principle that the well-being and development of such peoples form a sacred trust of civilization. (1957, "Expanding International Concern with Human Rights," pp. 650–51).

170. Ibid., pp. 653–54.

## CHAPTER SEVEN

1. Bingham 1954, *Shirt-Sleeve Diplomacy*, pp. 243–44.
2. Glick 1957, *The Administration of Technical Assistance*, pp. 30–31.
3. Some of the figures supporting these generalizations are given in chap. 4. Others may be found in OECD, *Development Cooperation, 1984*, and still others in the invaluable statistical compilation by Bach 1987, *Soviet Economic Assistance to the Less Developed Countries*. The totals on pp. 5–9 sum up many of the individual figures given later in his book.
4. Much of the information in this chapter about the origins of the Colombo Plan is drawn from Singh 1963, *The Colombo Plan*. The dates and framework for the meeting are given on p. 5.
5. At this time, the international programs were very small, while early U.S. aid funding was over 50% of the aid total.
6. Acheson 1969, *Present at the Creation*, pp. 249–51, sees the third point, as well, as "breaking new ground," but agrees with others in seeing the fourth point as most innovative, although he says it was "by no means novel."
7. M. Truman 1973, *Harry S. Truman*, pp. 401–2.
8. Bingham 1954, *Shirt-Sleeve Diplomacy*, p. 10, states that "top State Department leaders, including Under Secretary Robert Lovett and Charles S. Bohlen, urged that [Hardy's idea] be deleted as vague and immature." Truman acknowledged Hardy's formative role after Hardy died in a plane accident during his later work for the Point Four program, as Bingham explains in a note, p. 268.
9. Glick 1957, *The Administration of Technical Assistance*, pp. 30–31, discusses this suggestion made to Truman by Benjamin Hardy in relation to the programs of assistance to Latin America from 1939 to 1949, which Glick describes in his book.
10. In his memoirs, Truman comments on what he thought these bases were, and on the basis on which aid ought to be given, in words that illustrate the characteristic juxtaposition of altruistic and self-interest language in describing aid programs. In successive paragraphs, he states:

The assistance then asked amounted to little more than one tenth of one percent of the $341 billion the United States had contributed toward the winning of World War II. It was common sense that we should safeguard our investment.

The American people have always been traditionally altruistic, and the spirit of neighborliness has been a characteristic of our society since the earliest days. . . .

. . . I knew Americans would respond to Point Four, as they respond to all realistic calls for help. The program was thoroughly practical because it would open up new opportunities for development and prosperity to all nations. (H. Truman 1956, *Memoirs*)

11. Glick comments along these same lines:

President Truman's call in January, 1949, for a program to assist the underdeveloped countries must have been one of those historic events that occurred precisely when the situation was ripe. This speculation is prompted by the fact that the response was instantaneous, deep, and world-wide. It led not only to the institution of the Point 4 program by the United States government but also to the inauguration of similar programs under other auspices. (1957, *The Administration of Technical Assistance*, p. 217)

which he then goes on to list. Van Soest 1978, *The Start of International Development Cooperation in the United Nations*, pp. 96–100, also discusses the reaction to Truman's speech.

12. This is from Article 55. The discussion draws on Glick 1957, *The Administration of Technical Assistance*, pp. 217ff.

13. The Rao efforts are discussed by Van Soest 1978, *The Start of International Development Cooperation*, pp. 102–4; and by Baldwin 1966, *Economic Development and American Foreign Policy*, pp. 88–90.

14. See Resolution 222 (IX); and Van Soest 1978, *The Start of International Development Cooperation*, pp. 107–8.

15. United Nations (Hakim et al.) 1951, *Measures for the Economic Development of Under-Developed Countries*.

16. H. Wilson 1953, *The War on World Poverty*, p. 114.

17. Singh 1966, *The Politics of Economic Cooperation in Asia*, p. 174.

18. This clearly is the opinion of Arnold 1962, *Aid for Developing Countries*, p. 81, and it is a fairly common-sense deduction from the structure of and participation in the plan.

19. Keenleyside 1966, *International Aid*, pp. 127f.

20. Singh 1966, *The Politics of Economic Cooperation in Asia*, p. 178. Singh goes into the meeting in detail.

21. For instance, Rubin 1966, *Conscience of the Rich Nations*, p. 17.

22. British Information Services 1964, *The Colombo Plan*, p. 2. The pamphlet (83 pp.) refers to the origins as linked to the Marshall Plan in Europe, as well as to events in Asia.

23. While there can be no full certainty about why this occurred, Truman, in his memoirs, notes Eisenhower's lack of enthusiasm for the aid program as expressed to Truman in personal conversations. Truman implicitly attributes this to a difference in philosophy between Democrats and Republicans, seeing Kennedy's interest in foreign aid as a continuation of his own (H. Truman 1956, *Memoirs*).

24. Rostow 1985, *Eisenhower, Kennedy, and Foreign Aid*, p. 92.

25. A discussion of this is given in ibid., pp. 58ff.

26. Kennedy's motives, like Truman's, are not part of the argument being developed here. However, it is evident, both from Rostow 1985, *Eisenhower, Kennedy, and Foreign Aid*, and from a report of Kennedy's interest in foreign aid during his campaign, that Kennedy had been deeply moved and influenced by exposure to poverty in visiting some less developed countries. See Weidner 1969, *Prelude to Reorganization*.

27. United Nations (Hakim et al.) 1951, *Measures for the Economic Development of Under-Developed Countries*.

28. This section draws heavily on the section on flow targets in OECD, *Development Cooperation, 1985*, pp. 135–37.

29. Ibid., p. 136.

30. Ibid., pp. 45–49.

31. Ibid., p. 47.

32. However, for a critical account of what influence McNamara succeeded in having on the Bank, see Ayres 1983, *Banking on the Poor*.

33. British Government, Ministry of Overseas Development 1975, *The Changing Emphasis in British Aid Policies*.

## CHAPTER EIGHT

1. *United Nations Review*, May 30, 1956, quoted (with ellipsis shown), pp. 120–21, in Faris 1958, *To Plow with Hope*, New York: Harper and Brothers.

2. Myrdal 1973, *Against the Stream*.

3. See for instance the accounts in the historical section of OECD, *Development Cooperation, 1985*, pp. 39–64; especially Thorp 1985, "The DAC's Expanding Influence," pp. 45–49. See also in the same volume the section on the evolution of resource aid targets, pp. 135–37.

## CHAPTER NINE

1. Taken from King 1983, *The Words of Martin Luther King*, quoted in a 1986 Newmarket Press calendar.

2. Of course, aid was very imperfect, sometimes used for donors' own selfish ends, sometimes botched, far from perfectly sensitive to the issues of poverty and human dignity which it was meant to address.

3. See, for instance, Kreuger et al. 1989, *Aid and Development*; Cassen and Associates 1986, *Does Aid Work?*; and Riddell 1987, *Foreign Aid Reconsidered*.

4. This kind of affinity between domestic and international politics, it should be clearly noted, is entirely distinct from any notion that domestic political demands impinge upon international politics, limit international rationality or pursuit of national interests, or force policymakers to engage in a two-level bargaining game. Rather, I am arguing a similar set of political analyses, perceptions, practices, principles, and values tended to constitute a country's or individual's domestic and international ideas of wise political practice.

5. I am not arguing that aid was adequate, pure, ideal, or highly effective. It was, in my view, highly flawed; and the developed countries did not do, by any means, all they were bound to do to combat poverty at home or abroad. But

dissatisfaction with the performance of the developed countries all too often becomes a kind of naive cynicism which, beginning by judging efforts to build a better world by standards of unattainable perfection, ends by denying the value of what was accomplished at great labor, even when that was a remarkable departure from the sorry past, and by denying the possibility of working for attainable change.

Of course aid programs, once in place, became a target of opportunity for many other groups, as any large program will: many interests tried to get what they could from aid, usually with some success. But there are very few indications that there were ever any other strong or consistent bases of support for foreign aid programs than commitment to the welfare of the world's poor and attempts to build a viable and just world society.

6. Robert S. McNamara, Preface, in World Bank 1975, *The Assault on World Poverty*, p. v.

7. Ward 1962, *The Rich Nations and the Poor Nations*, p. 159.

8. For instance, in Myrdal 1970, *The Challenge of World Poverty*, pp. 336ff. and 452ff.

9. Pearson et al. 1969, *Partners in Development*, p. 11.

10. This paragraph is a close paraphrase, and moral reinversion, of key sentences out of the opening chapters of Morgenthau's *Politics Among Nations*. Morgenthau opens chap. 3 with the words, "International politics, like all politics, is a struggle for power. Whatever the ultimate aims of international politics, power is always the immediate aim" (1954, p. 25). He opens chap. 4 with the words, "Domestic and international politics are but different manifestations of the same phenomenon: the struggle for power" (p. 35). In chap. 1, in his discussion of Realism's awareness of the moral significance of political action, among his six principles of Realism, he states that "Realism maintains that universal moral principles cannot be applied to the actions of states in their abstract universal formulation, but that they must be filtered through the concrete circumstances of time and place. The individual may say for himself: '*Fiat justitia, pereat mundum*' (Let justice be done, even if the world perish), but the state has no right to say so in the name of those who are in its care. . . . The state has no right to let its moral disapprobation of the infringement of liberty get in the way of successful political action, itself inspired by the moral principle of national survival. There can be no political morality without prudence: that is, without consideration of the political consequences of seemingly moral action" (p. 9). Added at the end of my paragraph is a paraphrase of another well-known sentence, from Robert Bolt's play about Thomas More, *A Man for All Seasons*: "When statesmen forsake their own private conscience for the sake of their public duties . . . they lead their country by a short route to chaos" (Bolt [1960] 1990, *A Man For All Seasons*, p. 22, original ellipsis marks).

# Bibliography

Acheson, Dean, 1969, *Present at the Creation: My Years in the State Department*, New York: W. W. Norton.

Addams, Jane, 1922, "Peace and Bread in Time of War," reprinted in Christopher Lasch, ed., [1965] 1982, *The Social Thought of Jane Addams*, New York: Irvington Publishers.

Aiken, William, and Hugh La Follette, 1977, *World Hunger and Moral Obligation*, Englewood Cliffs, N.J.: Prentice-Hall.

Alcalde Gonzalo, Javier, 1987, *The Idea of Third World Development: Emerging Perspectives in the United States and Britain, 1900–1950*, Lanham, Md.: University Press of America (for the Miller Center of the University of Virginia).

Alessandrini, Sergio, 1984, "Italian Aid: Policy and Performance," in Olav Stokke, 1984a, *European Development Assistance*.

Antonides, Harry, 1985, *Stones for Bread: The Social Gospel and Its Contemporary Legacy*, Jordan Station, Ont.: Paideia Press.

Arndt, H. W., 1944 (1965), *The Economic Lessons of the Nineteen-Thirties*, New York: August M. Kelley; 1944 edition, Oxford: Oxford University Press.

———, 1987, *Economic Development: The History of an Idea*, Chicago: University of Chicago Press.

Arnold, H. J. P., 1962, *Aid for Developing Countries: A Comparative Study*, Chester Springs, Pa.: Dufour Editions.

Arthur, Brian W., 1985, "Competing Technologies and Lock-in by Historical Small Events: The Dynamics of Allocation under Increasing Returns," CEPR publication no. 43, Stanford: Stanford University, Center for Economic Policy Research.

Asher, Robert E., 1957, "Problems of the Underdeveloped Countries," in Robert E. Asher et al., 1957, *The United Nations and Promotion of the General Welfare*.

Asher, Robert E., Walter Kotschnig, William Adams Brown, Jr., James Frederick Green, Emil J. Sady, and Associates, 1957, *The United Nations and Promotion of the General Welfare*, Washington, D.C.: Brookings Institution.

Auerbach, Kenneth D., 1976, "The Distribution of Multilateral Assistance: A Five Organization Study," *Social Science Quarterly* 56, 4 (March): 644–59.

Axelrod, Robert, 1984, *The Evolution of Cooperation*, New York: Basic Books.

Axelrod, Robert, and Robert O. Keohane, 1986, "Achieving Cooperation under Anarchy: Strategies and Institutions," in Kenneth Oye, 1986, *Cooperation under Anarchy*, Princeton: Princeton University Press.

Ayres, Robert L., 1983, *Banking on the Poor: The World Bank and World Poverty*, Cambridge: MIT Press.

Bach, Quintin V. S., 1987, *Soviet Economic Assistance to the Less Developed Countries: A Statistical Analysis*, Oxford: Clarendon Press.

Baldwin, David A., 1966, *Economic Development and American Foreign Policy, 1943–1962*, Chicago: University of Chicago Press.

Baldwin, Peter, 1990, *The Politics of Social Solidarity: Class Bases of the European Welfare State, 1875–1975*, Cambridge: Cambridge University Press.

Bartholomew, Mark, 1989, "Social Welfare Policy: Canada," in Jack Paul DeSario, 1989, *International Public Policy Sourcebook*.

Bates, Robert H., 1981, *Markets and States in Tropical Africa*, Berkeley and Los Angeles: University of California Press.

Beer, Samuel H., 1964, *Modern British Politics: A Study of Parties and Pressure Groups*, London: Faber and Faber.

Beitz, Charles R., 1979, *Political Theory and International Relations*, Princeton: Princeton University Press.

———, 1988, "Recent International Thought," *International Journal* 43, 2 (Spring): 183–204.

Bencivenga, Valerie R., 1984, "An Econometric Model of the Geographical Distribution of Foreign Aid," Ph.D. diss., University of Toronto.

———, 1985a, "Explaining the Foreign Aid Policies of the OECD Donors," Working Papers in Economics, no. 257, Santa Barbara: University of California.

———, 1985b, "Motives for Bilateral OECD Aid to Developing Countries," Working Papers in Economics, no. 256, Santa Barbara: University of California.

Berthelot, Yves, with D. Besnaiou, 1983, "France's New Third World Policy: Problems of Change," in Christopher Stevens, 1983, *EEC and The Third World (3)*.

Bertholet, Christiaan, Peter de Clercq, and Leon Janssen, 1984, "Dutch Development Cooperation: Policy and Performance," in Olav Stokke, 1984a, *European Development Assistance*.

Bingham, Jonathan B., 1954, *Shirt-Sleeve Diplomacy: Point 4 in Action*, New York: John Day Company.

Bock, Edwin A., 1954, *Fifty Years of Technical Assistance: Some Administrative Experiences of U.S. Voluntary Agencies*, Chicago: Public Administration Clearing House.

Bolt, Robert, [1960] 1990, *A Man for All Seasons: A Play in Two Acts*, New York: Vintage Books.

Boudreau, Frank G., 1945, "The International Food Movement in Retrospect" in Theodore W. Schultz, 1945, *Food for the World*.

Brandt Commission, 1980, *North-South: a Program for Survival. Report of the Independent Commission on International Development Issues*, Cambridge: MIT Press.

———, 1983, *Common Crisis: North-South. Cooperation for World Recovery*, London: Pan Books.

Brandt, Willy, 1986, *World Armament and World Hunger: A Call for Action*, trans., Anthea Bell, London: Victor Gollancz.

Bremner, Robert, 1956, *From the Depths: The Discovery of Poverty in the United States*, New York: New York University Press.

———, 1960, *American Philanthropy*, Chicago: University of Chicago Press.

Brilmayer, Lea, 1989, *Justifying International Acts*, Ithaca: Cornell University Press.

British Government, Ministry of Overseas Development, 1975, *The Changing Emphasis in British Aid Policies: More Help for the Poorest*, Presented to Parliament by the Minister of Overseas Development by Command of Her Majesty, London: Her Majesty's Stationery Office.

British Information Services, 1964, *The Colombo Plan*, Reference Division, Central Office of Information, London: Her Majesty's Stationery Office.

Brown, William Adams, 1957, "The Inheritance of the United Nations," in Robert E. Asher et al., *The United Nations and the Promotion of the General Welfare*.

Carnegie, Andrew, 1909, *Armaments and Their Results*, New York: Peace Society of the City of New York.

Carnegie Endowment for International Peace, 1936, *World Economic Progress*, pamphlet.

Carr, Edward Hallett, [1946] 1964, *The Twenty Years' Crisis, 1919–1939: An Introduction to the Study of International Relations*, 2d ed., New York: Harper Torchbooks.

Carter, Paul, 1954, *The Decline and Revival of the Social Gospel: Social and Political Liberalism in American Protestant Churches, 1920-1940*, Ithaca: Cornell University Press.

Cassen, Robert, and Associates, 1986, *Does Aid Work? Report to an Intergovernmental Task Force*, Oxford: Clarendon Press.

Cassen, Robert, Richard Jolly, John Mathieson and John Sewell, 1982, "Overview," in Robert Cassen et al., 1982, *Rich Country Interests*.

Cassen, Robert, Richard Jolly, John Sewell, and Robert Wood, eds., 1982, *Rich Country Interests and Third World Development*, New York: St. Martin's Press, Institute of Development Studies (Sussex).

Castle, Eugene, 1957, *The Great Giveaway: The Realities of Foreign Aid*, Chicago: Henry Regnery Company.

Clunies Ross, Anthony, 1969, "Economic Responses and the Question of Foreign Aid," in Max Teichmann, 1969, *New Directions in Australian Foreign Policy*.

Coase, Ronald, 1960, "The Problem of Social Cost," *Journal of Law and Economics* 3:1–44.

Cole, G. D. H., 1932, *A Guide through World Chaos*, New York: Alfred A. Knopf.

Curti, Merle, 1963, *American Philanthropy Abroad: A History*, New Brunswick, N.J.: Rutgers University Press.

Curti, Merle, and Kendall Birr, 1954, *Prelude to Point Four: American Technical Missions Overseas, 1838–1938*, Madison: University of Wisconsin Press.

David, Paul A., 1985, "Clio and the Economics of QWERTY," *American Economic Review* 75, 2 (May):332–37.

Davis, Allen F., 1967, *Spearheads for Reform: The Social Settlements and the Progressive Movement, 1890–1914*, New York: Oxford University Press.

Davis, Harriet Eager, ed., 1944, *Pioneers in World Order: An American Appraisal of the League of Nations*, New York: Columbia University Press.

Davis, J. Merle, 1944, *The Preparation of Missionaries for Work in the Post-War*

*Era*, New York: Department of Social and Economic Research and Counsel, International Missionary Council, *International Review of Missions*, reissued as a pamphlet, July 1944.

DeSario, Jack Paul, 1989, ed., *International Public Policy Sourcebook*, vol. 1, *Health and Social Welfare*, New York: Greenwood Press.

Dixon, John, and Robert P. Scheurell, eds., 1989, *Social Welfare in Developed Market Countries*, London and New York: Routledge.

Donnelly, Jack, 1991, "Thucydides and Realism," convention paper delivered at the International Studies Association 1991 meeting, Vancouver, B.C.

Dore, Ronald, 1982, "Japan and the Third World: Coincidence or Divergence of Interests," in Robert Cassen et al., 1982, *Rich Country Interests*.

Dowling, J. M., and Ulrich Hiemenz, 1985, "Biases in the Allocation of Foreign Aid: Some New Evidence," *World Development* 13, 4:534–41.

Draper, G. I. A., 1988, "The Development of International Humanitarian Law," in UNESCO, 1988, *International Dimensions of Humanitarian Law*, Geneva: Henry Dunant Institute; Paris: Unesco; Dordrecht, Boston, and London: Martinus Nijhoff Publishers.

Dunant, J. Henry, [1862] 1939, *A Memory of Solferino*, Washington, D.C.: American National Red Cross.

Einhorn, Eric S., and John Logue, 1988, *Modern Welfare States: Politics and Policies in Social Democratic Scandinavia*, New York: Praeger.

Eldridge, Philip J., 1980, "Diplomacy, Development and 'Small Government': Conflicting Directions in Australia's Overseas Aid Program," CSAAR Research Paper no. 23, Brisbane: Centre for the Study of Australian-Asian Relations, School of Modern Asian Studies, Griffith University.

Esman, Milton J., and Daniel S. Cheever, 1967, *The Common Aid Effort: The Developmental Assistance Activities of the Organization for Economic Cooperation and Development*, Columbus: Ohio State University Press.

Everts, Ph. P., 1983, *Public Opinion, the Churches, and Foreign Policy: Studies of Domestic Factors in the Making of Dutch Foreign Policy*, Leiden: University of Leiden, Institute for International Studies.

Faris, Donald K., 1958, *To Plow with Hope*, New York: Harper and Brothers.

Farnsworth, Lee W., 1981, "Japan and the Third World," in Phillip Taylor and Gregory A. Raymond, eds., 1981, *Third World Policies of Industrialized Nations*.

Fellner, C. H., and J. R. Marshall, 1968, "Twelve Kidney Donors," *Journal of the American Medical Association* 206:2703–7.

Ferejohn, John, 1990, "Rationality and Interpretation: Parliamentary Elections in Early Stuart England," mimeo.

First Assembly of the World Council of Churches, Amsterdam, 1948, *The Ten Formative Years, 1938–1948: Report on the Activities of the World Council of Churches during Its Period of Formation*, Geneva: World Council of Churches.

Flora, Peter, ed., 1986, *Growth to Limits: The Western European Welfare States Since World War II*, vols. 1–4, Berlin and New York: Walter de Gruyter, European University Institute.

Flora, Peter, and Arnold J. Heidenheimer, eds., 1981, *The Development of Welfare States in Europe and America*, New Brunswick, N.J.: Transaction Books.

Forster, Jacques, 1984, "Swiss Aid: Policy and Performance," in Olav Stokke, 1984a, *European Development Assistance.*

Forsythe, David P., 1977, *Humanitarian Politics: The International Committee of the Red Cross,* Baltimore: Johns Hopkins University Press.

Forsythe, M. G., H. M. A. Keens-Soper, and P. Savigear, eds., 1970, *The Theory of International Relations: Selected Texts from Gentili to Treitschke,* London: George Allen and Unwin.

Forward Movement Commission, [1938], *"Into All The World": Aids in Presenting Missions,* Cincinnati, Ohio: Forward Movement Commission, booklet.

Frank, Robert, 1988, *Passions within Reason: The Strategic Role of the Emotions,* New York: Norton.

Franks, Lord, 1978, "The Lessons of the Marshall Plan Experience," in OECD, 1978, *From Marshall Plan to Global Interdependence.*

Freeman, Gary P., 1989, "Social Welfare Policy: France," in Jack Paul DeSario, 1989, *International Public Policy Sourcebook,* vol. 1.

Friedlander, Walter A., 1975, *International Social Welfare,* Englewood Cliffs, N.J.: Prentice Hall.

George, Alexander, and Juliet George, 1956, *Woodrow Wilson and Colonel House: A Personality Study,* New York: John Day Company.

Ghebali, Victor-Yves, 1989, *The International Labour Organization: A Case Study on the Evolution of U.N. Specialized Agencies,* vol. 3 of *International Organization and the Evolution of World Society,* Dordrecht and Boston: Martinus Nijhoff Publishers.

Gilbert, Felix, 1984, *The End of the European Era, 1890 to the Present,* 3d edition, New York: Norton.

Gilchrist, Huntington, 1944, "Dependent Peoples and Mandates," in Harriet Eager Davis, 1944, *Pioneers in World Order.*

Gilpin, Robert, 1987, *The Political Economy of International Relations,* Princeton: Princeton University Press.

Glick, Philip M., 1957, *The Administration of Technical Assistance: Growth in the Americas,* Chicago: University of Chicago Press.

Goldstein, Judith, 1988, "Ideas, Institutions, and Trade Policy," *International Organization* 42, 1 (Winter): 179–217.

——, 1989, "The Impact of Ideas on Trade Policy," *International Organization* 43, 1 (Winter): 31–71.

Goldstein, Judith, and Robert O. Keohane, 1990, "Ideas and Foreign Policy," mimeo.

Goldwater, Barry M., [1960] 1961, *Conscience of a Conservative,* New York: MacFadden Books.

Goodin, Robert E., 1985, *Protecting the Vulnerable: A Reanalysis of Our Social Responsibilities,* Chicago: University of Chicago Press.

Gould, Stephen Jay, 1985, *The Flamingo's Smile,* New York: Norton.

Gould, Stephen Jay, and N. Eldredge, 1977, "Punctuated Equilibria: The Tempo and Mode of Evolution Reconsidered," *Paleobiology* 3:115–151.

Grady, Henry F., 1944, "World Economics," in Harriet Davis, 1944, *Pioneers in World Order.*

Green, James Frederick, 1957, "Expanding International Concern with Human

Rights," in Robert E. Asher et al., 1957, *The United Nations and Promotion of the General Welfare.*

Greenberg, Jerald, and Ronald Cohen, eds., 1982, *Equity and Justice in Social Behavior*, New York: Academic Press.

Grieco, Joseph, 1988, "Anarchy and the Limits of Cooperation: A Realist Critique of the Newest Liberal Institutionalism," *International Organization* 42, 3 (Summer): 485–507.

———, 1990, *Cooperation among Nations*, Ithaca: Cornell University Press.

Haas, Ernst, 1990, *When Knowledge Is Power*, Berkeley: University of California Press.

Haas, Peter, 1989, "Do Regimes Matter? Epistemic Communities and Mediterranean Pollution Control," *International Organization* 43, 3:377–404.

———, 1990, *Saving the Mediterranean: The Politics of International Environmental Cooperation*, New York: Columbia University Press.

Hage, Jerald, Robert Hanneman, and Edward T. Gargan, 1989, *State Responsiveness and State Activism: An Examination of the Social Forces and State Strategies that Explain the Rise in Social Expenditures in Britain, France, Germany, and Italy, 1870–1968*, London: Unwin Hyman.

Haggard, Stephan, and Beth A. Simmons, 1987, "Theories of International Regimes," *International Organization* 41, 3 (Summer): 491–517.

Hallie, Philip, 1979, *Lest Innocent Blood Be Shed: The Story of the Village of Le Chambon and How Goodness Happened There*, New York: Harper and Row, Harper Colophon Books.

Hanke, Lewis, 1949, *The Spanish Struggle for Justice in the New World*, Philadephia: University of Pennsylvania Press; London: Oxford University Press.

———, 1974, *All Mankind Is One: A Study of the Disputation between Bartolome de Las Casas and Juan Gines de Sepulveda in 1550 on the Intellectual and Religious Capacity of the American Indians*, DeKalb: Northern Illinois University Press.

Hansen, Alvin H., 1942, *Economic Problems of the Post-War World: Democratic Planning for Full Employment*, (with teaching aids by Laurence E. Leamer, Unit no. 10 in Problems in American Life, Washington, D.C.: National Education Association.

Havighurst, Alfred F., 1979, *Britain in Transition: The Twentieth Century*, 3d ed., Chicago: University of Chicago Press.

Hayter, Teresa, 1971, *Aid as Imperialism*, Baltimore: Penguin Books.

Hayter, Teresa, and Catherine Watson, 1985, *Aid: Rhetoric and Reality*, London: Pluto Press.

Hayward, J. E. S., 1959, "Solidarity: The Social History of an Idea in Nineteenth-Century France," *International Review of Social History* 4:261–84.

Harvey, Heather, 1942, "War-Time Research in Great Britain on International Problems of Reconstruction," *Agenda* (April).

Hinsley, F. H., 1973, *Nationalism and the International System*, Dobbs Ferry, N.Y.: Oceana Publications.

Hoadley, Steve, 1989, *The New Zealand Foreign Affairs Handbook*, Oxford: Oxford University Press.

Hoffman, Mark J., 1985, "Normative Approaches," in Margot Light and A. J. R. Groom, 1985, *International Relations*.

Hoffman, Paul G., 1962, *World without Want*, New York: Harper and Row.

Hoffmann, Stanley, 1977, "An American Social Science: International Relations," *Daedalus* 106, 3:41–60.

———, 1978, *Primacy or World Order*, New York: McGraw Hill.

———, 1981, *Duties Beyond Borders: On the Limits and Possibilities of Ethical International Politics*, Stanford: Stanford University Press.

Hofmeier, Rolf, and Siegfried Schultz, 1984, "German Aid: Policy and Performance," in Olav Stokke, 1984a, *European Development Assistance*.

Holland, Kenneth M., 1989, "Social Welfare Policy: Germany," in Jack Paul DeSario, 1989, *International Public Policy Sourcebook*, vol. 1, *Health and Social Welfare*.

Hoover, Herbert, and Hugh Gibson, 1942, "The Problems of Lasting Peace," in *Prefaces to Peace*, 1943.

Horesh, Edward, 1984, "British Aid: Policy and Performance," in Olav Stokke, 1984a, *European Development Assistance*.

Hornstein, H. A., E. Fisch, and M. Holmes, 1968, "Influence of a Model's Feelings about His Behavior and His Relevance as a Comparison on Other Observers' Helping Behavior," *Journal of Personality and Social Psychology*, 10:222–26.

Hugon, Philippe, 1984, "French Development Cooperation: Policy and Performance," in Olav Stokke, 1984a, *European Development Assistance*.

Humphrey, Hubert H., [1964] 1965, *The Cause Is Mankind: A Liberal Program for Modern America*, New York: MacFadden Books.

International Committee of the Red Cross and League of Red Cross Societies, 1983, *International Red Cross Handbook*, 12th ed., Geneva: International Committee of the Red Cross, League of Red Cross Societies, and Henry Dunant Institute.

International Federation of League of Nations Societies, Bulletins, Box: Ozd 844 In 8d, Mudd Library, Yale University.

International Labour Organization, 1950, *Fourth Report of the International Labour Organization to the United Nations*, Geneva: International Labour Office.

———, 1969, *The ILO in the Service of Social Progress*, Geneva: International Labour Office.

International Missionary Council, 1934, *The International Missionary Council: Its History, Purpose and Activities*, London: International Missionary Council, pamphlet.

International Monetary Fund, annual, *Direction of Trade Statistics, 1948–1990*, a machine-readable data set, Washington, D.C.: International Monetary Fund.

Jellinek, Sergio, Karl-Anders Larsson, and Christina Storey, 1984, "Swedish Aid: Policy and Performance," in Olav Stokke, 1984a, *European Development Assistance*

Jervis, Robert, 1978, "Cooperation under the Security Dilemma," *World Politics* 30 (January): 167–214.

Jones, S. Shepard, 1939, *The Scandinavian States and the League of Nations*, Princeton: Princeton University Press.

Judge, Anthony J. N., 1978, "International Institutions: Diversity, Borderline Cases, Functional Substitutes and Possible Alternatives," in Paul Taylor and A. J. R. Groom, 1978, *International Organization*.

Kalshoven, Frits, ed., 1988, *Assisting the Victims of Armed Conflict and Other Disasters*, Dordrecht and Boston: Martinus Nijhoff.

Kant, Immanuel, 1795, "Perpetual Peace: A Philosophical Essay," and 1784, "Idea for a Universal History from a Cosmo-Political Point of View," in M. G. Forsythe et al., 1970, *The Theory of International Relations*.

Keenleyside, Hugh L., 1966, *International Aid: A Summary. With Special Reference to the Programmes of the United Nations*, New York: James H. Heineman.

Keohane, Robert O., 1984, *After Hegemony*, Princeton: Princeton University Press.

———, ed., 1986a, *Neorealism and Its Critics*, New York: Columbia University Press.

———, 1986b, "Realism, Neorealism and the Study of World Politics," in Robert O. Keohane, 1986a *Neorealism and Its Critics*.

———, 1988, "International Institutions: Two Approaches," *International Relations Quarterly*, 32, 4:379–96.

Keynes, John Maynard, 1935, *The General Theory of Employment, Interest and Money*, New York: Harcourt, Brace, and World.

Kiljunen, Kimmo, 1984, "Finnish Development Cooperation: Policy and Performance," in Olav Stokke, 1984a, *European Development Assistance*.

King, Martin Luther, Jr., 1983, *The Words of Martin Luther King, Jr.*, selected by Coretta Scott King, New York: Newmarket Press.

Kohn, Alfie, 1989, *The Brighter Side of Human Nature: Altruism and Empathy in Everyday Life*, New York: Basic Books.

Kotshnig, Walter M., 1957, "Organizational Setting," in Robert E. Asher et al., 1957, *The United Nations and the Promotion of the General Welfare*.

Krasner, Stephen D., 1985, *Structural Conflict*, Berkeley and Los Angeles: University of California Press.

———, 1988, "Sovereignty: An Institutional Perspective," *Comparative Political Studies* 21, 1 (April): 66–94.

———, ed., 1983, *International Regimes*, Ithaca: Cornell University Press.

Kratochwil, Friedrich, 1986, "Of Systems Boundaries and Territoriality: An Inquiry into the Formation of the State System," *World Politics* 39:27–52.

Kratochwil, Friedrich, and John G. Ruggie, 1986, "International Organization: A State of the Art on an Art of the State," *International Organization* 40:753–76.

Krebs, Dennis, 1982, "Prosocial Behavior, Equity, and Justice," in Greenberg and Cohen, 1982, *Equity and Justice in Social Behavior*.

Kreuger, Anne O., Constantine Michalopoulos, and Vernon Ruttan, with Keith Jay et al., 1989, *Aid and Development*, Baltimore: John Hopkins University Press.

Lange, Chr. L., 1937, "Introduction, Part I," *Resolutions Adopted by Interparlia-*

*mentary Conferences and Principal Decisions of the Council, 1911–1936*, Geneva: League of Nations.

Lappe, Frances Moore, and Joseph Collins, 1979, *World Hunger: Ten Myths*, 4th ed., San Francisco: Institute for Food and Development Policy.

Lappe, Frances Moore, Joseph Collins, and David Kinley, 1980, *Aid as Obstacle: Twenty Questions about Our Foreign Aid and the Hungry*, San Francisco: Institute for Food and Development Policy.

Laudicina, Paul A., 1973, *World Poverty and Development: A Survey of American Opinion*, Washington, D.C.: Overseas Development Council.

Lauren, Paul Gordon, 1988, *Power and Prejudice: The Politics and Diplomacy of Racial Discrimination*, Boulder, Colo.: Westview.

Lewis, W. Arthur, 1949, *Economic Survey, 1919–1939* London: George Allen and Unwin.

Light, Margot, and A. J. R. Groom, eds., 1985, *International Relations: A Handbook of Current Theory*, London: Francis Pinter; Boulder, Colo.: Lynne Reinner.

Lindholm, Stig, 1971, *The Image of the Developing Countries: An Inquiry into Swedish Public Opinion*, Uppsala: Almqvist and Wiksell, (Dag Hammarskjöld Foundation).

Liss, Peggy, 1983, *Atlantic Empires: The Network of Trade and Revolution, 1713–1826*, Baltimore: Johns Hopkins University Press.

Little, Ian M.D., 1982, *Economic Development: Theory, Policy, and International Relations*, New York: Basic Books, Twentieth Century Fund Books.

Little, I. M. D., and J. M. Clifford, 1966, *International Aid: A Discussion of the Flow of Public Resources from Rich to Poor Countries*, Chicago: Aldine Publishing Company; London: George Allen and Unwin.

Loescher, Gil, and Bruce Nichols, 1989, *The Moral Nation: Humanitarianism and U.S. Foreign Policy* Notre Dame, Ind.: University of Notre Dame Press.

Lorwin, Lewis L., 1933, *The World Economic Conference and World Organization*, New York: National Committee on the Cause and Cure of War, pamphlet, in box: Nc66 1 1933, Mudd Library, Yale University.

———, 1941, *Economic Consequences of the Second World War*, New York: Random House.

Loufti, Martha F., 1973, *The Net Cost of Japanese Foreign Aid*, New York: Praeger Publishers.

Luard, Evan, ed., 1966, *The Evolution of International Organizations*, London: Thames and Hudson.

Lumsdaine, David H., 1992, "Relative Gains and the Pursuit of Cooperation under Anarchy," mimeo.

Macalister-Smith, Peter, 1985, "Red Cross and Humanitarian Assistance," in Peter Macalister-Smith, 1985b, *International Humanitarian Assistance*.

Macalister-Smith, Peter, 1985b, ed., *International Humanitarian Assistance: Disaster Relief Actions in International Law and Organization*, Dordrecht, Boston, Lancaster: Martinus Nijhoff.

Maddox, James G., 1956, *Technical Assistance by Religious Agencies in Latin America*, Chicago: University of Chicago Press.

Maizels, Alfred, and Michiko K. Nissanke, 1984, "Motivations for Aid to Developing Countries," *World Development* 12, 9: 879–900.

Malek, Mohammed H., ed., 1991, *Contemporary Issues in European Development Aid*, Aldershot, Hants, England: Avebury; Brookfield, Vt.: Gower Publishing Group.

Mangone, Gerard J., 1954, *A Short History of International Organization*, New York: McGraw-Hill.

Mather, Kirtley F., 1944, *Enough and to Spare: Mother Earth Can Nourish Every Man in Freedom*, New York: Harper and Brothers.

May, Henry, 1949, *Protestant Churches and Industrial America*, New York: Harper.

May, Herbert L., 1944, "Dangerous Drugs," in Harriet Eager Davis, 1944, *Pioneers in World Order*.

May, James, 1977, "Cooperation between Socialist Parties," in William E. Patterson and Alastair H. Thomas, 1977, *Social Democratic Parties in Western Europe*.

May, Ranald S., Dieter Schumacher, and Mohammed H. Malek, 1989, *Overseas Aid: The Impact on Britain and Germany*, New York: Harvester Wheatsheaf.

McGillivray, Mark, 1989, "The Allocation of Aid among Developing Countries: A Multi-Donor Analysis Using a Per Capita Aid Index," *World Development* 17, 4:561–68.

McKinlay, R. D., 1979, "The Aid Relationship: A Foreign Policy Model and Interpretation of Official Bilateral Economic Aid of the United States, the United Kingdom, France, and Germany, 1960–1970," *Comparative Political Studies* 11, 4 (January):411–63.

McKinlay, R. D., and A. Mughan, 1984, *Aid and Arms to the Third World: An Analysis of the Distribution and Impact of US Official Transfers*, London: Francis Pinter.

Minkin, Lewis, and Patrick Seyd, 1977, "The British Labour Party," in William E. Patterson and Alastair H. Thomas, 1977, *Social Democratic Parties in Western Europe*.

Mooney, Christopher F., 1982, *Inequality and the American Conscience: Justice through the Judicial System*, New York: Paulist Press.

Morgenthau, Hans J., 1946, *Scientific Man vs. Power Politics*, Chicago: University of Chicago Press.

———, 1954, *Politics Among Nations*, New York: Alfred A. Knopf.

Morris, James, 1963, *The Road to Huddersfield*, New York: Pantheon.

Mosley, Paul, 1985, "The Political Economy of Foreign Aid: A Model of the Market for a Public Good," *Economic Development and Cultural Change* 33 (January): 373–93.

Mosley, Paul, 1987, *Foreign Aid: Its Defense and Reform*, Lexington: University Press of Kentucky.

Myrdal, Gunnar, [1958] 1960, *Beyond the Welfare State*, New Haven, Conn.: Yale University Press.

———, 1970, *The Challenge of World Poverty: A World Anti-Poverty Program in Outline*, New York: Vintage Books.

———, 1973, *Against the Stream: Critical Essays on Economics*, New York: Random House, Pantheon Books.

National Conference of Catholic Bishops, 1983, *The Challenge of Peace: God's Promise and Our Response. A Pastoral Letter on War and Peace by the National Conference of Catholic Bishops*, Washington, D.C.: National Conference of Catholic Bishops.

Nicholson, Marjorie, 1986, *The TUC Overseas: The Roots of Policy*, London: Allen and Unwin.

North, Robert C., 1976, *The World That Could Be*, New York: W. W. Norton.

O'Neill, Helen, 1984, "Irish Aid: Policy and Performance," in Olav Stokke, 1984a, *European Development Assistance*.

OECD (Organization for Economic Cooperation and Development), *Development Assistance*, various years, Paris: OECD.

———, *Development Cooperation*, various years, Paris: OECD.

———, *Geographical Distribution of Financial Flows*, various years, Paris: OECD.

———, 1978, *From Marshall Plan to Global Interdependence: New Challenges for the Industrialized Nations*, Paris: OECD.

———, 1982, *Historical Statistics of Foreign Trade, 1965–1980*, Paris: OECD.

———, 1985, *Social Expenditure, 1960-1990: Problems of Growth and Control*, Paris: OECD Social Policy Studies.

———, 1988, *The Future of Social Protection*, Social Policy Studies, no. 6, Paris: OECD.

OECD, annual, *Public Data Base on Financial Flows to Developing Countries, 1968–1982*, a machine-readable data set, Paris: Development Assistance Committee.

Orr, Robert M., Jr., 1990, *The Emergence of Japan's Foreign Aid Power*, New York: Columbia University Press.

Osgood, Robert Endicott, 1953, *Ideals and Self-Interest in America's Foreign Relations*, Chicago: University of Chicago Press.

Oye, Kenneth, ed., 1986, *Cooperation under Anarchy*, Princeton: Princeton University Press.

Packenham, Robert A., 1971, *Liberal America and the Third World: Political Development Ideas in Foreign Aid and Social Science*, Princeton: Princeton University Press.

Pakistan Red Crescent Society (Punjab Provincial Branch, Lahore), [1981] *Dissemination of International Humanitarian Law*.

Patterson, William E., and Alastair H. Thomas, eds., 1977, *Social Democratic Parties in Western Europe*, New York: St. Martin's Press.

Pearson, Lester B., Sir Edward Boyle, Roberto de Oliviera Campos, C. Douglas Dillon, Wilfried Guth, W. Arthur Lewis, Robert E. Marjolin, and Saburo Okita, 1969, *Partners in Development: Report of the Commission on International Development*, New York: Praeger Publishers.

Pictet, Jean, [1982], *Development and Principles on International Humanitarian Assistance*, Dordrecht and Boston: Martinus Nijhoff; Geneva: Henry Dunant Institute.

Poe, Stephen C., 1991, "U.S. Economic Aid Allocation: The Quest for Cumulation," *International Interactions* 16, no. 4:295–316.

Pratt, Cranford, 1989a, "Canada: An Eroding and Limited Internationalism," in Cranford Pratt, 1989b, *Internationalism under Strain*.

Pratt, Cranford, ed., 1989b, *Internationalism under Strain: The North-South Policies of Canada, the Netherlands, Norway, and Sweden*, Toronto: University of Toronto Press.

*Prefaces to Peace*, 1943, Cooperatively published by Simon and Schuster; Doubleday; Doran and Co.; Reynal and Hitchcock; Columbia University Press.

Proceedings and Resolutions from the Plenary Congress of the International Federation of League of Nations Societies, in Folder: Ozd844 In8a, Mudd Library, Yale University.

Puffert, Douglas J., 1991, "The Economics of Spatial Network Externalities and the Dynamics of Railway Gauge Standardization," Ph.D. diss., Stanford University.

Putnam, Robert D., 1988, "Diplomacy and International Politics: The Logic of Two-Level Games," *International Organization* 42:427–60.

Rabier, Jacques-René, Helene Riffault, and Ronald Inglehart, principal investigators, 1983, *Euro-Barometer 13: Regional Development and Integration*, 2d ed., in ICPSR codebook, Ann Arbor, Mich.: Inter-University Consortium for Political and Social Research, 1980, and machine-readable data set.

———, 1985, *Euro-Barometer 20: Aid to Developing Nations*, in ICSPR codebook, Ann Arbor, Mich.: Inter-University Consortium for Political and Social Research, 1983 and machine-readable data set.

Raucher, Alan R., 1985, *Paul G. Hoffman: Architect of Foreign Aid*, Lexington: University Press of Kentucky.

Rauta, I(rene), 1971, *Aid and Overseas Development: A Survey of Public Attitudes, Opinions, and Knowledge*, London: Her Majesty's Stationery Office, Office of Population, Censuses, and Surveys; Social Survey Division.

Rawls, John, 1953, "Two Concepts of Rules," *The Philosophical Review* 64, 1 (January):3–32.

Renard, Robrecht, 1984, "Belgian Aid: Policy and Performance," in Olav Stokke, 1984a, *European Development Assistance*.

Rich, Norman, 1977, *The Age of Nationalism and Reform, 1850-1890*, 2d ed. New York: Norton.

Riddell, Roger, C., 1987, *Foreign Aid Reconsidered*, Baltimore: Johns Hopkins University Press.

Rielly, John E., ed., 1983, *American Public Opinion and U.S. Foreign Policy*, 1983, Chicago: Chicago Council on Foreign Relations.

Rippy, J. Fred, 1958, "Historical Perspective," in James W. Wiggins and Helmut Schoeck, 1958, *Foreign Aid Reexamined*.

Robertson, John D., 1984, "Foreign Aid and Political-Economic Change in Advanced Industrial States: Implications for LDCs," *Scandinavian Journal of Development Alternatives* 3, 4 (December): 38–60.

Robson, W. A., 1976, *Welfare State and Welfare Society*, London: Allen and Unwin.

Roemer, William Francis, 1929, *The Ethical Basis of International Law*, Chicago: Loyola University Press.

Romanofsky, Peter, ed., 1978, *Social Service Organizations*, 2 vols., Westport, Conn.: Greenwood Press.

Rostow, W. W., 1985, *Eisenhower, Kennedy, and Foreign Aid*, Austin: University of Texas Press.

Rousseau, Jean-Jacques, "Abstract of the Abbé de Saint-Pierre's Project for a Perpetual Peace," and "Judgment on Saint-Pierre's Project for Perpetual Peace," in M. G. Forsythe et al., 1970, *The Theory of International Relations*.

Royce, Josiah, [1886] 1970, *California: From the Conquest in 1846 to the Second Vigilance Committee in San Francisco. A Study of American Character*, Santa Barbara, Calif.: Peregrine Publishers.

Rubin, Seymour J., 1966, *The Conscience of the Rich Nations: The Development Assistance Committee and the Common Aid Effort*, New York: Harper and Row.

Ruggie, John G., 1983, "International Regimes, Transactions, and Change: Embedded Liberalism in the Postwar Economic Order," in Stephen Krasner, 1983, *International Regimes*.

Rushton, J. Philippe, 1980, *Altruism, Socialization and Society*, Englewood Cliffs, N.J.: Prentice-Hall.

Rushton, J. Philippe, and Richard M. Sorrentino, eds., 1981, *Altruism and Helping Behavior: Social, Personality, and Developmental Perspectives*, Hillsdale, N.J.: Lawrence Erlbaum Associates.

Russell, Bertrand, in collaboration with Dora Russell, 1923, *The Prospects of Industrial Civilization*, New York: Century Co.

Russell, Bertrand, [1910] 1917, *Political Ideals*, New York: Century Co.

Russett, Bruce M., 1990, *Controlling the Sword: The Democratization of National Security*, Cambridge: Harvard University Press.

Sady, Emil J., 1957, "Colonial Setting of the United Nations Charter," in Robert E. Asher et al., 1957, *The United Nations and Promotion of the General Welfare*.

Sahlins, Marshall D., 1972, *Stone Age Economics*, Chicago: Aldine-Atherton Press.

Sanford, Jonathan, 1982, *U.S. Foreign Policy and Multilateral Development Banks*, Boulder, Colo.: Westview Press.

———, 1988, "The World Bank and Poverty: The Plight of the World's Impoverished Is Still a Major Concern of the International Agency," *American Journal of Economics and Sociology* 47, 3 (July): pp. 257–75.

———, 1989, "The World Bank and Poverty: A Review of the Evidence on Whether the Agency Has Diminished Emphasis on Aid to the Poor," *American Journal of Economics and Sociology* 48, 2 (April): 151–64.

Schelling, Thomas, 1960, *The Strategy of Conflict*, Cambridge: Harvard University Press.

Schultz, Theodore W., ed., 1945, *Food for the World*, Chicago: University of Chicago Press.

Scott, David, 1969, "Some Aspects of Overseas Aid," in Max Teichmann, 1969, *New Directions in Australian Foreign Policy*.

Service, Elman R., 1962, *Primitive Social Organization*, New York: Random House.

Sharp, Paul, 1990, *Irish Foreign Policy and the European Community: A Study of the Impact of Interdependence on the Foreign Policy of a Small State*, Aldershot, Hants, England: Dartmouth Publishing.

Shenton, Herbert R., 1933, "Cosmopolitan Conversation: The Language of International Conferences," in Gerard J. Mangone, 1954, *A Short History of International Organization*.

Shivute, Tomas, 1980, *The Theology of Mission and Evangelism: In the International Missionary Council from Edinburgh to New Delhi*, Helsinki: Finnish Society for Missiology and Ecumenics and the Finnish Missionary Society.

Shue, Henry, 1980, *Basic Rights: Subsistence, Affluence, and U.S. Foreign Policy*, Princeton: Princeton University Press.

Singh, L. P., 1963, *The Colombo Plan: Some Political Aspects*, working paper no. 3, Canberra: Department of International Relations, Australian National University.

———, 1966, *The Politics of Economic Cooperation in Asia: A Study of Asian International Organizations*, Columbia: University of Missouri Press.

Skuhra, Anselm, 1984, "Austrian Aid: Policy and Performance" in Olav Stokke, 1984a, *European Development Assistance*.

Smith, Brian, 1990, *More than Altruism: The Politics of Private Foreign Aid*, Princeton: Princeton University Press.

Smith, Michael, Steve Smith, and Brian White, eds., 1988, *British Foreign Policy: Tradition, Change and Transformation*, London: Unwin Hyman.

Södersten, Bo, 1989, "Sweden: Towards a Realistic Internationalism," in Cranford Pratt, 1989, *Internationalism under Strain*.

Spykman, Nicholas John, 1942, *America's Strategy in World Politics*, New York: Harcourt, Brace and Co.

Staley, Eugene, 1940, *This Shrinking World: World Technology vs. National Politics*, Chicago: World Citizens Association, reprint of pt. 1 of Eugene Staley, 1939 *The World Economy in Transition*, New York: Council on Foreign Relations.

Stamp, Elizabeth, 1982, "Oxfam and Development," in Peter Willets, 1982, *Pressure Groups in the Global System*.

Staub, Ervin, 1978, *Positive Social Behavior and Morality: Social and Personal Influences*, vol. 1, New York: Academic Press.

Stevens, Christopher, ed., 1983, *EEC and The Third World: A Survey*, vol. 3, *The Atlantic Rift*, New York: Holmes and Meier, for the Overseas Development Institute and the Institute for Development Studies.

Stokke, Olav, 1984b, "Norwegian Aid: Policy and Performance," in Olav Stokke, ed., 1984a, *European Development Assistance*

Stokke, Olav, ed., 1984a, *European Development Assistance*, vol. 1, *Policies and Performance*, Tilburg: European Association of Development Research and Training Institutes; Oslo: Norwegian Institute of International Affairs.

Stone, D. A., 1984, *The Disabled State*, Philadelphia: Temple University Press.

Suarez, Francisco, S.J. [1611–21] 1944, *Selections from Three Works: De Legibus, Ac Deo Legislatore, 1612; Defensio Fidei Catholicae, et Apostolicae Adversus Anglicanae Sectae Errores, 1613; De Triplicati Virtute Theologica, Fide,*

*Spe, et Charitate, 1621*, edited by James Brown Scott, Oxford: Clarendon Press.

Sundelius, Bengt, ed., 1982, *Foreign Policies of Northern Europe*, Boulder, Colo.: Westview Press.

Svendsen, Knud Erik, 1984, "Danish Aid: Consolidation and Adjustments in the 1980s," in Olav Stokke, ed., 1984a, *European Development Assistance*.

Tarlton, Charles David, 1964, "Internationalism, War, and Politics in American Thought, 1898–1920," Ph.D. diss., University of California at Los Angeles, Ann Arbor: University Microfilms.

Tawney, R. H. [1931] 1965, *Equality*, New York: Barnes and Noble.

Taylor, Michael, 1976, *Anarchy and Cooperation*, New York: Wiley.

———, 1982, *Community, Anarchy and Liberty*, Cambridge: Cambridge University Press.

———, 1987, *The Possibility of Cooperation*, Studies in Rationality and Social Change, edited by Jon Elster, Cambridge: Cambridge University Press.

Taylor, Paul, and A. J. R. Groom, 1978, eds., *International Organization: A Conceptual Approach*, London: Francis Pinter; New York: Nichols Publishing.

Taylor, Phillip, and Gregory A. Raymond, eds., 1981, *Third World Policies of Industrialized Nations*, Westport, Conn.: Greenwood Press.

Teichmann, Max, ed., 1969, *New Directions in Australian Foreign Policy: Ally, Satellite or Neutral?* Harmondsworth, Middlesex, England: Penguin.

Tendler, Judith, 1975, *Inside Foreign Aid*, Baltimore: Johns Hopkins University Press.

Thomson, Janice Eileen, 1988, "The State, Sovereignty, and International Violence: The Institutional and Normative Basis of State Control over External Violence," Ph.D. diss., Stanford University.

Thorp, Willard L., 1985, "The DAC's Expanding Influence," in OECD, *Twenty Five Years of Development Cooperation*.

Thucydides, *The Peloponnesian War*, translated by Richard Crawley, revised by T. E. Wick, New York: Modern Library.

Titmuss, Richard M., 1958a, Essays on *"The Welfare State,"* London: Allen and Unwin.

———, 1958b, "The Social Division of Welfare: Some Reflections on the Search for Equality," in Richard M. Titmuss, 1958a, *Essays on The Welfare State*.

———, 1971, *The Gift Relationship*, New York: Pantheon Books.

Todorov, Tzvetan, 1984, *The Conquest of America: The Question of the Other*, translated by Richard Howard, New York: Harper and Row.

Townley, Ralph, 1966, "The Economic Organs of the United Nations," in Evan Luard, 1966, *The Evolution of International Organizations*.

Truman, Harry S., 1956, *Memoirs*, 2 vol., Garden City, N.Y.: Doubleday.

Truman, Margaret, 1973, *Harry S. Truman*, New York: William Morrow.

United Nations, 1945, *Five Technical Reports of Food and Agriculture: Submitted to the United Nations Interim Commission on Food and Agriculture by Its Technical Committees on Nutrition and Food Management, Agricultural Production, Fisheries, Forestry and Primary Forest Products, and Statistics*, Washington, D.C.: United Nations Interim Commission on Food and Agriculture.

United Nations (George Hakim, Alberto Baltra Cortez, D. R. Gadgil, W. Arthur

Lewis, Theodore W. Schultz), 1951, *Measures for the Economic Development of Under-Developed Countries: Report by a Group of Experts Appointed by the Secretary-General of the United Nations*, New York: United Nations, Department of Economic Affairs.

United Nations Conference on Food and Agriculture, 1943a, *The Final Act of the United Nations Conference on Food and Agriculture*, Hot Springs, Va., May 18–June 3, 1943, London: His Majesty's Stationery Office.

United Nations Conference on Food and Agriculture, 1943b, *Section Reports of the Conference* (Hot Springs, Va.), London: His Majesty's Stationary Office.

U.S. *Overseas Loans and Grants, and Assistance from International Organizations*, 1983, Statistical Annex 1 to the Annual Development Coordination Committee Report to Congress, CONG-R-0105.

Van Soest, Jaap, 1978, *The Start of International Development Cooperation in the United Nations, 1945–1952*, Assen, Netherlands: Van Gorcum and Co.

Victoria, Francisco de [1557 and 1696], 1917, *De Indis et de Jure Belli Relectiones*, translated by John Pawley Bate, edited by Ernest Nys, Oxford: Clarendon.

Vogler, John, 1988, "Britain and North-South Relations," in Michael Smith et al., 1988, *British Foreign Policy*.

Walters, F. P., 1966, "The League of Nations," in Evan Luard, 1966, *The Evolution of International Organizations*.

Waltz, Kenneth N., 1959, *Man, the State and War*, New York: Columbia University Press.

———, 1979, *Theory of International Politics*, Reading, Mass.: Addison-Wesley Publishing Co.

Walzer, Michael, 1977, *Just and Unjust Wars: A Moral Argument with Illustrations*, New York: Basic Books.

Ward, Barbara, 1962, *The Rich Nations and the Poor Nations*, New York: W. W. Norton and Company.

Weidner, Edward W., 1969, *Prelude to Reorganization: The Kennedy Foreign Aid Message of March 22, 1961*, Syracuse, N.Y.: Inter-University Case Program.

Welles, Sumner, 1943, "Blueprint for Peace," in *Prefaces to Peace*, 1943.

Wendt, Alexander E., 1987, "The Agent-Structure Problem in International Relations Theory," *International Organization* 41, 3 (Summer): 335–70.

———, 1992, "Anarchy Is What States Make of It: The Social Construction of Power Politics," *International Organization* 46, no. 2.

White, Lyman Cromwell, assisted by Marie Ragonetti Zocca, 1951, *International Non-Governmental Organizations: Their Purposes, Methods, and Accomplishments*, New Brunswick, N.J.: Rutgers University Press.

Wiggins, James W., and Helmut Schoeck, eds., 1958, *Foreign Aid Reexamined: A Critical Reappraisal*, Washington, D.C.: Public Affairs Press.

Willemin, Georges, and Roger Heacock, 1984, *The International Committee of the Red Cross*, Boston: Martinus Nijhoff, vol. 2 of *International Organization and the Evolution of World Society*, under the direction of Jacques Freymond, under the auspices of the Graduate Institute of International Studies, Geneva, and Società Italiana per la Organizzazione Internazionale, Rome.

Willets, Peter, ed., 1982, *Pressure Groups in the Global System: The Transnational Relations of Issue-Oriented Non-Governmental Organizations*, London: Francis Pinter.

Willkie, Wendell, 1943, "One World," in *Prefaces to Peace*, 1943.

Wilson, Harold, 1953, *The War on World Poverty: An Appeal to the Conscience of Mankind*, London: Victor Gollanz.

Wilson, Thomas, and Dorothy J. Wilson, 1982, *The Political Economy of the Welfare State*, Boston: Allen and Unwin.

Wittkopf, Eugene R., 1990, *Faces of Internationalism: Public Opinion and American Foreign Policy*, Durham, N.C.: Duke University Press.

Wood, Bernard, 1982, "Canada and Third World Development: Testing Mutual Interests," in Robert Cassen et al., 1982, *Rich Country Interests*.

Wood, Robert E., 1986, *From Marshall Plan to Debt Crisis: Foreign Aid and Development Choices in the World Economy*, Berkeley: University of California Press.

World Bank, 1975, *The Assault on World Poverty: Problems of Rural Development, Education, and Health*, preface by Robert McNamara, Baltimore: Johns Hopkins University Press for the World Bank.

World Citizens' Association, 1941, *The World's Destiny and the United States: A Conference of Experts in International Relations*, Chicago: World Citizens' Association.

World Council of Churches, 1948a, *First Assembly of the World Council of Churches: Amsterdam, Holland, August 22nd–September 4th, 1948. Findings and Decisions*, Geneva, London, New York: World Council of Churches.

————, 1948b, *The Ten Formative Years, 1938–1948: Report on the Activities of the World Council of Churches during its Period of Formation*, Geneva: World Council of Churches.

World Council of Churches, n.d. [1954?], *Commission of the Churches on International Affairs*, Lausanne, Switzerland: Commission of the Churches on International Affairs, World Council of Churches, and International Missionary Council.

World Council of Churches, [early to middle 1950s], "Refugees," pamphlet, (Yale Divinity Special Collection: B011.22, Geneva: World Council of Churches, Oikumene.

Yasutomo, Dennis T., 1986, *The Manner of Giving: Strategic Aid and Japanese Foreign Policy*, Lexington, Mass.: Lexington Books.

Yoder, Amos, 1989, *The Evolution of the United Nations System*, New York: Crane Russak.

Zarjevski, Yefime, 1988, *A Future Preserved: International Assistance to Refugees*, Oxford: Pergamon Press, for the Office of the United Nations High Commissioner for Refugees.

# Index

acknowledgment of human neediness, xiii, xiv, 293
Addams, Jane, 188
affirmative action, 11
Africa, 285
African Development Bank (AFDB), 244
African Development Fund, 245
aid. *See* foreign aid
Alliance for Progress, 239, 241–42
altruism: in human nature and society, 9–11, 138, 185, 321–22n.10; private voluntary contributions to poor nations, 121–25, 122t, 123f, 124t. *See also* egoism; human nature; humanitarianism; private charity and philanthropy
America. *See* Latin America; United States
American Council of Voluntary Agencies for Foreign Service (ACVAFS), 192
Amnesty International, 11
anarchy, 12–21: cooperation under, 6–8, 13–15, 29, 57–60, 145, 200–202, 269, 287; structural implications of, 7–8, 14–15, 16, 21, 287. *See also* determinism, structural; moral choice and responsibility; social construction of international politics; survival pressures
anticommunism: as determinant of support for foreign aid, 53, 55–57, 144, 309n.22; as reason for forming aid programs, 225–27, 237; and U.S. security-supporting assistance, 50, 109–11, 134. *See also* security interests
anti-war sentiment, 190, 196, 217
Arab countries. *See* OPEC aid
Arndt, H. W., 200
Asia. *See* Colombo Plan; *individual countries*
Asian Development Bank, 245
Asian Development Fund, 245
Atlantic Charter, 65, 201, 203–4, 206, 210–11, 219. *See also* United Nations
Auerbach, Kenneth D., 98
Australia, foreign aid of: group and party support for, 158, 160, 162; motivations for, 106, 108, 110, 124–25, 132, 170, 171; public opinion about, 116–17, 144; regional relationships in, 86–87, 87t, 108
Austria, foreign aid of, 109, 121, 125, 142, 170, 171; support for, 116–17, 158, 165–66, 175
Axelrod, Robert, 16, 18–19, 57, 296nn.33 and 34

balance of payments, 111
Basic Human Needs strategy, 248
Belgian Relief, 68, 208, 218; Hoover's efforts regarding, 192, 205–6, 208
Belgium: foreign aid of, 105–6, 108, 121, 170; colonial ties in, 83, 84; domestic support for, 116, 166
Bencivenga, Valerie R., 99–100
Beveridge, William Henry, 185
Beveridge Report, 185–86
Bevin, Ernest, 189–90, 217
bilateral assistance, 40t2.2, 52, 99–100; and colonial ties, 85–86, 100; and trade patterns, 77t3.3, 78t, 79t; U.S. non-SSA, 99–100, 102
bipolar world. *See* anticommunism; security interests; Soviet bloc aid
Black, Eugene, 235
Blake, Eugene Carson, 158
Blanqui, Jerome Adolphe, 193–94
Bourgeois, Leon (Prime Minister), 184
Brandt, Willi (Chancellor), 42, 140, 165, 172
Brandt Commission Report, 31, 51, 162, 165
Bretton Woods conference, 46, 214–15, 274. *See also* International Monetary Fund; World Bank
Britain: Colonial Development Acts of 1929, 1940 and 1948, 204, 209; colonial ties in aid, 99–100, 102, 108, 170; foreign aid policy and program, 82, 83–84, 85, 105, 132, 170, 243, 249; group and party support for, 160–61, 161–62, 219, 239; Lend-Lease program with U.S., 211, 215; poverty orientation, 168; public opinion on, 116, 144, 149–50, 151; so-

cial welfare and labor policies of, 184–
88. *See also* Thatcher, Margaret
Bruce Commission, 213
burden-sharing, 256
Bush, George (President), 249

Canada, 106; party and group support for
aid, 160–61, 162–63; public opinion on
aid, 142; social welfare policies of, 184
capital resources, in foreign aid, 235
capitalism: actions of business firms, 15,
159; and humanitarianism, 284; and
poverty, 184; preserving world, 53–54,
112–14
CARE, 192, 218
Carnegie Foundation and Endowment for
International Peace, 10, 201, 217
Carr, E. H. (Edward Hallett), 8
CEEC. *See* Committee for European Economic Cooperation
Chamberlain, Neville (Prime Minister), 198
change in the international system: based on
meaningful practices, 26–28, 68–69,
207–10, 230, 233–34; description of
major, 182–220, 221–52, 253–69; evolution of cooperation, 16–17, 18–19,
112–14; explanations of, 3–6, 16–17,
223–27, 272, 275–77, 283. *See also* international system
charitable organizations and individuals.
*See* private charity and philanthropy
China, 202, 208
choice. *See* change in the international system; determinism, structural; moral
choice and responsibility
church attendance. *See* religion
Churchill, Winston (Prime Minister), 65,
203, 210
CMEA. *See* Council for Mutual Economic
Assistance
cold war. *See* anticommunism
Cole, G. D. H., 202
Colombo Plan, 47, 217, 222, 230, 236–38,
250, 274–75; basis for initiating, 190,
275
Colonial Development Acts of 1929 and
1940 (British), 204, 209
colonial ties, of aid donors and recipients,
82–86, 83t, 100, 108, 305n.4; Belgian,
Dutch, and Italian, 83–84, 108; British,
99–100, 102, 108; French, 85–86, 99–
100, 102, 108, 303n.7, 310n.55; French

territories (DOM and TOM), 85,
306n.12; as motive for aid, 73, 107–9,
209, 310n.55. *See also* decolonization;
Third World
Committee for European Economic Cooperation (CEEC), 216
common good. *See* international cooperation
communism. *See* anticommunism; security
interests; Soviet bloc aid
comparative analysis of donor aid policies.
*See* anarchy: cooperation under; foreign
aid, comparisons of donor states
concessional loans, 38, 48t2.10
Congress of Vienna (1815), 190
conservative politics, 119, 137, 145, 159,
161–62, 163, 166–67, 228, 250; critique
of foreign aid, 31; instances of aid support, 205
cooperation. *See* international cooperation
"cooperative internationalism," 5, 145,
147t
Council for Mutual Economic Assistance
(CMEA) aid, 128–30, 129t. *See also* Soviet bloc aid
cross-national comparisons in foreign aid.
*See* foreign aid, comparisons of donor
states

DAC. *See* Development Assistance Committee of the OECD
de Gaulle, Charles (President), 169
Declaration of the United Nations, 46, 211,
218
decolonization, 224–25
democracy, 10, 16, 19, 20; democratic
states not fighting each other, 16; imper-
fections in, 32; promoting international
order, 20, 23, 287–88. *See also* developed
democracies; public opinion; social philosophies of donor states
Denmark, foreign aid of: 121, 124, 133,
135, 158; poverty focus in, 102, 168;
public support for, 116, 141, 166
dependency theory, 24, 299n.74, 302n.2.
*See also* Third World
determinism, structural (in international
system): arguments against, 5–6, 8–9,
11–12, 14–17, 19, 28, 219, 227–28, 273,
287; based on objective laws, 7–8, 12–
14. *See also* moral choice and responsibility; survival pressures

developed democracies, 178, 243; fostering international institutions, 5, 230–31, 280, 289; of the West, compared with OPEC, 130–32; of the West, compared with Soviet bloc (CMEA), 127–30. *See also* foreign aid, comparisons of donor states

development assistance. *See* foreign aid

Development Assistance Committee (DAC) of the OECD, 113–14, 216, 271, 300n.7; adoption of stricter standards, 244; change of name of annual report, 171; expanded membership, 243; increasing influence of standards, 245–48; variation in state compliance to standards, 113–14, 271. *See also* foreign aid, comparisons of donor states; foreign aid, motives for; *individual countries*

Development Loan Fund (DLF), 239

DOM and TOM. *See under* France

domestic influence on international politics, systematic: apart from foreign aid, 5, 19, 24, 45–46, 189, 200; and concern about poverty, 126–27, 140, 217, 288–89, 323n.4; influencing foreign aid, 5, 63–65, 69, 104, 135, 137–40, 156–61; in public opinion on foreign aid, 43, 116–18, 143–44, 148, 152, 154; theory of, 8, 13, 16–17, 19–20, 22–24, 278–79; welfare policy and aid policy, 41–42, 119–21, 120f, 125, 122t, 124t. *See also* political views and parties; social philosophies of donor states; welfare state

domestic special interests, 23, 50–51, 159, 323–24n.5

Donnelly, Jack, 19

donor states. *See* foreign aid, comparisons of donor states

Dunant, J. Henry, 11, 168, 190–91

Dutch aid policy and program. *See under* Netherlands

Dutch Anti-War Council, 196

Economic and Social Council of the UN (ECOSOC), 213–14, 215, 219, 234, 274. *See also* Expanded Programme of Technical Assistance

economic and social justice, 189, 202, 293; expressed in political ideas and programs, 45, 68, 140, 165, 189, 219. *See also* egalitarianism

Economic and Social Rights Charter (of the UN), 218

economic assistance. *See* foreign aid

economic basis of security, 198–204, 205–6, 210–13, 221–23, 286–87. *See also* justice and world order

Economic Commission for Asia and the Far East (ECAFE), 214

Economic Commission for Latin America (ECLA), 214, 234

economic development: of recipient nations as motive for aid, 94, 95t3.12, 98–99; special UN fund for (SUNFED), 244–45; of Third World nations, 64, 93–94, 99, 100, 233–34, 245–48, 283; UN subcommission on, 234–35; and world poverty, 285–86

economic interests, 39–41, 40tt.2.2 and 2.3, 50, 74, 270; and donor giving patterns, 59, 105–7, 106t, 107t; as predictor of aid spending, 3, 6, 51–52, 57–60, 104, 133–36, 224

economic need, aid levels related to, 94, 95t3.12

ECOSOC. *See* Economic and Social Council of the UN

Edinburgh World Missionary Conference, 197

education, and support for foreign aid, 145, 146t

egalitarianism, 29, 30, 115–16, 119–25, 223–24; domestic sources of, 138, 144, 148, 154, 179; favoring egalitarian LDCs, 54, 55, 110; power of idea of, 184, 185–87, 313n.4; social democracy, labor, and, 188–90, 193, 217

egoism, 8, 17, 19, 148, 269. *See also* human nature

Eisenhower, Dwight (President), 43, 206, 228–39

elites, views on aid, 138, 169

England. *See* Britain

EPTA. *See* Expanded Programme of Technical Assistance

ethics and ethical beliefs. *See* moral convictions; social philosophies of donor states

Euro-Barometer surveys, 117, 139, 141, 143–45, 151–52, 180–81

European foreign aid: egalitarian values in, 54; non-DAC countries providing, 249; and public opinion, 138, 141, 143–48, 151–56. *See also* developed democracies; Euro-Barometer surveys; foreign aid,

European foreign aid (*cont.*)
  comparisons of donor states; *individual countries*
European Recovery Program (ERP). *See* Marshall Plan
European Relief Council, 192
Expanded Programme of Technical Assistance (EPTA), 212, 222, 235–36; initiation of, 47, 230–31, 234–36, 275. *See also* technical assistance; United Nations Development Program
exports. *See* trade relationships

financial terms for international loans, 47, 264–66, 300–301n.11
Finland, foreign aid of, 106, 109, 121, 125, 133, 238, 249; influence of international society 25–26, 66, 172–73, 177; influence of public opinion, 117, 141–42, 167; joining DAC, 58; percentage movement, 158
foreign aid: advocates of, 137, 140, 156, 158–61, 164–68; defined and characterized, 33, 36, 37–39, 68–69, 290, 299n.74, 300n.7, 323–24n.5; financial importance to LDCs, 4, 30, 34–36, 35t, 69; larger than investment by multinationals, 34, 35t, 105, 106t; opponents of, 31, 42, 43, 137, 140, 159, 162–64; policies reflecting national values, 167–70; public scrutiny of, 38, 276; role in North-South relations, 4. *See also* bilateral assistance; multilateral assistance
foreign aid, comparisons of donor states, 41–41, 63–64, 106t, 107t, 119–21, 120f, 122t, 124t, 133t, 301–2n.16; domestic social spending and charity explain differences, 118–27; emphasis on poverty, 99–100, 102; public support for, 58, 116–18, 121–25, 140–43; similarities among, 42, 114–15, 127–28, 132–34, 154; social philosophies, 116–18, 119; variable compliance with international standards, 58, 113–14, 271. *See also* colonial ties; developed democracies; regional relationships; social philosophies of donor states
foreign aid, history of, 29, 34–37, 35t, 221–252, 230, 274, 284; emergence of after World War II, 30, 216–20; gradual further institutionalization (seventies), 244–49; institutionalization, 221–23,

230–38, 273, 278, 279–80, 287, 300–301n.11; recent changes (eighties), 249–50; reinstitutionalization (sixties), 239–44; timing as test of hypotheses, 223–29. *See also* foreign aid, long-term trends in; foreign aid regime
foreign aid, long-term trends in, 253–80, 254, 268–69, 271, 272; focus on poorest nations, 50t, 52, 68, 94–103, 95tt.3.11 and 3.12, 96t, 97t; focus on poverty sectors within LDCs, 52, 68, 101tt.3.15 and 3.16; growing volume, 254–55, 255t; increase in diversity of supply, 256, 257t; increasing multilateral assistance, 41t2.4, 47–50, 52, 102, 159, 244–45, 257–60, 259tt.8.4 and 8.5, 261tt.8.6 and 8.7; reduced concentration of recipients, 257, 258t, 259tt.8.4 and 8.5; softened financial terms, 264–66; untying, 48t.2.9, 48, 69, 260, 262–64, 263t, 265tt.8.9 and 8.10
foreign aid, motives for, 30–32, 39–50, 143–49, 178–79; competition for influence, 60–62; direct evidence about, 137, 149–51; domestic ideals, 63–65, 182–95, 217; international society, 65–67, 173–78, 195–98, 207–16, 289; justice as a basis for order, 198–207, 279–80, 283, 287; influence of international society, 25–26, 174–78, 289; national ideals, 167–73; preservation of capitalist order, 53–54, 112–14; and strength of support for aid, 36, 134–36, 151–52. *See also* altruism; anticommunism; colonial ties; economic development; economic interests; egalitarianism; foreign aid, comparisons of donor states; humanitarian internationalism; humanitarianism; international cooperation; justice and world order; mixed motives for foreign aid programs; regional relationships; security interests
foreign aid, origins and antecedents, 45–47, 115n.115, 182–220, 182–83, 216–20, 274; growth of internationalism, 188, 190–93, 195–98; humanitarian and religious roots, 186–88, 196–98; interwar period, 46, 193, 196, 197, 199, 200–202, 207–10; labor movements and social democracy, 184–85, 188–90, 193–95; lessons drawn, consolidating internationalism, 198–207; in origins and rise of the

welfare state, 183–86, 186–88; postwar period (late forties), 37, 69, 199, 204–5, 212–16; wartime thought and collaboration, 202–7, 210–12

foreign aid, recipients of: colonial ties with donors, 82–86, 83t; cutting off of aid to, 74; poorest nations, 50t, 52, 68, 94–103, 95tt.3.11 and 3.12, 96t, 97t; poverty sectors within poor nations, 52, 68, 101tt.3.15 and 3.16; special or regional ties with donors, 86–90, 87t; as trading partners, 75–82, 76t, 77tt.3.2 and 3.3, 78t, 79t, 80t, 81t. See also Africa; Asia; Latin America; least developed countries; less developed countries; low income countries; Third World

foreign aid regime: benefits of, 285; changes in characterized, 239–44, 268–69, 271–72; effects of processes and institutions, 245–48, 251, 269, 276–67; influenced by beliefs and moral values, 253, 271–74, 287–93; origins and basis of emergence, 30, 216–20, 224–25, 227–29, 275; professional personnel in, 27–28, 50, 276; reinforced through international cooperation, 228–29; solidity of over time, 132–34, 133t; underlying processes of changes in, 273–77. See also foreign aid, comparisons of donor states; international economic institutions

Four Freedoms, 46, 202, 206, 210–11, 218; from hunger and want, 201, 211, 223

France, foreign aid of: and advocacy for Third World, 102; and colonial ties, 82–86, 99–100, 102, 108, 209, 303n.7, 310n.55; to DOM and TOM, 85, 164, 306n.12; funding level, 105, 108, 125–26, 132–34; Jeanneny report, 243; public support for, 116, 118; revival under Mitterand, 102, 118, 164–65, 169, 249; social welfare and, 121, 124

France, social welfare and labor policies, 184, 188

Frank, Robert, 298n.62, 307–8n.2

freedom from want, and from fear. See Four Freedoms; justice and world order

Friedman, Milton, 43

Fukuda (Prime Minister), 175

Gandhi, Mohandas K., 11

GATT (General Agreement on Tariffs and Trade), 57

Geneva Convention, 191

Germany: foreign aid of, 99, 116–18; party and group support for aid, 158, 165; poverty orientation of aid, 169; social welfare policies, 184. See also Brandt, Willi; Brandt Commission Report; Hallstein Doctrine

global community. See international society

global security interests. See anticommunism

global system. See international system

Goldwater, Barry (Senator), 42, 137, 163, 228

Gompers, Samuel, 194

Goodin, Robert E., 104, 183–84, 185

Green Corps, 176

Hague conferences of 1899 and 1907, 196

Hallstein Doctrine, 51, 74

Hansen, Alvin H., 204–5, 318nn.114 and 115

Hardy, Benjamin, 210, 321nn.8 and 9

Hayter, Teresa, 140

hegemonic power, 53–54, 57, 111–12

Hobson, John Atkinson, 188

Hoffman, Paul G., 43, 140, 177

Hoover, Herbert (President), 192, 205–6, 208

Hull, Cordell (Secretary of State), 202, 219

human nature, 6–12, 13, 292–93; complexity of 8, 12; destructive side of, 6, 8–9, 11, 18–19, 19–20; idealistic and constructive side of, 9–11

humanitarian internationalism, 22–28, 45–47, 137, 171, 178–81, 180–81t, 182, 254, 277; as basis of aid, 3–6, 29–32, 68–69, 178–79, 216–20; as basis for foreign aid regime, 216–20, 227–29, 283–84; correlated with support for aid, 63–65, 124–25, 134–35, 145, 147t, 148; stated rationale for aid, 118, 137–38, 149–51, 163, 167–69. See also idealism; moral convictions; poverty: public concern over; social philosophies of donor states

humanitarianism, 9–11, 148, 193, 223, 283. See also humanitarian internationalism

Humphrey, Hubert H. (Senator), 42–43, 137, 163–64

hunger, world, 69, 158, 161, 206

IBRD. *See* World Bank

IDA. *See* International Development Association

IDB. *See* Inter-American Development Bank

idealism. 8, 167–70, 241–44 *See also* altruism; human nature; humanitarianism; justice and world order; Wilson, Woodrow; Wilsonian internationalism

ideas and ideals, shaping international politics: concepts implicit in practices, 26–28; influencing national policies, 12, 19–20, 167–73; political and ethical, 143–49, 161–67, 299n.74; Realist view of, 6–8, 20–21; staying power, 253–55, 272–78; structuring interests, 4–6, 21–22, 155–56, 198–200, 200–202. *See also* moral convictions; moral vision; political views and parties

IIAA. *See* Institute of Inter-American Affairs

ILO. *See* International Labour Organization

IMF. *See* International Monetary Fund

imports. *See* trade relationships

India, 82, 149, 238

individual charitable giving. *See* private charity and philanthropy

Institute of Inter-American Affairs (IIAA), 210, 232–33

institutions: effects and processes of, 245–48, 251, 269, 276–77; persistence of, 15

Inter-American Development Bank (IDB), 239, 244

Inter-Parliamentary Union, 195, 196

Interdepartmental Committee on Scientific and Cultural Cooperation, 210

interdependence, 195, 201, 204, 206, 210, 213; related to ethical concerns, 170–73, 273; unaffordable costs of ignoring, 205, 286. *See also* Brandt Commission Report; Philadelphia Declaration

interest groups supporting for foreign aid, 156, 158–61

International Bank for Reconstruction and Development (IBRD). *See* World Bank

international community. *See* international society

international cooperation: based on beliefs and values, 17, 28–29, 139, 223, 272–74; based on mutual gain, 12–21, 57–58, 112–14, 270; evolving, 16–17, 18–19, 112–14; increasing returns to, 15, 16; reinforcing aid regime, 228–29. *See also* anarchy: cooperation under

International Development Association (IDA), 239–40

international economic institutions, 212–14, 228–29, 280; coordinating functions of, 240; formation of, 212–14, 230–31; fostered by developed democracies, 5, 230–31, 280, 289. *See also* Expanded Programme of Technical Assistance; United Nations Development Program; World Bank; *individual organizations*

international economy, 200–202, 204–5

International Finance Corporation (IFC), 239

International Labour Organization (ILO), 45–46, 65, 194–95, 201, 207, 209, 218, 320–21n.169. *See also* labor associations, and trade unions; Philadelphia Declaration

International Missionary Council, 45, 197, 218

International Monetary Fund (IMF), 33, 57, 214. *See also* Bretton Woods conference; World Bank

international relations, history of, 195–200, 216–20; consolidation of internationalism, 198–200; growth of international law and collaboration, 190–93; growth of internationalist sentiment, 45, 46, 195–98, 200–202; institutionalization, 207–10, 230; lessons of the interwar period on, 200–207; lessons of the twenties and thirties on, 200–207; wartime collaborative efforts, 210–12, 214–15. *See also* foreign aid, history of

international relations, theories of change in, 20–21, 22, 34, 112–14; based on common economic interests, 112–14, 270; emphasis on power and violence, 6, 8, 11, 291; structural determination, 12, 14, 16, 17, 20, 137, 296n.26; structural-institutional, 251–52. *See also* humanitarian internationalism; international cooperation; rationality; Realist view of international relations

international society: influencing state behavior, 24, 25–26, 29, 245–48; national aid policies linked to, 170–73, 177, 228; and world public opinion, 173–78

international system, 4, 223–227, 284; change processes in, 16–17, 268–69, 272, 275–77, 290; choice and variability within, 14–15, 21, 113–14, 271, 291–92, 302n.22; ideas and ideals purposively

shaping, 3–6, 269, 272–78, 283, 288–89. *See also* anarchy; change in the international system; regimes, international
internationalism: consolidation of, 198–200; rise of, 45–47, 190–93, 195–98, 200–207, 217. *See also* humanitarian internationalism
interpretivist view of international relations. *See* social construction of international politics
interwar period, 46, 185, 186, 193, 199, 200–207. *See also* World War I
Ireland, foreign aid of: international society and, 58, 109, 172, 174; missionary impulse, 161; motivations for, 25–26, 66–67; policy and program of, 117, 249, 311–12n.94
isolationism, 200, 285
Italy, foreign aid of, 83, 84, 108, 121, 132; and basic human needs, 168–69; and public opinion, 116–17, 141–42

Japan, foreign aid of, 108, 121, 134, 166, 249; economic self-interest in, 50–51, 88–89, 93, 99; idealism and improved quality of, 159, 160tt.5.7 and 5.8, 249; international opinion and, 66, 102, 175–77; public opinion and, 117–18, 141–42; regional relationships of, 87t, 88–90; security objectives in, 110
Johnson, Lyndon B. (President), 242
Just War theory, 24
justice and world order, 155–56, 170–73, 286–87, 290–91, 293, 321–22n.10. *See also* economic basis of security

Kant, Immanuel, 16, 20
Kekkonen, Urho (President), 167, 172–73
Kennan, George Frost, 55
Kennedy, John F. (President), 241–42
Keohane, Robert O., 57, 58, 297–98n.55
Keynes, John Maynard, 3, 219
Keynesian economics, 189, 199
King, Martin Luther, Jr., 10–11, 283
Krasner, Stephen D., 15, 57
Kreisky, Chancellor, 165, 171, 177
Kuwait, aid policy and program of, 130, 131

labor associations, and trade unions: international, 193–95, 207, 217, 320–21n.169; and social democracy, 45–46, 188–89; supporting aid, 65, 144, 158–59, 194–95, 277
Labour Party and governments, 161, 219, 239
laissez-faire policies, 139, 187, 199, 200, 273
Lappé, Frances Moore, 140
Latin America, 24, 234; role in international institutions, 46, 215, 219. *See also* Alliance for Progress; Institute of Inter-American Affairs; Inter-American Development Bank
Laudicina, Paul A., 144–45, 149, 150
League of Nations, 46, 190, 196, 207–9, 217, 320–21n.169; Health Organization of, 207–8; U.S. failure to join, 202
least developed countries (LLDCs): increasing orientation of DAC to aid of, 96, 97, 245–48, 304n.21; public support for helping, 149–51, 151; U.S. funding to, 91–93, 92t; worsening conditions in, 285–86. *See also* low income countries
left political views. *See* liberal politics; New Deal and social-democratic programs; socialism
Leo XII (Pope), 194
less developed countries (LDCs), 221; disbursements among, 50t2.13, 96t, 96–98, 97t; financial importance of foreign aid to, 4, 30, 34–36, 35t, 69. *See also* least developed countries; low income countries
lessons of history, perceived: of interwar period, 198–200, 200–203, 206; of postwar period, 199; problems of competitive nationalism, 201; worldwide responsibility, 200, 202
Lewis, Sir W. Arthur, 200, 236
liberal politics, 119, 137, 139–40, 145, 152, 161–63, 163–64, 165–66
Lindholm, Stig, 145, 148, 150
Lloyd George, David (Prime Minister), 184
loans, international, 49t.2.12, 49, 99, 208, 264, 265t, 266t; for capital resources, 235; commercial, 33; concessional or "soft," 38, 47, 48t.2.10, 264–66, 300–301n.11
long-term self-interest. *See* economic basis of security; justice and world order
Lorwin, Lewis L., 201, 203–4
low income countries, 30, 40; increasing shift in aid to, 29, 36, 38–39, 48–49, 52,

243–49, 246t, 250, 266–69, 267t. *See also* least developed countries; poverty
Luxembourg, 117

McKinlay, R. D., 90, 91
McNamara, Robert S. (Secretary of State), 73, 242, 248, 251, 276, 290
Maizels, Alfred, 98
Mandates System, of League, 209, 218
market system. *See* capitalism
Marshall, Alfred, 186
Marshall, George C., Secretary of State, 215
Marshall Plan, 5, 46–47, 55, 68, 177–78, 215–16, 232, 274
Mather, Kirtley, 204
May, James, 189
military assistance, 33, 90
military interests, 145, 146t, 147t; and expenditures, 16, 51, 286; "militant internationalism," 5, 145. *See also* security interests
Mitterand, François, 43, 86, 118, 164–65, 169, 249
mixed motives for foreign aid programs, 4, 31–32, 42, 47, 73–74, 86, 89, 135, 169–70. *See also* justice and world order
moral aspects of international relations. *See* humanitarian internationalism; idealism; justice and world order; moral choice and responsibility; moral convictions; moral vision; religion; social philosophies of donor states
moral choice and responsibility, xiv, 3, 4–5, 9–11, 19–20, 62–63, 283–90, 302n.22. *See also* determinism, structural; moral convictions
moral convictions, 145, 146t, 148, 154, 157tt.5.5 and 5.6, 192–93; combined with political pressure, 185–86; constituting interests and debate, 140, 220, 238, 275, 277–78; related to worldview, 273, 291; shaping international regime, 3, 5, 27, 29, 62–63, 68, 283–85, 287–93; and support for foreign aid, 44tt.2.6 and 2.7, 64, 309n.27. *See also* idealism; ideas and ideals; moral vision; religion
moral vision: author's worldview, xiii–xiv, 283–90; behind foreign aid, 104, 137, 163–64, 176, 221–24, 228–29; behind foreign aid, sources of, 42–45, 45–50, 182–220, esp. 216–220; shapes interna-

tional politics, 3–4, 12, 19–22, 137–40, 250–51, 277, 283–84; structuring rationality, 26–29, 155–56, 272–73, 278–79, 287–92
Morgenthau, Hans J., 8, 62, 137, 295n.12
Mosley, Paul, 117–18
Mother Theresa, 10, 32
motives for foreign aid. *See* foreign aid, motives for
Mughan, A., 90, 91
multilateral assistance: features of, 41, 235, 299–300n.6; increasing role of, 41t.2.4, 47–50, 52, 102, 159, 244–45, 254, 257–60, 259tt.8.4 and 8.5, 261tt.8.6 and 8.7; opposition or harm to, 160, 164; shift toward, and increased poverty orientation in aid, 245–46, 250; and trade relationships, 75, 77t.3.2
Myrdal, Gunnar, 30, 43, 140, 170, 290–91; on the power of ideas, 56, 254–55; on the welfare state, 185–86

Nansen, Fridtjof, 11, 191–92
National Committee on the Cause and Cure of War, 201
National Council of Churches, 158
national interest, 11–12, 45t, 61; broad, 36–37, 114–15, 137, 139, 155–56, 159, 278–79, 284, 287, 298n.63; role in international affairs, 4, 7, 287; shaped by ideas and ideals, 12, 19–20, 167–73, 303n.5. *See also* self-interest; social philosophies of donor states
neo-Realism. *See* international relations, theories of change in; Realist view of international relations
Netherlands, the, foreign aid of: international society, and image, 66, 162, 177–78; motivations for, 166, 168; party differences, 166; policy and program, 83, 105, 106, 108–9, 133, 135, 168, 172; poverty focus of aid, 102, 166; public support for, 58, 116–17, 142; social welfare and, 121, 124
New Deal and social-democratic programs, 140, 219. *See also* Roosevelt, Franklin Delano; "World New Deal"
"New Directions" legislation, 91, 164
New Zealand, foreign aid of, 106, 108, 121; joining DAC, 58, 66; party and group support, 159–60, 162; public opinion in, 116–17, 142, 159–60; and

regional relationships, 87t, 87–88, 108, 110
Nightingale, Florence, 188
Nissanke, Michiko K., 98
norm-governed change, 223–24, 269, 271–72
Norway, foreign aid of, 105, 121, 124, 133; international society and, 174; poverty focus, 41, 102; support for, 141, 167

OECD. *See* Organization for Economic Cooperation and Development
Official Development Assistance (ODA). *See* foreign aid
ongoing change: growing sense of international responsibility, 207, 216–20; growth of aid norms, 40–41, 47–50, 227–49, 253, 254–69; guided by moral meanings, 5, 68–69, 212–13, 272–79; leading up to aid, 45–47, 182–220; rhetorical momentum, 219, 274, 277; theory of, 26–28, 68–69, 222–24, 253–54, 269–72; welfare outlays steadily increase, 183, 185
OPEC aid, analysis of, 130–32
Organization for Economic Cooperation and Development (OECD): controversy within over anticommunist aid policies, 55, 59; evolution of, 27, 216, 240–41; U.S. motives in founding, 256. *See also* Development Assistance Committee (DAC) of the OECD; foreign aid, comparisons of donor states
Osgood, Robert Endicott, 19
Overseas Resources Development Act of 1948 (British), 209
Owen, Charlotte, 192
Owen, Robert, 193
Oxfam, 140, 160–61, 218
Oxford Missionary conference (1937), 188

Packenham, Robert A., 170
Peace Corps, 239, 241
peace, 202, 303n.5; and anti-war sentiment, 190, 196, 217
Pearson, Lester B., 42
Pearson Commission Report, 247, 291
Philadelphia Declaration, 45–46, 300n.9, 217–18, 316n.76; quoted explicitly, 65, 195; quoted implicitly, 34, 201, 206, 223. *See* interdependence; International Labour Association

philanthropy. *See* private charity and philanthropy
Poe, Stephen C., 90–91
Point Four Program, 27, 31, 47, 55, 163, 178, 210, 219, 221–23, 230, 231–33, 250, 275, 322n.11
political views and parties, 119, 137, 139–43, 144, 145, 146, 161–63, 161–67; conservative, 159, 166, 228, 250; initial conservative idealism about aid, 205; liberal promotion of aid, 152, 163–64, 165–66; social-democratic, 45, 68, 140, 165, 189. *See also* domestic influence on international politics; public opinion; welfare state
poorest nations. *See* least developed countries; low income countries
post-World War I. *See* interwar period
postwar period: decolonization during, 224–25; emergence and growth of aid regime during, 37, 69, 199, 204–5, 212–14, 273, 278, 279–80, 287, 300–301n.11. *See also* World War II
poverty, 120f.4.1, 285–86; aid increasingly oriented to, 29, 36, 38–39, 48–49, 243–49, 246t, 250, 267t; and capitalism, 184; donors with highest emphasis on, 98, 102; public concern over, 5, 116, 120f, 123f, 187, 208, 217, 223, 241, 290; public concern over worldwide and domestic linked, 5, 24, 69, 273–74; world hunger, 69, 158, 161, 206. *See also* economic development; foreign aid, recipients of; least developed countries; low income countries
Pratt, Cranford, 162–63
prehistory of aid. *See* foreign aid, origins and antecedents of
principles. *See* moral convictions
private charity and philanthropy, 158, 192, 217; associated with government policies, 28, 41t.2.5, 121–25, 122t, 123f, 124t
project aid vs. program aid, 38, 301n.15
prosocial behavior, 10–11, 17, 289
public opinion: on aid, 43, 138–39; on aid related to moral convictions and social philosophy, 43, 116–18; concern over poverty, 5, 116, 120f, 123f, 217; cross-national analyses of, 116, 117, 140–45, 141, 142, 159–60, 162–63, 166, 167; influence of international, 67–68, 173–78;

levels of public support for aid, 63–65, 116–18, 140–43; predictors of, favoring aid, 31, 43–45, 44t.2.7, 45t, 143–55, 146–47t, 149t, 153t; and scrutiny of foreign aid programs, 38, 276. *See also* democracy; social philosophies of donor states

quality of aid, covarying with quantity, 117–18, 139, 151, 157–60, 162–67, 169, 176–77

Rao proposal, 235–36
Rao, V. K. R. V., 234–35, 240
rationality: not independent of philosophical outlook, 20–21; responding to broader values, 278–79; role of values in, 8, 12, 14, 19–22, 44–45, 62–63, 65, 272–74, 278–79, 283–84, 287–92; as self-interested calculation, 8, 18–19, 57–58, 269, 271, 278, 307–8n.2; unbridled pursuit of self-interest undermines, 18–20, 298n.62, 307–8n.2
Rauta, I(rene), 144, 150
Reagan, Ronald, 42, 119, 164, 249
Realist view of international relations, 4, 6–8, 13–14, 25–26, 31, 67–68; classical, 7–8, 137, 295n.12; evaluation of, 28–29, 114, 269–70, 273, 298n.62, 307–8n.2; on moral and ideological factors, 6, 8, 13, 20. *See also* international relations, theories of change in; rationality
realpolitik, 16, 17, 21, 269–70. *See also* Realist view of international relations
recipient nations. *See* less developed countries
Red Cross, 11, 68, 168, 190–91, 218
reflectivist view of international relations. *See* social construction of international politics
reform in aid, 254
refugees, 46, 191, 218, 315n.52
regimes, international, 18; based on beliefs and values, 3, 5, 27, 29, 62–63, 68, 272–74, 283–85, 287–93; based on self-interest 17–19, 269–72; change processes in, 16–17, 221–52, 253–69, 269–77; as meaningful practices, 26–28, 68–69; with ongoing change 269–78. *See also* foreign aid regime; norm-governed change; ongoing change

regional relationships of Australia, Japan, and New Zealand, with aid recipients, 86–90, 87t, 108
reinstitutionalization of aid regime, 47, 239–44;
relative gains, 17, 297n.46
religion: support for foreign aid, 44t2.6, 145, 146t, 148, 149t, 158–59, 161, 167, 193; support for relief and for structural change, 186–88, 193, 196–98
rhetorical momentum, 275
right, the. *See* conservative politics
Rockefeller, Nelson, 210
Rockefeller Foundation, 188, 192
Roosevelt, Franklin Delano (President), 65, 201–2, 206, 210–11, 219; Four Freedoms speech, 210
Royce, Josiah, 14–15
Russell, Bertrand, 196

Saint-Pierre, Bernardin, Abbé de, 16
sanctions, 26
Sato, Eisaku (Prime Minister), 176
Saudi Arabia, 130, 131
Scandinavia, 67, 141, 166, 177, 184, 189. *See also* Denmark; Finland; Norway; Sweden
scientific aid. *See* technical and scientific assistance
security interests: as basis for formation of aid regime, 9, 50, 232; and Japanese foreign aid, 110; as motive for foreign aid, 32, 109–11; and New Zealand aid, 110; promoted by politicians and officials, 64; U.S. aid related to, 42, 55, 90–92, 92t, 286; in U.S. foreign aid policy, 50, 109–11, 134
selection pressures, natural. *See* survival pressures
self-interest, 3, 7–9, 155–56; and egoism, 8, 17, 19, 148, 269; in international relations, 3, 6, 8, 31–32; testable implications of, 82, 270. *See also* economic interests; human nature; military interests; national interest; security interests; trade relationships; tied aid
settlement house movement, 188, 217
Sisters of Charity, 10
small-country bias, 97–98
social construction of international politics, 22, 26–28, 297–98n.55

social Darwinism, 6
social democracy, 115, 119, 125–27, 135, 140, 165, 167, 188–90
Social Gospel movement, 187–88, 217
social justice, 189, 202, 293; expressed in political ideas and programs, 45, 68, 140, 165, 189, 219. See also egalitarianism
social philosophies of donor states: comparative measures of, 116–18, 119; linking domestic and foreign policy, 5, 28–29, 41t.2.5, 115–16, 291–92; reflected in commitment to domestic welfare, 119–21, 120f; reflected in politics and parties, 45, 68, 140, 165, 189, 219; reflected in private voluntary contributions, 121–25, 122t, 123f, 124t, 324n.10. See also moral convictions; national interest; political views and parties; public opinion
socialism: critique of aid, 31; critique of political economy, 24; parties of, 189, 217
soft loans, 47, 264, 300–301n.11
Solferino, battle of, and book about. See Dunant, J. Henry
Soviet bloc aid, 33, 55–56, 128–30, 129t, 225–26
special interests (domestic), 23, 50–51, 323–24n.5
Special United Nations Fund for Economic Development (SUNFED), 244–25. See also United Nations Development Program
Spykman, Nicholas John, 7
statesmanship, 8, 19–20
Streeten, Paul, 248
Sub-Commission on Economic Development (of UN), 234–35
SUNFED. See Special United Nations Fund for Economic Development
survival pressures, and natural selection, 4–5, 7, 12–20, 21–22
Sweden, foreign aid of, 105, 109, 121, 124, 133, 135, 238; party differences, 167; policy and programs, 61, 66, 109–10, 249; poverty focus, 41, 102, 173; public opinion, 141, 150–51
Switzerland, foreign aid of, 105, 106, 109, 117, 124, 133; distinctive factors in, 125, 126–27; idealism in, 102, 168, 170–71; party differences in, 166

Tanzania, 54
targets for foreign aid performance, 245, 266, 268, 276; history of, 212, 247–48, 323n.28, 323n.3; one percent target, 69, 166, 167, 174, 175, 212, 244, 249, 250, 256; other volume targets, 86, 89, 162, 163, 164–65, public response to, 141, 142, 151, 155, 158
Tawney, R. H., 183, 197, 313n.4
Taylor, Michael, 14
technical and scientific assistance, 47, 209–10, 221, 231–32, 234–36
technological progress, 284–85
Temple, William (Archbishop), 185
Thatcher, Margaret, 43, 119, 161–62, 175, 249
Third World: attitudes toward, 24, 139, 146t, 151, 153t, 154; decolonization of, 224–25; development of, as focus for foreign aid, 64, 93–94, 99, 100, 233–34, 245–48, 283; economic stagnation in, 285; emphasis on interdependence with, 51; extent of aid to top importers of, 77t.3.3; France's advocacy for, 102; Marxist countries in, 56; North-South relations, 4. See also colonial ties; dependency theory; less developed countries; individual countries
Thorp, Willard L., 247
tied aid, 48t.2.9, 48, 260, 262–64, 263t, 265tt.8.9 and 8.10
trade relationships: in bilateral aid, 77t.3.3, 78t, 79t; of donor states, 39, 75–80, 76t, 77tt.3.2 and 3.3; and interests of the hegemon, 111–12; relationship to aid giving, 39, 75–80, 76t, 77tt.3.2 and 3.3, 93–94
trade unions. See labor associations
Truman, Harry S (President), 42, 178, 206–7, 210, 219, 221, 231–32, 320n.167. See also Marshall Plan; Point Four Program

UN. See United Nations
UNDP. See United Nations Development Program
UNHCR. See United Nations High Commission for Refugees
UNICEF. See United Nations Children's Emergency Fund
unions. See labor associations
United Kingdom. See Britain

United Nations (UN), 66, 213–14, 244–45, 274, 287; Special Fund, 177; Universal Declaration of Human Rights of, 218. *See also* Expanded Programme of Technical Assistance

United Nations Children's Emergency Fund (UNICEF), 192

United Nations Conference on Food and Agriculture, 211–12, 217, 319n.148

United Nations Conference on Trade and Development (UNCTAD), 247

United Nations Development Program (UNDP), 59, 245

United Nations Expanded Programme of Technical Assistance. *See* Expanded Programme of Technical Assistance

United Nations High Commission for Refugees (UNHCR), 191, 315n.52

United Nations Relief and Rehabilitation Administration (UNRRA), 68, 206–7, 208, 211–12, 218, 319n.130

United Nations Special Fund for Economic Development (SUNFED), 244–45. *See also* United Nations Development Program

United Nations Sub-Commission on Economic Development, 234–35

United States, foreign aid of: declining, 42, 57, 58, 111–12, 117, 132–34, 242, 249, 254, 256, 286, 306n.17; economic self-interest in, 105, 111–12, 262–63; extent of tying, 262, 263t; and hegemony, 53–54, 57, 111–12; to Israel and Egypt, 82, 158, 303n.15; laggardly among DAC donors, 36–37, 41, 286; party and group support for, 42–43, 137, 158–59, 163–64; Peace Corps, 239, 241; poverty orientation, 99–100, 102; public support for, 116–17, 142, 144–45, 149–50; resurgence in sixties, 241; role in growth of internationalism, 202–7, 256; and social welfare policies, 121, 124–25, 187–88, 228; special factors affecting, 125, 127, 130; strategic interests in, 42, 55, 74, 82, 90–93, 92t, 132–35, 286; strategic interests, proportion of, 50, 109–11, 134; to Vietnam, 82

U.S.-British Mutual Aid Agreement (Lend-Lease program), 211, 215

Universal Declaration of Human Rights (UN), 218

UNRRA. *See* United Nations Relief and Rehabilitation Administration

untying of aid. *See* tied aid

values. *See* moral convictions; social philosophies of donor states

vision. *See* moral vision

volume of aid: increase in, 254–55, 255t; largest financial flow to Third World, 34–36, 38; as percentage of GNP, 254. *See also* targets for foreign aid performance

Wallace, Henry (Vice President), 46, 203, 219

Wallenberg, Raoul, 10

Waltz, Kenneth N., 13–14, 16, 17, 20, 296n.26, 298n.63

Walzer, Michael, 27

war: and anti-war sentiment, 190, 196, 217; debts from World War I, 279; need to justify, 24, 27; neo-Realist view of, 13; relief efforts after World War II, 192, 199, 207, 208, 219; world, fear of, 208. *See also* military interests; United Nations Relief and Rehabilitation Administration; World War I; World War II

Ward, Barbara, 43, 140, 170, 290

welfare state, 251–52; basis of support for, 185–86; disillusionment with, 250; rise of, 45, 183–84, 217, 228. *See also* domestic influence on international politics; New Deal and social-democratic programs; welfare state

Welles, Sumner (Undersecretary of State), 203, 206

White, Harry Dexter, 219

WHO. *See* World Health Organization

Willkie, Wendell, 203

Wilson, Harold (Prime Minister), 42, 161, 182

Wilson, Woodrow (President), 196; on colonial possessions, 208–9; as idealist and visionary, 14, 20, 280, 287

Wilsonian internationalism, 219, 287

Wittkopf, Eugene R., 145, 309n.22

Women's International League for Peace and Freedom, 188, 196

World Bank, 27, 47, 59, 68, 214–15, 218, 222, 232, 251, 274, 276, 287; Bretton Woods conference, 46, 215–16; change in direction of, 230, 233–34; establishment of, 214–15; International Finance Corporation (IFC) of, 239; and the International Monetary Fund (IMF), 33, 57, 214; resources going to poverty-sectors, 101t.3.16. *See also* International Development Association

World Citizens Association, 203, 217

world community. *See* international society

World Council of Churches, 197, 218, 247

world economy, 200, 200–202, 204–5. *See also* international economic institutions

World Food Program, 245

World Health Organization (WHO), 234

world hunger, 69, 158, 161, 206

"World New Deal," 46, 203–4

world peace, 202; and anti-war sentiment, 190, 196, 217

world politics. *See* anarchy; international cooperation; international relations, theories of change in

World War I, postwar policies leading to collapse, 206, 279, 280. *See also* interwar period

World War II, 198–99; collaborative efforts during, 46, 210–12, 214–15; as turning point for internationalism, 218. *See also* postwar period